P9-DWG-628

EDITED AND WITH ESSAYS BY IRENE DIAMOND
AND GLORIA FEMAN ORENSTEIN

REWEAVING THE WORLD

The Emergence of Ecofeminism

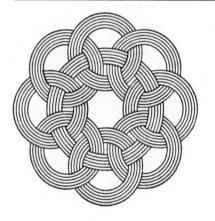

SIERRA CLUB BOOKS
SAN FRANCISCO

The Sierra Club, founded in 1892 by John Muir, has devoted itself to the study and protection of the earth's scenic and ecological resources—mountains, wetlands, woodlands,
wild shores and rivers, deserts and plains. The publishing program of the Sierra Club
offers books to the public as a nonprofit educational service in the hope that they may
enlarge the public's understanding of the Club's basic concerns. The point of view
expressed in each book, however, does not necessarily represent that of the Club. The
Sierra Club has some sixty chapters coast to coast, in Canada, Hawaii, and Alaska. For
information about how you may participate in its programs to preserve wilderness and
the quality of life, please address inquiries to Sierra Club, 730 Polk Street, San Francisco, CA 94109.

Copyright © 1990 by Irene Diamond and Gloria Feman Orenstein
All rights reserved under International and Pan-American Copyright Conventions. No
part of this book may be reproduced in any form or by any electronic or mechanical
means, including information storage and retrieval systems, without permission in writing
from the publisher.

"Development as a New Project of Western Patriarchy" originally appeared in *Staying
Alive* (New Delhi: Kali for Women, 1988).
"Searching for Common Ground: Ecofeminism and Bioregionalism" originally appeared
in *The New Catalyst*, Winter 1987/88.
In Sally Abbott's essay, the excerpt from "The Second Coming" is reprinted with permission of Macmillan Publishing Company from *The Poems of W. B. Yeats: A New Edition*,
edited by Richard J. Finneran; copyright © 1924 by Macmillan Publishing Company,
renewed 1952 by Bertha Georgie Yeats. The untitled shamanic poem beginning "Otso,
thou my well-beloved . . ." is quoted from "The Shamanic Universe," by Peter T. Furst,
in *Stones, Bones, and Skin* (Society for Arts Publications in Canada, 1977).
The poetry in Starhawk's essay originally appeared in her book *Truth or Dare: Encounters
with Power, Authority, and Mystery* (Harper & Row, 1987).
In Susan Griffin's essay, "The Lion in the Den of the Prophets" is reprinted from her
book *Woman and Nature: The Roaring Inside Her* (Harper & Row, 1978), and "Hunger"
is reprinted from her book *Unremembered Country* (Port Townsend, Wash.: Copper
Canyon Press, 1987).

Library of Congress Cataloging-in-Publication Data
Reweaving the world : the emergence of ecofeminism / edited by Irene
    Diamond and Gloria Feman Orenstein.
        p. cm.
    Includes bibliographical references (p.).
    ISBN 0-87156-694-X ISBN 0-87156-623-0 (pbk.)
    1. Human ecology. 2. Feminist criticism. I. Diamond, Irene,
1947-   . II. Orenstein, Gloria Feman, 1938-   .
GF50.R49 1990   89-29295
304.2—dc20   CIP

Editors: Marie Cantlon, Linda Gunnarson
Production: Susan Ristow
Cover/jacket design: Bonnie Smetts
Cover painting: Susan Seddon Boulet
Book design: Abigail Johnston
Drawing on page 81: Amy Evans

Printed in the United States of America
10 9 8 7 6 5 4 3 2 1

The text of this book is printed on recycled paper.

This book is dedicated to that remarkable and modest woman Rachel Carson, who, loving the natural world, had to move from the exquisite accuracy of her books The Sea Around Us *and* The Edge of the Sea *to the true story of our toxic times,* Silent Spring. *Men of science have believed for hundreds of years that naming preceded owning, that owning preceded using, and that using naturally preceded using up. Some even believed that scientific understanding of the world would, if shrewdly managed, become something human beings could with considerable financial profit do to one another.*

Rachel Carson thought that loving the world was what science had to be about. That it is essential to love the natural world before you can understand it. This was not sentimentality. She knew it would be dangerous to undertake understanding without that love, as well as love's classy child—awe—and its everyday child—responsibility. She lived in opposition to gross curiosity and greed. She taught us that the life of a bug cannot be taken without silencing songbirds. And finally the songbird cannot be silenced without poisoning the human child. She lived to see some results of her work. The beginning of the washing of the waters of the Hudson, the Connecticut, and other rivers, the beginning of the ecological movement. We have lived to see our great oceans lined and littered with plastic, our trees dying under the industrial showers of acid rain, the great net of nuclear terror thrown over the whole world. We have so many hard jobs ahead of us, so much education, so much organizing, so much action. But we do have that other way of understanding, a revolutionary understanding that we call feminist and ecological, in which we share the world with all creatures and all living things and know that their stories are our own.

SACE PALEY

GRACE PALEY

Contents

3 Healing Ourselves: Healing the Planet

Preface

THIS VOLUME, with its chorus of voices reflecting the variety of concerns flowing into ecofeminism, challenges the boundaries dividing such genres as the scholarly paper and the impassioned poetic essay. In so doing, it acknowledges poetic vision as a form of knowledge and as one of the important steps in the process of global transformation.

Ecofeminist philosophy and creation have brought about changes in consciousness, political action, and spiritual practice. This collection is composed of writings by poets, novelists, scholars, scientists, ecological activists, and spiritual teachers, many of which were first presented at the conference "Ecofeminist Perspectives: Culture, Nature, and Theory," held at the University of Southern California in March 1987 and sponsored by the California Council for the Humanities. We also invited others who did not attend the original conference to contribute to the volume, thus making a more comprehensive statement about the global emergence of ecofeminism.

We hope to dispel the notion that poetry and politics, spirituality and activism, scholarship and vision are to remain forever divided, either from each other or within the same person. The writers and activists represented here share a multicultural and diversified global vision of healing for life on Earth. Their voices have been inspiring to us, and our fervent wish is that this volume will be a catalyst for further change.

IRENE DIAMOND AND GLORIA FEMAN ORENSTEIN

Acknowledgments

WE WISH TO EXPRESS our deepest thanks to the following people, who helped bring our vision of a book on ecofeminism to realization.

Without Marie Cantlon's dedication to our work from the very beginning, and without her patient, thoughtful commentary on our collection of essays, this project never would have emerged as a book. For her steadfast personal and professional nurturance of the manuscript throughout the many stages of its transformation over time, we extend to her our sincerest gratitude.

We also wish to express our heartfelt appreciation to Linda Gunnarson and Betty Berensen, whose insightful editorial expertise and attention to detail so perfected the volume's final form.

We extend a special "thank you" to Jeffrey Land, whose unflagging Green energy expedited endless matters concerning the creation and vision of *Reweaving the World*.

We would also like to acknowledge all of our authors, whose concern for life on our planet inspired us as we rewove the contents of our book so that ecofeminism could emerge with the clarity and strength of their many voices.

Finally, we would like to give special thanks to Grace Paley, whose dedication so beautifully expresses the debt we all owe to Rachel Carson.

Introduction

TODAY, MORE THAN TWENTY-FIVE YEARS after Rachel Carson's *Silent Spring* first raised a passionate voice of conscience in protest against the pollution and degradation of nature, an ecofeminist movement is emerging globally as a major catalyst of ethical, political, social, and creative change. Although Carson was not an avowed feminist, many would argue that it was not coincidental that a woman was the first to respond both emotionally and scientifically to the wanton human domination of the natural world. Carson's 1962 text prefigured a powerful environmental movement that culminated in the nationwide Earth Day of 1970, but the notion that the collective voices of women should be central to the greening of the Earth did not blossom until the mid to late 1970s.

Ecofeminism is a term that some use to describe both the diverse range of women's efforts to save the Earth and the transformations of feminism in the West that have resulted from the new view of women and nature. With the birth of the Women's Movement in the late 1960s, feminists dismantled the iron grip of biological determinism that had been used historically to justify men's control over women. Feminists argued that social arrangements deemed to be timeless and natural had actually been constructed to validate male superiority and privilege. They asserted that women had the right to be full and equal participants in the making of culture. In this process writers and scholars documented the historical association between women and nature, insisting that women would not be free until the connections between women and the natural world were severed.

But as the decade advanced and as women began to revalue women's cultures and practices, especially in the face of the twin threats of nuclear annihilation and ecocide, many women began to understand how the larger culture's devaluation of natural processes was a product of masculine consciousness. Writers as diverse as Mary Daly, Elizabeth Dodson Gray, Susan Griffin, Carolyn Merchant, Maria Mies, Vandana Shiva, Luisah Teish, and Alice Walker demonstrated that this masculine consciousness denigrated and manipulated everything defined as "other" whether nature, women, or Third World cultures. In the industrialized world, women were impelled to act, to speak out against the mindless spraying of chemicals, the careless disposal of toxic wastes, the unacknowledged radiation seepage from nuclear power plants and weapons testing, and the ultimate catastrophe—the extinction of all life on Earth. In the Third World, women had still more immediate concerns. For women who had to walk miles to collect the water, fuel, and fodder they needed for their households, the devastation wrought by patriarchal fantasies of technological development (for example, the Green revolution, commercial forest management, and mammoth dam projects) was already a daily reality.

In many ways, women's struggle in the rural Third World is of necessity also an ecological struggle. Because so many women's lives are intimately involved in trying to sustain and conserve water, land, and forests, they understand in an immediate way the costs of technologies that pillage the Earth's natural riches. By contrast, in the industrialized world, the connections between women's concerns and ecological concerns were not immediately apparent to many feminists. Community activists such as Rachel E. Bagby, Lois Gibbs, and Carol Von Strom, who were struggling to protect the health of their families and neighborhoods, were among the first to make the connections. Women who are responsible for their children's well-being are often more mindful of the long-term costs of quick-fix solutions. Through the social experience of caretaking and nurturing, women become attentive to the signs of distress in their communities that might threaten their households. When environmental "accidents" occur, it is these women who are typically the first to detect a problem. Moreover, because of women's unique role in the biological regeneration of the species, our bodies are important markers, the sites upon which local, regional, or even planetary stress is often played out. Miscarriage is frequently an early sign of the presence of lethal toxins in the biosphere.

Feminists who had been exploring alternatives to the traditional "woman is to nature as man is to culture" formulation, who were seeking a more fundamental shift in consciousness than the acceptance of women's participation in the marketplace of the public world, began to question the nature versus culture dichotomy itself. These activists, theorists, and artists sought to consciously create new cultures that would embrace and honor the values of caretaking and nurturing—cultures that would not perpetuate the dichotomy by raising nature over culture or by raising women over men. Rather, they affirmed and celebrated the embeddedness of all the Earth's peoples in the multiple webs and cycles of life.

In their hope for the creation of new cultures that would live *with* the Earth, many women in the West were inspired by the myths and symbols of ancient Goddess cultures in which creation was imaged as female and the Earth was revered as sacred. Others were inspired by the symbols and practices of Native-American cultures that consider the effects on future generations before making any community decision. The sources of inspiration were many and varied and led to a diverse array of innovative practices—from tree-planting communities, alternative healing communities, organic food coops, performance art happenings, Witchcraft covens, and the retelling of ancient myths and tales to new forms of political resistance such as the *Chipko* (hugging) tree actions and women's peace camps. Through poetry, rituals, and social activism that connected the devastation of the Earth with the exploitation of women, these activists reinvigorated both feminism and social change movements more generally. The languages they created reached across and beyond the boundaries of previously defined categories. These languages recognized the *lived* connections between reason and emotion, thought and experience. They embraced not only women and men of different races, but all forms of life—other animals, plants, and the living Earth itself. The diverse strands of this retelling and reframing led to a new, more complicated experiential ethic of ecological interconnectedness.

Ecofeminist politics does not stop short at the phase of dismantling the androcentric and anthropocentric biases of Western civilization. Once the critique of such dualities as culture and nature, reason and emotion, human and animal has been posed, ecofeminism seeks to reweave new stories that acknowledge and value the biological and cultural diversity that sustains all life. These new stories honor, rather than fear, women's biological particularity while simultaneously affirming women as subjects and makers of history. This understanding that biological particularity need not be antithetical to historical agency is crucial to the transformation of feminism.

We can discern three important philosophical strains from the many paths that peoples in the West and postcolonial societies are taking in their efforts to defend the Earth against the encroachments of life-denying imperialism:

1. One position emphasizes that the Earth is sacred unto itself, that her forests, rivers, and different creatures have *intrinsic* value. The

abstract "whole Earth" is not posed as being superior to or more valuable than the particular life of any one of her individual creatures.

2. Another strain emphasizes that because human life is dependent on the Earth, our fates are intertwined. Social justice cannot be achieved apart from the well-being of the Earth—we must care for the Earth as our survival and well-being are directly linked to her survival and well-being.

3. Finally, from the perspective of indigenous peoples, whose connection to native lands is essential to their being and identity, it is both true that the Earth has intrinsic value and that we are also dependent on her. Thus, we are led to understand the many ways in which we can walk the fine line between using the Earth as a natural resource for humans and respecting the Earth's own needs, cycles, energies, and ecosystems.

The presence of these different strains indicates that ecofeminism is not a monolithic, homogeneous ideology. Indeed, it is precisely the diversity of thought and action that makes this new politics so promising as a catalyst for change in these troubled times. The planet is in crisis, as evidenced so clearly by the impending greenhouse effect and the concomitant droughts and loss of crops, the vanishing of rain forests and the extinction of so many species, the pollution of rivers, lakes, and beaches, and the poisoning of the food chain. One response to this crisis is to reduce all these problems to one by arguing that there are simply too many people. Others say we are on the brink, that doomsday is at our door, and that only Draconian measures of control will see us through. Ecofeminist politics stands against any such monological, reductionist, apocalyptic thought processes. In contrast, this tapestry in green embraces heterogeneous strategies and solutions. While ecofeminism recognizes the severity of the crisis, it also recognizes that the methods we choose in dealing with problems must be life affirming, consensual, and nonviolent. The process of creating new cultures that honor the Earth and her peoples is not something we can postpone. Moreover, because the creation of new images of living with the Earth is viewed as an essential element of the process of transformation, creative artists are an integral part of this new constellation. In short, ecofeminism radically alters our very notion of what constitutes political change.

This volume is divided into three sections. Part one, "Histories and Mysteries: In the Beginning," introduces the development of ecofeminism as a social movement and philosophy. For some, the power of ecofeminism derives from the way in which it articulates new stories of origins and the place of humans in the world. This section explores several of these narratives of sacred meaning that profoundly transform the ways in which we define the cosmos, the Earth, and society. Part two, "Reweaving the World: Reconnecting Politics and Ethics," elaborates both the development of ecofeminism and some of the important political, philosophical, and scientific questions that have been sparked by this new constellation. And part three, "Healing Ourselves: Healing the Planet," exposes some of the specific problems that the current life-denying system has produced and documents some of the creative efforts of repair and healing.

In the first essay of part one, Charlene Spretnak discusses the origins and roots of ecofeminism. Spretnak's organic metaphors about the roots and flowering of ecofeminism situate its historical birth at the contemporary moment of planetary crisis in which we face the threat of ecocide. In pleading for a new ecophilosophy to restore health to the biosphere, Spretnak names themes that reappear in many of the essays in this volume: the interconnectedness of all life, the need for a nonandrocentric basis to our philosophy and practice, and the importance of reclaiming those values associated with ancient prepatriarchal and contemporary tribal cultures. In the second essay, Brian Swimme relates the story of the origins of the cosmos. Swimme shows us how deeply fragmented the ideas of most scientists are, how alienated their models are, and how urgent it is for us to change our story of origins. Riane Eisler's "Ecofeminist Manifesto" sweeps back into prepatriarchal history in order to reclaim the more than 20,000 years of life in which the "dominator model" of hierarchy and oppression did not prevail.

Sally Abbott's experiential narrative suggests that human guilt in response to killing animals led to the development of religions that distance us from a feeling of kinship with all forms of life. Mara Keller reclaims the ancient female mysteries of Demeter and Persephone as metaphors for our current descent to and rebirth from the underworld. She sees the Eleusinian mysteries as a powerful myth for our time. Paula Gunn Allen's meditation on the planet envisages our grandmother Earth passing through a sacred transformation. Carol Christ suggests that we make our connection with the web of life a basis for a new theology that would realign "the divine/Goddess/God/Earth/Life/It" humanity and nature.

Part two documents the rich political imagination of this new constellation. In the first essay, Starhawk's poetic, magical voice emphasizes the importance of a spiritually empowered community in the process of political action. For Starhawk, our politics will be strengthened if we see time as cyclical, avoid idealizing suffering, and are open to mystery. Susan Griffin's essay articulates the way in which we create the world in the image of our thoughts. Griffin eloquently speaks to how we have built a world of deprivation out of words of deprivation and how we must create a world of light out of images of the possible.

Carolyn Merchant demonstrates that liberal, radical, and socialist feminism have all been concerned with improving the human/nature relationship and that each has contributed to an ecofeminist perspective. Ynestra King further explores the attitudes toward nature within the different strains of feminism. For King, each strain of feminism has capitulated to dualistic thinking; thus, the task of ecofeminism is to forge a genuinely antidualistic, or dialectical, theory and praxis. Lee Quinby, drawing on the insights of Michel Foucault, examines ecofeminism as a politics of resistance. Quinby contends that the questions of a politics of resistance can counter the essentialist tendencies within ecofeminism.

The essays by Marti Kheel and Michael Zimmerman explore the differences and similarities between ecofeminism and deep ecology. Kheel critically examines deep ecology's concept of an expanded self. She brings into focus the centrality of the hunting instinct to Aldo Leopold's famous land ethic and cautions that the identification with the larger biotic community that deep ecologists call for risks obliterating the uniqueness and importance of individual beings. Zimmerman's essay, which calls for new forms of individuation for both women and men, attempts to bring about a reconciliation between the two perspectives. In her essay, Judith Plant argues that bioregionalism, the practice of "learning to become native to place, fitting ourselves to a particular place, not fitting a place to our predetermined tastes," could enable us to realize ecofeminism's full potential as part of a practical social movement.

Part three analyzes some of the specific problems the current cultural system has created at the same time that it points to creative efforts of repair. Arisika Razak's essay powerfully reminds us of the importance of the event of birth, an event that has been profoundly devalued by patriarchy. Lin Nelson's essay demonstrates that as the planet suffers systematic and increasing pollution, women find themselves in an array of troubling predicaments; however, women are also resisting this victimization in both hazardous workplaces and environmentally threatened communities. Turning more directly to the Third World, Vandana Shiva demonstrates how patriarchy and gender oppression have taken on new and more virulent forms with "development"—or what may more appropriately be called patriarchal "maldevelopment"— projects. In her essay, Irene Diamond focuses on the potential indus- trialization of human procreation, arguing that the seemingly benign goals of helping infertile women to have babies and all mothers to have "normal" babies pose profound threats to the dignity and well-being of human life itself.

The next four essays look upon city-dwellers as potential catalysts for what is perhaps the most difficult kind of ecological change of all. Irene Javors, a therapist in Manhattan, teaches us how to apprehend the sacred and the holy in the midst of urban decay. Cynthia Hamilton presents the concrete case history of a group of poor Black women in Los Angeles who said "no" to the installation of a solid waste in- cinerator in their residential community. And while it may seem im- possible to live ecologically in Los Angeles, Julia Russell's vision and commitment to transforming personal life-style have resulted in the creation of Eco-Home, a demonstration home for ecological living. When we understand that all of our acts have political ramifications that affect life, we realize that we can only heal the planet by healing our own lives and life-styles first. Finally, Rachel Bagby's interview with her mother, Rachel E. Bagby of Philadelphia, shows us how vacant lots can be recycled into gardens, and vacant houses into shared homes for elders. This is her story of how her gardens and others' efforts grow.

Catherine Keller's essay speaks to us about the effects of the biblical prophecies of the end of time on our current doomsday mentality. For Keller, it is only by changing our myth of the end of time to one of cyclical rebirth that we can stop wasting the world. Yaakov Garb probes the issue of how we know nature, asking what the "whole Earth" im- age means for contemporary perceptions of nature. The volume closes with Gloria Feman Orenstein's essay documenting how ecofeminist concerns are being expressed in contemporary visual and literary arts.

Ecofeminism, a new term for an ancient wisdom, is a great and difficult idea. Great because it finds hope and power in our bonds to each other and the Earth, difficult precisely because these bonds have been so tattered in the contemporary era. As we relocate ourselves on the planet we must re/place ourselves. Thus, we will forge new under- standings which this book's many essays help us to begin.

1

HISTORIES AND MYSTERIES: IN THE BEGINNING

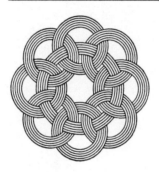

mention the present and pending environmental disasters at all. When the opposition party was given response time on national television and radio, no one mentioned this absence in the president's account of our problems. When members of the media, female and male, commented on the address, the glaring absence of ecological concern, let alone ecological wisdom, again went unmentioned. In the State of the Union addresses for the previous 2 years, the story was the same, except for the president's brief tip of the hat in 1986 to the Superfund (ridiculously underfunded for the cleanup of toxic dump sites) and his promising the previous year not to grant drilling and mining leases inside the national park system!

That politicians, the media, and the public barely noticed the crucial omission in the president's annual assessment of our national situation is merely one indication of pervasive alienation from the realities of nature. A powerful industrial giant like us lives on *top* of nature, it is understood, free to do with it what we will. The arrogance and ignorance behind that deadly folly are being challenged to varying extents by environmentalist organizations and to a much deeper extent by a loose aggregate of movements whose members are sometimes called the "new" ecologists: ecofeminism, deep ecology, Green politics, bioregionalism, creation-centered spirituality, animal rights, and others. Their numbers are not a large portion of our 242 million, but they are carrying on extremely significant work, feeling their way out of alienation toward a way of being that is infused with ecological wisdom. *Something* connected those people with nature; some event or accumulation of experiences woke them up to the centrality of ecology.

In the case of ecofeminism, there are many paths into our rich and fertile garden, each with its own occasions for awakening. What cannot be said, though, is that women are drawn to ecology and ecofeminism simply because we are female. The very first issue of *Audubon Magazine* in 1887 contained an article by Celia Thaxter titled "Woman's Heartlessness," on the resistance she and other activists met in trying to get women to stop wearing on their hats the feathers and stuffed bodies of birds: "Not among the ignorant and uncultured so much as the educated and enlightened do we find the indifference and hardness that perplexes us . . . I think I may say in two-thirds of the cases to which we appeal. One lady said to me, 'I think there is a great deal of sentiment wasted on the birds. There are so many of them, they will never be missed, any more than mosquitoes.'" Clearly those ladies were team players, defenders of patriarchal, anthropocentric values, which is exactly what we were raised to be, too—until we figured out that the game was dreadfully wrong.

Ecofeminism grew out of radical, or cultural, feminism (rather than from liberal feminism or socialist feminism), which holds that identifying the dynamics—largely fear and resentment—behind the dominance of male over female is the key to comprehending every expression of patriarchal culture with its hierarchical, militaristic, mechanistic, industrialist forms. The first tendrils of ecofeminism appeared not in the exuberant season of Earth Day 1970—for feminists were quite preoccupied with the birthing of our own movement then—but in middecade. Our sources of inspiration at the time were not Thoreau, John Muir, or even Rachel Carson (though we have certainly come to appreciate those beacons since then) but, rather, our own experiential explorations.

One path into ecofeminism was the study of political theory and history. Radical/cultural feminists who had been exposed to Marxist analysis in the 1960s as well as those who had gone on to study critical theory and social ecology in the early 1970s built upon the framework of dominance theory. They rejected the Marxist assertion that domination is based solely on money and class: if there is a universally dominated class, surely it is women. Experiencing and naming the inadequacies of classical dominance theory, which ignores nature as well as women, such radical feminists moved in the direction of ecofeminism. Another source of radical/cultural feminist dominance theory was the work of cultural historians who explored the roots of patriarchy.[1]

A second path into ecofeminism is exposure to nature-based religion, usually that of the Goddess. In the mid-1970s many radical/cultural feminists experienced the exhilarating discovery, through historic and archaeological sources, of a religion that honored the female and seemed to have as its "good book" nature itself. We were drawn to it like a magnet, but only, I feel, because both of those features were central. We would not have been interested in "Yahweh with a skirt," a distant, detached, domineering godhead who happened to be female. What was cosmologically wholesome and healing was the discovery of the Divine as immanent in and around us. What was intriguing was the sacred link between the Goddess in her many guises and totemic animals and plants, sacred groves, and womblike caves, in the moon-rhythm blood of menses, the ecstatic dance—the experience of *knowing* Gaia, her voluptuous contours and fertile plains, her flowing waters that give life, her animal teachers. For who among us would ever again see a snake coiled around the arms of an ancient Goddess statue, teaching lessons of cyclic renewal and regeneration with its shedding of skins, as merely a member of the ophidian order in the reptilian class of the vertebrate phylum? That period of discovery—which would certainly not have been news to primal peoples, but was utterly earthshaking for us Judeo-Christian women of a thoroughly modern culture—inspired art, music, poetry, and the resurrection of long-forgotten sacred myth and ritual, usually held out of doors, of course, often on the Earth's holy days of cosmic alignment, the solstices and equinoxes. They are rituals of our own creation that express our deepest feelings of a spirituality infused with ecological wisdom and wholeness. At the beginning of that period, ecology was not on our minds; since moving out of that period into activism, ecology has never left our minds. Today we work for ecopeace, ecojustice, ecoeconomics, ecopolitics, ecoeducation, ecophilosophy, ecotheology, and for the evolution of ecofeminism.

A third path into ecofeminism comes from environmentalism. For many women with careers in public policy, science and technology, public-interest environmental organizations, and environmental studies programs in universities, their initial connection with feminism was the liberal-feminist attention to how and why their progress on the career ladder was blocked. From there they eventually encountered a book, an article, or a lecture with ecofeminist analysis—and suddenly their career work was framed with a radically different meaning. Similarly, women and men who become involved with Green politics for environmental reasons discover ecofeminism and deep ecology there. College students, male and female, who feel that feminism was merely an issue for their mothers' generation and who enroll in an environmental studies course are often exposed to ecofeminist analysis and recognize a depth not present in their textbooks.

There are many variations of these three well-trodden paths into our garden, and perhaps other paths altogether. I have delineated them in order to acknowledge our diversity, which brings strength, but also in the hope that the social and political theory evolving within ecofeminism will address not only the interlinked dynamics in patriarchal culture of the terror of nature and the terror of the elemental power of the female but also the ways *out* of the mesmerizing conditioning that keeps women and men so cut off from our grounding in the natural world, so alienated from our larger sense of self in the unfolding story of the universe. If we look into this matter further, I think we'll find that many people connected with nature on a deep level through a ritual moment of awakening, or perhaps several of them. These moments may have occurred in the context of spiritual practice. They may have occurred in childhood. They are the precious moments we need to acknowledge and to cultivate, to refuse to let the dominant culture pave them over any longer with a value system made of denial, distancing, fear, and ignorance.

The moment of awakening, however, is only the beginning. After that comes a great deal of work if we really want to transform patriarchal culture into new possibilities informed by justice, wisdom, and compassion. We have to be willing to do intellectual work—to explore the books and articles, the speeches and debates that contribute to the evolving social and political theory of ecofeminism. We have to be willing to seek a holistic understanding of ecofeminism, to make an effort to learn about the priorities and experiential wisdom of ecofeminists who came from paths different from our own. We have to be willing to pursue self-education in ecology since our schooling for the most part failed us in that, to read an ecology textbook, for instance.[2] We have to be willing to educate ourselves about the major ecological issues of our day and to understand the economic and political forces at work.

Extremely important is a willingness to deepen our experience of communion with nature. This can be done in the mountains, at the ocean, in a city park, or a backyard garden. My own life is a rather embarrassing example of how long one can be absorbed in ecofeminist intellectual thought, political activism, and ritual honoring of nature *after* the moment of awakening and still know almost nothing of the richness and profound depth of communion that nature can offer. Several years ago I was invited to a conference on bioregionalism and Green politics in Santa Fe and met the environmental editor of the journal that was then called *CoEvolution Quarterly*. We went for a walk, conversing all the while, and when we returned a colleague asked if the editor, who was wearing a large pair of binoculars on a strap around his neck, had seen any birds. "I didn't see any, but I heard four," he replied. "What?!" I thought to myself, "Four birds? On that walk? Just now? I didn't hear anything. Four birds?!" It was at that moment that I realized that, despite my intellectual and political understanding of ecofeminism, I was a tourist in the natural world. In the intervening years, I have gone on many birding hikes, which I love, as well as canoe and backpacking trips into the wilderness. Nature has given me gifts, teachings, and revelations, but none more intense than those times in the wilderness I approached in silence, simply observing and being aware of the sensations I was experiencing, until eventually I was enfolded by the deep, deep silence and the oneness that is almost palpable. At that moment the distinction between inner and outer mind dissolves, and we meet our larger self, the One Mind, the cosmic unfolding. I feel that various intensities of that mystery are revealed to us during the postorgasmic state and during certain kinds of meditation and also ritual, but the grandeur and majesty of oneness I have found only in nature. A starting point for ecofeminists who are as backward in their direct knowledge of nature as I certainly was might be to learn about ten birds and ten plants native to their bioregion. The rest will come quite naturally.

All these kinds of work are the nutrient-rich compost that has yielded the vibrant flowering of ecofeminism today. Composting good soil takes time, and the work of ecofeminism goes back more than a dozen years. In fact, it goes back to a number of feminist writers (including Simone de Beauvoir in 1947) who mentioned in passing the attitudes of men (under patriarchy) to nature and to women and the connection between the two. The first conference to address this idea was "Women and the Environment," organized by Sandra Marburg and Lisa Watson at the University of California, Berkeley, in 1974. In 1980, spurred by the Three Mile Island catastrophe, Ynestra King, Celeste Wesson, Grace Paley, Anna Gyorgy, Christina Rawley, Nancy Jack Todd, and Deborah Gaventa organized a conference in Amherst, Massachusetts, on "Women and Life on Earth: Ecofeminism in the 1980s." Prior to learning of that gathering, Susan Adler and other spiritually aware women at Sonoma State University in California began planning a 1981 conference entitled "Women and the Environment: The First West Coast Ecofeminist Conference." In London, an ecofeminist conference called "Women and Life on Earth" was also held that year. The number of ecofeminist books and articles as well as running debates in anthologies and journals is far too great to cite here, but certainly *Woman and Nature* by Susan Griffin (New York: Harper & Row, 1978) and *The Death of Nature* by Carolyn Merchant (San Francisco: Harper & Row, 1980) were particularly important contributions. Both of those books were begun many years earlier, but they were immediately recognized as the ecofeminist classics that they are because so many radical/cultural feminists had moved in that direction during the second half of the 1970s.

OUR FLOWERING

So those are our roots. Today ecofeminists address the crucial issues of our time, from reproductive technology to Third World development, from toxic poisoning to the vision of a new politics and economics—and much more. We support and join our sisters fighting for equal pay, for battered women's shelters, for better child care, and for all the efforts to stop the daily exploitation and suffering of women. But we see those efforts as bandages on a very unhealthy system. Radical/cultural feminism is sometimes called "big-picture" feminism because we examine the deepest assumptions, values, and fears that inform the structures and expectations of patriarchal culture. The reason we insist on integrating radical analysis with ecological perspective is best understood in the larger framework of the fate of our species and all life on Earth: *What is the purpose of cultivating ecological wisdom at this postmodern moment in human history?*

Our society is facing a crisis in agriculture, a crisis in education and literacy, a crisis in national security and the arms race, a crisis in the international debt situation, and a crisis in the state of the global environment. For the first time in the modern era, there is widespread agreement that something is very wrong. The assumptions of modernity, the faith in technological "progress" and rapacious industrialism, along with the militarism necessary to support it, have left us very lost indeed. The quintessential malady of the modern era is free-floating anxiety, and it is clear to ecofeminists that the whole culture is free floating—from the lack of grounding in the natural world, from the lack of a sense of belonging in the unfolding story of the universe, from the lack of a healthy relationship between the males and females of the species. We are entangled in the hubris of the patriarchal goal of dominating nature and the female. On August 29, 1986, the *New York Times* published a lead editorial titled "Nature as Demon," reminding everyone that the proper orientation of civilization is to advance itself *in opposition to* nature. The editorial advised that disasters such as "Hiroshima, DDT, Bhopal, and now Chernobyl" simply require "improving the polity," that is, fine-tuning the system. Such smugness, of course, is the common response of guardians of the status quo: retrenchment and Band-Aids.

But ecofeminists say that the system is leading us to ecocide and species suicide because it is based on ignorance, fear, delusion, and greed. We say that people, male or female, enmeshed in the *values* of that system are incapable of making rational decisions. They pushed nuclear power plants when they did not have the slightest idea what to do with the plutonium wastes—because, after all, someone always comes along later to clean up like Mom. They pushed the nuclear arms race because those big phallic missiles are so "technologically sweet." They are pushing reproductive technology with the gleeful prediction that children of the future, a result of much genetic selection, will often have a donor mother, an incubator mother, and social mother who raises them—making motherhood as disembodied and discontinuous as fatherhood, at last! They are pushing high-tech petroleum-based agriculture, which makes the soil increasingly brittle and lifeless and adds millions of tons of toxic pesticides to our food as well as our soil and water, because *they* know how to get what they want from the Earth—a far cry from the peasant rituals that persisted in parts of Europe even up to World War I where women would encircle the fields by torchlight and symbolically transfer their fertility to the land they touched. Women and men in those cultures participated in the cycles of nature with respect and gratitude.

Such attitudes have no place in a modern, technocratic society fueled by the patriarchal obsessions of dominance and control. They have been replaced by the managerial ethos, which holds efficiency of production and short-term gains above all else—above ethics or moral standards, above the health of community life, and above the integrity of all biological processes, especially those constituting the elemental power of the female. The experts guiding our society seek deliverance from their fears of nature, with which they have no real communion or deep connection, through their seeming victories over the great forces: their management of the vast watersheds and forests of the planet and its perilously thin layer of topsoil; their management of the economics and daily conditions of people of color throughout the Third World (the so-called developing nations) and the Fourth World (the indigenous peoples); their management of "improved animal tools" for agribusiness; their management of women's economic status; and finally—so very technologically sweet—their management of women's birthing power, beginning first with control over labor and delivery, then control over breastfeeding (which the AMA almost succeeded in phasing out between the 1930s and the mid-1970s), and now control over conception and gestation, with the prediction that they will one day colonize the universe by sending frozen human embryos or cells for clones into space to colonize planets.

The technological experts of the modern era, with their colleagues in business, government, and the military, are waging an antibiological revolution in human conduct. The moral systems of Western ethics and religion are nearly powerless in this struggle because those systems themselves are largely devoid of ecological wisdom. The crying need right now—if we have any hope of charting a postmodern, posthumanist, and postpatriarchal transition to the Age of Ecology—is for a new philosophical underpinning of civilization. We need an ecophilosophy that speaks the truth with great immediacy in language that everyone can understand.

That work has already been started by ecofeminists and by the deep ecology movement, many of whose pioneering members are philosophy professors drawing on ecology, ethics, philosophy, and religion. There has been little serious contact between these two movements, a situation that I hope both parties will work to change, for ecofeminism has a great deal to add to the evolution of ecophilosophy. The following are a few examples. Deep ecologists write that Western philosophy, religion, and culture in general are estranged from nature, being anthropocentric. Ecofeminists say, "Yes, but surely you've noticed something else about them, haven't you? They're intensely *andro*centric. And surely you've noticed that Western conquest and degradation of nature are based on fear and resentment; we can demonstrate that that dynamic is linked closely to patriarchal fear and resentment of the elemental power of the female." Deep ecologists write that our estrangement from nature began with classic Greek humanism and the rise of Judeo-Christian culture. But ecofeminists say, "Actually, it began around 4500 B.C. with the Indo-European invasions of nomadic tribes from the Eurasian steppes, who replaced the nature-based and female-honoring religion of the Goddess in Europe, the Near East, Persia, and India with their thunderbolt God, removing that which is held sacred and revered from the life processes of the Earth to the distant realm of an omnipotent, male Sky-God. It is in the Indo-European Revolution, not in the Scientific Revolution of the sixteenth and seventeenth centuries, that one finds the earliest sources of desacralized nature, the foundation of a mechanistic worldview." Deep ecologists write that the only incidence of ecological wisdom in Christianity was Saint Francis of Assisi. But ecofeminists say, "There were many other creation-centered great mystics of the medieval era, including Hildegard of Bingen, Mechtild of Mageburg, Julian of Norwich, and Meister Eckhart, who said he learned much from the Beguines, a female lay order." Deep ecologists write that the well-being and flourishing of human and nonhuman life on Earth has value in itself and that humans have no right to reduce the richness and diversity of life forms except to satisfy vital human needs. Ecofeminists agree but wonder how much one's concept of "vital needs" is shaped by the values of patriarchal culture.

There are also some philosophical ecologists who favor abstract schemes such as "ecological process analysis" to explain the natural world. But ecofeminists find such approaches alone to be sterile and inadequate, a veiled attempt, yet again, to distance oneself from wonder and awe, from the emotional involvement and caring that the natural world calls forth.

To care empathetically about the person, the species, and the great family of all beings, about the bioregion, the biosphere, and the universe is the framework within which ecofeminists wish to address the issues of our time. The problem of world population, for example, is one that attracts no dearth of single-minded solutions. The New Left claims that any population-control program proposed for the Third World is genocide of people of color. The Reagan administration cut off U.S. money for abortion operations in Third World countries and talked of cutting off support for contraception on the grounds that growth always brings prosperity—meaning, I suspect, that Third World fetuses are viewed as future markets. Ecologists point out that the Earth's ecosystems are strained almost beyond their carrying capacity and that a major collapse is imminent if human population continues to soar. Radical feminists say that any population control is patriarchal domination of women's wombs.

The reality that many Third World countries are facing is one with half of their populations under age 18, roaming shanty towns in overcrowded cities looking for food and work while ecosystems die around them. An ecofeminist response to this suffering would involve the following elements: (1) the health of the biosphere demands that the rate of population growth level off *everywhere* and then decline (with the exception of tribal peoples in danger of extinction); (2) Third World women have made it clear that they are not interested in contraception unless health and economic conditions are improved (studies have shown that when the death rate of children goes down, the birth rate goes down); (3) women at the regional level must be involved with the planning of population-control programs, health care, education, and nonexploitative small-scale economic opportunities; (4) the political struggles between indigenous cultural nations and the capitalist or socialist states that have been created around them (a freedom fight that accounts for 78 percent of the current wars globally, according to one study) must be resolved so that the women of the ethnic nations are no longer pressured to have many babies in order to outnumber their oppressors; (5) governments and institutions must address the patriarchal attitudes that condition men to demand a large number of offspring in order to prove their virility—as well as the patriarchal attitudes that bring such misery, and sometimes death, to young mothers who give birth to a female under China's "successful" one-child-only policy.

It is our refusal to banish feelings of interrelatedness and caring from the theory and practice of ecofeminism that will save our efforts from calcifying into well-intentioned reformism, lacking the vitality and wholeness that our lives contain. We need to find our way out of the technocratic alienation and nihilism surrounding us by cultivating and honoring our direct connections with nature.

In my own life I have found that many of those connections have been long since buried. In thinking about ecofeminism recently, I remembered an event that took place 16 years ago, which I had nearly lost from memory. When my daughter was about 3 days old and we were still in the hospital, I wrapped her up one evening and slipped outside to a little garden in the warmth of late June. I introduced her to the pine trees and the plants and the flowers, and they to her, and finally to the pearly moon wrapped in a soft haze and to the stars. I, knowing nothing then of nature-based religious ritual or ecofeminist theory, had felt an impulse for my wondrous little child to meet the rest of cosmic society. Perhaps it was the ultimate coming-out party! The interesting thing is that that experience, although lovely and rich, was so disconnected from life in a modern, technocratic society that I soon forgot all about it. Last year when I heard about a ritual of the Omaha Indians in which the infant is presented to the cosmos, I waxed enthusiastic and made copies of the prayer for friends who were planning a baptism—but forgot completely that I, too, had once been there, so effective is our cultural denial of nature.

I cannot imagine a challenge greater than that addressed by ecofeminism. We know that we are of one fabric with all life on this glorious blue-green planet, that the elements in our bodies and in the world around us were forged by the fireball at the moment the universe was born, and that we have no right to destroy the integrity of the Earth's delicately balanced ecosystems, whose histories are far longer than our own. Around us we see the immensely destructive thrashing of patriarchal leaders *who cannot even name the pain and ignorance that drive their greed.* In their frenzy, they push 10,000 species into extinction each year, a figure that is ever increasing. Can ecofeminism and the related grassroots movements heal those people, heal ourselves, and heal the planet?

Our society is lost and very confused. Perhaps the most effective strategy for us—and certainly the most difficult—is to lead by example: to contribute to the new philosophical base and to work in its new ecopolitics and ecoeconomics; to organize around the concrete issues of suffering and exploitation; to speak out clearly but without malice against those who further policies of injustice and ecological ignorance; to nurture the relationships with our colleagues, never feeling that we must ridicule and crush those with whom we disagree—but most of all, to unlock our memories; to follow the "body parables" of our sexuality; to cultivate our spiritual impulses; to act, as best we can, with pure mind/pure heart; to celebrate with gratitude the wonders of life on Earth; and to seek intimate communion with the natural world. All of these are the flowering of ecofeminism.

Brian Swimme

HOW TO HEAL
A LOBOTOMY

On September 27, 1986, a conference was sponsored by the U.S.'s most prestigious scientific organizations—the Smithsonian Institution and the National Academy of Sciences. Three facts reported by scientists bear repeating. Sociobiologist E. O. Wilson claimed that our accelerating extinction spasm now takes at least 10,000 species each year and the numbers will increase rapidly in the next century. Ecologist Paul Ehrlich predicted that in its folly, "humanity will bring upon itself consequences depressingly similar to those expected from a nuclear winter." And in biologist Norman Myer's estimate, our assault on the Earth constitutes the worst trauma life has suffered in all its 4 billion years of existence.

These facts seem newsworthy, don't they? And yet, in the *New York Times*, this story was printed on page 28. This is puzzling. If news of life's termination isn't fit for the front page, what possibly could be? Life's most imperiled moment in 4 billion years, and we tuck this fact onto page 28 between ads for mink furs?

In our age of slaughter, madness threatens every thinking person. To dwell on the absurdity of a culture that congratulates itself on its "progress" while carrying out geocide is to risk hearing your mind go *spronnnng* while spending the rest of your days gnawing bark off trees. To avoid this unhappy fate, I have had to make some fundamental adjustments toward my society, and toward my profession, science.

The perspective I've settled on is this: the patriarchal mind-set of our culture is very similar to a frontal lobotomy. I think it is important that this be understood once and for all, for otherwise one is condemned to eternal soul-rotting fury. We need to remember the basic helplessness associated with individuals who have had significant portions of their brains removed. One can expect only so much from such people. All the moral indignation in the world will get you nowhere if you're dealing with someone whose mind has been shut down in its fundamental cognitive and sentient powers.

I speak here from my own experience as a scientist. It is quite possible that the lobotomizing taking place in the standard scientific training surpasses that carried out in all other educational processes, even seminaries and business schools, and that's saying something. In any event, this much is certain: by the time they are done training us as leaders for our major institutions, we have only a sliver of our original minds still operative. What sliver is left? As Susan Griffin powerfully delineates (see her essay, "Curves Along the Road," in this volume), it is the sliver chiseled to perfection for controlling, for distancing, for calculating, and for dominating. The rest has been sacrificed in the surgery of patriarchal initiation.

Our entire difficulty is easy to describe. By "our" I should say that I mean scientists in particular and all others who have been strongly influenced by the basic scientific outlook, including presidents, senators, corporate executive officers, generals, journalists, media leaders, lawyers, engineers, city planners, educators at every level, to name some of us. Trapped inside our mind splinter, *we are unable to see what is right there before us.* We see something, no doubt, but it's at best a gnarled illusion of the actual reality enveloping us.

Perhaps it seems odd that I insist that we do not see what is before us. Don't the scientific facts I quoted at the beginning refer to "what is there before us"? Unquestionably so, but they capture only a fragment, which is then further warped when held by minds abused by patriarchal shaping. We have these scientific facts, but we as a society can feel neither the full terror they reveal, nor the pervasive majesty of this Earth they announce. Instead, all the universe is seen as crass material, as a barren mechanism. Even such impressive scientists as E. O. Wilson and Paul Ehrlich regard organisms and nature as "machinery," seemingly unaware that their own basic orientation promotes the very destruction they decry.

Our insistence on analysis, on computation, on categorization has blinded us to the reality of the whole. We have been seated at a table heavy with food, and instead of realizing that this is a feast we are meant to join, we occupy our minds with counting the silverware over and over as we starve to death.

Dorothy Dinnerstein explains our ruin as "the killing split—the split between male and female sensibilities."[1] Until we overcome this splintering of the mind, the destruction will only get worse. But how can we proceed? How do we overcome this split? What do we do to enter the journey that all must take—the journey into seeing what is actually right here before us?

My proposal is that we learn to interpret the data provided by the fragmented scientific mind within the holistic poetic vision alive in ecofeminism. What is this holistic vision? I don't know that I should even attempt a definition. Instead, I would simply point to the perspective, awareness, and consciousness found most clearly in primal peoples and women generally. I am saying quite bluntly that only when the scientific facts are interpreted by an ecofeminist consciousness will we even begin to see where we are, who we are, and what we are about.

This proposal will no doubt be greeted with skepticism by many scientists. They will argue that the scientific facts can only be understood by scientists and therefore must be interpreted by scientists; that without question anyone ignorant of differential equations or organic chemistry would be the very last person one would expect to have something of value to say about the universe. There's something to be said for this point of view, obviously. But in a basic sense, my own understanding is nearly the opposite. My conviction is that the fragmentation of mind that is seemingly *required* to produce the massive knowledge sets of scientific enterprise *disqualifies* these very minds from a full understanding of what they have discovered. To get knowledge of the parts, we had to become partial. But the one-eyed vision of partial minds is exactly what is killing us. To understand the scientific facts we need the wisdom of the whole, the wisdom germane to the consciousness celebrated by ecofeminism.

What would be the result of this union? Poet and novelist Deena Metzger speaks to us of this future work with great feeling; she can already sense the magnificence of this new synthesis, one that will gather together "both branches and roots" of the human world, a vision of tremendous healing power that rises up from the depths of the unconscious and stretches out to include every galaxy.[2] The work of creating this vision will require many minds and will reinvent along the way even what it means to know and to understand.

What I would like to do here is to take a couple of central and extraordinary facts provided by scientists and interpret them according to the vision of some brilliant ecofeminists. I hope in this way to provide some indication of what this work of integration promises.

THE ORIGIN OF THE UNIVERSE

By focusing their razor-sharp intellects and their vastly magnified sensory awareness at the heavens, twentieth century physicists have actually discovered the very origin of all things. Imagine. Throughout all history, this event has been speculated upon, wondered about, prayed to, celebrated in song and chant; and now, in our century, we learn that some of our own species have actually interacted in a direct physical way with the very fire from the beginning of time. That they can actually touch the remnants of this primordial creativity. But what was their response? How did they interpret these facts?

Albert Einstein, who first discovered the universe's birth in a theoretical way, rejected it entirely. It was just too alarming, so he changed his famous field equations. (Eventually the empirical evidence accumulated to the point where he realized he never should have doctored his equations.) Arthur Eddington, another gifted physicist, was just as repulsed. He regarded the discovery of the universe's beginning 15 billion years ago as "abhorrent." Even more revealing is the phrase chosen to name it, the "Big Bang." When one learns that most of us physicists work on weapons research, it comes as no great surprise that we would automatically come up with images of shrapnel and exploding bombs. But that's my whole point. Lodged in the mechanized mind-set of our culture, we scientists are ill-equipped to see what is right before us.

What happens if the sensibility of ecofeminism confronts this scientific discovery? Does it perhaps have something essential to say? Faced with the news of the origin of the universe, Starhawk sings: "Out of the point, the swelling, out of the swelling, the egg, out of the egg, the fire, out of the fire, the stars."[3] Not bombs, not explosions, not abhorrence; rather, she sees the event for what it is, a birthing moment, the Great Birth. The elementary particles rushed apart in their trillion degree heat, yes, and became stars, yes, and all of this is a swelling, an egg, a mysterious engendering that is the root reality behind all the various facts.

To miss the reality of birth in these scientific facts is to miss everything. It is to sit at the heavily laden table and starve. For here is a great moment in human consciousness. Now for the first time in all of human history we have empirical and theoretical evidence of a reality that has been celebrated by primal people for millennia—the great cosmic egg out of which the universe comes forth. The mathematics of this initial singularity of space/time are not enough. We require song and festival and chanting and ritual and every manner of art so that we can establish an original and felt relationship with the universe

Starhawk intuits effortlessly what remained beyond the grasp of these scientists. Our universe is quite clearly a great swelling birthing event, but why was this hidden from the very discoverers of the primeval birth? The further truth of the universe was closed to them because central regions of mind were closed. On the other hand, this sentience is awake in Starhawk because of her life as a woman, as one who has the power to give birth herself, and because of her work as a scholar who has studied the archetypal symbols of primal peoples with their intuitive feeling for the sacred egg at the beginning of time. I emphasize this because I am sensitive to the charge that poetry such as Starhawk's is just an "addendum"—that what are real are the empirical facts, while the rest is commentary. On the contrary, what is true is that this universe is a stupendous birth process, an engendering reality. And we would never have noticed this without the ecofeminist dimensions of mind necessary to respond to this maternal dimension of the universe.

THE EXPANSION OF THE UNIVERSE

As we got used to the idea that the universe really is expanding out in all directions, we scientists did what we do best—we measured it. We calculated just how fast the galaxies were expanding away from each other. But after determining this value, called the Hubble constant, we discovered that this was not just an arbitrary number. It was physicist Stephen Hawking[4] who first noticed something extraordinary: if the expansion rate had been even slightly different, the ensuing universe would have been drastically different. For if the initial expansion of the universe had been even the least fraction of a percent slower, the universe would have collapsed back into chaos without ever having produced anything like a star; or if the expansion had been infinitesimally faster, the particles would have rushed away so quickly that here, too, nothing like a galaxy or a living being would ever have emerged.

One must understand that this was a complete shock to the scientific community. This discovery went counter to everything we had taken for granted—namely, that the universe was just this great backdrop reality, devoid of anything like this sort of subtlety in its large-scale dynamism.

How did the scientific community respond? In various ways—confusion, wonderment, disbelief—but perhaps nowhere more characteristically than in the hypothesis immediately forthcoming that explained the discovery as completely meaningless. We were suddenly asked to believe in an infinity of universes all of which came before us, all of which had different expansion rates, and all of which therefore remained completely barren of life—until finally there was this one universe that accidentally had the right expansion rate so that life just happened to bloom. So long as scientists remain trapped in a total insistence upon reductionism, such uninspired interpretations are inevitable.

What would be the response within the ecofeminist vision? Here I refer to Charlene Spretnak's seminar on Goddess myths, presented as part of the 1987 ecofeminist conference at the University of Southern California. For Charlene, the scientific discovery of the elegance in the cosmic expansion speaks of a reality long honored and celebrated within primal cultures, that of the mystery that weaves the universe. But as soon as I mention this, I hear the cry from scientists: "What mystery?! Show us! That's fantasy!"

It's the same difficulty throughout. So long as a mind insists that reality can only be approached through analyzing events into their component parts, the reality of the whole—obviously—can never appear in its consciousness. So we have the scientists dissecting the universe and insisting that the protons and the strong nuclear interaction and so forth are the only realities. Rather than give up their partial vision, they are willing to invent fantastic scenarios of multiple hypothetical universes concerning which we have not the least shred of evidence.

In fact, nothing is more obvious than Spretnak's assertion that weaving is a fundamental dynamic of this universe. Picture it: From a single fireball the galaxies and stars were all woven. Out of a single molten planet the hummingbirds and pterodactyls and gray whales were all woven. What could be more obvious than this all-pervasive fact of cosmic and terrestrial weaving? Out of a single group of microorganisms, the Krebs cycle was woven, the convoluted human brain was woven, the Pali Canon was woven, all part of the radiant tapestry of being. Show us this weaving? Why, it is impossible to point to anything that *does not* show it, for this creative interlacing energy envelops us entirely. Our lives in truth are nothing less than a further unfurling of this primordial ordering activity.

I say it's obvious, this primordial weaving. But what am I saying? Simply that once the mystery of weaving has been pointed out with power, as by someone like Charlene Spretnak, it is impossible not to see it. This is the way with all truth. The point to emphasize here is that it is women and the ecofeminist consciousness that speak of this dimension of the universe. It is not the physicists, even armed with the best computers. Women are beings who know from the inside out what it is like to weave the Earth into a new human being. Given that experience and the congruent sensitivities seething within body and mind, it would be utterly shocking if ecofeminists *did not* bring forth meanings to the scientific data that were hidden from the scientists themselves.

CONCLUSION

I have tried to show, with a couple of examples taken from physics, what happens when our scientific data come alive within ecofeminist consciousness. These examples were chosen as a way of indicating what I think will be taking place in every area of science. Through time this synthesis will transform our physical, biological, sociological, anthropological, historical data into bodies of living knowledge, with the power to awaken and to regenerate the war-torn depths of the human psyche.

What does it all mean? I have said that we will learn to overcome the split in our sensibilities; that we will activate the atrophied areas of human sentience; that we will learn to see what is before us. What does this amount to but entering a new world. Dare we hope for this? Professor Gloria Orenstein thinks we can. As she explains, "We are learning to tell a new cosmogonic myth, a new myth of creation. And as the fundamental myth of all other myths this promises healing."[5]

What healing does she envision? A healing that touches everyone. We might consider education as an illustration. We need to imagine this cosmogonic myth as alive in our educational processes. What then would our children learn? To exploit? To dominate? No. From Starhawk's poetry they will learn that they and all beings and every thing in existence come from a common birth. That kneaded into their lives is the very fire from the stars and the genes from the sea creatures and that everyone, utterly everyone, is kin. Kin. Not an external relationship; not a legal bond set up by the state. Rather a deep and undeniable communion, from within, even from the center of the DNA.

And from Charlene Spretnak's celebration of the weaving dynamic of the universe, what will we teach? We will teach our children at a young age the central truth of everything: that this universe has been weaving itself into a world of beauty for 15 billion years, that everything has been waiting for their arrival, for they have a crucial if unknown role to play in this great epic of being. We will teach that their destinies and the destinies of the oak trees and all the peoples of Earth are wrapped together. That the same creativity suffusing the universe suffuses all of us, too, and that together we as a community of beings will fashion something as stupendous as the galaxies.

The Native-American writer Paula Gunn Allen insists that we will never be healed, we will never be sane, until we recognize that we are a tribal people.[6] A tribal people of many many clans. I'm convinced she's right. My own hope is that what is happening in our time in this synthesis of scientific knowledge within the ecofeminist and indigenous consciousness is the emergence of the common myth necessary for us to feel and act as kin to everything.

Riane Eisler

THE GAIA TRADITION AND THE PARTNERSHIP FUTURE: AN ECOFEMINIST MANIFESTO

THE LEADING-EDGE social movements of our time—the peace, feminist, and ecology movements, and ecofeminism, which integrates all three—are in some respects very new. But they also draw from very ancient traditions only now being reclaimed due to what British archaeologist James Mellaart calls a veritable revolution in archaeology.

These traditions go back thousands of years. Scientific archaeological methods are now making it possible to document the way people lived and thought in prehistoric times. One fascinating discovery about our past is that for millennia—a span of time many times longer than the 5,000 years conventionally counted as history—prehistoric societies worshipped the Goddess of nature and spirituality, our great Mother, the giver of life and creator of all. But even more fascinating is that these ancient societies were structured very much like the more peaceful and just society we are now trying to construct.

This is not to say that these were ideal societies or utopias. But, unlike our societies, they were *not* warlike. They were *not* societies where women were subordinate to men. And they did *not* see our Earth as an object for exploitation and domination.

In short, they were societies that had what we today call an ecological consciousness: the awareness that the Earth must be treated with reverence and respect. And this reverence for the life-giving and life-sustained powers of the Earth was rooted in a social structure where women and "feminine" values such as caring, compassion, and non-violence were not subordinate to men and the so-called masculine

23

values of conquest and domination. Rather, the life-giving powers incarnated in women's bodies were given the highest social value. In the words of Greek archaeologist Nicolas Platon, who for 50 years excavated the civilization of Minoan Crete where this type of social organization survived until approximately 3,300 years ago, it was a social organization where "the whole of life was pervaded by an ardent faith in the goddess Nature, the source of all creation and harmony."[1]

THE GAIA TRADITION

Most accounts of Western civilization start with Sumer or with the Indo-European Greeks. These accounts generally describe anything prior to Judeo-Christian religion as "pagan." And they usually leave us with the impression that prior societies were both technologically and morally "primitive." But the new knowledge now accumulating from archaeology shows that this is a highly misleading view.

The Paleolithic period, about 25,000 years ago, is generally considered to mark the beginning of Western culture. It is thus the logical place to begin the reexamination of our past. And it is also a good place to begin to reassess our present—and potential future—from a new perspective.

Under the conventional view of Paleolithic art as the story of "man the hunter and warrior," the hundreds of highly stylized carvings of large-hipped, often pregnant women found in Paleolithic caves were dubbed "Venus figurines"—objects in some ancient, and presumably obscene, "fertility cult." They were often viewed as obese, distorted erotic symbols; in other words, as prehistoric counterparts of *Playboy* centerfolds.

But if we really look at these strangely stylized oval figures, it becomes evident that they are representations of the life-giving powers of the world. As UCLA archaeologist Marija Gimbutas and other archaeologists now point out, they are precursors of the Great Goddess still revered in historic times as Isis in Egypt, Ishtar in Canaan, Demeter in Greece, and later, as the Magna Mater of Rome and the Catholic Virgin Mary, the Mother of God.

Similarly, earlier scholars kept finding in Paleolithic drawings and stone and bone engravings what they interpreted as barbed weapons. But then they could not figure out why in these pictures the arrowheads or barbs were always going the wrong way. Or why these "wrong-way weapons" regularly seemed to miss their mark. Only when these pictures were reexamined by an outsider to the archaeological establishment (someone not conditioned to see them as "failed hunting magic") did it become clear that these were not pictures of weapons. They were images of vegetation: trees and plants with their branches going exactly the *right* way.

This same view of human nature—or "man's nature"—as a self-centered, greedy, brutal, "born killer" has long shaped what we have been taught about the next phase of human culture: the Neolithic or agrarian age (approximately 8000–1500 B.C.). The conventional view, still perpetuated by most college survey courses, is that the most important human invention—the development of the technology to domesticate plants—was also the beginning of male dominance, warfare, and slavery. That is, with "man's" invention of agriculture—and thus the possibility of sustaining civilization through a regular and even surplus food supply—came not only male dominance but also warfare and a generally hierarchic social structure.

But once again, the evidence does not bear out the conventional view of civilization as the story of "man's" ever more efficient domination over both nature and other human beings. To begin with, anthropologists today generally believe that the domestication of plants was probably invented by women. Indeed, one of the most fascinating aspects of the current reclamation of our lost heritage is the enormous contribution women have made to civilization. If we look closely at the new data we now have about the first agrarian or Neolithic societies, we actually see that all the basic technologies on which civilization is based were developed in societies that were *not* male dominated and warlike.

As James Mellaart writes, we now know that there was not one cradle of civilization in Sumer about 3,500 years ago.[2] Rather, there were many cradles of civilization, all of them thousands of years older. And thanks to far more scientific and extensive archaeological excavations, we also know that in these highly creative societies women held important social positions as priestesses, craftspeople, and elders of matrilineal clans. Contrary to what we have been taught of the Neolithic or first agrarian civilizations as male dominated and highly violent, these were generally peaceful societies in which both women and men lived in harmony with one another and nature. Moreover, in all these peaceful cradles of civilization, to borrow Merlin Stone's arresting phrase from the book of the same title, "God was a woman" (New York: Dial Press, 1976).

There is today much talk about the Gaia hypothesis (so called because Gaia is the Greek name for the Earth). This is a new scientific theory proposed by biologists Lynn Margulis and James Lovelock that our planet is a living system designed to maintain and to nurture life. But what is most striking about the Gaia hypothesis is that in essence it is a scientific update of the belief system of Goddess-worshipping prehistoric societies. In these societies the world was viewed as the great Mother, a living entity who in both her temporal and spiritual manifestations creates and nurtures all forms of life.

This consciousness of the essential unity of all life has in modern times been preserved in a number of tribal cultures that revere the Earth as our Mother. It is revealing that these cultures have often been described as "primitive" by anthropologists. Equally revealing is that frequently in these cultures women traditionally hold key public positions, as shamans or wise women and often as heads of matrilineal clans. This leads to an important point that once articulated may seem obvious. The way a society structures the most fundamental human relations—the relations between the female and male halves of humanity without which our species could not survive—has major implications for the *totality* of a social system. It clearly affects the individual roles and life choices of both women and men. Equally important, though until now rarely noted, is that it also profoundly affects all our values and social institutions—whether a society will be peaceful or warlike, generally agalitarian or authoritarian, and living in harmony with or bent on the conquest of our environment.

MYTH AND REALITY

Previously unknown prepatriarchal societies have been coming to light since World War II. Rich evidence has been yielded by the excavation of important sites such as Catal Huyuk in Turkey (the largest neolithic site ever excavated) and what Marija Gimbutas calls the civilizations of Old Europe in the Balkans and Greece (which even had a written language thousands of years before Sumer, which she is now deciphering). But perhaps most fascinating is that, in fact, we actually have known about these societies all along. That is, almost all societies have legends about an earlier, more harmonious time. For example, one of the most ancient Chinese legends comes to us from the *Tao Te Ching*, which tells of a time when the *yin* or feminine principle was not yet subservient to the male principle or *yang*, a time when the wisdom of the mother was still honored above all. Hesiod, the Greek poet (ca. 800 B.C.), also writes of an age when the Earth was inhabited by a golden race who "tilled their fields in peaceful ease" (in other words, the Neolithic) before a lesser race brought with them Ares, the Greek god of war.

Not so long ago people rejected the scientific finding that the Earth is round rather than flat even though, according to ancient records, Greek scholars had come to this conclusion centuries earlier. Similarly, the new archaeological findings of a more harmonious and peaceful past are today viewed by some people as impossible, even though they, too, are verified by ancient records.

In fact, we all know of this earlier time from no less a source than the best known story of Western civilization: the story of the Garden of Eden. This biblical story explicitly tells us there was an earlier time when woman and man (Adam and Eve) lived in harmony with one another and with nature. The Garden is probably a symbolic reference to the Neolithic period, since the invention of agriculture made possible the first gardens on Earth. Even the question of what ended this peaceful era is explicitly answered in the biblical story. This lost paradise was a time when society was *not* male dominated: as the Bible has it, it was a time before a male god decreed woman to be subservient to man.

We have been taught that our fall from paradise is an allegory of God's punishment of man—and particularly woman—for the sin of disobeying the command not to eat from the tree of knowledge. But what the archaeological evidence reveals is that this story (like the Babylonian myths from which it derives) is based on folk memories of a time before (as the Bible also tells us) brother turned against brother and man trod woman down under his heel.

If we look at both the archaeological and mythic record from this new perspective, we begin to understand many otherwise incomprehensible aspects of the Garden of Eden. Why, for example, would Eve take advice from a serpent? The answer is that the serpent was in ancient times a symbol of oracular prophecy (as in the Greek temple of Delphi, where a woman, the high priestess or Pythoness, was still in historical times inspired by a serpent, the Python, to prophesy the future). Moreover, because the serpent was for millennia associated with the worship of the Goddess (as a symbol of cyclic regeneration, since it sheds and regrows its skin), Eve's continued association with the serpent also represents a refusal to give up the old Goddess-centered religion.

The punishment of Eve for her refusal to acknowledge Jehovah's monopoly of the tree of knowledge is a mythical device to justify male dominance and authoritarian rule. But the underlying story—with critical significance for our time—is that it records a major social shift. This shift, now being extensively verified by the archaeological evidence, is the dramatic change that occurred in our prehistory from an egalitarian and peaceful way of living to the violent imposition of male dominance.

THE LOST CIVILIZATION

Even in the nineteenth century, when archaeology was still in its infancy, scholars found evidence of societies where women were not subordinate to men. But their interpretation of this evidence was that if these societies were not partriarchies, they must have been matriarchies. In other words, if men did not dominate women, then women must have dominated men. However, this conclusion is not borne out by the evidence. Rather, it is a function of what I have called a *dominator* society worldview. The real alternative to patriarchy is not matriarchy, which is only the other side of the dominator coin. The alternative, now revealed to be the original direction of our cultural evolution, is what I call a *partnership* society: a way of organizing human relations in which beginning with the most fundamental difference in our species—the difference between female and male—diversity is *not* equated with inferiority or superiority.

What we have until now been taught as history is only the history of dominator species—the record of the male dominant, authoritarian, and highly violent civilizations that began about 5,000 years ago. For example, the conventional view is that the beginning of European civilization is marked by the emergence in ancient Greece of the Indo-Europeans. But the new archaeological evidence demonstrates that the arrival of the Indo-Europeans actually marks the truncation of European civilization. That is, as Marija Gimbutas extensively documents, there was in Greece and the Balkans an earlier civilization, which she calls the civilization of Old Europe.[3] The first Indo-European invasions (by pastoralists from the arid steppes of the northeast) foreshadow the end of a matrifocal, matrilineal, peaceful agrarian era. Like fingerprints in the archaeological record, we see evidence of how wave after wave of barbarian invaders from the barren fringes of the globe leave in their wake destruction and what archaeologists call cultural impoverishment. And what characterizes these invaders is that they bring with them male dominance along with their angry gods of thunder and war.

The archaeological record shows a dramatic shift after these invasions. We see the disappearance of millennial traditions of art and pottery, a sharp decrease in the size of settlements, the appearance of "suttee" chieftain tombs (so called because with the male skeleton are sacrificed women, children, and animals to serve him even after death). Warfare now becomes endemic, along with "strongman" rule, since these invaders, as Gimbutas writes, "worshipped the power of the lethal blade."

One of the most striking manifestations of this change is found in the art. Now begins something dramatically absent before: the idealization of male violence and male dominance in an art that glorifies killing (scenes of "heroic" battles) and rapes (as in Zeus's fabled rapes of both mortal women and goddesses). And equally striking is the transformation of myth. Here, too, "strongman" rule is idealized and even presented as divinely ordained, as the bards, scribes, and priests of the ruling men systematically distort and gradually expunge the myths and images of the civilization of Old Europe from their sacred and secular tales. But although these, too, become distorted, memories of an earlier and better time still linger in folk stories and legends.

In the nineteenth century, the archaeological excavations of Sophia and Heinrich Schliemann established that the Homeric story of the Greek sacking of Troy was historically based. Similarly, the probable historical basis for the legend of Atlantis is now being revealed by twentieth century archaeological excavations. The fabled civilization of Atlantis was said to have ended when large land masses sank into the sea. What geologists and archaeologists now reveal is that approximately 3,500 years ago massive earthquakes and tidal waves in the Mediterranean caused large land masses to sink into the sea. For example, as in the legend of Atlantis, most of the island of Thera, or Santorini, was swallowed by the sea.

These cataclysmic events seem to have marked the end of what scholars call Minoan civilization, a highly technologically developed Bronze Age civilization centered in the Mediterranean island of Crete. Minoan Crete had the first paved roads in Europe, and even indoor plumbing. In sharp contrast to other "high civilizations" of antiquity (such as Sumer and dynastic Egypt), Crete had a generally high standard of living, with houses built for both beauty and comfort. Its art, too, is very different from that of Sumer and Egypt: it is so natural, so free, so full of the celebration of life in all its forms, that sober scholars have described it as unique in the annals of civilization for its grace and exuberant joy.

But what really makes Minoan Crete unique is that it was neither a male-dominant nor warlike culture. Archaeologist Nicolas Platon, the former head of the Acropolis Museum and director of antiquities in Crete, notes that this was a "remarkable peaceful society." He also notes that here descent was still traced through the mother and that "the influence of women is visible in every sphere."[4] For example, the only Minoan fresco of tribute is not the conventional picture of an aggrandized king with a sword in his hand and kneeling figures at his feet characteristic of male-dominant ancient civilizations. It is rather the picture of a woman. And instead of sitting on an elevated throne, she is standing with her arms raised in a gesture of benediction as men approach with offerings of fruits, wine, and grains.

In other words, in this highly creative and peaceful society, masculinity was *not* equated with domination and conquest. Accordingly, women and the "soft" or "feminine" values of caring, compassion, and nonviolence did not have to be devalued. Power was seen as *actualizing* power—as the capacity to create and nurture life. It was power to, rather than power over: the power to illuminate and transform human consciousness (and with it reality) that is still in our time symbolized by the "feminine vessel," the chalice or Holy Grail.

NATURE, CULTURE, TECHNOLOGY,
AND SPIRITUALITY

We have been taught that in "Western tradition," religion is the spiritual realm and that spirituality is separate from, and superior to, nature. But for our Goddess-worshipping ancestors, spirituality and nature were one. In the religion of Western partnership societies, there was no need for the artificial distinction between spirituality and nature or for the exclusion of half of humanity from spiritual power.

In sharp contrast to "traditional" patriarchal religions (where only men can be priests, rabbis, bishops, lamas, Zen masters, and popes), we know from Minoan, Egyptian, Sumerian, and other ancient records that women were once priestesses. Indeed, the highest religious office appears to have been that of high priestess in service of the Goddess. And the Goddess herself was not only the source of all life and nature; she was also the font of spirituality, mercy, wisdom, and justice. For example, as the Sumerian Goddess Nanshe, she sought justice for the poor and shelter for the weak. The Egyptian Goddess Maat was also the goddess of justice. The Greek Goddess Demeter was known as the lawgiver, the bringer of civilization, dispensing mercy and justice. As the Celtic Goddess Cerridwen, she was the goddess of intelligence and knowledge. And it is Gaia, the primeval prophetess of the shrine of Delphi, who in Greek mythology is said to have given the golden apple tree (the tree of knowledge) to her daughter, the Goddess Hera. Moreover, the Greek Fates, the enforcers of laws, are female. And so also are the Greek Muses, who inspire all creative endeavor.

In fact, this association of woman with the highest spirituality— with both wisdom and mercy—survived well into historical times. Even though women were by then already barred from positions of spiritual power, Sophia (the Greek word for wisdom) is still female. So also is the Hebrew word for wisdom, *hochmah*. And even though we have not been taught to think of her this way, the Catholic Virgin Mary (now the only mortal figure in the Christian holy family of divine Father and Son) still perpetuates the image of the Goddess as the Merciful Mother.

We also know from a number of contemporary tribal societies that the separation between nature and spirituality is not universal. Tribal peoples generally think of nature in spiritual terms. Nature spirits must be respected, indeed, revered. And we also know that in many of these tribal societies women as well as men can be shamans or spiritual healers and that descent in these tribes is frequently traced through the mother.

In sum, *both* nature and woman can partake of spirituality in societies oriented to a partnership model. In such societies there is no need for a false dichotomy between a "masculine" spirituality and a "feminine" nature. Moreover, since in ancient partnership societies woman and the Goddess were identified with *both* nature and spirituality, neither woman nor nature were devalued and exploited.

It is often said that the answer to our mounting environmental crises is a "return to nature." According to this view, the roots of our ecological problems lie in the shift from a religious to a secular or scientific/technological worldview. We are told that with the Renaissance, and later the Enlightenment, "modern man" became alienated from both himself and nature.

But if we carefully examine both our past and present, we see that many peoples past and present living close to nature have all too often been blindly destructive of their environment. While many indigenous societies have a great reverence for nature, there are also both non-Western and Western peasant and nomadic cultures that have overgrazed and overcultivated land, decimated forests, and, where population pressures have been severe, killed off animals needlessly and indifferently. And while there is much we can learn today from tribal cultures, it is important not to indiscriminately idealize all non-Western cultures and/or blame all our troubles on our secular-scientific age. For clearly such tribal practices as cannibalism, torture, and female genital mutilation (which continue into our time under the guise of ethnic or religious tradition) antedate modern times. And some indigenous and/or highly religious societies (whether in reaction to an extremely harsh environment or to conquest by a foreign culture) have been as barbarous as the most "civilized" Roman emperors or the most "spiritual" Christian inquisitors.

Another widely held notion is that technology is causing our global problems. But technology is integral to the human condition. Indeed, the story of human culture is to a large extent the story of human technology. It is the story not only of the fashioning of material tools but also of the fashioning of our most important and unique non-material tools: the mental tools of language and imagery, of human-made words, symbols, and pictures. Advanced technologies are the extension of human functions, of our hands' and brains' capacity to alter our environment, and ourselves. Indeed, technology is itself part of the evolutionary impulse, the striving for the expansion of our potential as human beings within both culture and nature.

Once we look at technology from the new perspective provided by the gender-holistic analysis of our past and present, it is clear that the problem is not now nor has it ever been simply that of technology. The same technological base can produce very different types of tools: tools to kill and oppress other humans or tools to free our hands and minds from dehumanizing drudgery. The problem is that in dominator societies, where "masculinity" is identified with conquest and domination, every new technological breakthrough is basically seen as a tool for more effective oppression and domination. That is, what led to the nineteenth century's exploitation of women, children, and men in sweat shops and mines and the twentieth century factories of dehumanizing assembly lines where workers became cogs in industrial machines was *not* the invention of machines. Rather, it was the use to which that mechanization was put in a dominator system. Similarly, the use of modern technologies to devise ever more effective and costly weapons is *not* a requirement of modern technology. It is, however, a requirement of dominator systems, where throughout recorded history the highest priority has been given to technologies fashioned not to sustain and enhance life, but technologies to dominate and destroy.

In sum, the basic issue is not one of technology versus spirituality or nature versus culture. The fundamental issue is how we define nature, culture, technology, and spirituality—which in turn hinges on whether we orient to a dominator or a partnership model of society.

It is not science and technology, but the numbing of our innate human sensibilities that makes it possible for men to dominate, oppress, exploit, and kill. What passes for "scientific objectivity" in a dominator society is the substitution of detached measuring for an inquiry designed to enhance and advance human evolution. Even beyond this, what often passes for "higher" spirituality in a dominator society is equally stunted and distorted. For what this system requires is that spirituality be equated with a detachment that often condones and encourages indifference to avoidable human suffering—as in most Eastern religions. Or it leads to the Western dualism that justifies the domination of culture over nature, of man over woman, of technology over life, and of high priests and other so-called spiritual leaders over "common" women and men.

RECLAIMING OUR PARTNERSHIP TRADITIONS

In ancient times the world itself was one. The beating of drums was the heartbeat of the Earth—in all its mystery, enchantment, wonder, and terror. Our feet danced in sacred groves, honoring the spirits of nature. What was later broken asunder into prayer and music, ritual and dance, play and work, was originally one.

For many thousands of years, millennia longer than the 5,000 years we count as recorded history, everything was done in a sacred manner. Planting and harvesting fields were rites of spring and autumn celebrated in a ritual way. Baking bread from grains, molding pots out of clay, weaving cloth out of fibers, carving tools out of metals—all these

ways of technologically melding culture and nature were sacred cere
monies. There was then no splintering of culture and nature, spirituality, science, and technology. Both our intuition and our reason were
applied to the building of civilization, to devising better ways for us
to live and work cooperatively.

The rediscovery of these traditions signals a way out of our alienation from one another and from nature. In our time, when the nuclear
bomb and advanced technology threaten all life on this planet, the
reclamation of these traditions can be the basis for the restructuring
of society: the completion of the modern transformation from a dominator to a partnership world.

Poised on the brink of ecocatastrophe, let us gain the courage to
look at the world anew, to reverse custom, to transcend our limitations, to break free from the conventional constraints, the conventional
views of what are knowledge and truth. Let us understand that we
cannot graft peace and ecological balance on a dominator system; that
a just and egalitarian society is impossible without the full and equal
partnership of women and men.

Let us reaffirm our ancient covenant, our sacred bond with our
Mother, the Goddess of nature and spirituality. Let us renounce the
worship of angry gods wielding thunderbolts or swords. Let us once
again honor the chalice, the ancient symbol of the power to create and
enhance life—and let us understand that this power is not woman's
alone but also man's.

For ourselves, and for the sake of our children and their children,
let us use our human thrust for creation rather than destruction. Let
us teach our sons and daughters that men's conquest of nature, of
women, and of other men is not a heroic virtue; that we have the
knowledge and the capacity to survive; that we need not blindly follow
our bloodstained path to planetary death; that we can reawaken from
our 5,000-year dominator nightmare and allow our evolution to resume
its interrupted course.

While there is still time, let us fulfill our promise. Let us reclaim
the trees of knowledge and of life. Let us regain our lost sense of
wonder and reverence for the miracles of life and love, let us learn again
to live in partnership so we may fulfill our responsibility to ourselves
and to our Great Mother, this wondrous planet Earth.

Sally Abbott

THE ORIGINS OF GOD
IN THE BLOOD
OF THE LAMB

And what rough beast, its hour come round at last,
Slouches towards Bethlehem to be born?
                    YEATS, "THE SECOND COMING"

As SOMEONE WHO HAS been studying the scholarship
on Goddess worship for the past 13 years, I have been painfully aware
of the connection between the demise of the Goddess, the rise of patriarchy, and the rape of the environment. But while in general I had
a bad feeling about hunting and about raising animals for slaughter,
I did not focus my attention on animals per se until 5 years ago when
I went on a 4-day fast to obtain a vision.

The vision quest is a traditional form of seeking guidance among
Native Americans, for a young person desiring to find out how to live
and for an older person facing a difficult task. In my own case, I had
a general, uneasy feeling that there was something wrong with the
way I was living, something I was unable to apprehend in my ordinary
state, and I hoped to find out what this was.

The first few days of the fast passed uneventfully, although pleas-
antly enough. I went to work during the day in a weakened condition
and in the evenings I went to bed early and slept easily. My vision
did not come until the last night and, at that, was more of a feeling
than a vision, but one so strong that it caused me to see differently.
The general uneasiness that had caused me to go on the vision quest
escalated that night into a crescendo of terror. Finally, at 2:30 A.M., I
rushed next door and spent the rest of the night at my neighbor's, seeking protection from imagined killers.

In the fasting state, I had a sense of myself as a sacred person waiting to be sacrificed and, alternatively, as a tethered animal waiting to be slaughtered, and, in fact, I could not distinguish between the two. I was terrified that I would be put to death by God or the collective animal kingdom—and here again I could not distinguish between God and the animal spirits—to avenge the animals I had eaten.

About 8 years earlier, I had had a vision of myself leaving my leather shoes and purse by the gate before entering the Garden of Eden. The image had impressed me at the time, but now the feelings were strong enough to act on, and by dawn I was determined to become a vegetarian.

I adjusted quickly to my new diet and didn't think much more about my "vision" until a year and a half later, when I began doing research on shamanism.

Shamanic tribal religion, which is still practiced today in many areas, including the United States, had its origins in hunting magic at the onset of the Ice Age, close to 40,000 years ago. Scenes on the walls of caves in Europe depict the slaying of the "souls" of animals through art, to be followed by capturing their bodies in the hunt. After the hunt, the slain animals' bones were ritually buried to appease their souls. Thus, I believe occurred the first separation of body and soul, and that the term *anima* means soul is, I think, no coincidence.

The shamanic worldview with its reverence for animal spirits and guardians resonated with the vision I had had and led me to speculate on the relation of religion to humanity's feelings of guilt about killing animals. Since shamanism (along with Goddess worship) is the world's oldest religion, I wondered whether the gods themselves hadn't come into being as the avenging voices of the slain animals and were thenceforth with us in the form of conscience and moral law, at first demanding our own blood and later demanding right action. I began to feel that ritual and religion themselves might have been brought to birth by the necessity of propitiation for the killing of animals, and, based on my research, I developed the following ideas for this essay.

RITUAL AND PROPITIATION IN SHAMANIC CULTURES

In the shamanic worldview, the human relationship to animals is central. In modern shamanic societies, animals are frequently referred to as relatives—as "father" and "grandmother."[1] The Bororo people of

South America believe that every "tapir and every wild pig and every alligator" shelters the shade of one or another of their departed tribes people.[2] There are myths about times when there were "marriages between human beings and beasts, of commerce and conversation . . . and of specific covenanting episodes from which the rites and customs of the people derive."[3] Given this proximity with the animals, early peoples' feeling about hunting was likely to have been at best highly conflicted. Among the Ainu of Japan, for instance, there was the belief that in killing and eating a bear, they were freeing its spirit to return to the bear's native homeland. Joseph Campbell sees this notion as "an obvious psychological defense against the guilt feelings and fears of revenge of a primitive hunting and fishing folk whose whole existence hangs upon acts of continual, merciless killing."[4]

In the *Origins of Sacrifice*, O. E. James points out that killing and eating an animal to which early peoples felt deep kinship was an "anomaly calling forth an emotional situation to be approached by an appropriate ritual." He reports that when a dead bear was brought into a Tlingit camp in Alaska, for instance, it was spoken to as a human, with such sayings as: "I am poor, that is why I am hunting you." Or, "My father's brother-in-law, have pity upon me, let me be in luck."[5] Among the Koryaks of northeastern Siberia, a sacred dance was held after the killing of a bear, during which a woman put on the skin of the slain animal and danced, entreating it not to be angry.[6]

In the following poem, a Finnish shaman addresses a slain bear in a ritual, trying to talk the bear-spirit out of revenge and promising better things to come in the hereafter:

> Otso, thou my well-beloved
> honey-eater of the woodlands,
> let not anger swell thy bosom;
> I have not the force to slay thee,
> willingly thy life thou givest
> as a sacrifice to Horthland.
> We shall never treat thee evil,
> thou shallt dwell in peace and plenty,
> thou shallt feed on milk and honey . . . [7]

Eskimo rites and taboos related to the killing of animals are dramatic and complex, especially emphasizing the familial bonds between humans and animals, as reported by Rasmussen of the Ilulik:

When a whale, bear, or bearded seal had been killed, for example, no man's or woman's work could be done for three days. Special food dishes had to be used. Bearded seals required particular sacrifice, for the Mother of the Sea Animals was especially fond of bearded seals. . . . No one could step where a dead seal's head had lain. If a seal was caught in a freshwater lake, the same sacrifices were required as in the case of a man who had lost a brother . . . if a white caribou were brought down, the hunter had to observe the same taboos as one who had lost a sister.[8]

Violation of the taboo would mean that the spirit of the animal could take revenge on the hunter, or that the entire band of animals might leave the area in which the hunter and his people lived.

THE SOUL OF ANIMALS IN THE WESTERN TRADITION
AND THE JUDEO-CHRISTIAN ETHIC

Given their almost familial relations with animals, the conflict faced by early humans might have been just the archetypal situation that Aristotle points to as arousing terror and pity, and catharsis, and perhaps therein lies the birth of religion—bearing the unbearable, bringing into play some other reality in which all could be made over. In terms of modern-day psychology, this would parallel the "splitting off" experience of a psychotic break, as likely felt then as now as a religious experience. Along similar lines, according to Julian Jaynes, the first instance of schizophrenia being considered an illness did not occur until 400 B.C., and he believes that before 2000 B.C. "everyone was schizophrenic."[9]

Andreas Lommel quotes an Eskimo shaman who states that the greatest danger in life "lies in the fact that man's food is made up of souls."[10] As we have seen, people in shamanistic societies follow taboos and enact assiduous rituals for the spirits of slain animals. In reindeer Eskimo cultures, the shaman in the course of initiation experiences a ritual dismemberment and has to make a dangerous journey down to Sedna, the mother of the sea, to fetch the souls of the animals to be hunted. In the shamanistic system, nothing is taken from the animal world without putting something back.

If we accept the notion that ritual was developed to assuage the fear of reprisal and the guilt about killing animals, the creationist doctrine of the Judeo-Christian tradition that flatly denies the evolutionary link and the familial connectedness to animals may be seen as a further defense against that fear or guilt—an attempt to completely erase animals from consciousness. But there is a toll, nonetheless, in the form of free-floating guilt and a sense of original sin.

The biblical expulsion from the paradisiacal state resulted in enmity between humans and animals and a sense of shame about nudity and sexuality—our "animal" nature. Interestingly enough, the Cherokee have a similar myth that in the beginning "we find all creatures alike living and working together in harmony and mutual helpfulness until man, by his aggressiveness and disregard for the rights of others, provokes their hostility, when insects, birds, fishes, reptiles, and four-footed beasts join forces against him. Henceforth, their lives are apart, but the difference is always one of degree only."[11] Undoubtedly, the enmity is caused by consciousness of guilt for killing animals. The Christian view that the blood of Jesus is shed in atonement for the sin of Adam further suggests that original sin might be related to killing, since a death is exacted in atonement. Jesus's epithet as the "lamb of God" imagistically strengthens this association, as does his birth in a stable.

IMPLICATIONS

We have seen how early humans developed ritual and religion to help them cope with terrifyingly conflicted feelings about hunting animals and have speculated that these early emotions gave rise to the origin of religions. We have also speculated that the cross-cultural myth of the expulsion from paradise relates to the enmity between humans and animals caused by hunting and by raising animals for slaughter.

I would like to close with the idea that the cultural recognition of animal rights could conversely bring about the fulfillment of a new covenant with animals and a restoration to the paradisiacal state. Such recognition would eliminate the suffering of factory farm animals as well as experiments on animals. The cultural adoption of a vegetarian diet would eliminate the needless death of 15 million animals a year and enable the feeding of the world's human population because, as Frances Moore Lappé has argued, a diet centered around meat requires six to seven times as much land as does a vegetarian diet.[12]

Finally, if ritual and religion were brought into the world specifically to meet the need to propitiate animals because of hunting, the liberation of animals would negate the need and inaugurate an enlightened secularism that could heal the false division of body and soul. The night after I'd developed most of the ideas for this article, I had a wonderful dream. I was lying out in the woods and heard a rustling in the bushes. Out came a couple of mangy, moth-eaten-looking wolves, followed by some sheep. One of the sheep bent over and kissed me gratefully on the mouth. It was only a dream, but I am still reeling from that kiss.[13]

Mara Lynn Keller

THE ELEUSINIAN MYSTERIES: ANCIENT NATURE RELIGION OF DEMETER AND PERSEPHONE

ANCIENT GREEK PEOPLES voiced their understanding of nature, themselves, their community, and the cosmos through sacred stories called myth or *mythos*. The myth of Demeter and Persephone illuminated the experiences of life that through all times remain the most mysterious—birth, sexuality, death—and the greatest mystery of all, enduring love. In ceremonies devoted to the two Goddesses, people expressed their joy in the beauty and abundance of nature, including the provident harvest of their crops; in personal love, sexuality, and procreation; and in the rebirth of the human spirit, even through suffering and death. Cicero wrote of these rites: "We have been given a reason not only to live in joy, but also to die with better hope."[1]

The Mother Earth religion did not glorify the sacrifice of her children, but celebrated their birth, enjoyment of life, and loving return to her in death. As Aeschylus (525–456 B.C.) wrote in *The Libation Bearers*, "Yea, summon Earth, who brings all things to life / and rears, and takes again into her womb.[2]

Demeter's rites were celebrated most elaborately at Eleusis, 14 miles northwest of Athens, where they flourished for almost 2,000 years. Here people of the Mycenaean era built their first shrine to Demeter about 1450 B.C.[3] The Eleusinian mysteries were the greatest of all ancient Greek religious festivals. During the Archaic period, celebrants came to Eleusis from all of Greece; during Hellenistic and Roman times, as many as 30,000 celebrants gathered together from around the known world.[4] During the later eras, the rites remained open to all, women and men, young and old, slave and free. The main requirement for initiation was that a person have no unatoned blood guilt on his or her hands.

The most ancient of the Greek Goddesses, according to the Greek poet Hesiod (about 800 B.C.) was Gaia, Mother Earth. The poet of the Homeric "Hymn to Gaia" praises the primal Goddess with this song:

> Mother of us all, oldest of all, of the earth,
>   the sacred ground,
> nourishing all out of her treasures—children,
>   fields, cattle, beauty . . .
> Mistress, from you come our fine children and
>   bountiful harvests;
> Yours is the power to give mortals life and to
>   take it away . . .
> Hail to you, mother of Gods.[5]

Demeter, like her grandmother Gaia, was the Earth Mother. She was One-in-Many, Many-in-One, the Earth and the fruits of the Earth. Demeter's rites were fertility festivals, praising Demeter the Great Mother, giver of children and crops, and her daughter Kore, also called Persephone, the Grain Maiden, who embodied and in turn would bear the new crop.

Demeter was revered as the Goddess who taught the cultivation of grain to the Greek people, enabling them to enhance with their own ingenuity and energy the fruitfulness of the Earth and the material abundance of their lives. During Demeter's ancient ritual, the peoples of the farming community, standing first at one side of their fields, then the opposite side, fervently invoked the creative forces of nature for their crops, calling to the sky: "HYE!, rain!, pour down!"; then to the Earth, "KYE!, conceive!, bring forth!"

Demeter was invoked by many names: *Carpophorus*, Fruit-bearer; *Thermasia*, Warmth; *Chloe*, Green; *Anesidora*, Sender-up of Gifts; *Thesmophoria*, Lawgiver; and in her aspect of healer, *Phosphoros*, Light-bearer. In Arcadia she was sometimes addressed as Demeter *Erinyes*, the Furious, and sometimes as Demeter *Lousia*, the Gentle.[6] The rhetorician Isocrates in the fourth century B.C. explains that: "Demeter bestowed on us two gifts, the greatest gifts of all: first, the fruits of the earth, thanks to which we have ceased to live the life of beasts; and second, the mysteries; and they who are initiated therein have brighter hopes both for the end of their life and for all eternity."[7]

Demeter was closely related to the Goddess Isis of Egypt. On the Aegean island of Delos, Demeter and Isis were worshipped side by side. Both Goddesses were worshipped as giver of grain and of the laws of civilization; as healer; as queen of the dead; and as the one who provided the mystery of resurrected life. According to the myths, Demeter brought her daughter back from the underworld, while Isis brought her beloved partner Osiris back to life after he had been killed by his brother Seth, who wished to take over Osiris's kingdom. According to the Greek historian Herodotus (fifth century B.C.), the knowledge of agriculture was first brought to the peoples of Greece by the women of Egypt.[8]

At Eleusis, and in other sacred precincts, priestesses of Demeter were called *melissae*—bees, producers of sweetness. Various plants were especially sacred to Demeter: wheat and barley, basic food sources; the many-seeded pomegranate, symbol of fertility and sexual pleasure; and poppies, symbol of sleep and death. The prolific and nurturant pig was also sacred to Demeter; as were the playful dolphin, the peaceful dove, and the powerful, graceful horse. Snakes, too, were frequently included in ritual ceremonies of the Earth Goddess religion. Snakes protected the grain harvest from being eaten by rodents. And because snakes shed their skin, they were closely linked to healing and reincarnation. The sphinx, with its lion's body, great wings, and woman's head, was another symbol found in the artwork of Eleusis, combining elemental physical, psychic, and spiritual powers. I see the sphinx, like the snake, as a major symbol of the early mother-clan or mother-rite Goddess cultures.

Along with the Earth Mother's rituals for farming, ancient peoples also celebrated their community's renewal through sexual union and the birthing of new human life. Demeter's rites, we are told, were "performed with the same intent concerning the growth of crops and of human offspring."[9] One of the major purposes of the mother-daughter Goddess religion was to instruct girls about their fertility and the unfolding patterns of women's lives. As Demeter was protectress of childbearing, so one of Persephone's names was "midwife."

Ecofeminist philosopher Charlene Spretnak, drawing upon the classical scholarship of Jane Ellen Harrison, Louis Farnell, Sir Arthur Evans, and others, has created a prepatriarchal version of the Demeter/Persephone myth that does not include Persephone's abduction and rape, the aspect so greatly emphasized during the patriarchal epoch:

> Demeter and Persephone share the bountiful fields, enjoying the beautiful earth, and watching over the crops together. One day, Persephone asks her mother about the restless spirits of the dead she has seen hovering about their earthly homes. "Is there no one in the underworld to receive the newly dead?" she asks. Demeter explains that she rules over the underworld as well as the upper world, but her more important work is above ground, feeding the living.
>
> Reflecting on the bewilderment and pain she has seen in the ghostly spirits, Persephone replies, "The dead need us, Mother. I will go to them." After trying to persuade Persephone to stay with her, Demeter relents: "Very well. . . . We cannot give only to ourselves. I understand why you must go. Still, you are my daughter, and for every day you remain in the underworld, I will mourn your absence."
>
> Persephone gathers three sheaves of wheat and three poppies, favorite flower of Demeter, takes the torch that Demeter has prepared for her, and begins her descent down into a deep chasm into the underworld. After a long journey, she comes to a place where many spirits are milling about, moaning. She moves among them, and after preparing an altar, she beckons them to her, saying, "If you come to me, I will initiate you into your new world. You have waxed into the fullness of life, and waned into darkness; may you be renewed in peace and wisdom."
>
> Meanwhile, Demeter has grown sorrowful, her bountiful energies draining from the earth, leaving it barren, with no crops growing to feed the humans. After some months, Persephone decides she will return to the upper world. As she approaches her mother, the flowers of the earth rise up in joyful song, and as Demeter and Persephone run to embrace each other, the birds and animals begin to sing, "Persephone returns, Persephone returns." And as the mother and daughter dance and dance, new growth springs up in the fields, and the humans join in the rejoicing.
>
> Each time Persephone goes back down into the underworld, the mortals share with Demeter the bleak season of her daughter's absence; and as she rejoins her mother in the spring, they are renewed by the signs of Persephone's return.[10]

This sacred story, while describing the relationship of the two Goddesses, mother and daughter, also explains nature's seasonal cycles of earthly abundance, barrenness, and renewal, as well as the seasons of human experience, from birth and maturation to death and beyond.

In the Homeric "Hymn to Demeter," the poet describes the mother and daughter's reunion this way:

> Then all day long, with their hearts in
>   agreement, they basked
> In each other's presence, embracing with love and
>   forgetful of sorrow
> And each received joy from the other and gave joy in
>   return.

Such amazing love between mother and daughter has rarely been articulated or celebrated in the major patriarchal religions or literature of the world.

The hymn continues: "Then smooth-coifed Hecate came and lovingly kissed / The holy child of Demeter, and . . . from that time on / [was] Persephone's . . . faithful companion."[11] This part of the Demeter/Persephone myth lets us see the reverence among early farming peoples for the Goddess as girl, mother, and wise grandmother, an honoring of women in all stages of life.

Respect for the triple-aspected Goddess was also expressed in devotions to the moon, Selene, who passes through three phases—waxing youth, maturing fullness, and waning toward darkness and the unknown—before beginning another cycle. As we know, women's fertility cycles are closely tied to lunar cycles, and these in turn are linked to the measuring of seasonal cycles for the favorable planting and harvesting of crops.

Kore or Persephone, Demeter, and Hecate were names frequently given the triple Goddess. She was also called the three Fates, the three Graces, the nine Muses—and, as the customs of patriarchy grew, the three Furies.

Pausanias in the second century A.D. wrote that the three Fates were named Birth, Death, and Love; Love being the eldest.[12] And so we may assume, of these three destinies, love was primary, and the most honored.

SEXUALITY AND MARRIAGE

For the ancients, sexual love was considered one of life's deepest mysteries. It was experienced as the participation of the human body and spirit in the creative energies of nature, of the universe.

Demeter was first a Goddess in Crete before arriving in Greece. Homer writes that the Goddess herself made love in the fields: "So too fair-haired Demeter once in the spring did yield / To love, and with Iason lay in a new-ploughed field."[13]

The offspring of Demeter and Iason of Crete, according to Hesiod, was a son named Plutos. It seems fitting that the offspring of Demeter would be named Plenty, and that he be associated with Irene, Goddess of peace, who was often represented in art holding the infant Plutos in her arms. Abundance was also one of the names for Demeter. It is ironic, then, that Pluto, the "rich one" or "wealth-giver" became a name given to Hades, abductor of Persephone and brother of the war god, Zeus.

In Homer's account, Demeter yielded not to Iason, but to her own feelings of love, an experience conveyed by one word, *thoumos*, translated as spirit/passion/feeling: "Demeter yielded to her spirit/passion/feeling . . . and mingled with him in lovemaking and sleep."[14] But in later versions of the story of Demeter and Iason, Demeter is raped by Iason. And into the religion of Demeter and Persephone itself come accounts of the rape of the Goddess by Zeus, Poseidon, or Hades.

In the lyrical language of a Homeric poet, the story unfolds: Persephone was

> . . . playing far from gold-bladed Demeter of the harvest . . . gathering flowers with the daughters of Ocean, roses and crocuses and beautiful violets, iris, hyacinth, and the narcissus . . . a . . . lure for the blossoming girl according to Zeus's plan to please Hades, who receives all. It was an object of awe for all to see, both the immortal gods and mortal men. And from its root grew a hundred heads smelling a smell so sweet that the whole broad sky above and all the earth laughed and the salty swell of the sea. The girl was amazed and stretched out both her hands to take the marvelous bauble. But as she did, the earth gaped open and Lord Hades, whom we all meet, burst forth with his immortal horses . . . Begging for pity and fighting him off, she was dragged into his golden chariot. She screamed the shrill cry of a maenad . . . [15]

Demeter searched for her daughter for 9 days without food or rest, without success, and then lapsed into grief. The fields withered, and humanity was threatened by famine. Zeus finally reversed his decision and ordered that Persephone be returned to her mother. Because Demeter refused to abandon her daughter to her abductor, because of her uncompromising refusal to accept Zeus's will, she did win back her daughter, but only for two-thirds of the year. For the other third, because Persephone tasted the pomegranate seed, symbol of sexuality and fertility, she must return to Hades in the underworld.

In the patriarchal version of the Demeter/Persephone myth, and in the rituals of the Athenian and subsequent patriarchal periods, Demeter became increasingly less the Goddess of divine sexuality and procreation that she was in Crete. Her dual role of lover and mother became dichotomized. She became the grieving mother, while the virgin daughter became the focus of male sexual desire. In the later period, the "sacred union" or "holy marriage" of the Goddess and her partner, Persephone and Pluto, differed drastically from the more spontaneous and earthy sacred union between Demeter and Iason.

Finally, there also developed in the myth and ritual and legends associated with Demeter and Persephone increasing emphasis on the importance of a "holy son."[16] In the Homeric hymn we are told that after Demeter lost her daughter she attempted to adopt a human son, Demophoon (his name makes him the symbolic representative of the people). Demeter sought to make Demophoon immortal by placing him at night in a sacred fire. But his mortal mother interrupted Demeter's efforts, and the Goddess departed angrily with these words: "Unknowing are ye mortals and thoughtless: ye know not whether good or evil approaches."[17]

Having lost her daughter, and now a son, Demeter fell into an even deeper grief than before, sitting in isolation in the temple she commanded to be built for her at Eleusis. She ignored all the pleadings of the Gods and Goddesses to return to the heights of Mount Olympus until Zeus decided to have Persephone returned to her. Then, according to the Homeric hymn, calling the people of Eleusis to her,

> . . . Demeter made known her holy order of service,
> teaching to all her most sacred rites . . .
> When she had thoroughly taught them,
> the queen among goddesses
> Went with Persephone up to Olympus
> among the assembly of gods . . .
> Greatly blessed of men upon earth is the mortal
> these goddesses favor with love.

In the rites of the Eleusinian mysteries, despite the increasing dominance of male Gods, the mother and daughter Goddesses remained primary. Sexual union was honored and celebrated as sacred. And the holy child—whether daughter or son—was joyfully welcomed and lovingly praised, as offspring of the Great Mother who graciously gives both new crops and new life to the human community.

Although Hades of the Olympian religion became lord of the underworld, his domain was for the Greeks one of pale and restless shades, and they built no temples to honor him. It was to Persephone, queen of the underworld, that the people prayed for guidance and courage in their journey into death. As it was to the Earth Mother, Demeter, that they prayed for abundance of life on this Earth.

DEATH AND REBIRTH

The belief of ancient peoples in the resurrection of life was closely related to their experience of nature, their experience of love. The reunion of the daughter with the mother/Goddess in the Demeter/Persephone myth must have been seen as a symbol of the human soul's return, after the death of the body, to its universal origin or loving source. In Athens, those who had died were called *Demetrioi*, the people of Demeter.

The precise secrets of the mysteries are not known. The Homeric poet said of these rites: "The essential gift of the ceremonies no man may describe or utter; / Blessed is he among men on earth who has beheld this."[18]

During the classical Athenian era, and later, the rites took place in the fall at the time of the equinox and lasted 9 days—the length of time Demeter spent searching for her lost daughter. Heralds were sent from Athens and Eleusis throughout Greece proclaiming the festival. All warfare was to cease for 2 months, and no legal proceedings were to be conducted during the 9 days of the rites.[19]

To begin the festival, the priestesses of Demeter carried her sacred objects in baskets on their heads from her temple at Eleusis along the sacred way, which was strewn with flowers and fruits, to the Eleusinian temple at the foot of the Athenian acropolis.

The opening of the festival during the Athenian era was officially proclaimed by the *hierophant*, the high priest. He invited those who had been initiated the previous spring into the lesser mysteries to become initiated now into the greater mysteries.

On the second day, the initiates, or *mystai*, were sent to the sea to bathe and purify themselves in the refreshing saltwater of the Aegean.

The third day was a day of ceremonies and special prayers for women and children and for state leaders and citizens.

The fourth day was devoted to Asclepius, God of healing; it was a day for more prayers and for healing dreams. It was also devoted in part to a ritual identification with Demeter in her grief, her sense of inexplicable loss—an experience keenly felt, we might imagine, by the indigenous Goddess peoples who must have looked upon the period of the patriarchal class takeover, at least in part, as a descent into hell.

On the fifth day, the initiates and the community journeyed westward from Athens to Eleusis, carrying at the head of the great procession the boychild "Iacchus." Toward evening, they bathed and refreshed themselves in special waters at the outskirts of Eleusis, before finally gathering by torchlight for the rituals of collective purpose.

This *pannycheis*, or nightlong revelry, included dancing by the women near Callichoron, the Well of Fair Dances. According to Euripides (about 484–406 B.C.) in his play *Ion*, all of nature responded to the dance of the women:

> the starry ether of Zeus takes up the dance
> the moon Goddess dances, and with her
> the fifty daughters of Nereus dance in the sea
> and in the eddies of the ever-flowing streams
> so honoring the Daughter with the golden crown
> and the holy Mother [Demeter]. . . .

The ancients believed that if these rituals were suppressed, if the collective purpose of the community would no longer find expression, the cosmos would fall apart.[20]

On the sixth day, the *mystai* entered the sacred grounds of Demeter's sanctuary one by one across a bridge called the Bridge of Jests while the townspeople teased or ridiculed or told secrets about the initiate. This may have served to help the initiates rid themselves of whatever overbearing pride or arrogance might prevent them from opening themselves to the illumination of the mysteries.

The next day was a final day of preparation, of resting, purification, fasting, and sacrifice, of "making oneself holy," offering up to the Goddess whatever might still be hindering the soul's journey along its path.

The seventh and eighth nights were the nights of the mysteries, when the *mystai* entered the *Telesterion*, the temple of Demeter, the hall of initiation. (Perhaps in more ancient days they had gone down into a womblike cave, the cave at the edge of the sanctuary, later named the *Ploutonion*, doorway to Hades.) During these 2 nights the initiates received the central experience of the mysteries.

No special creed was required of the initiates. The rites may have included a simple invitation to a communion of first fruits, a partial dramatization of the Demeter/Persephone myth, and perhaps a singing of the Hymn to Demeter relating the sacred story of the two Goddesses, and certain objects sacred to Demeter that exemplified the fertile forces of nature, such as symbols of human genitals or a single grain of wheat, may have been shown. The only detail we know with certainty is that during their initiation, the *mystai* witnessed a great blazing fire.

No doubt the fasting, prayers, and anticipation of the initiates helped clarify their inner vision. We are told that the initiates experienced a special seeing, the "opening of the eyes."

During initiation, the *mystai* may have felt abducted into the underworld, there remembering whatever they had lost to disease, pain, or death (remembering even the suffering stored beneath memory, in the recesses of the subconscious or in the collective unconscious of race history); felt overwhelming grief; and then experienced the healing, joyful embrace of the sacred union and the arrival of a new life.

Perhaps the initiate had a vision of the Goddess as Earth Mother; of Persephone returning from the dead; of the reunion of mother and child; of the essential nature of life and death. It may have been a vision of a vast sea of love all around, described by Diotima of Mantinea when she instructed Socrates into the lesser and greater mysteries of love, as related in Plato's *Symposium*. It may have been the experience of dying and being reborn, circled by a flow of love far beyond human ability to express in words.

Perhaps, finally, the initiates simply came out of the darkness at the moment of sunrise into a new day, into the upper world with its fertile land and waiting community of family and friends.

In all the years of the mysteries' celebration, the central experience of the initiation was never revealed. I believe this is because the mystical insight itself was beyond naming, ineffable.

The ninth day was for further prayers, pouring libations to the dead, and returning home.

An individual was initiated only once into the lesser mysteries, and only once into the greater mysteries. But these celebrations were repeated in the community generation after generation, century after century, millennium after millennium.

Pindar (518–438 B.C.) wrote: "Happy is he who has seen the Mysteries, he knows the source and the end of life."[21] And Cicero, an initiate of the first century B.C., wrote that if Greece had existed for no other reason than to have brought into existence the mysteries of Eleusis, that would have been sufficient reason for her existence.[22]

In a final sense, we may interpret the Eleusinian mysteries as a myth for our own time. There is a way in which the teaching of the journey of the soul transcends any particular time and place, age or gender.

The meaning I wish to evoke for us here is the remembrance of the early epoch of mother-centered life; followed by the separating away, the abduction, the death of this ancient way of life. That time has been followed by an epoch we might think of as the long period of patriarchal class rule, a long dark age reaching until this point where we stand poised between star wars and star peace, between the nuclear and ecological omnicide of the planet or the survival of our planetary community into a new world.

The renewal I long for is the return of a reverence for Mother Earth and her abundant forces of creation; an affirmation of the sacredness of sexuality and enduring human love; and the belief in the inevitability of death and the immortality of the soul.

It is a longing for the rebirth of the abundant love and nourishment of the ancient Earth Mother Gaia, Demeter, Persephone, Hecate, and for all the Great Grandmothers to be with us now, as comforters and guides, into the next stage of our journey in this life, with one another, on this beautiful planet Earth.[23]

Paula Gunn Allen

THE WOMAN I LOVE IS A PLANET; THE PLANET I LOVE IS A TREE

OUR PHYSICALITY—which always and everywhere includes our spirituality, mentality, emotionality, social institutions and processes—is a microform of all physicality. Each of us reflect, in our attitudes toward our body and the bodies of other planetary creatures and plants, our inner attitude toward the planet. And, as we believe, so we act. A society that believes that the body is somehow diseased, painful, sinful, or wrong, a people that spends its time trying to deny the body's needs, aims, goals, and processes—whether these be called health or disease—is going to misunderstand the nature of its existence and of the planet's and is going to create social institutions out of those body-denying attitudes that wreak destruction not only on human, plant, and other creaturely bodies but on the body of the Earth herself.

The planet, our mother, Grandmother Earth, is *physical* and therefore a spiritual, mental, and emotional being. Planets are alive, as are all their by-products or expressions, such as animals, vegetables, minerals, climatic and meteorological phenomena.

Believing that our mother, the beloved Earth, is inert matter is destructive to yourself. (There's little you can do to her, believe it or not.) Such beliefs point to a dangerously diseased physicality.

Being good, holy, and/or politically responsible means being able to accept whatever life brings—and that includes just about everything you usually think of as unacceptable, like disease, death, and violence. Walking in balance, in harmony, and in a sacred manner requires staying in your body, accepting its discomforts, decayings, witherings, and blossomings and respecting them. Your body is also a planet, replete with creatures that live in and on it. Walking in balance requires knowing that living and dying are twin beings, gifts of our mother, the Earth, and honoring her ways does not mean cheating her of your flesh, your pain, your joy, your sensuality, your desires, your frustrations, your unmet and met needs, your emotions, your life. In the end you can't cheat her successfully, but in the attempt to do so you can do great harm to the delicate and subtle balance of the vital processes of planetary being.

A society based on body hate destroys itself and causes harm to all of Grandmother's grandchildren.

In the United States, where milk and honey cost little enough, where private serenity is prized above all things by the wealthy, privileged, and well-washed, where tension, intensity, passion, and the concomitant loss of self-possession are detested, the idea that your attitudes and behaviors vis-à-vis your body are your politics and your spirituality may seem strange. Moreover, when I suggest that passion—whether it be emotional, muscular, sexual, or intellectual—IS spirituality, the idea might seem even stranger. In the United States of the privileged, going to ashrams and centers to meditate on how to be in one's immediate experience, on how to be successful at serenity when the entire planet is overwrought, tense, far indeed from serene, the idea that connected spirituality consists in accepting overwroughtness, tension, yes, and violence, may seem not only strange but downright dangerous. The patriarchs have long taught the Western peoples that violence is sin, that tension is the opposite of spiritual life, that the overwrought are denied enlightenment. But we must remember that those who preached and taught serenity and peacefulness were teaching the oppressed how to act—docile slaves who deeply accept their place and do not recognize that in their anguish lies also their redemption, their liberation, are not likely to disturb the tranquillity of the ruling class. Members of the ruling class are, of course, utterly tranquil. Why not? As long as those upon whose labor and pain their serenity rests don't upset the apple cart, as long as they can make the rules for human behavior—in its inner as well as its outer dimensions—they can be tranquil indeed and can focus their attention on reaching nirvanic bliss, transcendence, or divine peace and love.

And yet, the time for tranquillity, if there ever was time for it, is not now. Now we have only to look, to listen, to our beloved planet to see that tranquillity is not the best word to describe her condition. Her volcanic passions, her hurricane storms of temper, her tremblings and shakings, her thrashings and lashings indicate that something other than serenity is going on. And after careful consideration, it must occur to the sensitive observer that congruence with self, which must be congruence with spirit, which must therefore be congruence with the planet, requires something more active than serenity, tranquillity, or inner peace.

Our planet, my beloved, is in crisis; this, of course, we all know. We, many of us, think that her crisis is caused by men, or White people, or capitalism, or industrialism, or loss of spiritual vision, or social turmoil, or war, or psychic disease. For the most part, we do not recognize that the reason for her state is that she is entering upon a great initiation—she is becoming someone else. Our planet, my darling, is gone coyote, *heyoka*, and it is our great honor to attend her passage rites. She is giving birth to her new consciousness of herself and her relationship to the other vast intelligences, other holy beings in her universe. Her travail is not easy, and it occasions her intensity, her conflict, her turmoil—the turmoil, conflict, and intensity that human and other creaturely life mirror. And as she moves, growing and learning ever closer to the sacred moment of her realization, her turmoil, intensity, agony, and conflict increase.

We are each and all a part of her, an expression of her essential being. We are each a small fragment that is not the whole but that, perforce, reflects in our inner self, our outer behavior, our expressions and relationships and institutions, her self, her behaviors, her expressions and relationships, her forms and structures. We humans and our relatives the other creatures are integral expressions of her thought and being. We are not her, but we take our being from her, and in her being we have being, as in her life we have life. As she is, so are we.

In this time of her emergence as one of the sacred planets in the Grandmother galaxy, we necessarily experience, each of us in our own specific way, our share or form of her experience, her form. As the initiation nears completion we are caught in the throes of her wailings and contractions, her muscular, circulatory, and neurologic destabilization. We should recognize that her longing for the culmination of the initiatory process is at present nearly as intense as her longing to remain as she was before the initiation ceremony began, and our longing for a new world that the completion of the great ceremony will bring, almost as great as our longing to remain in the systems familiar to us for a very long time, correspond. Her longing for completion is great, as is ours; our longing to remain as we have been, our fear that we will not survive the transition, that we will fail to enter the new age, our terror at ourselves becoming transformed, mutated, unrecognizable to ourselves and all we have known correspond to her long-ing to remain as she has been, her fear that she will fail the tests as they arise for her, her terror at becoming new, unrecognizable to her-self and to all she has known.

What can we do in times such as these? We can rejoice that she will soon be counted among the blessed. That we, her feathers, talons, beak, eyes, have come crying and singing, lamenting and laughing, to this vast climacteric.

I am speaking of all womankind, of all mankind. And of more. I am speaking of all our relatives, the four-leggeds, the wingeds, the crawl-ers; of the plants and seasons, the winds, thunders, and rains, the rivers, lakes, and streams, the pebbles, rocks, and mountains, the spirits, the holy people, and the Gods and Goddesses—of all the in-telligences, all the beings. I am speaking even of the tiniest, those no one can see; and of the vastest, the planets and stars. Together you and I and they and she are moving with increasing rapidity and under ever increasing pressure toward transformation.

Now, now is the time when mother becomes grandmother, when daughter becomes mother, when the living dead are released from en-tombment, when the dead live again and walk once again in her ways. Together we all can rejoice, take up the tasks of attending, take up the joy of giving birth and of being born, of transforming in recogni-tion of the awfulness of what is entailed, in recognition of what it is we together can and must and will do. I have said that this is the time of her initiation, of her new birth. I could also say it is the time of mutation, for transformation means to change form; I could also say it is the climacteric, when the beloved planet goes through menopause and takes her place among the wise women planets that dance among the stars.

At a time such as this, what indeed can we do? We can sing *Heya-hey* in honoring all that has come to pass, all that is passing. Sing, honoring, *Heya-hey* to all the beings gathering on all the planes to witness this great event. From every quadrant of the universe they are coming. They are standing gathered around, waiting for the emer-gence, the piercing moment when she is counted among those who are counted among the wise. We can sing *Heya-hey* to the familiar and the estranged, to the recognized and the disowned, to each shrub and tree, to each flower and vine, to each pebble and stone, to each moun-tain and hill. We can sing *Heya-hey* honoring the stars and the clouds, the winds and the rains, the seasons and the temperature. We can think with our hearts, as the old ones do, and put our brains and muscles in the service of the heart, our Mother and Grandmother Earth, who is coming into being in another way. We can sing *Heya-hey,* honoring.

What can we do, rejoicing and honoring, to show our respect? We can heal. We can cherish our bodies and honor them, sing *Heya-hey* to our flesh. We can cherish our being—our petulances and rages, our anguishes and griefs, our disabilities and strengths, our desires and passions, our pleasures and delights. We can, willingly and recognizing the fullness of her abundance, which includes scarcity and muchness, enter inside ourselves to seek and find her, who is our own dear body, our own dear flesh. For the body is not the dwelling place of the spirit—it is the spirit. It is not a tomb, it is life itself. And even as it withers and dies, it is born; even as it is renewed and reborn, it dies.

Think: How many times each day do you habitually deny and deprive her in your flesh, in your physicality? How often do you willfully prevent her from moving or resting, from eating or drinking what she requests, from eliminating wastes or taking breath? How many times do you order your body to produce enzymes and hormones to further your social image, your "identity," your emotional comfort, regardless of your actual situation and hers? How many of her gifts do your spurn, how much of her abundance do you deny? How often do you interpret disease as wrong, suffering as abnormal, physical imperatives as troublesome, cravings as failures, deprivation and denial of appetite as the right thing to do? In how many ways do you refuse to experience your vulnerability, your frailty, your mortality? How often do you refuse these expressions of the life force of the Mother in your lovers, your friends, your society? How often do you find yourself interpreting sickness, weakness, aging, fatness, physical differences as pitiful, contemptible, avoidable, a violation of social norm and spiritual accomplishment? How much of your life is devoted to avoiding any and/or all of these? How much of her life is devoted to avoiding any and all of these?

The mortal body is a tree; it is holy in whatever condition; it is truth and myth because it has so many potential conditions; because of its possibilities, it is sacred and profane; most of all, it is your most precious talisman, your own connection to her. Healing the self means honoring and recognizing the body, accepting rather than denying all the turmoil its existence brings, welcoming the woes and anguish flesh is subject to, cherishing its multitudinous forms and seasons, its unfailing ability to know and be, to grow and wither, to live and die, to mutate, to change. Healing the self means commiting ourselves to a wholehearted willingness to be what and how we are—beings frail and fragile, strong and passionate, neurotic and balanced, diseased and whole, partial and complete, stingy and generous, safe and dangerous, twisted and straight, storm-tossed and quiescent, bound and free.

What can we do to be politically useful, spiritually mature attendants in this great transformation we are privileged to participate in? Find out by asking as many trees as you meet how to be a tree. Our Mother, in her form known as Sophia, was long ago said to be a tree, the great tree of life: Listen to what they wrote down from the song she gave them:

> I have grown tall as a cedar on Lebanon,
> as a cypress on Mount Hermon;
> I have grown tall as a palm in Engedi,
> as the rose bushes of Jericho;
> as a fine olive on the plain,
> as a plane tree I have grown tall.
> I have exhaled perfume like cinnamon and acacia;
> I have breathed out a scent like choice myrrh,
> like galbanum, onzcha and stacte,
> like the smoke of incense in the tabernacle.
> I have spread my branches like a terebinth,
> and my branches are glorious and graceful.
> I am like a vine putting out graceful shoots,
> my blossoms bear the fruit of glory and wealth.
> Approach me, you who desire me,
> and take your fill of my fruits.[1]

Carol P. Christ

RETHINKING THEOLOGY
AND NATURE

WITH MANY SPIRITUAL FEMINISTS, ecofeminists, ecologists, antinuclear activists, and others, I share the conviction that the crisis that threatens the destruction of the Earth is not only social, political, economic, and technological, but is at root spiritual. We have lost the sense that this Earth is our true home, and we fail to recognize our profound connection with all beings in the web of life. Instead, many people uncritically accept the view that "man" is superior to "nature" and has the right to "use" the natural world in any way "he" sees fit. Although often clothed in the garb of modern science, such a view has its root in theological conceptions that separate both God and humanity from nature and from finitude, change, and death.[1] The preservation of the Earth requires a profound shift in consciousness: a recovery of more ancient and traditional views that revere the profound connection of all beings in the web of life and a rethinking of the relation of both humanity and divinity to nature. I will explore some of the dimensions of this shift in consciousness by contrasting the work of Protestant theologian Gordon Kaufman with a variety of feminist voices that challenge the Western theological notion that human creation in the image of God sets us apart from the rest of nature.

Gordon Kaufman articulates a version of the Western theological separation of humanity and nature when he states:

> The great religious struggle between Israel and Canaan was over the relative metaphysical importance of natural power and process on the one hand and personal moral will on the other. When Yahweh won that struggle it meant that the object of ultimate loyalty and devotion for humans in the West would be conceived increasingly in terms of models rooted in our moral and personal experience, not in our sense of dependence upon and unity with the orders and processes of nature.[2]

He states further that Western theological tradition considers nature to be without purpose or value:

> Nature appears to be a nonteleological, nonaxiological order within which emerges purposive valuing activity. . . . [that] the conceptions of God and humanity, as they have developed in Western religious traditions, work hand in hand toward distinguishing humankind from (the rest of) nature. Nature is *not* [my italics] conceived primarily as our proper home and the very source and sustenance of our being.[3]

Kaufman thus argues that in Western theology the concept of a personal moral will separates both humanity and God from nature. He states that human agency and morality cannot be explained without positing a God who stands outside the natural world as its source.

Feminist philosopher, poet, and mystic Susan Griffin challenges the Western tradition's assertion that humanity is separate from nature and that our value lies in this alleged separation. She concludes *Woman and Nature* with a passage that reverses the imagery of Plato's vision in the cave (where Plato equates the physical world and the body with darkness that can only be lit by the transcendent light of reason):

> I know I am made from this earth, as my mother's hands were made from this earth, as her dreams were made from this earth, and this paper, these hands, this tongue speaking, all that I know speaks to me through this earth and I long to tell you, you who are earth too, and listen as we speak to each other of what we know: the light is in us.[4]

Griffin's work is also imbued with what some might call a stunning moral consciousness and will. For example, she writes of the intrinsic value of other beings: "for the blackbird, which flies now over our heads, whose song reminds us of a flute, who migrates with the stars, who lives among reeds and rushes, threading a nest like a hammock, who lives in flocks, chattering in the grasses, this creature is free of our hands, we cannot control her."[5]

Griffin and Kaufman express two very different understandings of the human relation to nature: one asserts our ontological separation by virtue of personal moral will; the other names a felt connection. The voices, too, are different. One separates itself from whatever passions and emotions may have led to its assertions, affirming that only thus can we think clearly; the other tells us with its every word that "we have cause to feel deeply."[6] Those of us who have been trained in the language and thought forms of patriarchy but who have not entirely forgotten our connections to the powers of other beings understand both voices. Should we follow the voice of male philosophy and theology and assert that the woman whose words have named something we know deeply within ourselves is after all not a philosopher but at best a poet? Should we accept the assertion that she cannot adequately account for our differences from nature, for the moral projects we propose as persons? Or can we respond to her call to enter into dialogue and "listen as we speak to each other of what we know."[7]

Susan Griffin has named the passionate conviction that "we are nature" that I have always known deeply within myself but that I have found lacking from both the form and content of much of theology and philosophy. As a mystic, she also calls us to rethink the separation of the divine from nature. But before adopting her vision as a foundation for feminist theology, it is important to consider several typical misinterpretations of her work. One misreading asserts that she has simply reversed the dualisms we have inherited, naming men and rationality as essentially evil, and women, nature, and irrationality as essentially good. But Griffin explicitly counters this view when she begins her book with a Prologue which states: "He says that woman speaks with nature. That she hears voices from under the earth. That wind blows in her ears and trees whisper to her. But for him this dialogue is over. He says he is not part of this world, that he was set on this world as a stranger. He sets himself apart from woman and nature."[8] Close reading of this text indicates that it is man's choice that sets him apart from woman and nature, not his essence. Griffin underscores this point when she writes: "(And when we hear in the Navajo chant of the mountain that a grown man sits and smokes with bears and follows directions given to him by squirrels, we are surprised. We had thought only little girls spoke with animals.)"[9]

Because philosophy has been defined as a discipline in which reason is separated from passion and emotion, some have asserted that when Griffin affirms deep feeling as a source of knowledge, she accepts Western culture's designation of women as intuitive and irrational. But her poetic reflections on the human relation to nature have deep philosophical implications and demonstrate mastery of the language and thought forms of Western so-called rational thought. If Griffin had intended to state that women and nature are irrational and inarticulate, she would not have compared her consciousness of herself as a writer to the flight of a redwing blackbird:

Yet the blackbird does not fly in us but somewhere else free of our mind, and now even free of our sight, flying in the path of her own will, she wrote, the ink from her pen flowing on this paper, her words, she thought, having nothing to do with this bird, except, she thought, as she breathes in the air this bird flies through . . . all that I know, I know in this earth, the body of the bird, this pen, this paper, these hands, this tongue speaking, all that I know speaks to me through this earth . . . [10]

Griffin is playing with the expectations embedded in our language and way of thinking. We are used to thinking of the mystical experience with the bird, a bodily, preverbal experience, in relation to the Earth, which we think of as inarticulate. But we are not used to thinking of the book we read in relation to the paper it is written on, the hand that wrote it in a particular place on a particular day, and of the hand and the pen and the paper as Earth. We are used to hearing that women and girls speak with nature, but we are not used to hearing that those same girls and women put pen to paper, consciously shaping their experience into naming, into words.

Griffin is not proposing that women remain within a mystical, perhaps even mantic, but ultimately inarticulable and inarticulate relation with nature. She calls us rather to rethink the notions of rationality and articulation we have inherited as we rename the relation with nature we experience. She is clearly aware that this will require a deconstruction and reconstruction of language when she writes: "And we are nature. We are nature seeing nature. We are nature with a concept of nature. Nature weeping. Nature speaking of nature to nature."[11] Here she is consciously using words that are not adequate to her conceptions, deforming and stretching language.

Because the disjunction of divinity, humanity, and nature is deeply embedded in the words *God, humanity,* and *nature*—it is difficult to articulate new conceptions. The three terms in the triad "God, man, and nature" must be rethought together. It will not do, for example, simply to say that the divine is nature because concepts of nature have already been defined as excluding teleology and the kind of power commonly associated with divinity. Nor, on the other hand, will it do simply to say that nature is teleological since teleology has been defined as residing in the divine and human moral will that stand over and against nature. Similarly, it cannot be asserted that humanity is nature since to most people that would imply that humans are irrational, immoral, and inarticulate. What is required is a revolution in thought, a deconstruction and reconstruction of both theology and language.

In his recent work, *Theology for a Nuclear Age*, Kaufman takes some steps toward this reconstruction, departing from the notion of the separation between divinity, humanity, and nature that he had earlier characterized as constituting Western theology. In recognition of the very real possibility that human beings may destroy ourselves and much of the life on the planet, Kaufman writes: "We humans must understand ourselves in the first place, therefore, as one strand in the very ancient and complex web of life, a strand, moreover, which would not exist apart from this *context* [my italics] which has brought it forth and continues to sustain it at every point."[12]

But note that for Kaufman the "web of life" is "context." This leads me to ask whether the web of life is granted intrinsic value or whether it is valued because it supports and sustains human life. Kaufman confirms these suspicions when he asserts that understanding our connection to the biosphere is not sufficient for understanding human nature and its potentialities:

> Once an animal had evolved with a sufficiently complex nervous system to sustain linguistic and other symbolic activity, thus making possible primitive consciousness, memory, and imagination, a long and complicated *historical* development was required before anything that we would recognize as a truly human mode of existence could appear on earth. . . . Human creativity was born together with *intention* and *action* [my italics], as humans found they could themselves actualize some of these possibilities and hopes. Thus human existence gradually developed capacities not found in any other form of life.[13]

Although acknowledging that humans are rooted in and sustained by the web of life, Kaufman asserts that intention and action, self-reflection and choice, or finite freedom and self-consciousness, remain the marks of the distinctively human. This is expressed within an evolutionary perspective in which the two processes of nature and history have been guided by a "hidden creativity," symbolized by the name God, which has produced human beings who are essentially different from nature. As Kaufman writes:

> In the course of time the cosmic and divine order has brought forth a mode of being, a dimension of itself, that transcends in a significant way even the luxuriant fecundity of life, namely history—the symbolic order,

the realm of spirit—within which consciousness and meaning, self-conscious subjectivity and purposiveness and freedom have reality. We humans are the only creatures we know who are the living incarnations of that distinctive mode of being.[14]

In view of this statement, I wonder whether it would be misreading Kaufman to say that if self-consciousness and finite freedom could be sustained apart from continuing dependence on the web of life out of which it arose, then the death of the biosphere would not itself be a significant tragedy. If this conclusion is not intended, and I suspect it may not be, then a stronger affirmation needs to be made of the intrinsic value of the web of life and those parts of human nature that are similar to the rest of the web of life. As it is, there remains in *Theology for a Nuclear Age* a profound humanocentrism in regard to the web of life and the nature of God, as well as a focus on thought and choice as that which definitively characterize humanity and divinity. Although God for Kaufman is the hidden creativity behind both historical and biological evolution, one is left to conclude, perhaps despite Kaufman's intentions, that for the God he describes the primary goal in the creation of the universe is the creation of humanity. But it is precisely this notion that we must question and deconstruct.

Kaufman argues that theological positions ought to be judged by the following criterion: "the supreme test, one might say, of the ultimate viability, and thus finally of the truth . . . [of any] symbolic frame of orientation is [its] capacity to provide insight and guidance in our situation today, a situation in which humankind has come up against its own limits in a most decisive and paradoxical way: through gaining the power to obliterate itself."[15]

I agree, and add three other criteria: (1) a symbol system must aid us in overcoming the historic injustices between women and men, between races, and between peoples; (2) it must strike a deep chord in our experience; and (3) it must help us better to understand, love, and enjoy the life that has been given to us.

Kaufman argues that the symbol of God that comes to us through Christian tradition meets his test by playing a *relativizing* and a *humanizing* function. The relativizing function is provided by the symbol of God thusly: "God is understood as that ecological reality behind and in and working through all of life and history, and the service of God can consist thus only in universally oriented vision and work."[16] I agree that the relativizing function of God reminds us of the importance of universally oriented vision and work. But I am not happy with the asceticism and self-denial implicit in Kaufman's notion that "*service* of God can consist *only* [my italics] in universally oriented vision and work." I also agree with Shug, who, in Alice Walker's *The Color Purple*, says, "God love all them feelings. That's some of the best stuff God did."[17] And with Z Budapest, who says, "All pleasures are rituals to the Goddess."[18]

Kaufman proposes that the symbol of Christ serves a humanizing function that provides orientation by showing us that: "radical self-giving in the struggle with the worst evils of contemporary human life, culminating perhaps in complete self-sacrifice—crucifixion—is what is to be expected."[19] I wonder whether this image of Christ crucified can be separated from the other, more dangerous image of Christ exalted to the right hand of the Father, which Kaufman courageously criticizes and rejects because it has "laid foundations for later Christian imperialism, . . . crusades against infidels and inquisitorial tortures and executions of heretics, and . . . ultimately give[s] its blessing to Western imperialism."[20]

I am not convinced that one can change the way images of Christ have functioned in Christian imagination through theological, that is, intellectual, assertion. Images of Christ exalted as well as crucified remain embedded in the Christian Bible and liturgy and continue to mold and shape the Christian imagination. In addition, Kaufman's image of Christ crucified is tinged with a masochism that goes beyond recognizing that life has a tragic dimension. Kaufman states that Christ "understood himself as coming into the world to be trampled on by his fellow humans."[21] While it is true that the just do not always prosper, to me it is an overly pessimistic reading of life to say that we come into the world to be trampled upon. I am not persuaded that such an image of Christ provides a genuinely humanizing function.

In the remainder of this essay I will articulate and discuss the outlines of an alternative theological vision that I believe meets Kaufman's criterion of providing orientation for the lives we are living under the threat of nuclear war and ecological destruction. This vision resonates with many feminist voices. In Alice Walker's *The Color Purple*, Shug describes her vision of God to Celie in these words:

My first step from the old white man was trees. Then air. Then birds. Then other peoples. But one day when I was sitting quiet and feeling like a motherless child, which I was, it come to me: that feeling of being part of everything, not separate at all. I knew that if I cut a tree my arm would bleed. And I laughed and I cried and I ran all around the house. I knew just what it was. In fact, when it happen, you can't miss it. It sort of like you know what, she say, grinning and rubbing up on my thigh . . . I think it pisses God off if you walk by the color purple in a field and don't notice it. . . . Everything want to be loved. Us sing and dance, make faces and give flower bouquets, trying to be loved. You ever notice that trees do everything to git attention we do, except walk?[22]

Anthropologist Paula Gunn Allen, who comes from a Keres Pueblo background, expresses a strikingly similar understanding in her book, *The Sacred Hoop:*

We are the land. To the best of my understanding, that is the fundamental idea that permeates American Indian life; the land (Mother) and the people (mothers) are the same. As Luther Standing Bear has said of his Lacota people, "We are of the soil and the soil is of us." The earth is the source and being of the people and we are equally the being of the earth. The land is not really a place separate from ourselves, where we act out the drama of our isolate destinies; the witchery [disconnected power] makes us believe that false idea. The earth is not a mere source of survival, distant from the creatures it nurtures and from the spirit that breathes in us, nor is it to be considered an inert resource on which we draw in order to keep our ideological self functioning. Rather for the American Indians . . . the earth *is* being, as all creatures are also being: aware, palpable, intelligent, alive. . . . Many non-Indians believe that human beings possess the only form of intelligence in phenomenal existence (often in any form of existence). The more abstractionist and less intellectually vain Indian sees human intelligence as rising out of the very nature of being, which is of necessity intelligent in and of itself.[23]

For me the divine/Goddess/God/Earth/Life/It symbolizes the whole of which we are a part. This whole is the Earth and sky, the ground on which we stand, and all the animals, plants, and other beings to which we are related. We come from our mothers and fathers and are rooted in community. We come from the Earth and to the Earth we shall return. Life feeds on life. We live because others die, and we will die so that others may live. The divinity that shapes our ends is life, death, and change, understood both literally and as metaphor for our daily lives. We will never understand it all. We do not choose the conditions of our lives. Death may come at any time. Death is never early or late. With regard to life and death there is no ultimate justice, nor ultimate injustice, for there is no promise that life will be other than it is. There are no hierarchies among beings on Earth. Yes, we are different from the swallows that fly, from the many-faceted stones on the beach, from the redwood trees in the forest. We may have more capacity to shape our lives than other beings, but you and I will never fly with the grace of a swallow, live as long as a redwood tree, nor endure the endless tossing of the sea like a stone. Each being has its own intrinsic beauty and value. There will be no end to change, to death, to suffering. But life is as comic as it is tragic. Watching the sun set, the stars come out, eating, drinking, dancing, loving, and understanding are no less real than suffering, loss, and death. Knowledge that we are but a small part of life and death and transformation is the essential religious insight. The essential religious response is to rejoice and to weep, to sing and to dance, to tell stories and create rituals in praise of an existence far more complicated, more intricate, more enduring than we are.

How does this vision meet the test of the theological task proposed by Kaufman? God/Goddess/Earth/Life/It, the whole of which we are a part, the unnameable beneath naming, serves a profoundly relativizing function. The supreme relativizing is to know that we are no more valuable to the life of the universe than a field flowering in the color purple, than rivers flowing, than a crab picking its way across the sand—and no less. This vision of God/Goddess/Life/Earth/It has much to say to the ecological, social, and nuclear crises we face. The ethic that would follow from this vision is that our task is to love and understand, to live for a time, to contribute as much as we can to the continuation of life, to the enhancement of beauty, joy, and diversity, while recognizing inevitable death, loss, and suffering. To understand and value the life we enjoy is to understand and value the lives of all other beings, human and nonhuman. And to understand that we are limited by the values inherent in other beings. We cannot live without taking the lives of other beings, but when we understand our profound connection to other beings, we begin to understand that it is a violation of the web of life to take more than we need. To poison rivers and seas and the ground on which we stand so that we can have televisions and air conditioning, to engage in wars of conquest in order to exploit other people's labor and take the resources of their land is to forget that we are all connected in the web of life. Death and killing are part of life. But to imagine that something that we call "our way of life" justifies the creation of nuclear bombs with the capacity to destroy most of the life on this planet is ultimate arrogance. This ethic calls into question much of modern life, which is based on the acceptance of the inevitability of war and on the exploitation of other people, of plants, animals, and the rest of nature. But the difficulty of comprehending how to implement an ethic based upon reverence and respect for all life forms within the web of life should not lead us to dismiss it as romantic or impractical.

In addition to inspiring respect for all beings in the web of life, the vision of connection encourages greater appreciation for the diversity of human experience. If the essentially human is defined as consciousness and self-reflection, it is hard to avoid the conclusion that some humans, especially those educated within the Western intellectual tradition, are more human than others. This view has often been expressed through the naming of others—women, ethnic, cultural, and racial groups—as closer to nature, as barbarians, savages, peasants, slaves. However, *if the essentially human is to understand our connection to other people and to all other beings and to rejoice in the life that has been given to us,* then Western intellectuals are by no means self-evidently superior.

Further, this view offers a reason, rooted in vital feelings and instinct, to live. The great philosopher Simone de Beauvoir has written: "If we do not love life on our own account and through others, it is futile to seek to justify it in any way."[24]

To seek to perpetuate and preserve life because we enjoy it, because we love it, seems to me to be more life-affirming than the somewhat ascetic notion of "service to God" and the somewhat masochistic notion of "radical self-giving" proposed by Kaufman.[25] To choose life because we love it does not mean that life is without risk, inevitable suffering, loss, and death. It is life that can end in death at any moment that we must love. Such love must inspire an ethic rooted in a desire to enhance the life possibilities of all beings, both human and nonhuman.

Kaufman argues against this view in *Theology for a Nuclear Age:*

> We might, then, attempt to think of God in terms defined largely by the natural processes of cosmic and biological evolution. This would result in a God largely mute: one who, though active and moving with creativity and vitality, was essentially devoid of the kind of intentionality and care which was characterized by the heavenly father of tradition. Such a God could certainly evoke a piety of a profound awe and respect, and even, in its own way, of love and trust. But it is not a God who could provide

much guidance with respect to the great crises we today face, crises which are largely historical in character, not biological, crises of human motivation, policy, action, and institutions. . . . If we are to think of God as that reality which actually *humanizes* us, as well as *relativizes* us [my italics], these matters [history, language, human purpose] will have to be taken into account.[26]

Although there is a certain symmetry in this argument, I do not find it compelling. Let us approach the problem from the other side. Let us entertain the possibility that the divinity that shapes our ends is an impersonal process of life, death, and transformation. Let us imagine that the human spirit—history, language, human purpose—is not the goal of creation. Let us imagine that the life force does not care more about human creativity and choice than it cares about the ability of Bermuda grass to spread or moss to form on the side of a tree. The human species, like other species, might in time become extinct, dying so that other lives might flourish. But then is there nothing that should stop the human species from poisoning the Earth or blowing it up? Suppose there is no personal Goddess or God who would punish us for our act or even weep over what we had done? Does it therefore follow that there is no reason for humans not to destroy a universe that has been created through aeons of life, death, and transformation? I suggest that what can stop us is not knowledge that our self-reflection and freedom are in the image of God, nor that self-sacrifice is in the image of Christ. What can stop us, I propose, is a deeply felt connection to all beings in the web of life. What can stop us is that we love this life, this Earth, the joy we know in ourselves and other beings enough to find the thought of the end of the Earth intolerable. We do not need to know that our moral will is in the image of a personal God or Goddess in order to know that we have the capacity to create death or to love and preserve life.

But let us probe further. Is an image of Goddess/God that is based in our connection to all beings within the web of life necessarily impersonal and uncaring? Or is it our own Western consciousness that imparts the notion that nature is "devoid" of "intention and care." Let us return to the words of Paula Gunn Allen: "Many non-Indians believe that human beings possess the only form of intelligence in phenomenal existence (often in any form of existence). The more abstractionist and less intellectually vain Indian sees human intelligence as arising out of the very nature of being, which is of necessity intelligent in and of itself."[27]

Allen's view is that all beings have a similar nature, that all beings—including rocks and rain, corn and coyote, as well as the Great Spirit—have intelligence. In *Flight of the Seventh Moon*, the American Indian shaman Agnes Whistling Elk teaches Lynn Andrews how to listen to rocks: "Rocks are very slow and have sat around from the beginning, developing powers. . . . Rocks can show what you are going to become. They show you lost and forgotten things."[28]

The Great Spirit of the Native Americans is linked to the spirits of all beings, including rocks. When asked if a tree had consciousness, Martin Buber responded, "I have no experience of that."[29] Susan Griffin writes, "Behind naming, beneath words, is something else. An existence named, unnamed and unnameable."[30] There is a human tendency to name this unnameable with personal language, to believe that it cares as we care. I imagine, but I do not know, that the universe has an intelligence, a Great Spirit, that it cares as we care. I imagine that all that is cares. Sometimes I feel that I hear the universe weeping or laughing, speaking to me. But I do not know. What I do know is that whether the universe has a center of consciousness or not, the sight of a field of flowers in the color purple, the rainbow, must be enough[31] to stop us from destroying all that is and wants to be.[32]

2

REWEAVING THE WORLD: RECONNECTING POLITICS AND ETHICS

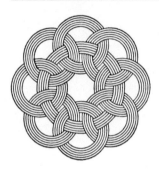

Starhawk

POWER, AUTHORITY, AND MYSTERY: ECOFEMINISM AND EARTH-BASED SPIRITUALITY

EARTH-BASED SPIRITUALITY is rooted in three basic concepts that I call immanence, interconnection, and community. The first—immanence—names our primary understanding that the Earth is alive, part of a living cosmos. What that means is that spirit, sacred, Goddess, God—whatever you want to call it—is not found outside the world somewhere—it's in the world: it *is* the world, and it is us. Our goal is not to get off the wheel of birth nor to be saved from something. Our deepest experiences are experiences of connection with the Earth and with the world.

When you understand the universe as a living being, then the split between religion and science disappears because religion no longer becomes a set of dogmas and beliefs we have to accept even though they don't make any sense, and science is no longer restricted to a type of analysis that picks the world apart. Science becomes our way of looking more deeply into this living being that we're all in, understanding it more deeply and clearly. This itself has a poetic dimension. I want to explore what it means when we really accept that this Earth is alive and that we are part of her being. Right now we are at a point where that living being is nearly terminally diseased. We need to reverse that, to turn that around. We really need to find a way to reclaim our power so that we can reverse the destruction of the Earth.

When we understand that the Earth itself embodies spirit and that the cosmos is alive, then we also understand that everything is interconnected. Just as in our bodies: what happens to a finger affects what happens to a toe. The brain doesn't work without the heart. In the

73

same way, what happens in South Africa affects us here: what we do to the Amazon rain forest affects the air that we breathe here. All these things are interconnected, and interconnection is the second principle of Earth-based spirituality.

Finally, when we understand these interconnections, we know that we are all part of a living community, the Earth. The kind of spirituality and the kind of politics we're called upon to practice are rooted in community. Again, the goal is not individual salvation or enlightenment, or even individual self-improvement, though these may be things and *are* things that happen along the way. The goal is the creation of a community that becomes a place in which we can be empowered and in which we can be connected to the Earth and take action together to heal the Earth.

Each of these principles—immanence, interconnection, and community—calls us to do something. That call, that challenge, is the difference between a spirituality that is practiced versus an intellectual philosophy. The idea that the Earth is alive is becoming an acceptable intellectual philosophy. Scientists have conferences on the Gaia hypothesis without acknowledging that this is exactly what people in tribal cultures, what Witches, shamans, and psychics, have been saying for thousands of years. But there's a difference between accepting it as a scientific philosophy and really living it. Living with the knowledge that the cosmos is alive causes us to do something. It challenges us. Earth-based spirituality makes certain demands. That is, when we start to understand that the Earth is alive, she calls us to act to preserve her life. When we understand that everything is interconnected, we are called to a politics and set of actions that come from compassion, from the ability to literally feel *with* all living beings on the Earth. That feeling is the ground upon which we can build community and come together and take action and find direction.

Earth-based spirituality calls us to live with integrity. Once we know that we're all part of this living body, this world becomes the terrain where we live out spiritual growth and development. It doesn't happen anywhere else, and the way we do it is by enacting what we believe, by taking responsibility for what we do.

These values are not limited to any particular tradition. They can be found in many, many different spiritual traditions and within many different political groups. For me, they come out of my tradition, which is the Pagan tradition, the Wiccan tradition, the old pre-Christian Goddess religion of Europe. We have a certain perspective that I believe can be valuable politically and that is, in some way, linked to what I see ecofeminism and the Green movement attempting. It's not that I think everyone has to be a Witch to be an ecofeminist, or that all Greens should be Witches—pluralism is vitally important in all our movements. It's that I do feel that Pagan values and perspectives can make important contributions to ecofeminist analysis and organizing.

A Pagan perspective might influence our approach to action. For example, I've participated in many political actions and organizations over the past 15 years. There have been times when it's been very exciting. In 1981, 1982, and 1983 the Livermore Action Group (LAG) was active in the Bay Area. We were constantly blockading, demonstrating, risking arrest, and mobilizing large numbers of people.

What happened to LAG, though, is very interesting. At a certain point—in fact, after what was really our strongest, most solid and successful action in 1983—things began to fall apart. Organizing began to get harder and harder, and we were never able to organize a large, cohesive action again. At the same time this was happening to LAG—and we were having meeting after meeting, asking, "Where did we go wrong?"—the same thing was happening to the peace movement in general. Everybody was asking, "What's wrong? Why are we burning out?"

In 1981 and 1982 we were very much focused on the Cruise and Pershing missiles, which were going to be deployed in Europe. There was a strong sense that if we didn't prevent the deployment from happening, that would be it. Russia would go to launch on warning, which meant that computers with approximately a 6-minute margin for error would essentially be in charge of blowing the world up. It made people more than nervous: we were terrified. This was a great impetus for action. If ever there was a time to put your personal life aside, to put your body on the line, to get dragged away, to go to jail, this was it. So our organizing was apocalyptic. Every meal, we feared, was the Last Supper. Without realizing it, we were acting out a Christian myth, expecting the end of the world, the end of time.

Of course, what happened is that the missiles went in, in spite of all the times we went to jail. And that's the way that political organizing and action often work. You go out, twelve hundred people performing civil disobedience, holding solidarity for 2 weeks, but President Reagan doesn't wake up the next day and say, "Gee, all these people are in jail. They're so sincere. They must have a point." It doesn't work that way.

But then, five years later, after long negotiations, Reagan and Gorbachev decide to take those missiles out of Europe. That is a victory, a victory that is the fruit of the organizing that we did all those years. But this kind of victory is not one we're going to see immediately. This is where the Pagan perspective comes in.

What Witches and Pagans do is practice magic. I like the definition of magic that says, "Magic is the art of changing consciousness at will." I also think that's a very good definition of political change—changing consciousness on a mass scale in this country. And one of the things we learn when we practice magic is that the results don't necessarily happen immediately. They unfold over time, and they always unfold in surprising ways, which is why we talk about our spiritual tradition in terms of mystery rather than answers and dogma and certainty. We talk about what it is we don't know and can only wonder about and be amazed at.

There is a certain way that magic works: it is, in a sense, a technology. When we want to do something, to change consciousness, for example, we first need an image of the change we want to create. We need a vision.

The same is true for political work. If we want to change consciousness in this nation, we first need to have a vision in our minds of what we want to change it into. We need to have an image, and we need to create that image and make it strong. And we need to direct energy and, in some way, ground it in reality.

The vision we want to create must also reflect a different model of power, one rooted in our understanding of the Earth as alive. We live in a system where power is *power-over*, that is, domination and control; it is a system in which a person or group of people has the right to tell other people what to do, to make their decisions, to set standards they have to live up to. The system may be overtly coercive, like a prison, or it may be benign on the surface, but it is still a system of power. And we internalize the system of domination. It lives inside us, like an entity, as if we were possessed by it.

Ecofeminism challenges all relations of domination. Its goal is not just to change who wields power, but to transform the structure of power itself. When the spirit is immanent, when each of us is the Goddess, is God, we have an inalienable right to be here and to be alive. We have a value that can't be taken away from us, that doesn't have to be earned, that doesn't have to be acquired. That kind of value is central to the change we want to create. That's the spell we want to cast.

The way we can embody that vision, can create the living image of that value, is in the groups we form and the structures we create. In some ways, especially in the Bay Area, we often have done this well. That is why so many people found organizing around Livermore and Diablo empowering. The Livermore Action Group and the Abalone Alliance (which organized the blockade at the Diablo nuclear power plant) were structured around small groups that worked by consensus. Now consensus can drive you out of your mind with frustration sometimes, but there is a very important principle in it. That is, everyone in the group has power, and everyone has equal power because everyone has value. That value is accepted, it's inherent, and it can't be taken away.

Along with the decision-making process goes a real care for the process that we use with each other. We listen to each other, we let each person have a say and hear each other and recognize that different people's opinions may be important, even if we disagree with them. Feminist process, as we call it, creates a strong sense of safety, and it changes people. I've known people in LAG who've said that their lives were profoundly changed by living for the first time in a society in which what they said was heard and considered important.

In a sense, that kind of decision making and organizing becomes a ritual. A ritual really is any kind of an intentional act we create that deepens our sense of value. The real heart of any ritual is telling our stories, that is, listening to each other and telling the sacred stories that we may have heard, that have been handed down and distilled from many people's experience, and telling the stories of our own experience.

Groups often seem to be most empowering when they are small. Only in a relatively small group can we really know each other as individuals. That's why LAG was organized in affinity groups, which are small, and why Witches are organized in covens, which traditionally have no more than thirteen members. When a group gets too large, people begin to become faceless. At the same time, small groups can also come together and form networks and coalitions and act together in larger ways. But the real base is always a small community of people who know and value each other personally.

We also need to have a sense of safety. A lot of people will say, "I feel unsafe in this group," meaning "I'm afraid someone's going to hurt my feelings." The truth is that someone will—someone always does—you can count on it. When we're honest, when we really interact with each other, there are always times when our needs or our style or our ways of communicating don't mesh. But when we each feel sure of our value to the group, conflict need not be devastating.

But real safety comes from something else. The groups we create and the ways we organize also have to be sustainable. If we weren't living in a state of denial all the time, the whole idea of sustainability would clearly be our first priority. How is it that we can live in a world where we use the Earth in ways that are destroying it and not worry? We all know we have to breathe; we all know we have to drink water; we all know we have to eat food; and, we all know it's got to come from somewhere. So why isn't the preservation of the environment our first priority? It makes such logical sense that it's irritating to have to say it.

In order to put the environment on the national agenda, we have to organize, but we also need to embody the principle of sustainability in our own groups. I think one of the flaws in our organizing, for example, in that period in the early 1980s, was exactly the apocalyptic sense coming out of that unconscious Christian myth that the end of time was near.

From a Pagan perspective, there is no end of time. Time is a cycle, and cycles come around and they go around and come back again. Our goal isn't to burn ourselves out as martyrs. Our model is the Earth, and the seed that is planted and springs up, grows, loses life, is planted and comes up again and again and again.

That, I think, is the kind of model we need for our politics. We need to see the process of changing our society as a lifetime challenge and commitment. Transforming consciousness so that we can preserve and sustain the Earth is a long-term project. We need the communities we create around that task to be sustainable. There are going to be times when we're active and it's exciting and we're obsessed by action, and there are going to be times when we pull back and nurture ourselves and heal and take care of ourselves. There are times when each of us gives a lot to a group, and times when each should get something back from the group, times when the giving and taking in a group balance out. Nobody should be stuck always having to be the leader, the organizer, or the one who pulls it all together. These tasks should rotate. And nobody should get stuck being the nurturer, the one everyone complains to, the mediator, the one who smooths everything over.

It is true that sometimes doing political work involves making sacrifices, and it may involve suffering. It's also true that around the world, people are suffering tremendously right now because of the policies of this country, the historical decisions and choices this country has made. We have to oppose and change these policies, and to do that we have to be willing to take risks. But sometimes in the nonviolence movement there's a kind of idealization of suffering. And I don't think that serves us. It comes out of the fantasy that people will see us suffering for our cause, be impressed by our nobility and sincerity, and be attracted to join and suffer with us.

Gandhi was a great man, but his ideas don't always fit for a lot of us, particularly for women. Gandhi said we have to accept the suffering and take it in. Women have been doing that for thousands and thousands of years, and it hasn't stopped anything much—except a lot of women's lives. In some ways, it's also not ecological. Rather than absorb the violence, what we need to do is to find some way to stop it and then transform it, to take that energy and turn it into creative change. Not to take it on ourselves.

The actual unsung truth about a lot of organizing is that it feels really good, and that's why people do it, again and again and again. It feels good because when we're actually organizing and taking action to stop the destruction of the Earth, we're doing an act of healing and we are free. There are few times when we are free in this culture and this is one of them. We need to speak about the joy and wildness and sense of liberation that comes when we step beyond the bounds of the authorities to resist control and create change.

Finally, I think that the spell we need to cast, the model we need to create, has to be open to mystery, to the understanding that we don't know everything about what's going on and we don't know exactly what to do about it. The mystery can be expressed in many ways. For one person it might be expressed through ritual, through celebration, chanting, and meditation; in some groups it might be expressed through humor, through making fun of what everybody else is doing. In some groups it might be expressed both ways. We can't define how a group or individual is going to experience it, but we can attempt to structure things so that we don't have dogmas and party lines, so we remain open to many possibilities of the sacred.

These are some ideas of how we build communities and what kinds of communities we might want to create. The other question is what we're going to organize these communities around. It's hard to get people together in a vacuum. One of the things that plagues our movements is that when we start looking at what's really going on with the

Earth and the people on it, it's overwhelming. All the issues seem so important that it's very, very hard to know what to focus on, and we can easily get fragmented.

I had dinner recently with a man named Terry Gips who heads a group called the International Alliance for Sustainable Agriculture. He was telling me that he'd come to the conclusion that we have about 3 years to turn around the environmental destruction or it'll be too late. He had expressed this idea to his friends and reactions were so bad that he'd decided not to talk about it any more. People got very depressed. I could understand that because I'd gotten terribly depressed myself.

I said, "Well, I don't know if it's useful to think in those terms. When you said 'three years,' it didn't sound like enough time. It reminds me of that period in the early 1980s when we thought we had to get rid of those missiles now or never. At the same time, if you really believe that, what do we need to do? Do we need to smash capitalism in 3 years and totally transform society? I don't think we can do that."

He said, "No. Actually, there are some very concrete things to do in the next 3 to 5 years—however long we might have—that would reverse the destruction enough to give us time to make the deeper kinds of changes and transformations we need to make." He sat there talking, and I started thinking, and we came up with a campaign for turning the tide.

So this is what I think we should do, and, if I were setting an ecofeminist or a Green agenda, this is how I would organize it, the beginning of which I look at as a sort of magic circle.

Illustrated on the opposite page are the tree of life and the magic circle. The magic circle is a circle of the elements: air, fire, water, and earth. The tree has roots and a core, a center, a heart that's the same as the circle, and it has branches. If we think about it, all of these issues that we see as being so interconnected can fit into that magic circle.

For example, let's talk about air. The ozone layer has holes in it and is rapidly being depleted. We should be organizing around this issue if we want our food crops and ocean plankton to survive, if we want to preserve the viability of the Earth. And such organizing has already had some success. Du Pont, which manufactures 25 percent of the world's chlorofluorocarbons, has voluntarily decided to phase out production. Several states, including Minnesota, are considering bills to ban these substances, and some fast-food franchises are phasing out packaging made from these substances. But even with these changes,

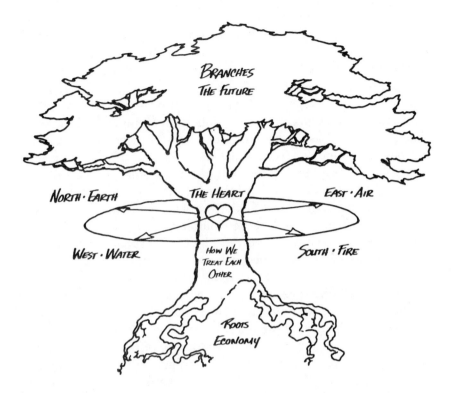

the ozone will continue to diminish since chlorofluorocarbons remain in the Earth's atmosphere for up to 80 years. Yet these positive steps show us that public pressure can bring about important changes.

Another air issue is the destruction of tropical rain forests. If you wonder why I put that under air, it's because these forests are the lungs of the world. They are being cut down, and they are key to systems that regulate the Earth's weather patterns. There *should* be an international commission on the rain forest, and there should also be pressure on institutions like the World Bank and the International Monetary Fund to stop funding the destruction of rain forests. A lot of the destruction comes as rain forests are cut down so cattle can graze and our fast-food restaurants can turn out hamburgers. That's another thing we can organize around. A boycott of one fast-food chain, Burger King, convinced it to stop buying rain forest beef.

Now look at fire: we have nuclear issues. Nuclear power—what do we do with all that waste? Nuclear weapons, we should be working to ban them. Fire represents energy, and we need renewable sources of energy. We need our money put into those sources rather than into things that pollute and kill.

There are also important water issues. Acid rain is also killing trees and forests. Canada wanted some very simple things from us, like smoke scrubbers and curbs on acid rain, and then-President Reagan refused. We need to set standards and see that they're enforced. (Bush's new proposals sound good but actually lack strict standards.) We need to be talking about groundwater pollution. In Minnesota, "Land of a Thousand Lakes" as the license plate says, wells were tested and 39 percent were found to be contaminated; similar statistics exist for many areas. We also need to stop the pollution of the ocean, the oil drilling off the coasts, the depletion of fisheries, and the killing of whales.

Then, of course, there's the Earth. One of the things that would push us toward sustainable agriculture would be simply to stop subsidizing pesticides, which we do now in a lot of very subtle ways. For example, if a pesticide is banned, who is it that pays for storing and destroying it? It's us. It's our tax money, not the company that produces it. In California beekeepers lose thousands of dollars every year to pesticides. The government reimburses them, but the pesticide companies should be paying the price. It's estimated that there are four pesticide poisonings a minute, three-fourths of them in the Third World. We could make it uneconomical to poison the Earth and the human beings who grow and eat the food the Earth produces. We could make alliances with the United Farmworkers of America, who've been calling for a boycott of grapes and focusing attention on pesticide issues and labor practices.

We also need to preserve sacred lands such as Big Mountain and end the destruction of indigenous peoples and cultures. If the Earth is sacred to us, we must preserve the wilderness that's left because that's the place we go for renewal, where we can most strongly feel the immanence of the Goddess.

Also with Earth go feeding the hungry, sheltering the homeless. One of the advantages of seeing issues as integrated, rather than fragmented, is that it can help us avoid false dichotomies. For example, environmental issues *are* social justice issues, for it is the poor who are forced to work directly with unsafe chemicals, in whose neighborhoods toxic waste incinerators are planned, who cannot afford to buy bottled water and organic vegetables or pay for medical care. Environmental issues are international issues, for we cannot simply export unsafe pesticides, toxic wastes, and destructive technologies without poisoning the whole living body of the Earth. And environmental issues are women's issues, for women sicken, starve, and die from toxics, droughts, and famines, their capacity to bear new life is threatened by pollution, and they bear the brunt of care for the sick and the dying, as well as for the next generation.

Environmental issues cannot be intelligently approached without the perspectives of women, the poor, and those who come from other parts of the globe, as well as those of all races and cultural backgrounds. To take only one example, we cannot responsibly approach questions of overpopulation without facing questions of women's power to make decisions about their own reproduction, to challenge traditional roles and restrictions.

If we approach any issue without taking into account the perspectives of all those it affects, we run the risk of accepting false solutions, for example, that famine or AIDS are acceptable answers to population problems. From a Pagan point of view, such "solutions" are entirely unethical because the ethics of integrity prevents us from accepting a solution for someone else that we are unwilling to accept for ourselves.

False solutions are also dangerous because they divert our attention from the real forces with which we must contend. Like an illusionist's tricks, they distract us from seeing what is really going on and from noticing what really works and what doesn't. What really works to stem population growth is not mass death—wars, famines, and epidemics have produced, at most, a ripple in the rising tide. What works is increasing the security of life for those who are already alive and, especially, increasing women's power and autonomy, women's control over our own bodies and access to work and economic compensation independent of our role in procreation. Feminists have been saying this for a long time, and environmentalists need to listen or their analysis will remain fragmented and shortsighted.

Unless we understand all the interconnections, we are vulnerable to manipulation. For example, we are often told that to end hunger we must sacrifice wilderness. But what will work to end hunger is not the further destruction of natural resources within the same system of greed and inequality that has engendered hunger. In their book, *World Hunger: Twelve Myths* (New York: Grove Press, 1986), Frances Moore Lappé and Joseph Collins make the point that people are hungry not because there isn't enough food in the world, but because they are poor. To end hunger we must restore control over land and economic resources to those who have been disenfranchised by the same forces that destroy, with equal lack of concern, the life of a child or a tree or an endangered species, in the name of profit.

And so we come to the roots of the tree—our economic base. Our economy reflects our system of values, in which profit replaces inherent value as the ultimate measure of all things. If we saw ourselves as interconnected parts of the living being that is the Earth, of equal existential value, we could no longer justify economic exploitation.

Our economy is one of waste. The biggest part of that waste is that it's an economy of war, which is inherently wasteful. We need to transform that into an economy that is truly productive and sustainable. To do that we need economic justice—economic democracy as well as political democracy.

Then we can support the branches of the tree, which reach out into the future, touching upon such issues as caring for our children, education, and the values that we teach people. Protecting the future also involves challenging potentially dangerous technologies like genetic engineering. It means basing our decisions, plans, and programs on our obligation to future generations.

In the heart of the tree, the center, is how we treat each other. To work on any of these issues, we must transform the power relationships and the hierarchies of value that keep us separate and unequal. We must challenge the relations of domination between men and women, between light people and dark people, between rich people and poor people; we must do away with all of those things that my friend Luisah Teish calls the "Ism brothers." Then we can really begin treating each other with that sense that each one of us has inherent value, that nobody's interests can be written off and forgotten.

These are the ways I see the issues as being interconnected. Ultimately, to work on any one of them, we need to work on all of them. To work on all of them, we can start at any place on that circle or part of the tree. What I would envision ecofeminist groups saying is: "Let's do it. Let's turn the environmental destruction around. Let's have a movement we call Turning the Tide and commit ourselves to it. Not as a short-term thing that we're going to do for a year and then burn out, but as a way of transforming and changing our lives."

We can begin this long-term commitment by first getting together with people in a small way and forming our own action groups, our own circles for support, which can take on their own characters and their own personalities. Maybe you will form a circle where members take off their clothes and go to the beach and dance around and jump in the waves and energize yourselves that way. And then you'll all write letters to your congresspersons about the ozone condition. Maybe somebody else will form a circle in their church where members sit on chairs and meditate quietly and then go out to Nevada and get in the way of the nuclear testing. But whatever we do, our spirituality needs to be grounded in action.

Along with seeing issues as interconnected, we need to all be able to envision new kinds of organizing. We need to envision a movement where our first priority is to form community, small groups centered around both personal support and action, and to make that what people see as their ongoing, long-term commitment. We don't have to commit ourselves to some big, overall organization. We can commit ourselves to eight other people with whom we can say, "We can form a community to do political and spiritual work and find support over a long period of time." Then our communities can network and form organizations around issues and around tasks as needed, and can dissolve the larger organizations and networks when they're not needed.

I want to end with my vision of where this might all bring us. It's an optimistic one because, ultimately, I do believe that we can do it. We really can turn the tide—we can reverse the destruction of the Earth.

> And so the time comes when all the people of the earth
>   can bring their gifts to the fire
>   and look into each other's faces
>   unafraid
>
> Breathe deep
> Feel the sacred well that is your own breath, and look
>   look at that circle
> See us come from every direction
>   from the four quarters of the earth
> See the lines that stretch to the horizon
>   the procession, the gifts borne
>   see us feed the fire
> Feel the earth's life renewed
> And the circle is complete again
>   and the medicine wheel is formed anew
>   and the knowledge within each one of us
>   made whole
> Feel the great turning, feel the change
>   the new life runs through your blood like fire

and all of nature rises with it
greening, burgeoning, bursting into flower
At that mighty rising
do the vines rise up, do the grains rise up
and the desert turns green
the wasteland blooms like a garden
Hear the earth sing
of her own loveliness
her hillock lands, her valleys
her furrows well-watered
her untamed wild places
She arises in you
as you in her
Your voice becomes her voice
Sing!
Your dance is her dance
of the circling stars
and the ever-renewing flame
As your labor has become her labor
Out of the bone, ash
Out of the ash, pain
Out of the pain, the swelling
Out of the swelling, the opening
Out of the opening, the labor
Out of the labor, the birth
Out of the birth, the turning wheel
the turning tide[1]

Susan Griffin

CURVES
ALONG THE ROAD

I WANT TO START with a concept from theoretical physicist David Bohm, who is among a group of British scientists who say that the universe does indeed have meaning. David Bohm points out that we in Western civilization have a fragmentary worldview. I am extending his insight into the social sphere to suggest that this fragmentary vision is expressed in the categories of gender, of masculine and feminine. What I mean by this is not the biological male and female, but the socially created categories, masculine and feminine. These categories reflect a deeper schism in the shared vision of our civilization: the separation between the natural world and the spiritual world.

Charlene Spretnak used a wonderful phrase about the importance of seeing the divine as immanent—the divine as filling all of life—a concept foreign to those raised in Judeo-Christianity. The view that we've grown up with is that the divine and matter are separate and that matter is really dangerous. The material world belongs to the devil. What's under your feet is closer to hell, and the more sensual you are, the more open you are to being corrupted by the devil. Women, being closer to the Earth, listened to serpents, made people eat apples, and made them commit other sins.

In splitting spirit from matter, human consciousness is divided. We think of intellectual knowledge as separate from sensual knowledge, and the spirit as belonging to a different realm entirely. In this way, our experience of the world is fragmented. And because of this we see fragments. Modern science, which in one way asserts the primacy of material knowledge, in a more subtle way preserves the same dividedness that preceded it. Using the scientific method, scientists attempt to be above sensual experience. But instead of being above experience, they are perceiving partially. They see the pieces clearly, with no feeling for the whole. When, for example, a drug is created that produces a predictable effect on birth, the illusion is created that science understands birth. As a scientific culture, we believe we have more knowledge and control than in truth we do. This produces a kind of hubris.

Bohm goes on to say that because we possess a fragmentary world-view we produce fragments. That is, we tend to make the way we see things become real. If you look at the way we view the world, it should be no surprise that we now have put billions of dollars into devising plans to blow it to smithereens. We are making the world into our own image, which is into little bits.

Consciousness is an integral part of nature. But we fail to under-stand this. We have stolen the soul from nature, or so we believe, because you really can't take away the spirit in nature. In our worldview we imagine that only human beings have souls, not other natural creatures, nor nature as a whole. In Descartes' *Meditations* he wrote that he came to see that animals do not have souls when he tried to think of sponges or shellfish having souls. That is why I dedicated *Women and Nature* to shellfish and sponges. When we take the soul from nature, what we are really doing is fragmenting human whole-ness. Most mystics will tell you that whatever you do to others you are doing to yourself in some sense. We lose the natural wholeness of vision that is given to us. Then we go to great lengths to regain what, in fact, we were born with and afterward rejected through an alienating assumption about the nature of the universe.

One of the more profound ways through which we fragment whole-ness is through the categories of masculine and feminine. We assign to the masculine the province of the soul, the spirit, or the transcendent, and we read the feminine as representing nature and the Earth. To some degree it's a system that functions because if you don't have somebody who is earthly, who's going to make the dinner? There have to be some people in the society to do the "dirty," material work. If you look at hierarchies in society, it's not only women, but people de-fined as "other," people of color, Jews in European tradition, who carry the burden of nature.

One of the reasons we do this is to shield ourselves from the fact of our complete participation with nature. It is a participation in which we are vulnerable to natural cycles and are mortal. Of course, the material stuff of our bodies as a part of the natural cycle is immortal, yet this particular form we are in changes with time, and we die. We're subject to the slings and arrows of outrageous fortune. But as a culture we have never learned how to understand or live with this knowledge. Instead, we deny the reality of death and create a masculine category of experience that is supposedly above the passage of time and therefore invulnerable. There's an old mystical lesson here, too: whatever you run from you meet. In running away from death (and from loss and from difficulty), we have in fact created the possibility of mass death, an unnatural atrocity for ourselves and all life on earth.

I want to read a passage in *Woman and Nature* called "The Lion in the Den of the Prophets." This telling reverses the usual story of the prophet in the lion's den. And in this case the "prophets" are scientists.

> She swaggers in. They are terrifying in their white hairlessness. She waits. She watches. She does not move. She is measuring their moves. And they are measuring her. Cautiously one takes a bit of her fur. He cuts it free from her. He examines it. Another numbers her feet, her teeth, the length and width of her body. She yawns. They announce she is alive. They wonder what she will do if they enclose her in the room with them. One of them shuts the door. She backs her way toward the closed doorway and then roars. "Be still," the men say. She continues to roar. "Why does she roar?" they ask. The roaring must be inside her, they conclude. They decide they must see the roaring inside her. They approach her in a group, six at her two front legs and six at her two back legs. They are trying to put her to sleep. She swings at one of them. His own blood runs over him. "Why did she do that?" the men question. She has no soul, they conclude, she does not know right from wrong. "Be still," they shout at her. "Be humble, trust us," they demand. "We have souls," they proclaim, "we know what is right." They approach her with their medicine, "for you." She does not understand this language. She devours them.[1]

We are, in fact, devouring ourselves with our fear of natural power and our attempts to control it. We seek to save ourselves from our own experience. We refuse to be eaten in a sense that one ought to be and always is finally eaten by experience.

I would like to tell you another story that sounds mythic, though unfortunately it is not. This is a story about the *Challenger* that was not widely reported in the media. The *Challenger*, which exploded, was a test for a shot still planned for the future. This future rocket will send off another. The second rocket is meant to circle and take photographs of Jupiter. And this second rocket is to be powered with plutonium. Let that sink in. Because, had this first shot been made, an unimaginable number of people would have died, not to speak of genetic damage that would affect the Earth for countless generations. We do not know what the results of that much plutonium settling to Earth would be, now or over many generations, because plutonium causes genetic damage, as well as cancer, and a wide range of diseases.

The *Challenger* was made lighter to carry the plutonium encasement and the second rocket, so two items were removed. The shielding around the *Challenger*'s booster rockets was made thinner, making them more vulnerable to freezing. And a mechanical device on the booster rockets that measured the temperature was also removed.

If you are like me, you might ask yourself, "Why are these scientists and statesmen doing this?" This kind of carelessness is beyond the "banality of evil" because plutonium is not going to say to itself, "I'm going to get working-class people and feminists and Black people and I'm going to leave the president and his advisers alone." The guys planning this are going to be affected, too, and their children and their children's children. Who are these free-floating "space cases"? What are they thinking of? Where are their heads?[2]

Let me tell you another story. This is from Robert Scheer's *With Enough Shovels* (New York: Random House, 1982). This title comes from the civil defense policy developed under Reagan's first administration by a man called T. K. Jones. This man I'm certain had a degree from a distinguished university in some distinguished discipline. He was an informed human being, and his job was civil defense. What he recommended was that everyone go out and buy a shovel. And with the shovel, you just dig a hole for yourself and get down in there when the bomb hits. He's right, to an extent. The soil would protect people from a certain amount of impact, if you do not take radiation into account. But then we do not, unfortunately, always take radiation into account.

It took an 8-year-old boy who had not yet earned an academic degree to point out to T. K. Jones and the Reagan administration that somebody was going to have to be above ground covering up the hole, right? They hadn't thought of that.

I was talking about this kind of thing with the American Friends Service Committee. Somebody came up afterward, a young man, who reminded me of something. The people planning nuclear strategy and space flights (we were talking specifically about Enrico Fermi) are very practical. It takes practical-minded people to get a missile up into space. They have to know how to measure and how to shape bits of metal. I can't do those things; I have trouble with light bulbs. So I began to think more about this question. Enrico Fermi combined the genius of a great theoretical physicist with engineering capacity, and he made the atomic bomb possible on a practical level. General Groves, the man in charge of the Manhattan Project, asked Fermi, just before the first chain reaction was to be set off on a playing field at the University of Chicago, "Are you certain that the chain reaction is going to stop? Are you certain it's not going to blow up the university, Chicago, Illinois, North America, the world?" Theoretically, a chain reaction could go on infinitely. Fermi said he'd made a number of calculations and that the possibility of the chain reaction going on and on and on was negligible. And to make this story even funnier, in this vein of gallows humor, the reactor he constructed to create the first chain reaction was a very crude model of a graphite reactor, much more crude than the sophisticated and safer model at Chernobyl. And before the meltdown at Chernobyl, scientists said that the possibility of that kind of accident happening was also negligible. Now they're changing their calculations. If you study the history of science, you realize that scientists always change their theoretical calculations when there are conflicting experimental results, and, in fact, such conflicts are often the sources for new theories.

Heinrich Himmler, who was Reichsführer SS under Hitler and therefore in charge of all the concentration camps, was also a very practical man. I do not mean to draw a moral comparison between Fermi and Himmler, who were very different men in very different circumstances, but to note a similarity in a caste of mind which we in this civilization share with both men. It is also important to understand that psychologically, technologically, and historically, the Nazi holocaust is the precedent of a nuclear holocaust. That we use the same word to refer to both events is a kind of cultural slip of the tongue that reveals a deep and largely unconscious association. To give you just one example of a technological and historical precedent: the first missiles, the V-1 and V-2 rockets, which are the prototypes of today's ICBM missiles, were manufactured at concentration camp Dora by prisoners who were worked to death in underground tunnels.

Himmler's power was based on his talent as a bureaucrat. He was very good at getting things done, at keeping records. He was a highly efficient organizer. He was in charge of what they called "security operations on the Eastern front," which in fact meant mass murder on the Russian front. He organized groups of SS men who were called

Einsatzgruppen, "mobile killing units" as the SS defined them. They went out into the Russian countryside, and they killed people who were partisans, or because they lived in a certain village, or because they were Jews. These young men found themselves shooting men, women, and children into open graves.

Himmler went out once to supervise these killings, and he was surprised to see actual death. He had it all arranged on paper, but when he actually saw people dying, he was very shaken, very upset. The captain of this particular SS group said to him, "You must realize how upsetting it is for the young men who have to do these killings, these shootings, every day."

Himmler said, "Yes. I'm going to do something about it." He went back to Berlin and hired an engineer, Walter Rauff, and had him design a mobile killing van, basically a gas chamber on the back of a truck. This was his solution—keep the process of death away from the eyes of the men who were committing the murders so they wouldn't know what they were doing. It was a kind of enforced fragmentation.

To return for a moment to Enrico Fermi. When he witnessed the first atomic bomb exploded at Alamogordo, New Mexico, he decided he would measure its effects by releasing two pieces of paper at the moment of detonation and watching their reaction to the blast as they floated to the ground. He was so focused on these papers that he did not hear a blast so loud that others described it as a force. He also underestimated the emotional effect the explosion would have on him. He was incapable of driving his car back to Los Alamos. He suffered from hallucinations that his car was jumping from point to point, skipping the curves along the road.

Why do these curves along the road vanish?

Hallucinations are like the ghosts of forgotten thoughts. They speak to us of whatever we have repressed.

Obviously, on a certain level, both Fermi and Himmler—Fermi the scientist who helped to create a weapon that killed hundreds of thousands of people and Himmler the mass murderer—had an intimate knowledge of nature. All existence *is* nature, and both men had an intimate knowledge of practical existence. But their awareness of what existence is, no matter how practical, was not embedded in the cycle of life. They distanced themselves from the wholeness of experience.

We have many institutions in this culture that help us do just that. One is science—which uses the concept of "objectivity" as a distancing device. One is bureaucracy—which keeps people from seeing the implications and direct consequences of their actions. These and other institutions reflect the basic way in which we understand consciousness within this culture; that is, not as a part of birth or the sustenance of life, or of emotions and the ecology of emotions, or as part of death; not as embedded in and inseparable from the process of life; but as separate and above it. It takes a bending of language at this point to speak of consciousness as embedded in the way we breathe, the way we stand, all the intricate numbers of relationships we have, where we live on the planet, the trees next to us.

Yet all experience of material existence threatens the imaginary schism between nature and consciousness; even language, which is itself a material experience, reflects the acoustical shape of mouth and tongue. The very word *culture* derives from the word for the cultivation of the soil. *Spirit* derives from the word for breath.

But we choose to forget this materiality of spirit and believe instead that culture has a transcendental power over nature. Yet, despite our denial, experience tells us otherwise, over and over again. There is one experience in particular that breaks through our illusion of separation from each other and from nature with an almost explosive force, and that is sexual experience. Perhaps this is why men call intensely attractive women "bombshells." Certainly the fear of sexual knowledge and the domination of women are part of the same psychology. Sexual intimacy locates consciousness in the body and at the same time challenges our fragmentary idea of the universe. By categorizing women as "other," sexual experience is defused; it is reduced to less than it is, to a sensuality stripped of its meaning. This is one of many ways by which pleasure is robbed of ontological significance. And it is not unrelated to the nuclear crisis we confront today.

I am going to quote a passage from a book I am writing, *A Chorus of Stones: The Private Life of War.* In this passage I picture a soldier on leave who goes to a prostitute. The men who were part of a special battalion charged with dropping the first atomic bomb were known as hell-raisers: they drank, gambled, and saw prostitutes. They did not know what mission they were being trained for, but they did know it was likely to be dangerous. I tried to imagine what it would be like to be one of these men:

A man, perhaps he is a soldier, and nearly ready to go into battle, goes to see a prostitute. He goes first to a bar, or to two or three or many bars, and drinks among men. Then when he is tight enough, but still able to walk, still able to feel himself in his sex, he searches, in the last bar, or neighborhood surrounding it. What is he looking for, a color of hair, the shape of a face, a way of moving, large breasts, or a lean body, light or dark skin, none of this matters. Some bit of her, her laugh, the way she looks will reach him and eat into his imagination until he is drawn. Not knowing this woman, he is drawn inevitably towards that which he remembers, or that which he has always dreamt of and learned in some way to associate with the turn of a head, the purely physical inflection of a voice. He follows as a force that seems to be hers takes him closer and closer. Who is she? He learns very little. Whatever she tells him she invents. In the darkened rooms where they meet he is not able to tell that she has taken drugs, enough to take the edge away from her awareness, or more, to make her nearly insensible. He will not have to remember her name. She only pretends to learn his name. He may ask to be beaten or to beat her. He may want to caress her, or pull her to him roughly and quickly. Perhaps he asks to put his sex in her mouth. He may want to swear at her or give her orders. As the sex comes into him a certain sharpness enters his mind, like windows, doors opening. There is a place in him, between his chest and his thighs, inside and through and in his belly, his penis, his testicles, that starts to unwind as he grows larger, as if space itself became larger, even infinite, and inside him like someone dying, images enter his mind unbidden, he is more drunken than drunk, perhaps he cries out, or shouts, he thinks of his own death, he puts his sex, large with wanting, inside her, and despite himself, his body sighs sinking into pleasure and then into more desire as he moves in her, wanting, his skin intense with feeling, he senses death, something in him almost breaking, he may shout again, and then it is warm, it breaks, it is sweet, it is gone. He rolls away from her. In a wordless place inside himself, he must know she is pretending. And he, he is feeling cold, his mind is racing back to where he came from. Saying nothing of what he has seen, what he has felt, he stands and puts on his clothes. He gives her money and makes his way back to the street where he will be among the other men, again.

The body, all earthy existence, has meaning. Metaphor derives its power from the intrinsic significance of the material world. Sexual feeling, orgasm, leads one to a sense of union, makes evident a kind of knowledge in the body, of the matrix of connections that defines all being. But through categorizing women as other, and within that category, creating further classifications, such as the virgin and the whore, culture is able to divorce this knowledge from conscious thought. Such a divorce is necessary, for instance, in order to wage war.

I want to close with a poem which talks about another kind of union—the connectedness on this Earth. Whether we want to or not, we share a social and biological matrix. We are connected. When we violate others or simply fail to feel this connection, we feel instead an emptiness, a mourning, an undefined grief.

I wrote "Hunger" after seeing an exhibition in Paris of a series of photographs taken by Sebastian Selgado. The photographs document the starvation in a region of Africa known as the Sahel. In the United States we have told ourselves that this is a natural calamity. But if we look more closely at the history of colonialism, we discover a different story. Disregard for the natural ecology of a region goes hand in hand with a disregard for the natural rights of people to determine their own fate and to live in the way they choose. This pattern of domination and disregard has created many of the famines in Africa.

Many African people in areas subject to drought used to grow millet and rotate it seasonally. Millet is an important crop because it can grow with very little water. When the White colonists came into Africa they uprooted the millet and substituted other crops, such as wheat. When the weather conditions changed, as the tribal societies that had lived there for centuries understood would happen, the wheat could not withstand the dry spells, and hence a famine was created. Seasons of drought would not have had such a devastating effect on millet, but because of the planting of wheat, terrible starvation resulted.

This pattern has been repeated over and over again and is still being repeated today, now not in the name of colonialism but in the name of development. It is part of the arrogance of this civilization to reduce nature to a materiality without meaning and to ignore the wisdom of more ancient cultures that see meaning as emanating from natural existence.

In "Hunger," I refer to the "old texts." These are the recorded teachings of Rabbi Nahem of Chernobyl. The reactor at Chernobyl was built over the ruins of a Hasidic temple. The reactor at Hanford, Washington, is built over a Native-American burial mound. Rabbi Nahem was a spiritual descendant of the Bal Shem Tov, who brought the natural soul and actual human experience back into theology. He was famous for teaching how to bring light out of the dark.

HUNGER

It is important to see this.

In the old texts

the world was made
after the image of justice

one photograph after another

I stood there
taking notes

(I who hunger
for love)

In one of the images
someone tries to feed
a small boy. He is
mostly bone. A clear tube
enters his nose.
His eyes draw everything
into them.
In the moment the camera captures
the world
spins about his terror

One could not reach out and touch him,
he was in another country,
only oneself
hand for a moment
shielding the eyes.

They say the world was created
by great love
yet for some reason
the letters were not written
in their proper order.

There was the breath of it
the hunger of these people
who were not in the room.

I wrote in my notebook
before I can stop myself
I am shaken
it is the sight
of the child's buttocks

so deprived of flesh
they appear
like an empty bag, crumpled
over his legs.

Language is filled
with words for deprivation
images so familiar
it is hard to crack language open
into that other country
the country of being.

I have felt many kinds of longing.
And also despair.
Wanting what did not exist
what I believed I could not
continue without
the sweet taste of
bliss covering me
like a blanket.

In one photograph
thirsty boys
hear the first sounds of water
moving through a pipe.

I know what is possible
what exists in and out of language.
Why is it one wishes
to feel the dimensions of
being outside
the dimensions
of self?

They sit waiting
under the beautiful trees
the hungry
with light striking them
and the trees
their beauty.

Malgre le nombre considérable des morts
Despite the considerable number of

deaths
les réfugiés gardent la dignité
the refugees hold onto dignity
et le respect des rites funéraires.
they practice burial rites.

Under this photograph I read
there is not enough wood
for coffins
so the bodies are wrapped
in the sacks
which have been used
to bring food.

Somewhere else it is written that
the love of creation
is a brilliantly shining light
and that it is the nature
of good to do good.

Behind these images
are many histories.
A long story traces
the beginning of hunger
past famine, past drought
to moments of blindness, places
where the full dimension
of being
was not known
and this led
to this image:
a small girl's body
webbed and spiny like an insect
hung in a scale,
this body
on which the light falls
as evenly
as any other,
the light
on this body
taken up by my eyes.

Where we see no image of justice

the word *injustice* reminds us of what we
want.

Inside, this word
makes circles like the
hungry who cannot
stop seeking, who stumble
over mountains, through deserts
Inside me this word
is like a lover
seeking the dimensions
of love.[3]

Carolyn Merchant

ECOFEMINISM AND FEMINIST THEORY

THE TERM *ecofeminisme* was coined by the French writer Françoise d'Eaubonne in 1974 to represent women's potential for bringing about an ecological revolution to ensure human survival on the planet.[1] Such an ecological revolution would entail new gender relations between women and men and between humans and nature. Liberal, radical, and socialist feminism have all been concerned with improving the human/nature relationship, and each has contributed to an ecofeminist perspective in different ways.[2] Liberal feminism is consistent with the objectives of reform environmentalism to alter human relations with nature through the passage of new laws and regulations. Radical ecofeminism analyzes environmental problems from within its critique of patriarchy and offers alternatives that could liberate both women and nature. Socialist ecofeminism grounds its analysis in capitalist patriarchy and would totally restructure, through a socialist revolution, the domination of women and nature inherent in the market economy's use of both as resources. While radical feminism has delved more deeply into the woman/nature connection, I believe that socialist feminism has the potential for a more thorough critique of the domination issue.

Liberal feminism characterized the history of feminism from its beginnings in the seventeenth century until the 1960s. Its roots are liberalism, the political theory that incorporates the scientific analysis that nature is composed of atoms moved by external forces with a theory of human nature that views humans as individual rational agents who maximize their own self-interest and capitalism as the optimal economic structure for human progress. Historically, liberal feminists have argued that women do not differ from men as rational agents and that exclusion from educational and economic opportunities have prevented them from realizing their own potential for creativity in all spheres of human life.[3]

For liberal feminists (as for liberalism generally), environmental problems result from the overly rapid development of natural resources and the failure to regulate environmental pollutants. Better science, conservation, and laws are the proper approaches to resolving resource problems. Given equal educational opportunities to become scientists, natural resource managers, regulators, lawyers, and legislators, women like men can contribute to the improvement of the environment, the conservation of natural resources, and the higher quality of human life. Women, therefore, can transcend the social stigma of their biology and join men in the cultural project of environmental conservation.

Radical feminism developed in the late 1960s and 1970s with the second wave of feminism. The radical form of ecofeminism is a response to the perception that women and nature have been mutually associated and devalued in Western culture and that both can be elevated and liberated through direct political action. In prehistory an emerging patriarchal culture dethroned the mother Goddesses and replaced them with male gods to whom the female deities became subservient.[4] The scientific revolution of the seventeenth century further degraded nature by replacing Renaissance organicism and a nurturing earth with the metaphor of a machine to be controlled and repaired from the outside. The Earth is to be dominated by male-developed and -controlled technology, science, and industry.

Radical feminism instead celebrates the relationship between women and nature through the revival of ancient rituals centered on Goddess worship, the moon, animals, and the female reproductive system. A vision in which nature is held in esteem as mother and Goddess is a source of inspiration and empowerment for many ecofeminists. Spirituality is seen as a source of both personal and social change. Goddess worship and rituals centered around the lunar and female menstrual cycles, lectures, concerts, art exhibitions, street and theater productions, and direct political action (web weaving in antinuclear protests) are all examples of the re-visioning of nature and women as powerful forces. Radical ecofeminist philosophy embraces intuition, an ethic of caring, and weblike human/nature relationships.

For radical feminists, human nature is grounded in human biology. Humans are biologically sexed and socially gendered. Sex/gender relations give men and women different power bases. Hence the personal is political. Radical feminists object to the dominant society's perception that women are limited by being closer to nature because of their ability to bear children. The dominant view is that menstruation, pregnancy, nursing, and nurturing of infants and young children should tie women to the home, decreasing their mobility and inhibiting their ability to remain in the work force. Radical feminists argue that the perception that women are totally oriented toward biological reproduction degrades them by association with a nature that is itself devalued in Western culture. Women's biology and nature should instead be celebrated as sources of female power.

Turning the perceived connection between women and biological reproduction upside down becomes the source of women's empowerment and ecological activism. Women argue that male-designed and -produced technologies neglect the effects of nuclear radiation, pesticides, hazardous wastes, and household chemicals on women's reproductive organs and on the ecosystem. They argue that radioactivity from nuclear wastes, power plants, and bombs is a potential cause of birth defects, cancers, and the elimination of life on Earth.[5] They expose hazardous waste sites near schools and homes as permeating soil and drinking water and contributing to miscarriage, birth defects, and leukemia. They object to pesticides and herbicides being sprayed on crops and forests as potentially affecting children and the childbearing women living near them. Women frequently spearhead local actions against spraying and power plant siting and organize others to demand toxic cleanups. When coupled with an environmental ethic that values rather than degrades nature, such actions have the potential both for raising women's consciousness of their own oppression and for the liberation of nature from the polluting effects of industrialization. For example, many lower-middle-class women who became politicized through protests over toxic chemical wastes at Love Canal in New York simultaneously became feminists when their activism spilled over into their home lives.[6]

Yet in emphasizing the female, body, and nature components of the dualities male/female, mind/body, and culture/nature, radical ecofeminism runs the risk of perpetuating the very hierarchies it seeks to overthrow. Critics point to the problem of women's own reinforcement of their identification with a nature that Western culture degrades.[7] If "female is to male as nature is to culture," as anthropologist Sherry Ortner argues,[8] then women's hopes for liberation are set back by association with nature. Any analysis that makes women's essence and qualities special ties them to a biological destiny that thwarts the possibility of liberation. A politics grounded in women's culture, experience, and values can be seen as reactionary.

To date, socialist feminists have had little to say about the problem of the domination of nature. To them, the source of male domination of women is the complex of social patterns called capitalist patriarchy, in which men bear the responsibility for labor in the marketplace and women for labor in the home. Yet the potential exists for a socialist ecofeminism that would push for an ecological, economic, and social revolution that would simultaneously liberate women, working-class people, and nature.

For socialist ecofeminism, environmental problems are rooted in the rise of capitalist patriarchy and the ideology that the Earth and nature can be exploited for human progress through technology. Historically, the rise of capitalism eroded the subsistence-based farm and city workshop in which production was oriented toward use values and men and women were economic partners. The result was a capitalist economy dominated by men and a domestic sphere in which women's labor in the home was unpaid and subordinate to men's labor in the marketplace. Both women and nature are exploited by men as part of the progressive liberation of humans from the constraints imposed by nature. The consequence is the alienation of women and men from each other and both from nature.

Socialist feminism incorporates many of the insights of radical feminism, but views both nature and human nature as historically and socially constructed. Human nature is seen as the product of historically changing interactions between humans and nature, men and women, classes, and races. Any meaningful analysis must be grounded in an understanding of power not only in the personal but also in the political sphere. Like radical feminism, socialist feminism is critical of mechanistic science's treatment of nature as passive and of its male-dominated power structures. Similarly, it deplores the lack of a gender analysis in history and the omission of any treatment of women's reproductive and nurturing roles. But rather than grounding its analysis in biological reproduction alone, it also incorporates social reproduction. Biological reproduction includes the reproduction of the species and the reproduction of daily life through food, clothing, and shelter; social reproduction includes socialization and the legal/political reproduction of the social order.[9]

Like Marxist feminists, socialist feminists see nonhuman nature as the material basis of human life, supplying the necessities of food, clothing, shelter, and energy. Materialism, not spiritualism, is the driving force of social change. Nature is transformed by human science

Feminism and the Environment

	NATURE	HUMAN NATURE	FEMINIST CRITIQUE OF ENVIRONMENTALISM	IMAGE OF A FEMINIST ENVIRONMENTALISM
LIBERAL FEMINISM	Atoms Mind/body dualism Domination of nature	Rational agents Individualism Maximization of self-interest	"Man and his environment" leaves out women	Women participate in natural resources and environmental sciences
MARXIST FEMINISM	Transformation of nature by science and technology for human use Domination of nature as a means to human freedom Nature is material basis of life: food, clothing, shelter, energy	Creation of human nature through mode of production, praxis Historically specific — not fixed Species nature of humans	Critique of capitalist control of resources and accumulation of goods and profits	Socialist/communist society will use resources for good of all men and women Resources will be controlled by workers Environmental pollution will be minimal since no surpluses will be produced Environmental research by men and women
RADICAL FEMINISM	Nature is spiritual and personal Conventional science and technology problematic because of their emphasis on domination	Biology is basic Humans are sexually reproducing bodies Sexed by biology/Gendered by society	Unaware of interconnectedness of male domination of nature and women Male environmentalism retains hierarchies Insufficient attention to environmental threats to women's reproduction (chemicals, nuclear war)	Woman/nature both valued and celebrated Reproductive freedom Against pornographic depictions of both women and nature Radical ecofeminism
SOCIALIST FEMINISM	Nature is material basis of life: food, clothing, shelter, energy Nature is socially and historically constructed Transformation of nature by production	Human nature created through biology and praxis (sex, race, class, age) Historically specific and socially constructed	Leaves out nature as active and responsive Leaves out women's role in reproduction and reproduction as a category Systems approach is mechanistic not dialectical	Both nature and human production are active Centrality of biological and social reproduction Dialectic between production and reproduction Multileveled structural analysis Dialectical (not mechanical) systems Socialist ecofeminism

and technology for use by all humans for survival. Socialist feminism views change as dynamic, interactive, and dialectical, rather than as mechanistic, linear, and incremental. Nonhuman nature is dynamic and alive. As a historical actor, nature interacts with human beings through mutual ecological relations. Socialist feminist environmental theory gives both reproduction and production central places. A socialist feminist environmental ethic involves developing sustainable, nondominating relations with nature and supplying all peoples with a high quality of life.

In politics, socialist feminists participate in many of the same environmental actions as radical feminists. The goals, however, are to direct change toward some form of an egalitarian socialist state, in addition to resocializing men and women into nonsexist, nonracist, nonviolent, anti-imperialist forms of life. Socialist ecofeminism deals explicitly with environmental issues that affect working-class women, Third World women, and women of color. Examples include support for the women's *Chipco* (tree-hugging) movement in India that protects fuel resources from lumber interests, for the women's Green Belt movement in Kenya that has planted more than 2 million trees in 10 years, and for Native-American women and children exposed to radioactivity from uranium mining.[10]

Although the ultimate goals of liberal, radical, and socialist feminists may differ as to whether capitalism, women's culture, or socialism should be the ultimate objective of political action, shorter-term objectives overlap. In this sense there is perhaps more unity than diversity in women's common goal of restoring the natural environment and quality of life for people and other living and nonliving inhabitants of the planet.

Ynestra King

HEALING THE WOUNDS: FEMINISM, ECOLOGY, AND THE NATURE/CULTURE DUALISM

NO PART OF LIVING NATURE can ignore the extreme threat to life on Earth. We are faced with worldwide deforestation, the disappearance of hundreds of species of life, and the increasing pollution of the gene pool by poisons and low-level radiation. We are also faced with biological atrocities unique to modern life—the existence of the AIDS virus and the possibility of even more dreadful and pernicious diseases caused by genetic mutation. Worldwide food shortages, including episodes of mass starvation, continue to mount as prime agricultural land is used to grow cash crops to pay national debts instead of food to feed people.[1] Animals are mistreated and mutilated in horrible ways to test cosmetics, drugs, and surgical procedures. The stockpiling of ever greater weapons of annihilation and the terrible imagining of new ones continues. The piece of the pie that women have only begun to sample as a result of the feminist movement is rotten and carcinogenic, and surely our feminist theory and politics must take account of this, however much we yearn for the opportunities that have been denied to us. What is the point of partaking equally in a system that is killing us all?

The contemporary ecological crisis alone creates an imperative that feminists take ecology seriously, but there are other reasons ecology is central to feminist philosophy and politics. The ecological crisis is related to the systems of hatred of all that is natural and female by the White, male, Western formulators of philosophy, technology, and death inventions. It is my contention that the systematic denigration of working-class people and people of color, women, and animals is

connected to the basic dualism that lies at the root of Western civilization. But the mind-set of hierarchy originates within human society.
It has its material roots in the domination of human by human, particularly of women by men. While I cannot speak for the liberation
struggles of people of color, I believe that the goals of feminism, ecology, and movements against racism and for the survival of indigenous
peoples are internally related and must be understood and pursued
together in a worldwide, genuinely pro-life,[2] movement.

There is at the root of Western society a deep ambivalence about
life itself, about our own fertility and that of nonhuman nature, and
a terrible confusion about our place in nature. But as the work of social
ecologist Murray Bookchin demonstrates, nature did not declare war
on humanity, patriarchal humanity declared war on women and on
living nature.[3] Nowhere is this transition more hauntingly portrayed
than by the Chorus in Sophocles' *Antigone:*

Many the wonders but nothing walks stranger than man.
This thing crosses the sea in the winter's storm,
making his path through the roaring waves.
And she, the greatest of gods, the earth—
ageless she is, and unwearied—he wears her away
as the ploughs go up and down from year to year
and his mules turn up the soil.

Gay nations of birds he snares and leads,
wild beast tribes and the salty brood of the sea,
with the twined mesh of his nets, this clever man.
He controls with craft the beasts of the open air,
walkers on the hills. The horse with his shaggy mane
he holds and harnesses, yoked about the neck,
and the strong bull of the mountain.

Language and thought like the wind
and the feelings that make the town,
he has taught himself, and shelter against the cold,
refuge from rain. He can always help himself.
He faces no future helpless. There's only death
that he cannot find an escape from. He has contrived
refuge from illnesses once beyond all cure.

Clever beyond all dreams
the inventive craft that he has
which may drive him one time or another to well or ill.

> When he honors the laws of the land and the gods' sworn right
> high indeed is his city; but stateless the man
> who dares to dwell with dishonor.[4]

So far have we gone from our roots in living nature that it is the living, and not the dead, that perplexes. The panvitalism of ancient and ancestral culture has given way to panmechanism, the norm of the lifeless.

But for a long time after the first echoes of this transition, the inroads human beings made on living nature were superficial and unable to fundamentally upset the balance and fecundity of the nonhuman natural world. And so appropriately, ethics, and ideas about how people should live, which took their instrumental form in politics, concerned the relationships of human beings to one another, especially in cities. But with the arrival of modern technologies the task of ethics and the domain of politics have changed drastically. The consideration of the place of human beings in nature, formerly the terrain of religion, becomes a crucial concern for all human beings. And with modern technologies, the particular responsibilities of human beings for nature must move to the center of politics.

Biological ethicist Hans Jonas says of this condition: "A kind of metaphysical responsibility beyond self-interest has devolved in us with the magnitude of our powers relative to this tenuous film of life, that is, since man has become dangerous not only to himself but to the whole biosphere."[5] Yet, around the world, capitalism, the preeminent culture and economics of self-interest, is homogenizing cultures and disrupting naturally complex balances within the ecosystem. Capitalism is dependent on expanding markets and therefore ever greater areas of life must be mediated by sold products. From a capitalist standpoint, the more things that can be bought and sold, the better. So capitalism requires a rationalized worldview, which asserts that human science and technology are inherently progressive, which systematically denigrates ancestral cultures, and which asserts that human beings are entitled to dominion over nonhuman nature.

Nonhuman nature is being rapidly simplified, undoing the work of organic evolution. Hundreds of species of life disappear forever each year, and the figure is accelerating. Diverse, complex ecosystems are more stable than simple ones. They have had longer periods of evolution and are necessary to support human beings and many other species. Yet in the name of civilization, nature has been desecrated in a process of rationalization sociologist Max Weber called "the disenchantment of the world."

The diversity of human life on the planet is also being undermined. The cultural diversity of human societies around the world developed over thousands of years and is part of the general evolution of life on the planet. The homogenizing of culture turns the world into a giant factory and facilitates top-down authoritarian government. In the name of helping people, the industrial countries export models of development that assume that the U.S. way of life is the best way of life for everyone.

A critical analysis of and opposition to the uniformity of technological, industrial culture—capitalist and socialist—is crucial to feminism, ecology, and the struggles of indigenous peoples. At this point in history, there is no way to unravel the matrix of oppressions within human society without at the same time liberating nature and reconciling that part of nature that is human with that part that is not. Socialists do not have the answer to these problems—they share the antivitalism and basic dualism of capitalism. Although developed within capitalism, the technological means of production utilized by capitalist and socialist states is largely the same. All hitherto existing philosophies of liberation, with the possible exception of some forms of social anarchism, accept the anthropocentric notion that humanity should dominate nature and that the increasing domination of non-human nature is a precondition for true human freedom. No socialist revolution has ever fundamentally challenged the basic prototype for the nature/culture dualism—the domination of men over women.

TO EMBRACE OR REPUDIATE NATURE?

Radical feminists, or feminists who believe that the biologically based domination of women by men is the root cause of oppression, have considered ecology from a feminist perspective because nature is their central category of analysis. They believe that the subordination of women in society is the root of human oppression, closely related to the association of women with nature. They see "patriarchy" (by which they mean the systematic dominance of men in society) as preceding and laying the foundation for other forms of human oppression and exploitation. Men identify women with nature and seek to enlist both in the service of male "projects" designed to make men safe from feared nature and mortality. The ideology of women as closer to nature is essential to such a project. So if patriarchy is the archetypal form of human oppression, then it follows that if we get rid of that, other forms of oppression will likewise crumble. But there are two basic differences within the radical feminist movement: whether the woman/nature connection is potentially emancipatory or whether it provides a rationale for the continued subordination of women.

How do women who call themselves radical feminists come to such divergent positions?[6] The first position implies a separate feminist culture and philosophy from the vantage point of identification with nature and a celebration of the woman/nature connection and is the position of *radical cultural feminists,* which I will address later. *Radical rationalist feminists* take the second position, repudiating the woman/nature connection. For these feminists, freedom is being liberated from the primordial realm of women and nature, which they regard as an imprisoning female ghetto. They deplore the appropriation of ecology as a feminist issue, seeing it as a regression that is bound to reinforce sex-role stereotyping. Anything that reinforces gender differences, or makes any kind of special claim for women, is problematic.

Thus, they think that feminists shouldn't do anything that would restimulate traditional ideas about women. They celebrate the fact that we have finally begun to gain access to male bastions by using the political tools of liberalism and the rationalization of human life, mythically severing the woman/nature connection as the humanity/nature connection has been severed. The mother of modern feminism, Simone de Beauvoir, represents this position. Recently she came out against what she calls "the new femininity":

> . . . an enhanced status for traditional feminine values, such as woman and her rapport with nature, woman and her maternal instinct, woman and her physical being . . . This renewed attempt to pin women down to their traditional role, together with a small effort to meet some of the demands made by women—that's the formula used to try and keep women quiet. Even women who call themselves feminists don't always see through it. Once again, women are being defined in terms of "the other," once again they are being made into the "second sex". . . . Why should women be more in favour of peace than men? I should think it a matter of equal concern for both! . . . being a mother means being for peace. Equating ecology with feminism is something that irritates me. They are not automatically one and the same thing at all.[7]

De Beauvoir thus reiterates the position she took almost 40 years ago in *The Second Sex*—that it is a sexist ploy to define women as beings who are closer to nature than men. She claims that such associations divert women from their struggle for emancipation and channel their energies "into subsidiary concerns," such as ecology and peace.

Radical cultural feminists, or cultural feminists, on the other hand, do not wish to obliterate the difference between men and women; instead, they take women's side, which, as they see it, is also the side of nonhuman nature. And, not surprisingly, they have taken the slogan "the personal is political" in the opposite direction, personalizing the political.

Cultural feminists celebrate the life experience of the "female ghetto," which they see as a source of female freedom rather than subordination. They argue, following Virginia Woolf, that they don't want to enter the male world with its "procession of professions."[8] They have attempted to articulate and even create a separate women's culture and have been major proponents of the identification of women with nature and feminism with ecology. The major strength of cultural feminism is that it is a deeply woman-identified movement. Cultural feminists celebrate what is distinct about women and have challenged the male culture rather than strategizing to become part of it. They have celebrated the identification of women with nature in music, art, literature, poetry, covens, and communes. But one problem that White cultural feminists, like other White feminists, have not adequately faced is that, in celebrating the commonalities of women and emphasizing the ways in which women are universal victims of male oppression, they have inadequately addressed the real diversity of women's lives and histories across race, class, and national boundaries. For women of color, opposing racism and genocide and encouraging ethnic pride are agendas they often share with men in a White-dominated society, even while they struggle against sexism in their own communities. These complex, multidimensional loyalties and historically divergent life situations require a politics that recognizes complexities. The connecting of women and nature has lent itself to a romanticization of women as good, and as apart from all the dastardly deeds of men and culture. The problem is that history, power, women, and nature are all a lot more complicated than that.

In the past 10 years, the old cultural feminism has given birth to the feminist spirituality movement, an eclectic potpourri of beliefs and

practices, with an immanent Goddess (as opposed to the transcendental God). I believe there has been a greater racial diversity in this movement than in any other form of feminism, and this is due in part to
the fact that this is a spiritual movement, based on the ultimate unity
of all living things. There is no particular dogma in this movement,
only a recognition of women as embodied, earth-bound living beings
who should celebrate their connection to the rest of life and, for some,
invoke this connection in public political protest actions. These beliefs
are supported by the Gaia hypothesis—the idea that the planet is one
single living organism, and the thesis of scientists Lynn Margolis and
James Lovelock (whose research corroborates Peter Kropotkin's mutual-
ism[9]) that cooperation was a stronger force in evolution than competition.[10]

Much of the iconography of the contemporary radical feminist peace
movement is inspired by the feminist spirituality movement. Actions
have featured guerrilla theater where the Furies ravage Ronald Reagan;
encircling military bases and war-research centers with pictures of
children, trees, brooks, and women; and weaving shut the doors of
stock exchanges while singing and chanting about spiders.

Cultural feminism and the women's spirituality movement have
been subjected to the same critique feminists of color have made of
the ethnocentricity of much White feminism.[11] This critique comes from
women of color who draw on indigenous spiritual traditions and who
argue that these White Western feminists are inventing and originating
an earth-centered prowoman spirituality while they are defending their
indigenous spirituality against the imperialism of Western rationalism.
For example, Luisah Teish, the first Voodoo priestess to attempt to explain her tradition to the public, advocates a practice that integrates
the political and spiritual and that brings together a disciplined understanding of the African spiritual tradition with contemporary feminist
and Black power politics.[12] Members of her group in Oakland are planning urban gardening projects to help the poor feed themselves and
to grow the herbs needed for the holistic healing remedies of her tradition while they engage in community organizing to stop gentrification.
Women in the Hopi and Navaho traditions are also attempting to explain their traditions to a wider public while they organize politically
to keep their lands from being taken over by developers or poisoned
by industry.

The collision of modern industrial society with indigenous cultures has decimated these ancestral forms but may have brought White Westerners into contact with forms of knowledge that are useful as we try to imagine our way beyond dualism, to understand what it means to be embodied beings on this planet. These traditions are often used as examples of ways of life that are nondualistic, at least that overcome the nature/culture dualism.[13] But human beings can't simply jump off, or jump out of history. These indigenous, embodied, Earth-centered spiritual traditions can plant seeds in the imaginations of people who are the products of dualistic cultures, but White Westerners cannot use them to avoid the responsibility of their own history.

The women's spirituality movement has changed in recent years, becoming more sophisticated and diverse as women of color articulate a powerful, survival-based feminism emerging from their experience in the crucible of multiple oppressions. From both the feminism of women of color (sometimes called "womanist" as opposed to "feminist" to convey the different priorities of women of color from White women) and ecofeminism has come a more holistic feminism, which links all issues of personal and planetary survival. The critique of cultural feminism advanced by women of color—that it is often ahistorical in that White women in particular need to take responsibility for being oppressors as well as oppressed and for having been powerful as White people or as people with class or national privileges—is crucial. In other words, women have a complexity of historical identities and therefore a complexity of loyalties. Instead of constantly attempting to make our identities less complex by emphasizing what we have in common as women, as has been the tendency of women who are feminists first and foremost, we should also pay attention to the differences among us.

SOCIALIST FEMINISM, RATIONALIZATION, AND THE DOMINATION OF NATURE

Socialist feminism is an odd hybrid—an attempt at a synthesis of rationalist feminism (radical and liberal) and the historical materialism of the Marxist tradition. In taking labor as its central category, Marxists have reduced human beings to *Homo laboran*, and the history of capitalism cries out with the resistance of human beings not only to being exploited but to being conceived of as essentially "workers." In

Marxism, revolutionary discourse has been reduced to a "language of productivity"[14] where a critique of the mode of production does not necessarily challenge the principle of production.

The socialist feminist theory of the body as a socially constructed (re)producer has informed a public discourse of "reproductive free-dom"—the freedom to (re)produce or not (re)produce with your own body—and it is in this area that socialist feminists have been a political force. But socialist feminists have an inadequate theory with which to confront the new reproductive technologies. Arguing that women have a right to "control our own bodies" does not prepare one to confront the issue of whether our reproductive capacities, like our productive capacities, should be bought and sold in the marketplace, as one more form of wage labor.[15]

Socialist feminists have criticized liberal feminists (just as socialists have criticized liberalism) for not going far enough in a critique of the political economy and class differences. But socialist feminists have shared the rationalist bias of liberal feminism, depicting the world primarily in exchange terms—whether production or reproduction—and have agreed with the liberal feminist analysis that we must strive in all possible ways to demonstrate that we are more like men than different. Some socialist feminists have even argued that liberal femin-ism has a radical potential.[16] For such feminists, the dualistic, overly rationalized premises of liberal feminism are not a problem. For them, too, severing the woman/nature connection is a feminist project.

In a sense, the strength and weakness of socialist feminism lie in the same premise—the centrality of economics in their theory and prac-tice. Socialist feminists have articulated a strong economic and class analysis, but they have not sufficiently addressed the domination of nature.[17] That is, they believe that the socialist feminist agenda would be complete if we could overcome systematic inequalities of social and economic power. They have addressed one of the three forms of domi-nation of nature—domination between persons—but they have not seriously attended to the domination of nonhuman nature, nor to the domination of inner nature.

In socialist feminism, women seek to enter the political world as articulate, historical subjects, capable of understanding and making history. And some socialist feminists, such as Alison Jagger and Nancy Hartsock, have drawn on historical materialism in very creative ways, attempting to articulate a position from which women can make special historical claims without being biologically determinist.[18] But even socialist feminists who are attempting a multifactored historical analysis of the oppression of women do not treat the domination of nature as a significant category for feminism, though they note it in passing.

In general, socialist feminists are very unsympathetic to "cultural feminism."[19] They accuse it of being ahistorical, essentialist (which they define as believing in male and female essences—male=bad, female= good), and antiintellectual. This debate partakes of the ontology versus epistemology debate in Western philosophy, where "being" is opposed to "knowing," and women are implicitly relegated to the realm of "being," the ontological slums. From an ecological (that is, antidualistic) standpoint, essentialism and ontology are not the same as biological determinism. In other words, we are not talking heads, nor are we unself-conscious nature. That is, socialist feminists are avoiding the important truths being recognized by cultural feminism, among them the female political imagination manifesting itself in political actions. They also forget that no revolution in human history has succeeded without a strong cultural foundation and a utopian vision. In part, I believe the myopia of socialist feminism with respect to cultural feminism is rooted in the old Marxist debate about the primacy of the base (economics/production) over the superstructure (culture/reproduction). This dualism also needs to be overcome before we can have a dialectical, or genuinely ecological, feminism.

The socialist feminist fidelity to a theory of history where women seek to understand the past in order to make the future is crucial to feminism. But belief in a direct relationship between the rationalization and domination of nature and the project of human liberation remains a central tenet of socialism.

The question for socialist feminists is whether they can accommodate their version of feminism within the socialist movement or whether they will have to move in a "greener" direction with a more radical critique of all forms of the domination of nature.

ECOFEMINISM:
BEYOND THE NATURE/CULTURE DUALISM

Women have been culture's sacrifice to nature. The practice of human sacrifice to outsmart or appease a feared nature is ancient. And it is in resistance to this sacrificial mentality—on the part of both the sacrificer and sacrificee—that some feminists have argued against the association of women with nature, emphasizing the social dimension of traditional women's lives. Part of the work of feminism has been asserting that the activities of women, believed to be more natural than those of men, are in fact absolutely social. For example, giving birth is natural (though how it is done is very social) but mothering is an absolutely social activity.[20] In bringing up their children, mothers face ethical and moral choices as complex as those considered by professional politicians and ethicists. In the wake of feminism, women will continue to do these things, but the problem of connecting humanity to nature will still have to be acknowledged and solved. In our mythology of complementarity, men and women have led vicarious lives, where women had feelings and led instinctual lives and men engaged in the projects illuminated by reason. Feminism has exposed the extent to which it was all a lie—that's why it has been so important to feminism to establish the mindful, social nature of mothering.

It is as if women were entrusted with and have kept the dirty little secret that humanity emerges from nonhuman nature into society in the life of the species and the person. The process of nurturing an unsocialized, undifferentiated human infant into an adult person—the socialization of the organic—is the bridge between nature and culture. The Western male bourgeois then extracts himself from the realm of the organic to become a public citizen, as if born from the head of Zeus. He puts away childish things. He disempowers and sentimentalizes his mother, sacrificing her to nature. But the key to the historic agency of women with respect to the nature/culture dualism lies in the fact that the traditional activities of women—mothering, cooking, healing, farming, foraging—are as social as they are natural.

The task of an ecological feminism is the organic forging of a genuinely antidualistic, or dialectical, theory and practice. No previous feminism has addressed this problem adequately, hence the necessity of ecofeminism. Rather than succumb to nihilism, pessimism, and an end to reason and history, we seek to enter into history, to a genuinely ethical thinking—where one uses mind and history to reason from the "is" to the "ought" and to reconcile humanity with nature, within and without. This is the starting point for ecofeminism.

Each major contemporary feminist theory, liberal, social, and cultural, has taken up the issue of the relationship between women and nature. And each in its own way has capitulated to dualistic thinking. Ecofeminism takes from socialist feminism the idea that women have been *historically* positioned at the biological dividing line where the organic emerges into the social. The domination of nature originates in society and therefore must be resolved in society. Thus, it is the embodied woman as social historical agent, rather than as a product of natural law, who is the subject of ecofeminism. But the weakness of socialist feminism's theory of the person is serious from an ecofeminist standpoint. An ecological feminism calls for a dynamic, developmental theory of the person—male *and* female—who emerges out of nonhuman nature, where difference is neither reified nor ignored and the dialectical relationship between human and nonhuman nature is understood.

Cultural feminism's greatest weakness is its tendency to make the personal into the political, with its emphasis on personal transformation and empowerment. This is most obvious in the attempt to overcome the apparent opposition between spirituality and politics. For cultural feminists, spirituality is the heart in a heartless world (whereas for socialist feminists it is the opiate of the people). Cultural feminists have formed the "beloved community" of feminism—with all the power, potential, and problems of a religion. And as an appropriate response to the need for mystery and attention to personal alienation in an overly rationalized world, it is a vital and important movement. But by itself it does not provide the basis for a genuinely dialectical ecofeminist theory and practice, one that addresses history as well as mystery. For this reason, cultural/spiritual feminism (sometimes even called "nature feminism") is not synonymous with ecofeminism in that creating a gynocentric culture and politics is a necessary but not sufficient condition for ecofeminism.

Both feminism and ecology embody the revolt of nature against human domination. They demand that we rethink the relationship between humanity and the rest of nature, including our natural, embodied selves. In ecofeminism, nature is the central category of analysis. An analysis of the interrelated dominations of nature—psyche and sexuality, human oppression, and nonhuman nature—and the historic position of women in relation to those forms of domination is the starting point of ecofeminist theory. We share with cultural feminism the necessity of a politics with heart and a beloved community, recognizing our connection with each other—and with nonhuman nature. Socialist feminism has given us a powerful critical perspective with which to understand, and transform, history. Separately, they perpetuate the dualism of "mind" and "nature." Together they make possible a new ecological relationship between nature and culture, in which mind and nature, heart and reason, join forces to transform the systems of domination, internal and external, that threaten the existence of life on Earth.

Practice does not wait for theory—it comes out of the imperatives of history. Women are the revolutionary bearers of this antidualistic potential in the world today. In addition to the enormous impact of feminism on Western civilization, women have been at the forefront of every historical, political movement to reclaim the Earth. For example, for many years in India poor women who come out of the Gandhian movement have waged a nonviolent campaign for land reform and to save the forest, called the *Chipko Andolan* (the hugging movement), wrapping their bodies around trees as bulldozers arrive. Each of the women has a tree of her own she is to protect—to steward. When loggers were sent in, one of the women said, "Let them know they will not fell a single tree without the felling of us first. When the men raise their axes, we will embrace the trees to protect them."[21] These women have waged a remarkably successful nonviolent struggle, and their tactics have spread to other parts of India. Men have joined in, though the campaign was originated and continues to be led by women. Yet this is not a sentimental movement—lives depend on the survival of the forest. For most of the women of the world, interest in preservation of the land, water, air, and energy is no abstraction but a clear part of the effort to simply survive.

The increasing militarization of the world has intensified this struggle. Women and children make up 80 percent of war refugees. Lands are often burned and scarred in such a way as to prevent cultivation for many years after the battles, so that starvation and hardship follow long after the fighting has stopped.[22] And, here, too, women—often mothers and farmers—respond to necessity. They become the protectors of the Earth in an effort to eke out a small living on the land to feed themselves and their families.

There are other areas of feminist activism that illuminate an enlightened ecofeminist perspective.[23] Potentially, one of the best examples of an appropriately mediated, dialectical relationship to nature is the feminist health movement. The medicalization of childbirth in the first part of this century and, currently, the redesign and appropriation of reproduction both create new profit-making technologies for capitalism and make heretofore natural processes mediated by women into arenas controlled by men. Women offered themselves up to the ministrations of "experts," internalizing the notion that they didn't know enough and surrendering their power. They also accepted the idea that maximum intervention in and domination of nature are inherently good. But since the onset of feminism in the 1960s, women in the United States have gone quite a way in reappropriating and demedicalizing childbirth. As a result of this movement, many more women want to be told what all their options are and many choose invasive medical technologies only under unusual and informed circumstances. They do not necessarily reject these useful technologies in some cases, but they have pointed a finger at motivations of profit and control in the technologies' widespread application. Likewise, my argument here is not that feminism should repudiate all aspects of Western science and medicine. It is to assert that we should develop the sophistication to decide for ourselves when intervention serves our best interest.

Another central area of concern in which women may employ ecofeminism to overcome misogynist dualism is that of body consciousness. Accepting our own bodies just as they are, knowing how they look, feel, and smell, and learning to work with them to become healthier is a basis for cultural and political liberation. In many patriarchal cultures, women are complicit in the domination of our natural bodies, seeking to please men at any cost. Chinese foot binding, performed by women, is a widely cited example of misogynist domination of women's bodies. But even as Western feminists condemn these practices, most of us will do anything to our bodies (yes, even feminists) to appear closer to norms of physical beauty that come naturally to about 0.2 percent of the female population. The rest of us struggle to be skinny, hairless, and, lately, muscular. We lie in the sun to get tan even when we know we are courting melanoma, especially as the accelerating depletion of the ozone layer makes "sunbathing" a dangerous sport. We submit ourselves to extremely dangerous surgical procedures. We primp, prune, douche, deodorize, and diet as if our natural bodies were our mortal enemies. Some of us living the most privileged lives in the world starve ourselves close to death for beauty, literally.

To the extent that we make our own flesh an enemy, or docilely submit ourselves to medical experts, we are participating in the domination of nature. To the extent that we learn to work with the restorative powers of our bodies, using medical technologies and drugs sparingly, we are developing an appropriately mediated relationship to our own natures. But even the women's health movement has not realized a full ecofeminist perspective.[24] It has yet to fully grasp health as an ecological and social rather than an individual problem, in which the systematic poisoning of environments where women live and work is addressed as a primary political issue. Here the community-based movements against toxic wastes, largely initiated and led by women, and the feminist health movement may meet.

A related critical area for a genuinely dialectical practice is a reconstruction of science, taking into account the critique of science advanced by radical ecology and feminism.[25] Feminist historians and philosophers of science are demonstrating that the will to know and the will to power need not be the same thing. They argue that there are ways of knowing the world that are not based on objectification and domination.[26] Here, again, apparently antithetical epistemologies, science and mysticism, can coexist. We shall need all our ways of knowing to create life on this planet that is both ecological and sustainable.

As feminists, we shall need to develop an ideal of freedom that is neither antisocial nor antinatural.[27] We are past the point of throwing off our chains to reclaim our ostensibly free nature, if such a point ever existed. Ecofeminism is not an argument for a return to prehistory. The knowledge that women were not always dominated and that society was not always hierarchical is a powerful inspiration for contemporary women, so long as such a society is not represented as a "natural order," apart from history, to which we will inevitably return by a great reversal.

From an ecofeminist perspective, we are part of nature, but not inherently good or bad, free or unfree. There is no one natural order that represents freedom. We are *potentially* free in nature, but as human beings that freedom has to be intentionally created by using our understanding of the natural world. For this reason we must develop a different understanding of the relationship between human and nonhuman nature, based on the stewardship of evolution. To do this we need a theory of history where the natural evolution of the planet and the social history of the species are not separated. We emerged from nonhuman nature, as the organic emerged from the inorganic.

Here, potentially, we recover ontology as the ground for ethics. We thoughtful human beings must use the fullness of our sensibility and intelligence to push ourselves intentionally to another stage of evolution. One where we will fuse a new way of being human on this planet with a sense of the sacred, informed by all ways of knowing—intuitive *and* scientific, mystical *and* rational. It is the moment where women recognize ourselves as agents of history—yes, even as unique agents—and knowingly bridge the classic dualisms between spirit and matter, art and politics, reason and intuition. This is the potentiality of a *rational reenchantment.* This is the project of ecofeminism.

At this point in history, the domination of nature is inextricably bound up with the domination of persons, and both must be addressed—without arguments over "the primary contradiction" in the search for a single Archimedes point for revolution. There is no such thing. And there is no point in liberating people if the planet cannot sustain their liberated lives, or in saving the planet by disregarding the preciousness of human existence not only to ourselves but to the rest of life on Earth.

Lee Quinby

ECOFEMINISM
AND THE POLITICS
OF RESISTANCE

IN A RECENT ARTICLE, "The Potential of the Green Movement," Howard Hawkins of the Vermont Greens laments that "Within the Green movement, there is no hegemonic theory that has the same standing in the new social movements that Marxism came to have in the workers' movement by the turn of the century"; as a result he calls for "coherent theory to guide [Green] practice."[1] Hawkins's analysis of the Green movement's potential to form alliances with and revitalize the Old Left is insightful in a number of respects. This is particularly so in its emphasis on the multiplicity of social movements—ecological, feminist, gay, antimilitarist—that have come together under the Green banner. But there is danger in his call for hegemonic theory. As the French theorist Michel Foucault has observed, "things never happen as we expect from a political programme," for "a political programme has always, or nearly always, led to abuse or political domination from a bloc, be it from technicians or bureaucrats or other people."[2] In other words, the move toward orthodoxy is complicitous with the tendency of power to totalize, to demand consensus, to authorize certain alliances and to exclude others—in short, to limit political creativity.

This movement toward totalization has already left its mark on the West German Green party. As Michael Hoexter writes in *New Politics*, within the West German Green party the philosophical and political hostilities between the "fundamentalists" and the "realists" over the power of the state "seem irreconcilable."[3] Yet Hoexter, like Hawkins, calls for "a comprehensive and comprehensible theory of the state," arguing that without such a program, "greens and socialists are doomed to repeat the disappointing, sometimes catastrophic, history of left parties and groups in government."[4] My argument, following Foucault, is that the demand for comprehensive theory and coherent practice leads to rather than avoids the kind of polarization that has occurred in the West German Green party. The call for comprehensive theory is not a new politics at all, but rather an old story. And this story—with its all-too-predictable ending—is now being told by the U.S. ecology movement, as attested to in the polarized debates between deep ecologists and social ecologists. The lines of argument between these two camps, made visible at the July 1987 gathering of Greens at Amherst, Massachusetts, have only widened and deepened.[5]

The radical feminist movement in the United States has also suffered from precisely this tendency of theory to become dogma and political practices of resistance to accordingly become less diverse. Over the last 20 years, we have witnessed a shift away from a wide-based, multiple-issues movement concerned with *women's* bodies toward a narrow-based, single-issue one, focused primarily on pornography and *woman's* body. This shift in practices was formalized in feminist legal scholar Catherine MacKinnon's call for coherence in feminism around sexuality.[6] Contemporary radical feminism's narrowed focus on sexuality and pornography has proven divisive and has abstracted and limited feminist debates to a simplified prosex or antisex polarity. As philosopher Jana Sawicki points out, these two camps, despite their antagonism toward each other's positions, actually share an essentialist notion that locates "identity within the psyche or body of the individual." Such a notion, which derives from power formations that have medicalized and confessionalized sexuality, places women in a precarious position and feminism in a co-optable one.[7]

In light of the splits that have taken place within the ecology and feminist movements, I want to argue against these calls for coherence, comprehensiveness, and formalized agendas and to cite ecofeminism as an example of theory and practice that has combated ecological destruction and patriarchal domination without succumbing to the totalizing impulses of masculinist politics. Ecofeminism as a politics of resistance operates against power understood, as Foucault puts it, as a "multiplicity of force relations," decentered and continually "produced from one moment to the next." Against such power, coherence in theory and centralization of practice make a social movement irrelevant or, worse, vulnerable, or—even more dangerous—participatory with forces of domination. As Foucault explains, decentered power requires decentered political struggle, for "there is no single locus of great Refusal, no soul of revolt, source of all rebellions, no pure law of the revolutionary. Instead there is a plurality of resistance, each of them a special case: resistances that are possible, necessary, improbable; others that are spontaneous, savage, solitary, concerted, rampant, or violent; still others that are quick to compromise, interested, or sacrificial."[8] And, indeed, the strength thus far of ecofeminism has been to target abuses of power at the local level, in a multiplicity of places.

Two works that bear witness to the significance of ecofeminism as resistance politics are the 1983 anthology *Reclaim the Earth* and the more recent work of Anne Garland called *Women Activists*.[9] Both of these books are politically astute and emotionally moving testaments of resistance politics operating at the microlevels where power is exercised. What we find in these pages is a recognition that struggling against specific sites of power not only weakens the junctures of power's networks but also empowers those who do the struggling. They show, for example, how contamination of women's wombs and breast milk leads to struggle against chemical dumping; how compromises to our immunity systems, which render our bodies vulnerable to a whole host of viruses that formerly we could withstand, leads to challenges against late-capitalist food industries and the practices of Western medicine; how logging practices in India lead to women there struggling against the multinational destruction of their culture; how the Pentagon's extravagant military funding leads to feminist actions that combine antimilitarism with demands that funds be channeled from war technology to day care, education, and environmental protection.

In short, such episodes of activism show how feminism's struggle for women's freedom and ecology's struggle for planetary well-being have come together in an alliance called ecofeminism. Because of shared concerns for health and freedom, a "we" has been formed. This we has not emerged from the prescriptions of a politically correct theory; it has resulted from ecologists and feminists combining forces in their challenges to institutions of power.[10] In these actions there have been activist/theorists speaking for themselves on their own terrain, discerning power's specific effects on them and conducting skirmishes against its operations. Ecofeminism as resistance politics has a great deal to tell us about the uses and abuses of theory itself as a power relation. It suggests that theory in the interrogative mode—as opposed to theory in the prescriptive mode—asks difficult questions; that is, it asks questions that pose difficulties, even, perhaps especially, for one's own practices. In fact, the we of ecofeminism is most formidable in its opposition to power when it challenges its own assumptions.

In "Roots: Black Ghetto Ecology," Wilmette Brown demonstrates the value of such questioning by combining the political insights of the Black civil rights movement, lesbian feminism, ecology, the peace movement, and the holistic health movement. Her analysis does not strive to synthesize these positions, but, instead, uses each to disrupt the assumptions of the others. Writing from a personal point of reference, she explains that she is "a Black woman, a cancer survivor," but is quick to reject the romance of the autonomous hero, so popular with the media, for "this is not 'the triumphant story of one woman's victory over cancer.'" Speaking as an activist/theorist, she states: "For me the issue is how to transform cancer from a preoccupying vulnerability into a vindicating power—for myself and for everyone determined to reclaim the earth."[11]

That transformation involves making visible the links among sex, race, class, and cancer. Brown discloses the disproportionate incidence of cancer among the poor who are forced to take jobs with greater risks of cancer, to live in "cancer-prone cities," and who are least able to afford the exorbitant costs of medical treatment. These conditions are exacerbated for Blacks, falling the heaviest on Black women and children. Against the backdrop of an international economic order that causes health hazards and a medical industry that profits from treatment, Brown brings into focus the political creativity, energy, and struggle of Black welfare mothers who "brought about the first concessions from the American state of anything approaching free health care for poor people [Medicaid] and for elderly people [Medicare]."[12]

Her analysis of convalescence from the perspective of a Black, working-class, lesbian feminist also explores the limits and limitations of the holistic health movement as defined largely by White, middle-class heterosexuals. Brown shows how, despite its critique of the medical industry, the holistic health movement has also been myopic to race, class, and gender issues. First, its emphasis on consciousness-raising ignored the necessity of organizing to struggle against the military-industrial complex. Second, holistic health assumes financial access to self-healing classes as well the time, skills, and money to obtain healthier diets. Finally, the holistic health movement has too often ignored traditions of herbal remedies that have been practiced for centuries among peoples of color. Her site of struggle—the geographic and bodily place from which she speaks—is the international women's peace movement, which she feels has learned to refuse "the sexist and racist assumptions and practices of the peace and holistic movements."

Brown's analysis and political activism exemplify a politics of resistance that runs counter to the will to totalize. It may serve as a challenge as well to the essentialist tendencies within ecofeminism, for, like the ecology and feminist movements from which it derives, ecofeminism is not devoid of impulses to develop a "coherent" theory. Essentialist ecofeminism speaks of a monovocal subject, Woman; of a pure essence, Femininity; of a fixed place, Nature; of a deterministic system, Holism; and of a static materiality, the Body. Writings that give homage to the Goddess as a symbol of *"the way things really are:* All forms of being are One, continually renewed in cyclic rhythms of birth, maturation, death,"* as Charlene Spretnak puts it, echo masculinist prescriptions about the way things "really" are—and must always be.[13]

As feminist critic Gayatri Spivak points out, "Essentialism is a trap. It seems more important to learn to understand that the world's women do not all relate to the privileging of essence, especially through 'fiction,' or 'literature,' in the same way."[14] Homogenizing women's diverse experiences and then romanticizing that "essence" blind us to the myriad ways in which the idea of "womanhood" is implicated in constraints on and brutality against women. Spivak cites a 1982 incident in Seoul, South Korea, involving a strike for higher wages by 237 women working in a factory owned by a Minnesota-based multinational corporation called Control Data. She juxtaposes the imprisonment of six of the union leaders and the injuries, including two miscarriages, of many others who were beaten by male workers, while Control Data's U.S. management watched, against the following quotation found in *Ms:* "Control Data is among those enlightened corporations that offer social-service leaves. . . . Kit Ketchum, former treasurer of Minnesota NOW, applied for and got a full year's pay to work at NOW's national office in Washington, D.C. She writes: "I commend Control Data for their commitment to employing and promoting women. . . . Why not suggest this to your employer?'" What bourgeois essentialism feminism fails to see, Spivak indicates, are the ways in which multinational exploitation of specific women is veiled through a rhetoric and "'clean' national practice" that declares itself an advocate of "women in general."[15]

The arrogance of speaking for others, so integral to the desire for hegemonic theory, is compounded by a diminished capacity to hear what others have to say about our circumstances as well as their own. Ecofeminism as a politics of resistance forces us to question the categories of experience that order the world and the truths we have come to know, even the truths of our radical politics, by confronting us with the truths of other women and men, differently acculturated, fighting against specific threats to their particular lands and bodies. This questioning must also extend to the anthropocentric assumption that only human beings have truths to tell about their and our experiences. The cries of factory farm animals, the suffocation of fish in poisoned waters, the sounds of flood waters rushing over deforested land—these are also voices we need to heed. Listening to all voices of subjugation and hearing their insurrectionary truths make us better able to question our own political and personal practices. This questioning may well risk the end of ecofeminism as currently constituted, for, like any social movement, ecofeminism is inevitably a provisional politics, one that has struck a chord of resistance in this era of ecological destruction and patriarchal power. And if another term and a different politics emerge from this questioning, it will be in the service of new local actions, new creative energies, and new alliances against power.

Marti Kheel

ECOFEMINISM AND DEEP ECOLOGY: REFLECTIONS ON IDENTITY AND DIFFERENCE

It is a sad irony that the destruction of the natural world appears to be proceeding apace with the construction of moral theories for how we should behave in light of this fact. Unable to trust or draw upon a felt sense of connection, most environmental theorists endorse reason as the sole guide in our dealings with the natural world. The vast majority of theories that constitute the field of environmental ethics are thus axiological or value theories whose primary purpose is the rational allotment of value to the appropriate aspects of the natural world.

Both ecofeminism and deep ecology share in common an opposition to these value theories with their attendant notions of obligations and rights. The emphasis of both philosophies is not on an abstract or "rational" calculation of value but rather on the development of a new consciousness for all of life. Both ecofeminism and deep ecology may therefore be viewed as "deep" philosophies in the sense that they call for an inward transformation in order to attain an outward change. Deep ecologists employ the notion of self-realization to describe this inward transformation. As environmental philosophers Bill Devall and George Sessions explain, this process:

> begins when we cease to understand or see ourselves as isolated and narrow competing egos and begin to identify with other humans from our family and friends to, eventually, our species. But the deep ecology sense of Self requires a further maturity and growth, an identification which goes beyond humanity to include the nonhuman world.[1]

There is a significant distinction between ecofeminism and deep ecology, however, in their understanding of the root cause of our environmental malaise. For deep ecologists, it is the anthropocentric worldview that is foremost to blame. The two norms of deep ecology— self-realization and biospherical egalitarianism—are thus designed to redress this self-centered worldview. Ecofeminists, on the other hand, argue that it is the androcentric worldview that deserves primary blame.[2] For ecofeminists, it is not just "humans" but men and the masculinist worldview that must be dismantled from their privileged place.

The key to understanding the differences between the two philosophies thus lies in the differing conceptions of self that both philosophies presuppose. When deep ecologists write of anthropocentrism and the notion of an "expanded Self," they ostensibly refer to a gender-neutral concept of self. Implicit in the feminist analysis of the androcentric worldview, however, is the understanding that men and women, under partiarchal society, experience the world, and hence their conceptions of self, in widely divergent ways. Whereas the anthropocentric worldview perceives humans as the center or apex of the natural world, the androcentric analysis suggests that this worldview is unique to men. Feminists have argued that women's identities, unlike men's, have not been established through their elevation over the natural world. On the contrary, under partriarchal society, women have been identified with the devalued natural world, an identification that they have often adopted as well.

One of the most thoroughgoing analyses of the masculine and feminine conceptions of self was formulated by Simone de Beauvoir in her monumental work *The Second Sex* (New York: Vintage, 1974). According to de Beauvoir, under patriarchal society, women's sense of self is inextricably tied to her status as the "other."

For de Beauvoir, the facts of pregnancy, menstruation, and childbirth have historically confined women to the world of immanence and contingency, a state of being in which life "merely" repeats itself. Authentic subjectivity is achieved to the extent that one raises oneself above biological necessity and hence above the animal world. Men have historically transcended the world of contingency through exploits and projects, that is, through attempts to transform the natural world. Thus, selfhood is an identity that emerges through an antagonistic relation to an "other." In order for women to achieve full human status or selfhood, they must join with men in exploits and projects that express this opposition to the natural world.

De Beauvoir developed her concept of the other from the writings of both Hegel and Sartre. Both of these philosophers considered antagonistic consciousness to be necessary for the establishment of the self. For Hegel, consciousness could only be achieved through recognition from an other. If the truth of self-certainty—the sustained sense of oneself as a part of the world—was to be achieved, the other must be overcome. This contradictory need for both recognition from and negation of the other could result in only two possible outcomes: the death of the other or the subjection of the other in the relation of master and slave.

Sartre went on to develop the notion of the antagonistic nature of consciousness with his concept of the "look." The struggle between two consciousnesses thus becomes one of competing looks. When one is looked at, according to Sartre, one becomes objectified; one is no longer the center of infinite possibilities. Each self struggles to attain transcendence by turning the other into an object.

De Beauvoir's contribution to Sartre's thought was to show that it was women, under patriarchal society, who had been assigned the role of the looked upon other.

While agreeing with much of de Beauvoir's analysis, many contemporary feminists reject the masculine norm of autonomy that she endorsed. The notion of an autonomous (masculine) self, established through the defeat of a female-imaged other, is viewed by many feminists as a central underpinning of the patriarchal world. Feminists have shown that many of the world's most sacred traditions depict stories of struggle and conquest. Typically, the conquest is of darkness or Chaos, usually symbolized by a female-imaged animal form—frequently a serpent or a snake. Through this struggle against unruly nature, the world of light and order is born.

The psychoanalytic theory of object relations presents a modern-day rendition of the same heroic struggle of the masculine self in opposition to the female world. According to this theory, both boys and girls experience their first forms of relatedness as a kind of merging with the mother figure. The child then develops a concept of self through the process of disengaging from this figure. Unlike girls, boys have a two-stage process of disidentification. They must not only disengage from the mother figure, but in order to identify as male, they must deny all that is female within themselves. The self-identity of the boy child is thus founded upon the negation and objectification of an other.[3]

Dorothy Dinnerstein extends this analysis to the masculine mode of interacting not only with women but with all of the natural world.[4] For Dinnerstein, since a child's self-identity is originally viewed as indistinct from the surrounding world, later self-identity is founded not only upon the notion of not being female but upon the notion of not being nature as well. Thus, object relations theory provides another interpretation of why the masculine self is conceived as the negation of both women and the natural world.

If men in our society are socialized to perceive their identity in opposition to a devalued, female-imaged world, we might expect that the process of reinstituting this forbidden identification might be fraught with problems along the way. At the very least, we might expect that such a process of identification would not be experienced in identical ways for women and men. The writings of three prominent male philosophers, who claim that their process of self-realization occurs through the act of hunting and killing animals, are suggestive in this regard.

According to the philosopher/biologist Randall Eaton:

> To hunt is to experience extreme oneness with nature. . . . The hunter imitates his prey to the point of identity. . . . hunting connects a man completely with the earth more deeply and profoundly than any other human enterprise. Paradoxical as it may appear at first glimpse, the hunter's feeling for his prey is one of deep passion, ecstacy and respect. . . . The hunter loves the animal he kills.[5]

Let us recall that according to psychoanalytic theory, the boy's yearning to identify with the mother figure is fueled by his feelings of alienation and the consequent urge to reexperience the original state of union. Eaton's words convey such a longing, which may be viewed as a longing for the original self:

> What do I mean at the deepest level when I say I want to know the behavior of the tiger? I really mean that I have affection for tigers and that I want to see the essential nature or being of the tiger. If the truth be known, I want to *be* a tiger, to walk in his skin, hear with his ears, flex my tiger body and feel as a tiger feels.[6]

José Ortega y Gasset, a well-known Spanish philosopher, reflects a similar urge toward unification with the animal, which he sees as a unification with the animal within himself. In his words: "Man can-not re-enter Nature except by temporarily rehabilitating that part of himself which is still an animal. And this, in turn, can be achieved only by placing himself in relation to another animal.[7]

For men such as Eaton and Ortega, the ultimate purpose of the hunt appears to be this reversion to an earlier state of being in which one's separateness not only from women, but from animals, has not yet oc-curred. Ortega, in fact, refers to hunting as a kind of "vacation from the human condition through an authentic 'immersion in Nature.'" He goes on to explain: "In that mystical union with the beast a contagion is immediately generated and the hunter begins to behave like the game."[8]

The erotic undertones of hunting can be found in sensuous descrip-tions of the hunt. Thus, the prominent environmental writer Aldo Leopold writes that he "tingled" at the recollection of the big gander that sailed honking into his decoys,[9] and Ortega writes of the "ex-quisite" feel of the air that "glides over the skin and enters the lungs."[10] At other times, both write of hunting in more heated terms, using such words as "hunting fever" and the "drama" and "contagion" of the hunt. Indeed, Ortega goes so far as to assert the "unequaled orgiastic power" of blood, contending that wildlife photography is to hunting what Platonic love is to the real thing.[11]

According to both object relations and Jungian theory it is the ongo-ing denial of the original union with the mother figure that creates the lifelong yearning to experience this original state. Hunting is, in fact, described by these writers as a permanent or instinctive longing. Ac-cording to Ortega, sport hunting is "however strangely a deep and permanent yearning in the human condition."[12] And according to Leopold: "The instinct that finds delight in the sight and pursuit of game is bred into the very fiber of the human race."[13] Desire for hunt-ing, according to Leopold, lies deeper than other outdoor sports: "Its source is a matter of instinct as well as competition. . . . A son of Robin-son Crusoe, having never seen a racket, might get along nicely without one, but he would be pretty sure to hunt or fish whether or not he were taught to do so."[14] In other words, a boy *instinctively* wants to hunt and kill!

It must be emphasized here that all three writers describe hunting not as a necessary means of subsistence but rather as a *desire* that fulfills a deep psychological need.

At times Leopold is unclear as to whether this instinct is universally held by all humans or only by men and boys. He writes that: "A man may not care for gold and still be human but the man who does not like to see, hunt, photograph or otherwise outwit birds and animals is hardly normal. He is supercivilized, and I for one do not know how to deal with him."[15]

In order to understand how the act of identification can coexist with the desire to kill the being with whom one identifies, it is important to understand the ambivalent nature of the hunt. Ortega refers to the "ambivalence" felt by every hunter, an ambivalence that results from "the equivocal nature of man's relationship with animals." As he explains: "Nor can it be otherwise, because man has never really known what an animal is. Before and beyond all science, humanity sees itself as something emerging from animality, but it cannot be sure of having transcended that state completely."[16]

The hunter is thus driven by conflicting desires to both identify with the animal and to deny that he is an animal himself. The "drama" of the hunt thus enables the hunter to experience both the yearning for a return to unity, while ensuring, through the death of the animal, that such a unification is never attained.

Deep ecologists caution that identification must entail a recognition of the "relative autonomy" of the other being, but it is precisely this autonomous existence that the above writers have failed to convey. According to object relations theory, it is only when the boy child transforms his mother into an object that his identity can be formed. In a similar way, animals have become objects in the eyes of these men. In fact, Leopold openly expresses this urge to reduce animals to object status: "Critics write and hunters outwit their animals for one and the same reason—to reduce that beauty to possession."[17] Interestingly, the original title of his famous *Sand County Almanac* was "Great Possessions."[18]

The significance of the reduction of the animal to object status is that the *relationship* to the animal becomes more important than the animal itself. The feelings of yearning for union, the urge to "outwit"—all these take precedence over the living being that will be killed. The animal is swallowed up in the act of merging. Even the death of the animal is considered incidental—it is a by-product of the more important desire that finds its expression in the hunt. As Ortega explains:

> To the sportsman the death of the game is not what interests him; that is not his purpose. What interests him is everything he had to do to achieve that death—that is the hunt. Therefore, what was before only

a means to an end is now an end in itself. Death is essential because without it there is no authentic hunting. To sum up, one does not hunt in order to kill; on the contrary, one kills in order to have hunted.[19]

Deep ecologists argue that a widened identification will ensure that one will want to minimize harm to individual beings, in that they will be viewed as part of the all-inclusive Self. However, it seems clear from the above examples of self-realization that for these men this was not the case. For all three, the killing of animals was an integral part of the process of self-realization. For them, the animal is seen not as a unique, living being but rather as a means to achieve a desired psychological state. The animal is thus reduced to the status of object or symbol.

For all three writers the desire to hunt is clearly of greater importance than the life of the animal they kill. For Leopold, the urge to hunt was strong enough to merit its enshrinement as an inalienable right. In his words:

> Some can live without the opportunity for the exercise and control of the hunting instinct, just as I suppose some can live without work, play, love, business or other vital adventure. But in these days we regard such deprivation as unsocial. Opportunity for the exercise of all the normal instincts has come to be regarded more and more as an inalienable right.[20]

Aldo Leopold is considered by many a pioneer of deep ecology and ecophilosophy. He is perhaps best known as an early promulgator of an ethic of nonanthropocentrism and biocentric equality. What is not widely recognized, however, is how paramount the hunting instinct was to Leopold's philosophy and to the land ethic for which he is so well known. Right after he writes of the inalienable right for the free exercise of the "normal" instinct to hunt, he goes on to deplore the fact that "The men who are destroying our wildlife are alienating one of these rights and doing a good job of it."[21] In other words, wildlife must be conserved not because of the animals' inalienable right to life but rather because of "man's" inalienable right to hunt and kill! As Leopold elaborates:

> His instincts prompt him to compete for his place in the community but his ethics prompt him also to cooperate (perhaps in order that there may be a place *to compete for*) [emphasis added]. . . . An ethic ecologically is a limitation on freedom of action in the struggle for existence. An ethic

philosophically is a differentiation of social from anti-social conduct. These two are two definitions of one thing. Good social conduct involves a limitation of freedom.[22]

Leopold's land ethic is thus conceived as a necessary restraint for a self that is driven by an inherently aggressive drive. All three of the above writers see such aggression and struggle as a fundamental fact of life. In Ortega's words: "Life is a terrible conflict, a grandiose and atrocious confluence."[23] This notion of life's inherent conflict can be understood as the result of the male's ongoing internal struggle to maintain his self-identity as distinct from the female-imaged natural world. This internal conflict then becomes projected onto the "outside" world. But not everyone's concept of self entails such an aggressive drive. For many women, this is, in fact, clearly not the case. Such women's process of identification and widening of the self finds expression in different ways.

For many women, identification with animals entails not an aggressive drive but rather the desire to avoid causing them harm. At times deep ecologists would seem to express this feeling as well. Thus, the Norwegian philosopher Arne Naess writes that: "There is a basic intuition in deep ecology that we have no right to destroy other living beings without sufficient reason. Another norm is that, with maturity, human beings will experience joy when other life forms experience joy, and sorrow when other life forms experience sorrow."[24] This statement, however, appears to be contradicted by Devall and Sessions, who suggest in *Deep Ecology* that hunting, along with such diverse activities as surfing, sailing, sunbathing, and bicycling, is "an especially useful activity" that, with the "proper attitude," can help encourage "maturity" of the self.[25]

In order to understand this seeming contradiction, we must recall that it is the *widest* sense of identification that deep ecologists ultimately call for—that is, an identification not with individual beings but rather the larger biotic community or whole. Australian environmental philosopher Warwick Fox expresses this relative prioritizing when he states that: "In terms of the wider identification approach, then, it can be seen that there is a strong sense in which community (e.g., the species or the ecosystem) is even more important than the individual expressions that constitute it since the community itself constitutes an entire *dimension* of the world with which I identify, i.e., of my self."[26]

And the poet Robinson Jeffers, whom deep ecologists cite with approval, expresses this relative prioritizing in even stronger terms: "I believe the universe is one being, all its parts are different expressions of the same energy, and they are all in communication with each other, therefore parts of an organic whole. . . . It seems to me that this whole *alone* is worthy of the deeper love [emphasis added]."[27]

Deep ecologists maintain that this primary identification with the "whole" is not at the expense of the individual beings since they, too, must be seen as part of the same all-inclusive Self. But, as we have seen, the danger with widening one's identification to the "whole" or biotic community (as in the case of Leopold) is that one may widen it beyond the reach of individual beings.[28] This preference for identification with the larger "whole" may reflect the familiar masculine urge to transcend the concrete world of particularity in preference for something more enduring and abstract.

Deep ecologists would have us believe that self-realization is a simple process of expanding one's identification to all of the natural world. But when deep ecologists write of expanding the self, ecofeminists must be prepared to examine more deeply the unconscious drives that fuel the self that one seeks to expand. We have seen that women and animals have been utilized as psychological instruments for the establishment of the masculine self. The conquest of the snake, the dragon, and other female-imaged monsters reflects the inner drives and needs of the masculine self. What we witness in the experiences of the writers discussed here is the same conquest mentality now operating on a seemingly "higher" plane. Nonetheless, animals are still used as instruments of self-definition—they are killed not in the name of an individual, masculine ego but instead in the name of a higher, abstract self. But whether one is establishing the self writ small or large, the experience of the animal—the loss of her or his life—remains the same.

The danger of an abstract identification with a larger "whole" is that it fails to recognize or respect the existence of independent, living beings. This has, in fact, been a major failing of both environmental philosophy and the environmental movement. By alternately raising the ecosystem or an aggrandized self to the level of supreme value, they have created a holism that risks obliterating the uniqueness and importance of individual beings. The disillusionment of many animal liberationists with both the environmental movement and environmental philosophy is a consequence of this fact.

Ecofeminist philosophy must be wary of a holistic philosophy that transcends the realm of individual beings. Our deep, holistic awareness of the interconnectedness of all of life must be a *lived* awareness that we experience in relation to *particular* beings *as well as* the larger whole.

If, as object relations theory argues, women's self-identity, unlike men's, is not bound up with the urge to negate one's dependence on the natural world, then we should not be surprised to find that women's experiences with nature may differ from those of men. Although it cannot be claimed that no women hunt or perhaps experience their sense of nature in the ways described by the writers discussed here, most people, I think, will recognize such behavior as primarily characteristic of men.[29] Throughout history hunting has, in fact, been an activity that has been pursued by and large by men.

Many women have found other ways to experience their oneness or identification with nature. Charlene Spretnak writes that women often have such experiences through the "body parables"—"reclaimed menstruation, orgasm, pregnancy, natural childbirth and motherhood."[30]

It is out of women's unique, felt sense of connection to the natural world that an ecofeminist philosophy must be forged. Identification may, in fact, enter into this philosophy but only to the extent that it flows from an *existing* connection with individual lives. Individual beings must not be used in a kind of psychological instrumentalism to help establish a *feeling* of connection that does not, in fact, exist. Our sense of oneness with nature must be connected with concrete, loving actions.

Ecofeminism and deep ecology have suggested, at times, that what each refers to is a consciousness of love. As we have seen, however, love can mean many things and be expressed in a variety of ways. As ecofeminism develops in relation to other philosophies, it must carefully examine the practical consequences of all abstract ideals. Only then will ecofeminism know how far our own identification can go.

Michael E. Zimmerman

DEEP ECOLOGY AND ECOFEMINISM: THE EMERGING DIALOGUE

IN THE SPRING OF 1987, a barge loaded with garbage from Islip, New York, made international headlines as it searched in vain for a place to dump its unwanted load. The garbage barge was a striking symbol for and symptom of the behavior of "advanced" industrial societies, which are poisoning themselves and the biosphere by their own wastes. One of today's leading issues is whether we can survive the very industrial practices that we have relied upon for material "progress." Some people, including deep ecologists and ecofeminists, maintain that the set of Western categories responsible for this "progress" must be transformed if we are to learn to dwell upon the Earth in an appropriate way. In what follows, I shall examine how deep ecologists, on the one hand, and ecofeminists, on the other, would explain how these Western categories have shaped society in a way that almost inevitably led to the appearance of the garbage barge. But despite apparent similarities in their critical appraisal of Western culture, the deep ecological and the ecofeminist views are not entirely in harmony. Ecofeminists argue that deep ecologists overlook the *real* source of the domination of nature: patriarchy. In developing a critical exchange between deep ecology and ecofeminism, my intention is to strengthen and to further the important dialogue that has been initiated between these two opponents of the domination of nature, of our own bodies, and of woman and man.[1]

DEEP ECOLOGY

Deep ecology, a radical stream of the environment movement, maintains that the environmental crisis is the inevitable outcome of the

138

history of Western culture. A primary distinction between deep ecology and reform environmentalism is that the former is nonanthropocentric in its attitude toward the natural world, while the latter is anthropocentric. It would be incorrect, however, to lump into one undifferentiated group all forms of environmentalism that are not "deeply" ecological. Environmental philosopher John Rodman, for example, differentiates four stages in ecological consciousness: (1) resource conservation, (2) wilderness preservation, (3) moral extensionism, and (4) ecological sensibility (Rodman's term for deep ecology).[2]

Resource conservation is the most obviously human-centered version of reform environmentalism. From its viewpoint, we must conserve "resources" because of our obligation to future generations of humanity. Although widespread, resource conservation is by no means universally accepted. Some people argue, for example, that we not only have no obligations to the natural world, we also have no obligations to so-called future generations of people.

Wilderness preservation seems at first glance to be oriented not toward human beings but instead toward protecting the wilderness itself from human "development." Rodman argues, however, that wilderness preservationists remain anthropocentric since they aim at protecting wilderness as the site for aesthetic or religious experiences in the grandeur of unspoiled wild places. Wilderness preservation, then, turns out to be subtly anthropocentric: we are to preserve the wilderness not so much for its own sake as for the sake of the experiences people have in it.

The third version of reform environmentalism is moral extensionism.[3] According to this approach, the environmental crisis stems in part from our unethical treatment of nonhuman beings. One way to protect the nonhuman world from human exploitation is to show that some (or perhaps all) nonhuman beings are worthy of moral "concern" and/or legal "standing." But there are problems with this approach, too. For example, the standards used to determine whether a nonhuman entity is morally "worthy" are all too often derived from criteria considered definitive of humanity, such as sentience, or consciousness. Anthropocentrism raises its ugly head once again.

Rodman's fourth stage of ecological consciousness is ecological sensibility, or deep ecology. While there are various approaches to deep ecology, there is one major issue on which virtually all deep ecologists agree: the industrial pollution, species extinction, biospheric degradation, and nuclear annihilation facing the Earth are all symptoms of anthropocentrism. Only by recognizing that humanity is no more, but also no less, important than all other things on Earth can we learn to dwell on the planet within limits that would allow other species to flourish and to follow out their own evolutionary destiny. Anthropocentric hierarchies would be replaced by biocentric egalitarianism. Disputes would necessarily arise in the face of difficult decisions ("Should these trees be cut down for the sake of building these houses?"), but such disputes would not paralyze human activity. The disputes would take place with the *presupposition* that all entities concerned have "rights" that must be taken into account during the decision-making process. According to the Norwegian philosopher and naturalist Arne Naess, living according to deep ecological principles would bring about the fulfillment of human existence as well as liberating nature from human exploitation.[4] Humanity's highest possibility is to bear witness to and to participate in the great process of life itself. Supposedly, only deep ecology points the way beyond abuse toward appreciation, beyond anthropocentrism toward a mature humanity living within appropriate limits that enable other entities to thrive as well.

According to the Australian environmental philosopher Warwick Fox, the "central intuition" of deep ecology is that there is no absolute divide between humanity and everything else.[5] Western humanity tends to think in terms of dualisms, such as that between mind and body, or between humanity and nature. Such dualism leads Western humanity to split off its "dark side"—its mortality, dependence, and finitude—and to project it upon the body and nature, which it then attempts to "dominate" and "control." Deep ecology, by way of contrast, thinks nondualistically; it looks instead to the rich internal relations that constitute the universe. Deep ecology also proposes an alternative to Newton's atomistic conception of the physical world, a conception that was extended by Hobbes and Locke into the social world. Far from being a social atom that is wholly independent of other people and the natural world, the human being is a "node" in the internal relations that compose everything.[6] A mature humanity would understand its interrelationship with everything else.

Many deep ecologists maintain that their view is consistent with both Eastern religions and mystical traditions within Western religions, namely, that the I and the not-I are ultimately a unity. Such realization also involves direct insight into the limitations of subject/object dualism and its calculating rationality. Rationality, according to deep ecology, is an important way of interpreting the world, but it is often used destructively in the service of the ego striving to deny its mortality by controlling all things. An enlightened humanity would use rationality in accordance with a more profound understanding or sensibility that transcends subject/object dualism. The discovery that all things are internally related would lead us to treat each other as well as the nonhuman world with profound respect instead of merely as raw material to enhance human power.

Deep ecology, then, seeks to overturn the major Western categories that are apparently responsible for humanity's destruction of the biosphere: *anthropocentrism, dualism, atomism, hierarchalism, rigid autonomy,* and *abstract rationalism.* A deep ecologist would see the garbage barge as merely the tip of the waste-and-pollution iceberg that is threatening the biosphere. The huge quantities of poisonous industrial and municipal wastes, the nuclear weapons, the destruction of the living Earth—all are manifestations of what amounts to human self-worship. Having "killed" God, humanity arrogated to itself the Divine position in the Great Chain of Being. Human beings became the origin and measure for all value, truth, and meaning. A "thing" had "value" only in economic or pragmatic terms—in relation to human needs. And because nature reminds us of our dependence on the body, we must "conquer" nature to reassure ourselves of our immortality. White Western humanity believes it has the "right" to dump its waste wherever it wants, instead of curbing its lavish consumption and recycling its wastes. The abstract, linear rationality at work in modern economies (be they capitalist or socialist) cannot comprehend the essentially cyclical character of natural processes. Despite the findings of the science of ecology, Western society plunges blindly ahead toward disaster in the name of infinite progress. Science can be an important part of the solution to anthropocentrism, but only if it is freed from its current enslavement to economic and nationalistic interests.

Deep ecologists agree that reform environmentalism—including stiff international laws against pollution, annihilation of species, expansion of human population, destruction of rain forests and marshes, nuclear power and nuclear weapons, and so on—is necessary in the short run. In the long run, however, mere reformism will not be sufficient to prevent the destruction of the Earth. Only a revolution in humanity's understanding of itself and its place within nature will bring about the dramatic changes in human behavior that are necessary at this critical juncture in human and terrestrial history.

ECOFEMINISM

At first glance, ecofeminism and deep ecology share many points in common. Both are critical of atomism, dualism, hierarchalism, rigid autonomy, and abstract rationality. According to feminist critics, however, because deep ecology has been formulated almost entirely by men, it is characterized by unintended patriarchal prejudices. Whereas the deep ecologist speaks of the drawbacks of anthropocentrism or *human*-centeredness, the ecofeminist speaks of the drawbacks of androcentrism or *man*-centeredness. According to many ecofeminists, patriarchalism leads to the destruction of the Earth.[7] Because deep ecologists fail to understand the *fundamental* role of patriarchy in the development of atomism, dualism, hierarchalism, rigid autonomy, and abstract rationality, deep ecologists mean something different by these categories than do ecofeminists. Ecofeminists believe that only when deep ecologists learn to appreciate the effects of patriarchal culture on their own awareness, only when they discover the extent to which their conceptions of self, body, nature, and other are shaped by patriarchal categories, will their ecology become truly deep.

Contemporary feminism is an extraordinarily complex movement. In the late 1960s and early 1970s, many Western feminists saw the problem as women being systematically denied the educational and economic opportunities necessary for them to compete on an equal footing with men. Feminism meant fighting for equal rights in the political and economic arenas. Gradually, however, feminists began to see that it might be unwise for women to emulate roles that had been defined and structured by and for men. Feminist theorists began to emphasize the *differences* between men and women. Still later, some feminists began to conclude that not only are women different from men, they are *better than* men. Whereas earlier feminists had insisted that differences between men and women were cultural in origin, some feminists now began taking an "essentialist" position, according to which patriarchal culture distorts or conceals the essential feminine that is the birthright of every woman.

Other feminists have been quick to point out the problems with this position. First, it seems to confirm the misogynist's viewpoint that women are essentially or naturally or biologically *different*. The misogynist concludes that such "natural" differences make women "inferior," while the feminist concludes that they make women "superior." And any talk of female "superiority" reinstalls the very hierarchy that feminists found and fought against in patriarchy. Some ecofeminists even speak as if men are so flawed that only women can solve the environmental crisis because women are more attuned to the cycles of nature and to their own feelings than are men. But women are also distorted by patriarchy, and some men are deeply appreciative of their relationship to the natural world. Most ecofeminists acknowledge that what is needed is the transformation of women *and* men. Ecofeminists, however, may be able to make a contribution that many men cannot because the marginal place of women in the history of patriarchy may have protected them from some of the crippling effects that it has had on so many men.

Many ecofeminists agree that the technological assault upon the Earth is the culmination of a direction in human history that took a particularly virulent form in Europe.[8] In the Europe of several thousand years ago, before the emergence of agriculturally based cities and before the onslaught of the Goddess-slaying, Sky-Father-worshipping nomadic horsemen, there was no patriarchy. Society was apparently nonhierarchical, nonauthoritarian, and nondualistic. Human worship was directed at the Goddess, the female divinity regarded by women and men alike as the source of all life and bounty and goodness. Gradually, however, the Goddess was displaced by the new Father God. Feminists have often interpreted this new God as the projection of the male's hierarchical, patriarchal, domineering, and authoritarian attitude. While the Goddess affirmed the goodness and primacy of the body and the Earth, the God affirmed the goodness and primacy of the spirit/soul and heaven. But this is not the only possible interpretation of the Father God.

C. G. Jung and psychotherapist Erich Neumann have argued that the emergence of the Father God was consistent with the development of human consciousness from out of a relatively collective state to one of increasing individuation.[9] They see the solar God as representing the clarity of the free-willed, self-assertive, rational ego-self. For this kind of individuated selfhood to be possible, according to Jung, the heroic ego had to escape from the embrace of the Great Mother, who represents both the organic-bodily and the subconscious domain of human existence. Transpersonal psychologist Ken Wilber, however, argues that the emergence of the Father God amounted to a new level in humankind's understanding of divinity, a level consistent with and made possible by the Great Goddess.[10] Wilber sees the Great Mother as representing early humanity's conception of "Mother Nature" as the now-bountiful, now-withholding source of life and death, who must be placated by ritual and blood sacrifice, while the Great Goddess represents the insight of a few into the transcendent Divine Unity that constitutes the creative source of all things. That is, the Great Goddess is the unifying principle of transcendence-in-immanence that makes even the Great Mother possible. Unlike the Great Mother, who demands ritual sacrifice, the Great Goddess requires not sacrifice of the body, but instead sacrifice or surrender of the separate self to the Divine Unity which is its source.

Rightly understood, the great Father can be regarded as a further development of the individuating and transcendent principles that first emerged with the Great Goddess. God did not *necessarily* have to become the basis for patriarchy. But as men became individuated by their identification with the Father God, the terror of individuation led them to construe him as an all-powerful, separate, other-worldly self. Men made God in their *own* image. This conception of God led men to dissociate themselves from women, from nature, and from their own bodies—from everything that reminded them of dependence. Hence, whatever corresponding process of individuation that might have occurred for women in association with the Great Goddess was feared and repressed by the newly individuated men. Men justified their deeds by portraying women as being too bound up with the Great Mother, the Earth, and with the subconscious, prerational, collective, material, and emotional realms. Women were simply "unfit" to follow the path of individuation. Worshippers of the "jealous" Father God destroyed the temples and killed the worshippers of the "false" dieties, the Great Mother and the Great Goddess.

Correctly intuiting that in some sense they shared in the eternal presence of what I prefer to call the God/dess, the ancient males mistakenly concluded that their own egos were immortal. Instead of surrendering their separate egos to the eternal God/dess, men embarked on what Wilber has called the "God project."[11] They invented immortality substitutes and symbols, such as money, war, science, art, and other activities of culture. The ego's logical-rational discourse projected an infinite future for unfolding its immortality projects. Hungry for the power that promised immortality, the God-worshipping urban kings invented full-scale war. They projected death and guilt upon the enemy—by slaying the enemy, they would also slay death and guilt. And they projected mortality and limitation on women, whom they regarded as seminatural beings incapable of participating in the "creative" domain of culture.

The "history of consciousness," then, has turned out to be the story of *man's* development. The heroic male struggles violently to free himself from the clutches of the subconscious and collective powers of the Great Mother. Only by the matricidal act of slaying the beast (representing the Great Mother) does the hero achieve individuation. The fierceness of the ego's repression of the female, the bodily, and the natural is directly proportional to the ego's recognition of its ultimate *dependent* status. But the anxious ego finally claims to be independent of everything, including the Divine. The ego in effect declares itself to be God.

According to ecofeminists, modern technology is simply the culmination of this male quest to conquer death and limitation by dominating his environment, his own body (through military and scientific "disciplines"), his women, and all other "subhuman" (that is, nonruling-class) types. The garbage barge represents man's refusal to own up to his own wastes, the disposal of which he has usually consigned to women. Organic wastes in particular remind man of his mortality, his connection to the Earth and to woman. By hoping to dump the barge's garbage in the U.S. South and then in Mexico, wasteful patriarchal culture again revealed its exploitative attitude toward the poor and dark-skinned. Even if a woman had ordered the barge to head south, she herself would be a victim of patriarchal thinking. Female bureaucrats, too, can be taught to think in linear terms, to conceive of the Earth not as a living entity with cyclical patterns but instead as an infinite resource for human projects and an endless dumping ground for excrement.

One may readily discern important similarities in the deep ecological and the ecofeminist account of the garbage barge as a symptom of the illness of Western culture. Ecofeminists charge, however, that patriarchal culture is governed not only by the categories of *dualism, abstract rationality, rigid autonomy,* and *atomism,* but also by the crucial category of *androcentrism* or *patriarchy.* Despite the fact that, except for androcentricism, the same categories are mentioned in the deep ecological critique of Western culture, ecofeminists argue that there are significant differences between the deep ecological and the ecofeminist perspec tive. That is, because of profound differences in the male and female sense of self, men and women experience the world differently. In the following section, I shall examine this assumption.

ECOFEMINIST CRITIQUES OF DEEP ECOLOGY

One ecofeminist, Ariel Kay Salleh, maintains that deep ecologists propose enforced birth control to solve the ecocrisis.[12] According to her, this drive to control reproduction betrays the long-standing patriarchal desire to dominate the female reproductive process. Moreover, she accuses deep ecologists of speaking in abstract terms, typical of males raised in patriarchy, instead of in terms of concrete, personal relationships to other people and to the Earth. Isolated from others and from nature, the alienated male ego invents deep ecology as another desperate attempt to become reattached to the world he denied during the matricidal process of individuation.

A male philosopher sympathetic to ecofeminism, Jim Cheney also argues that patriarchal categories can be discerned in the basic program of deep ecology.[13] For example, he notes that Arne Naess speaks about the importance of rights for all beings and about the inevitable conflict among bearers of such rights. But the vocabulary of rights is, according to Cheney, a conception of human beings seen as isolated, autonomous egos who choose to limit competition among themselves by according each other certain inalienable rights that each ego must respect. To conceive of biospheric egalitarianism in terms of rights, then, betrays an atomistic conception of human society that is inevitably linked to androcentrism and patriarchy.

Moreover, even the central intuition of deep ecology—the notion that we are all nodes in the fabric or web of internal relations—may be only *apparently* consistent with the view that while men think atomistically, women think relationally. What better way to overcome the effects of hierarchal and dualistic thinking than by doing away with atomism and by affirming a "contextual" metaphysics? While sympathetic to the aims of such an approach, Cheney maintains that it fails. For example, how are we to solve disputes among competing claims to rights? Ultimately, if it's a question of a human's right to life versus a squirrel's, won't we resort to some hierarchical consideration that undermines the commitment to biocentric egalitarianism?

> The infusion of the web-of-life concept into deep ecological ethics, then, may be seen to promise . . . a feminist ethical theory while in fact it serves *either* to flatten all issues of value and obligation into a normative egalitarianism which cannot serve to guide practice without reintroducing hierarchy *or* to shift the focus of ethical concern to the ecosystem as a whole, the result being a kind of ecological totalitarianism in which the good of individuals is subservient to the good of the whole. The concept of a moral community implied by the idea of a web-of-life in which selves are defined by means of relationships of care and responsibility cannot survive the attempt to fit it into the framework of a theory of rights, whether it be of the individualistic or holistic variety.[14]

Like Cheney, Marti Kheel maintains that we cannot solve the ecological crisis simply by ridding ourselves of metaphysical and social atomism and replacing such atomism with a metaphysical and social relationalism.[15] It is important to remember that relationships can only obtain between *individuals* that have some measure of importance and reality of their own. If we reduce individuals merely to the status of "nodes" in a field of internal relations, we run the danger of removing all obstacles to regarding the nexus of internal relations (for example, some particular biome) as being more important than the individual nodes comprising the biome. That is, for the sake of the "overall good" of the whole set of internal relations, individuals could justifiably be sacrificed since after all they are only temporary coagulations of the dynamic patterns at work in the vibrant field of life.[16]

Feminists are calling for a new version of selfhood or individuation, one that avoids isolated egos on the one hand and unconscious blending on the other. Earlier, I noted the masculinist bias in the prevailing Western account of individuation. In their path-breaking analyses of such individuation, Jung and Neumann recognized the destructive character of the patriarchal repression of the female principles of nature and divinity. Most feminists, however, have concluded that Jung and Neumann's history of individuation, despite its critique of the lopsidedness of patriarchal consciousness, is itself so colored by masculinist categories that it cannot be of help in developing an alternative conception of individuation. Recently, however, feminist theologian Catherine Keller has reinterpreted the approach of depth psychology to individuation to make it compatible with her own version of a feminist understanding of individuation.[17]

According to Keller, Jung's major achievement was his "discovery and charting of a collective unconscious."[18] Jung argued that the task of the ego in a person's later life was to reaffirm its relationship with the world, a relationship temporarily denied during the process of individuation:

> Sacrificing its own illusory claims to autonomy, the ego's task becomes that of reconnecting with the depth and breadth of life from which it had so early cut itself off. For the mother archetype symbolizes the ego's relation to its own deeper psyche, the transpersonal or collective unconscious. By its very nature, it belies the separate ego of the warrior-hero. . . .
>
> Reintegration of the psyche on the basis of its own transpersonal scope requires the process Jung calls "individuation." Authentic individuality can be gained only when I experience myself as fundamentally connected to all of life: this is the wisdom of the Jungian outlook. An ego-transcending selfhood is massively relational, exposing the individuality of the ego as the sham of individualism and a fabrication of persona . . . [Jung's] vision of a radical world-openness suggests the essence of a connective self.[19]

Where Keller speaks of the mother archetype as symbolizing the ego's relation to the transpersonal *or* collective unconscious, I would distinguish between the transpersonal and the collective unconscious. The transpersonal domain refers to the level of awareness opened up by the Great Goddess; the collective unconscious refers to the domain represented by the Great Mother. An integrated personality would be open to both domains. Both women and men are capable of such integration. Arguing against those feminists who adopt an essentialist view of the nature of woman and man, Keller maintains that women and men alike are originally relational beings. In early childhood, however, the boy is forced to separate in accordance with misguided patriarchal conceptions of individuation. But none of us is ever truly cut off from our relations with the world—the patriarchal quest to total autonomy and independence is an illusion. The task facing women and men today is to develop a nonpatriarchal, nonmatricidal version of individuation. Instead of slaying the "dragon," we need to integrate this disowned and denied aspect of ourselves:

This is not to step out of our skins, to subordinate gender-specific concerns to supposedly transcendent, humanistic ones, but rather to spin
a meaning of self out of our femaleness, without reducing it to anything
exclusively "feminine". . . .

[W]e are searching for some path of differentiation *in* relation. This
would permit women to remain faithful to the complex inner and outer
connectivity that we may sense as integral to our selves, while liberating
ourselves from the accompanying dependency and self-suppression. It
would challenge males to modes of relatedness that require not the
sacrifice of their maleness but of their ego rigidities and corollary manipulation of women. But then differentiation—becoming uniquely ourselves—must not be cast in the category of separation.[20]

Deep ecologists understand the relationship between the separa-
tistic, body-despising, "independent" ego-subject and the ego's quest
to control nature by technological means. As an alternative to this
separateness and its paranoid lust for power, deep ecologists have ap-
pealed to a wide variety of spiritual traditions, including Buddhism.
As mentioned earlier, however, critics of deep ecology claim that such
mystical traditions tend to "overcome" the dualism between self and
other by expanding the self to the status of a transcendental Self which
includes everything within itself. The danger of this transpersonal conception of enlightenment is twofold. First, the individual loses his or
her integrity as an individual; hence, he or she can then justifiably be
subordinated to the good of the "whole." Second, defining authentic
selfhood in terms of the identity of self and Self seems to omit what
many feminists regard as essential to selfhood: relationship.

While the Self spoken of by mystics and some deep ecologists may
appear to be an inflated version of the male ego, I believe that at least
some deep ecologists have something more in mind than this. Consider the contributions of the poet Gary Snyder to deep ecology.[21] A
long-time student of Zen Buddhism, Snyder takes seriously the Zen
critique of the "inflated self" conception of enlightenment. For the Zen
practitioner, insight into the Buddha-nature dwelling within all creatures frees a person from the dualistic-abstract domination imposed
by the ego. Enlightenment involves entering everyday life more deeply
than ever. Being awake means "chopping wood and carrying water."
This commitment to everyday life is made possible by the paradoxical
insight that as Buddha-nature, one is *both* this embodied person-in-
relationship *and* the "openness/emptiness" (*sunyata*) in which all spatio-

temporal events can unfold and thus "be." The more we surrender to the openness at work in us, the more we are liberated from the anxiety and insecurity produced by the illusion of radical separateness. The isolated ego defends itself against change and dependency; it despises the body as the bearer of limitation, sickness, and death. The Zen practitioner affirms and integrates the mortal-bodily realm and lives from the insight that "this very body is the body of Buddha." This leads to treating all creatures both with respect and with individualized attention. The Zen practitioner learns to care for each creature in a way consistent with its needs and possibilities. There is no abstract table of ethical judgments but a personalized compassion based upon insight into what is needed and into what can be done to help.

Such compassion provides the basis in which to situate the behavior of people toward each other and toward nonhuman beings. Compassion may begin with the members of one's own family; as it grows it may extend out to all our human sisters and brothers. Finally, it may extend to all beings. One may say that we should care for trees and plants, rocks and waters, animals and people because all things are both fundamentally related to each other and are manifestations of the same life principle. This compassion would be made concrete by reference to one's own particular geographical context and social history. Deep ecologists like Gary Snyder put such compassion into practice by attempting to "reinhabit" the land and to reestablish appropriate humanity-nature relationships in light of the particular character and possibilities of the area in which they find themselves. The bioregional movement, favored by deep ecologists, is an example of the growing conviction that only by living in a *particular* place, with *particular* relationships with people and the landscape, can humanity learn to produce goods and dispose of waste in ways that respect all who are affected.

Thus, discovering one's Buddha-nature means entering fully and deeply into one's particular body in particular relationships. Human beings are endowed with a degree of awareness and self-awareness that seems to differentiate us from the organic-biological realm in which animals dwell. Such awareness enables us to form a moral community to begin with, one that has the potential for expanding beyond the immediate limits of our own families and even of our own species.

The emergence of the Great Goddess and Father God can be regarded as crucial stages in the evolution of human awareness. The patriarchal perversion of this evolution, however, has led to terrible suffering for human and nonhuman beings alike. And yet, mystics in all religious traditions have known that no matter how profound our cosmic-transcendental insight might be, our understanding of ourselves and of the world in which we live is always a *human* understanding.

This insight, I assume, is behind Cheney's statement that "nonhuman nature must be located in the *ethical* space of the *moral* [human] community."[22] At first glance, some deep ecologists might say that such talk smacks of anthropocentrism. In their desire to curb anthropocentrism, deep ecologists have often relied upon metaphysical schemes that argue for the relative unimportance of humanity in the cosmic scheme of things. On the basis of such metaphysics, deep ecologists have developed moral principles such as biocentric egalitarianism, which are to curb the human tendency toward hubris. Ecofeminists, however, are wary of metaphysical and moral principles that downplay the role of humanity in the world. Perhaps they retain a sense of their connectedness with others in a way that leads them to have fewer suspicions and doubts about "human nature." And perhaps they also retain a more profound relationship with their own bodies, so that they take seriously the idea that "this very body is the body of Buddha." To be sure, some deep ecologists maintain that humanity has a crucial role to play in the scheme of things, as the witness and participant in cosmic evolution. Nevertheless, they sometimes have difficulty in formulating humanity's place in the world, partly because they are so concerned about lapsing into anthropocentrism.

Ecofeminists maintain that since we *are* human beings, we can only understand how to behave toward nonhuman beings in terms of principles and insights that are derived from the particular character of our humanity. According to Cheney, maintaining the human/nonhuman distinction appropriately "does not maintain moral hierarchy; it builds moral community."[23] Only within a fully textured moral community can people become aware first of how they can care for other people and for themselves and then how they can care for nonhuman beings. The atomistic individualism of patriarchy destroys much of the fabric of the human community. Such a damaged community is incapable of understanding the needs of its own members, much less of the nonhuman world. Before we can respond to the needs of the nonhuman world appropriately, we need to reestablish the fully textured human community in such a way that we learn to care for each other once again. Ecofeminists argue that then, and only then, will we be capable of extending our concern appropriately to the needs of non-human beings. Cheney maintains that

> Just as an answer to the question of what one's responsibilities are to one's friends is a highly contextual matter involving a detailed understanding of the precise threads of connectedness and intimacy involved, so an answer to what might be our moral relationship to the nonhuman environment depends upon (1) a complex understanding of what it means to be a human being, what it is to respond to another *as* a human being (whatever that might turn out to be), and (2) an understanding of how those complex webs of relationships that constitute the human moral community might expand to include the nonhuman. This sort of expansion of the moral community is not the extension of moral privilege to nonhuman creatures just because they happened to resemble us in desirable ways. . . . Rather, it is simply (or complexly) a matter of trying to come to an understanding of what it might mean to care, to respond to something in the nonhuman environment as a member of one's moral community.[24]

From the ecofeminist perspective it makes no sense to speak of caring for nonhuman beings apart from our capacity to care for each other. The moral context in which we can become concerned about nonhuman beings is made possible by particular human beings with needs and the capacities to take care of those needs.

This capacity for a deeply textured understanding of our particular human and environmental situation is by no means restricted to women, though under patriarchy far fewer men than women have retained this capacity in a healthy way.

Cheney concludes that ecofeminism involves

> a highly contextual attempt to see clearly what a human being is and what the nonhuman world might be, morally speaking, *for* human beings—i.e., what kinds of care, regard, and responsiveness might be possible for us in relationship to the nonhuman world. . . . [T]he limits of moral regard are set only by the limitations of one's own (or one's species' or one's community's) ability to respond in a caring manner, which, in turn, are a function of the depth of one's own understanding of the human moral community and the clarity and depth of one's understanding of, and relationship to, the nonhuman world or elements of that world.[25]

The danger of this approach to humanity's place in nature is that it may be used to reinforce the relative lack of concern that many feminists have traditionally displayed toward environmental issues. It may be true that our capacity to care for nonhuman beings is at least partly grounded in the human community that we must reproduce and sustain in everyday life. Feminists have understandably focused upon the needs of those members of the human community who have suffered most from the history of patriarchy. Nevertheless, increasing numbers of feminists are discovering the needs of the nonhuman world and their capacity to care for it, even as they continue to repair the human world.

CONCLUSION

It appears then that the emergence of concern for the nonhuman world has coincided with the rediscovery of the Great Goddess in particular and of the Divine in general. In the quest to rectify the mistreatment of women, many feminists tended to neglect both the Earth and the Divine. To more and more women and men alike, however, it is becoming clear that the Divine cannot be identified with the patriarchal understanding of divinity. Moreover, we are beginning to realize that our capacity for caring for other human beings is somehow related to our capacity to appreciate the divinity at work in all of us. By appreciating the Divine God/dess, the origin and destiny of all things, we also appreciate more fully both our own bodies and the Earth upon which those bodies so depend. Surrendering to the Divine, we simultaneously surrender to and affirm our own embodiment. This Divine God/dess is simultaneously and paradoxically transcendent and immanent. Perhaps this concept of a postpatriarchal God/dess is necessary for women and men alike to develop a form of individuation that does not involve dissociation from the body, from nature, and from woman. This God/dess may then provide the understanding and compassion necessary for women and men to care for each other in a way that encourages us to care for other people and for the Earth as well.

In this essay, I have attempted to develop a dialogue between deep ecology and ecofeminism. No doubt, masculine bias and phrasing color the writings of many deep ecologists, but a generous and compassionate interpretation of their work reveals an authentic concern to heal men and women and to heal the Earth that has been wounded by men and in some cases by women. Women and men alike have been distorted by the effects of patriarchy. What we need now is cooperation and trust, not animosity and suspicion, between deep ecologists and ecofeminists. We need each other in our common search for a way to be mature and complete human beings, so that the Earth can be freed from the burden of domination and exploitation.

Judith Plant

SEARCHING FOR COMMON GROUND: ECOFEMINISM AND BIOREGIONALISM

IT IS NO ACCIDENT that the concept of ecofeminism has emerged from the many elements of the movement for social change. Women and nature have had a long association throughout history, though it is only now that the deepest meanings of this association are being understood. Just as ecologists have paid critical attention to the attitudes, social structures, and rationalizations that have allowed the rape of the Earth, so have feminists dug deeply to understand why society has rendered them second-class citizens, at best.

Both schools of thought are now converging with similar analyses. The difference is that ecologists are scientists, basing their views of the interconnectedness of all things on the intellect, whereas feminists cannot help but come from the school of experience and have sought intellectual frameworks in order to try to make sense of their experience of subjugation. The coming together of the two gives us hope for an understanding of the world that has the potential to be rooted in "thinking feelingly."

ECOLOGY AND WOMEN

Ecology is the study of the interdependence and interconnectedness of all living systems. As ecologists look at the consequences of changes in the environment, they are compelled to be critical of society. Because the natural world has been thought of as a *resource*, it has been exploited without regard for the life that it supports. Social ecology seeks ways to harmonize human and nonhuman nature, exploring how humans can meet their requirements for life and still live in harmony with their environments.

Ecology teaches us that life is in a constant state of change, as species seek ways to fit in particular environments that are, in turn, being shaped by the diversity of life within and around them. Adaptation is a *process*. Ecology helps us develop an awareness of the need to incorporate these organic facts into our most general views of the world—those views that shape the way humans will *be* in the world.

Within human society, the idea of hierarchy has been used to justify social domination; and it has been projected onto nature, thereby establishing an attitude of controlling the natural world. The convergence of feminism with ecology is occurring because of an increasing awareness that there are, in fact, no hierarchies in nature. A belief in the virtues of diversity and nonhierarchical organization is shared by both views.

Women have long been associated with nature: metaphorically, as in "Mother Earth," as well as with the naming of hurricanes and other natural disasters! Our language says it all: a "virgin" forest is one awaiting exploitation, as yet untouched by man (sic). In society, too, women have been associated with the physical side of life. Our role has been "closer to nature," our "natural" work centered around human physical requirements: eating, sex, cleaning, the care of children and sick people. We have taken care of day-to-day life so that men have been able to go "out in the world," to create and enact methods of exploiting nature, including other human beings.

Historically, women have had no real power in the outside world, no place in decision making and intellectual life. Today, however, ecology speaks for the Earth, for the "other" in human/environmental relationships; and feminism speaks for the "other" in female/male relations. And ecofeminism, by speaking for *both* the original others, seeks to understand the interconnected roots of all domination as well as ways to resist and change. The ecofeminist's task is one of developing the ability to take the place of the other when considering the consequences of possible actions, and ensuring that we do not forget that we are all part of one another.

ECOFEMINISM:
ITS VALUES AND DIMENSIONS

Why does patriarchal society want to forget its biological connections with nature? And why does it seek to gain control over life in the form of women, other peoples, and nature? And what can we do about dismantling this process of domination? What kind of society could live in harmony with its environment? These questions form the basis of the ecofeminist perspective.

Before the world was mechanized and industrialized, the metaphor that explained self, society, and the cosmos was the image of organism. This is not surprising since most people were connected with the Earth in their daily lives, living a subsistence existence. The Earth was seen as female, with two faces: one, the passive, nurturing mother; the other, wild and uncontrollable. These images served as cultural constraints. The Earth was seen to be alive, sensitive; it was considered unethical to do violence toward her. Who could conceive of killing a mother, or digging into her body for gold, or mutilating her? But, as society began to shift from a subsistence economy to a market economy; as European cities grew and forested areas shrunk; and as the people moved away from the immediate, daily organic relationships that had once been their basis for survival, peoples' cultural values—and thus their metaphors—had to change. The image of Earth as passive and gentle receded. The "wrath and fury" of nature, as woman, was the quality that now justified the new idea of "power over nature." With the new technology, man (sic) would be able to subdue her.

The organic metaphor that once explained everything was replaced by mechanical images. By the mid-seventeenth century, society had rationalized the separation of itself from nature. With nature "dead" in this view, exploitation was purely a mechanical function, and it proceeded apace.

The new images were of controlling and dominating: having power over nature. Where the nurturing image had once been a cultural restraint, the new image of mastery allowed the clearing of forests and the damming and poisoning of rivers. And human culture that, in organic terms, should reflect the wide diversity in nature, was reduced to monoculture, a simplification solely for the benefit of marketing.

Since the subjugation of women and nature is a social construction, not a biologically determined fact, our position of inferiority can be changed. At the same time that we create the female as an independent individual, we can be healing the mind/body split.

Life struggles in nature become feminist issues within the ecofeminist perspective. Once we understand the historical connections between women and nature and their subsequent oppression, we cannot help but take a stand in the war against nature. By participating in these environmental standoffs against those who are assuming the right to control the natural world, we are helping to create an awareness of domination at all levels.

Ecofeminism gives women and men common ground. While women may have been associated with nature, they have been socialized to think in the same dualities as men have and we feel just as alienated as do our brothers. The social system isn't good for either of us! Yet, we *are* the social system. We need some common ground from which to be critically self-conscious, to enable us to recognize and affect the deep structure of our relations with each other and with our environment.

In addition to participating in forms of resistance, such as nonviolent civil disobedience in support of environmental issues, we can also encourage, support, and develop—within our communities—a cultural life that celebrates the many differences in nature and encourages thought on the consequences of our actions, in all our relations.

Bioregionalism, with its emphasis on distinct regional cultures and identities strongly attached to their natural environments, may well be the kind of framework within which the philosophy of ecofeminism could realize its full potential as part of a practical social movement

BIOREGIONALISM:
AN INTEGRATING IDEA

Bioregionalism means learning to become native to place, fitting ourselves to a particular place, not fitting a place to our predetermined tastes. It is living within the limits and the gifts provided by a place, creating a way of life that can be passed on to future generations. As Peter Berg and Raymond Dasmann have so eloquently stated, it

> involves becoming native to a place through becoming aware of the particular ecological relationships that operate within and around it. It means understanding activities and evolving social behavior that will enrich the life of that place, restore its life-supporting systems, and establish an ecologically and socially sustainable pattern of existence within it. Simply stated it involves becoming fully alive in and with a place. It involves applying for membership in a biotic community and ceasing to be its exploiter.[1]

By understanding the limitations of political change—revolution—bioregionalists are taking a broader view, considering change in evolutionary terms. Rather than winning or losing, or taking sides, as being the ultimate objective, *process* has come to be seen as key to our survival. *How* we go about making decisions and how we act them out are as important as *what* we are trying to decide or do.

In evolutionary terms, a species' adaptation must be sustainable if the species is to survive. How can humans meet their requirements and live healthy lives? What would an ecologically sustainable human culture be like? It is in dealing with these questions that the bioregional movement and the philosophy of ecofeminism are very much interconnected.

Human adaptation has to do with culture. What has happened with the rise of civilization, and most recently with the notion of mass culture, is that what could be called bioregionally adapted human groups *no longer can exist*. It is difficult to imagine how society could be structured other than through centralized institutions that service the many. In our culture almost every city exists beyond its carrying capacity; diverse regions are being exhausted and ecologically devastated.

Becoming native to a place—learning to live in it on a sustainable basis over time—is not just a matter of appropriate technology, home-grown food, or even "reinhabiting" the city. It has very much to do with a shift in morality, in the attitudes and behaviors of human beings. With the help of feminism women especially have learned an intimate lesson about the way power works. We have painfully seen that it is the same attitude that allows violence toward us that also justifies the rape of the Earth. Literally, the images are the same. We also know that we are just as capable, generally speaking, of enacting the same kind of behavior.

The ideas of bioregionalism are being practiced all over the world—though they are rarely referred to as such. The name gives us common ground, however, like ecofeminism. But bioregionalism gives us something to practice and together they offer a *praxis*—that is, a way of living what we're thinking. Here we can begin to develop an effective method of sharing with our male friends the lessons we have learned about power, as well as our hopes and aspirations for an egalitarian society—a society that would be based on the full participation and involvement of women and men in the process of adaptation and thus in the maintenance of healthy ecosystems.

HOMING IN ON A NEW IMAGE

One of the key ideas of bioregionalism is the decentralization of power: moving further and further toward self-governing forms of social organization. The further we move in this direction, the closer we get to what has traditionally been thought of as "woman's sphere"—that is, home and its close surroundings. Ideally, the bioregional view values home above all else, because it is here where new values and behaviors are actually created. Here, alternatives can root and flourish and become deeply embedded in our way of being. This is not the same notion of home as the bungalow in the suburbs of Western industrialized society! Rather, it is the place where we can learn the values of caring for and nurturing each other and our environments and of paying attention to immediate human needs and feelings. It is a much broader term, reflecting the reality of human cultural requirements and our need to be sustainably adaptive within our nonhuman environments. The word *ecology*, in its very name, points us in this direction: *oikos*, the Greek root of "eco," means home.

The catch is that, in practice, home, with all its attendant roles will not be anything different from what it has been throughout recent history *without* the enlightened perspective offered by feminism. Women's values, centered around life-giving, must be revalued, elevated from their once subordinate role. What women know from experience needs recognition and respect. We have had generations of experience in conciliation, dealing with interpersonal conflicts in daily domestic life. We know how to feel for others because we have practiced it.

At the same time, our work—tending to human physical requirements—has been undervalued. What has been considered material and physical has been thought to be "less than" the intellectual, the "outside" (of home) world. Women have been very much affected by this devaluation, and this is reflected in our images of ourselves and our attitudes toward our work. Men, too, have been alienated from childcare and all the rest of daily domestic life, which has a very nurturing effect on all who participate. Our society has devalued the source of its human-ness.

Home is the theater of our human ecology, and it is where we can effectively "think feelingly." Bioregionalism, essentially, is attempting to rebuild human and natural community. We know that it is nonadaptive to repeat the social organization that left women and children alone, at home, and men out in the world doing the "important" work.

The *real work* is at home. It is not simply a question of fairness or equality; it is because, as a species, we have to actually work things out—just as in the so-called natural world—with all our relations. As part of this process, women and nature, indeed *humans* and nature, need a new image, as we mend our relations with each other and with the Earth. Such an image will surely reflect what we are learning through the study of ecology, what we are coming to understand through feminism, and what we are experiencing by participating in the bioregional project

3

HEALING OURSELVES: HEALING THE PLANET

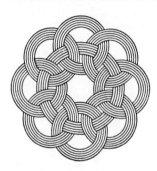

Arisika Razak

TOWARD
A WOMANIST
ANALYSIS OF BIRTH

I WOULD LIKE TO SHARE with you some of my thinking about the U.S. way of birth. I bring to this topic four perspectives that make me a critical and nonobjective observer: First of all, I am human. I have been born. Second, I am a woman. I have given birth. Third, I am a midwife—I help other women give birth. Fourth, I am a woman of color, and I bring new insights to paradigms devised by the "majority."

At one level this essay is about the cultural rape of women by the dominant health care model. It is about the collusion of women, through fear and ignorance, in their own oppression and their own diminishment. It is about birth and women—and the historical, psychological, and cultural significance that we have had for the human species. But, most of all, this essay is about the critical need our society has to make a new model for human interaction.

For all too long, we have allowed rape to exist as a dominant social and cultural metaphor for behavior. Ours is a culture where male participation in the acts of sexuality and procreation have become so equated with the acting out of hostility, physical oppression, and fear that rape, incest, and sexual abuse and murder of children, and the battering of women have become health issues of pandemic proportions.

The physical rape of women by men in this culture is easily paralleled by our rapacious attitudes toward the Earth itself. She, too, is female. With no sense of consequence and scant knowledge of harmony, we gluttonously consume and misdirect scarce planetary resources. With unholy glee we enter "virgin" territory. Nature is *naturally* threatening—she must be conquered, reduced, put in her place. She can be improved on. The Earth must be entered, emptied, changed. She can be made to "yield up her secrets." We *will* have from her what it is that we need.

This kind of rapacious attitude is also the primary model for the interactions between Third World peoples and the dominant Western cultures of the nineteenth and twentieth centuries. Many of the scarce resources that we have coveted and stolen are found in the indigenous habitats of peoples of color. We have all too often removed and destroyed both the peoples and their habitats.

Our psyches aren't really able to cope with these actions. All that we have psychically disowned and denied—sexuality, animality, natural innocence, and evil—has been projected onto peoples of color—and has been acted out upon them individually and en masse. Women of color have been particularly targeted.

The reversal of this cultural attitude of rape and rapaciousness is of fundamental importance to the issue of our societal health. Put quite simply, healthy humans do not rape one another. But we also need to develop new paradigms that articulate positive human interaction and functioning. We need models that are more inclusive and holistic. We need paradigms that are nurturing. We need models based on human cycles of growth and change, not mechanistic iterations of stasis and motion.

I would like to propose that birth is such a universal and central aspect of human existence that it can serve as the nucleus around which to build a paradigm for positive human interaction. Birth, the subsequent nurturing of the young, and the raising of the younger generation to adulthood are central tasks for all human societies, including the one in which we live.

The physical act of giving birth may be limited to women, but the process of birth has emotional significance for all human beings. When I say that birth can serve as the nucleus of a model for positive human interaction, I want us to remember the emotional bonding that happens at births—the bonding among men, women, and the newborn child. This spontaneous emotional bonding is a profound example of the human capacity for nurturing, love, and emotional attachment. All human beings, male and female, are capable of bonding.

Birth is important to all of us—whether we choose to bear children or not, for children are the future of every society that exists. It is our collective children who will inherit this Earth and manifest whatever visions they have found to be worthy from the previous generation.

The maternal womb is their first environment. The cultural paradigm of birthing is the first institution that receives our children. The child's family is the first society. Each of these elements—womb, birth culture, and family—has a profound effect upon the new human being. Each deserves our best thinking and analysis.

What would it be like if we envisioned a society in which positive, lifelong, nurturing support—from old to young, and young to old—were the dominant theme of human interaction? What would it be like if the human quest for adventure were linked to issues of social justice and individual empowerment?

I offer for your perusal the thinking of Alice Walker in *In Search of Our Mother's Gardens* as she defines the term *womanist*:

Womanist: (1) from womanish—(Opp. of "girlish," i.e., frivolous, irresponsible, not serious.) A black feminist or feminist of color . . . From the black folk expression of mothers to female children, "You acting womanish," i.e., like a woman. Usually referring to outrageous, audacious, and *willful* behavior. Wanting to know more and in greater depth than is considered "good" for one. Interested in grown-up doings. Acting grown up. Being grown up. Interchangeable with another black folk expression "You trying to be grown." Responsible. In charge. *Serious.* (2) *Also.* A woman who loves other women, sexually and/or nonsexually. Appreciates and prefers women's culture, women's emotional flexibility (values tears as a natural counterbalance of laughter), and women's strength. Sometimes loves individual men, sexually and/or nonsexually. Committed to survival and wholeness of entire people, male *and* female. Not a separatist, except periodically for health. Traditionally universalist, as in: "Mama, why are we brown, pink and yellow, and our cousins are white, beige and black?" Ans.: "Well you know the colored race is just like a flower garden with every color flower represented." Traditionally universalist, as in: "Mama, I'm walking to Canada and I'm taking you and a bunch of other slaves with me." Reply: "It wouldn't be the first time." (3) Loves music. Loves dance. *Loves the Moon.* Loves the Spirit. Loves love and food and roundness. Loves struggle. *Loves the folk.* Loves herself. *Regardless.* (4) Womanist is to feminist as purple is to lavender.

I feel that this definition of Walker's is incredibly important. It is important for all the social and human values it reclaims and articulates. It reclaims age groupings and the importance of intergenerational communication. It reclaims the concept of the people—and one's social responsibility to them. It articulates the notion of a distinct culture of women—and the importance of women's herstory, which is not always written but which we pass on and survive by. It includes the experiences of Third World and working-class people, and our experience of resistance and survival in the face of oppression. Most importantly, it reclaims love of self, love of the body, love of the Spirit, and love of the Earth.

As women in the United States, we have experienced a very profound alienation from our bodies. Our procreative abilities have been used to oppress us—our female bodies have become symbols of degradation. Under great force and pressure, we have yielded to unresolved male fears of animal physicality, women, and sexuality. We have sold our birthright as powerful female birth-givers for a mess of pottage that contains untested, invasive, dehumanizing, and nonproductive techniques and technologies. Some of this technology is certainly necessary, but we have failed to insist that all technology be developed within a culturally sensitive paradigm that stresses positive human nurturance, ethical behavior, intergenerational needs, and holistic and ecological analysis.

As feminists, we sought to repudiate patriarchal and sexist concepts of inferiority that were rooted in our biology. Biology would *not* be destiny for us; and we tried to deny the importance of birthing.

But birth is an event of incredible human significance. It has profound spiritual, psychological, and emotional importance. Not all of us give birth, but all of us who live have experienced being born. And all of us have entered life through the body of a woman.

Birth is *the* primary numinous event. It is our major metaphor for life and coming into being. We talk about the birth of the universe, the birth of galaxies. It is how the world came into being. It is the first act of magic—and physical testament to the continuity of human and all life.

Women are the only birth-givers in the human species. In cultures around the world we find preliterate evidence of the great sacredness with which birth was originally viewed. The fertility of women was linked to the fertility of the Earth—which produced the food upon which all life depended—and to the reproduction of the herds that also sustained humans.

In Paleolithic cave sites twenty and thirty thousand years old we find evidence of the earliest carvings and drawings of humans. The oldest images are those of women—women with large hips, full and pregnant bellies, pendulous breasts, and clearly defined or well-marked genitalia. These physical attributes were carved to emphasize the fertility and life-sustaining abilities of women.

Thousands of years later, in classical art from Egypt, Africa, and Central and South America, we find statues of the Goddess holding the Man-Child on her lap or offering her full breasts to the Child and to the world.

The early numinosity with which we view birth is indelibly embedded in the human psyche and the collective unconscious. Whether we access them or not, all of us store memories of our own birth experience. In *Beyond the Brain,* psychotherapist Stanislav Grof writes:

> The reliving of birth in experiential clinical work clearly indicates that from the introspective point of view this process is perceived and interpreted as an ordeal that requires extreme active struggle and effort, a true hero's journey. Thus the moment of birth is experienced under normal circumstances as a personal triumph. This can be illustrated by its characteristic association with images of victory in revolutions and wars, or the killing of wild and dangerous animals. It is not infrequent in the context of the birth memory that the individual experiences a condensed review of all his or her later success in life. The experience of birth thus functions psychologically as the prototype of all future situations that represent a serious challenge for the individual. It seems as if the experience of birth determines one's basic feelings about existence, image of the world, attitude toward other people, the ratio of optimism to pessimism, the entire strategy of life and even such elements as self-confidence and the capacity to handle problems and projects.[2]

Humankind's early veneration of woman in her role as birth-giver has persisted through the millennia, though it has been significantly changed by sexism and patriarchy. We find remnants of this attitude in contemporary nonindustrial societies where women are still valued for their ability to give birth. In many African societies, for example, a round belly and full figure are attractive because they denote potential fertility. Women in these cultures may dress in a way that adds girth to the waist.

One thing must be remembered: as women we experience great physical power in the process of giving birth. Birth is a physical ordeal that serves as a model for all subsequent rites of passage. It is a model for physical, emotional, and spiritual transcendence. As a woman who works with birth, I can truly attest to the strength of women. We are *not* the weaker sex.

But this is not the perception of the medical model. I speak to you as a midwife, and midwifery must certainly be the oldest profession in the world. Millennia before the first instruments were invented, we used our hands and our voices to help our sisters give birth; and we used the milk of our bodies to heal and to nurture. Midwifery was a woman-controlled and woman-dominated profession across the globe; it is the prototype of a field that is "of, by, and for the people." Like the earliest shaman-healers, the midwife was a person holistically rooted within her community. She was an integral part of popular religious, social, and cultural life. Most importantly, she had experienced what her clients experienced—for midwives traditionally are older women who have themselves given birth.

Feminist writers Barbara Ehrenreich and Dierdre English suggest that it was as midwives and healers that women in the Middle Ages engaged in scientific research.[3] We searched out, cataloged, and tested herbs for healing. And certainly our herb lore had very ancient antecedents.

Midwifery is also an example of a profession that uses human-scale technology. The use of gravity, positioning, and trust and support are still essential tools of the practicing midwife. Intuition, empathy, and touch are major components in our professional interactions. An intrinsic belief in the rightness of the process and the *natural* ability of women to birth are still at the core of even hospital-based midwifery.

I do not mean by this to indict the medical profession. Men were not involved in birth when birth occurred naturally, for worldwide, birth was a woman's institution. Men entered birth when the process failed and the child could not be born. They came in as priests or shamans who prayed for Divine intervention, or as barber surgeons who would dismember a child who could not be born. As the creators of forceps and Cesarean deliveries, they sought for alternatives to a process that had failed.

But our medical model has developed within a patriarchal context. In a society where the male is seen as normal, and the female as a defective male, men *choose* to disidentify with the feminine experience. Because their bodies do not experience firsthand the unifying dialectic of labor and pain, birth and resolution, they view our pain with fear, our opening with horror, and our bleeding with disgust. Much of the casual social oppression of women is reflected in the disgust with which our bodies, and our bodies' natural functions, are perceived. And much of the patriarchal oppression of women stems from fear and resentment of our birthing abilities. For the medieval church, pain in labor was God's punishment to wisdom-seeking Eve. And the bearing of children is part of her curse. Midwives in the Middle Ages were burned at the stake because they sought herbs that would reduce women's pain.

Under the Newtonian and Cartesian worldview, the body was seen as a functional machine. Man's body was the perfect expression of that machine—woman's body was most imperfect and barely worthy of study. Under this logic, which persists today, we casually remove the sexual parts of women. Today we remove breasts, uteri, and ovaries; a hundred years ago we also removed clitorises. We did it and do it to improve the imperfect body.

Where has this kind of thinking taken us in birth? We have a medical profession that rejects the relevance of the subjective experience of the person giving birth. We have an obstetric specialty that accepts the myth of the dangerous womb and the hostile vagina. We have a medical profession that advocates the routine use of electronic fetal monitors not because they have lowered infant mortality and morbidity, but because that profession has an *a priori* belief in the inability of the womb to safety nurture life. Despite all the scientific evidence against it, doctors view Cesareans as safer for the baby, for he or she is spared passage through a constricting vagina.

In the United States, we have a national Cesarean delivery rate of 25 to 30 percent—a rate that is significantly higher than in many other industrial nations whose infant mortality rates are a fraction of ours. Nor is this phenomenon confined to the United States: middle-class women in Argentina and Brazil are routinely encouraged to have Cesarean births, and their counterparts in Taiwan are told that modern humans have become so different from their long-ago ancestors that it is impossible for women today to give birth naturally.

We have excluded fathers from the birth rooms and denied them the experience of their own tenderness, their own protectiveness, and their empathetic abilities. They are now so disidentified with women that their projections about birth rest exclusively with the fetus. Like their medieval counterparts, they have reduced pregnant women to empty vessels that passively carry a child. These women, of course, have no natural love, interest in, or caring for the child. So laws must be made to effectively coerce them to righteous action. The recent attempted prosecution of a woman for failure to comply with medical advice during her pregnancy is an example of this.

Can we reverse these trends? For the health of our species, we had better say yes. The real plague that threatens us is our attitude toward one another. Why is birth not considered a major psychic event? Where is our birth art? Where are our birth stories? Why don't we celebrate birth instead of war? Why do we restrict fathers from participation in birth?

If we begin with loving care for the young, and extend that to social caring for all people and personal concern for the planet, we would have a different world. If we understood, and celebrated birth, we'd seek more humane alternatives to painful medical processes—we'd reclaim the importance of love and warmth and human interaction.

Nurturing is not a genetically feminine attribute. Tears and laughter are not the province of women only. The last time I looked, men had tear ducts. They had arms for holding babies. They cared about their children. And they cried at births.

In a society that wishes us to see men as devoid of feelings, let us hold an image of men as nurturers. Women are birth-givers, but men can care with them. Let us change our institutions. Let us demand that men come with us. Let birth teach them surrender. Let pain teach them transcendence. Let the shared experience of childbirth reclaim the human soul.

Lin Nelson

THE PLACE OF WOMEN
IN POLLUTED PLACES

1988:

drought in the Midwest
desertification in Africa
deforestation and flooding in Bangladesh
the greenhouse effect
the ozone hole
ozone smog in Acadia, Maine—precipitating the first health
  hazard alert issued in the National Park system
beaches littered with medical waste
World Health Organization warnings about urban air pollution,
  especially in the Third World
increasing poisonings and birth defects due to pesticides
epidemic disease and death among North Sea seals
and on, and on

And in and around Syracuse, New York, where I live—think about
your own home—

a lake, Onondoga Lake, its waters and banks once home to the
  Onondoga Nation, a lake some consider to be "the most
  polluted urban lake in the United States" (the world?)
solid waste and landfills encroaching upon what is left of
  relatively undeveloped land
a planned mass burn incinerator, which supporters say will not
  exceed the risk of four cigarettes in one lifetime
working people exposed to naptha, asbestos, toluene, formaldehyde
people, more and more, developing chemical sensitivities, leaving
  them incapacitated, angry, and in despair
to the south, the Onondoga Nation, its very limited land base
  occasionally the focus of landfill "offers"

to the north, the Mohawk Nation, its threatened land turned into
  a toxic soup from the effluence of nearby GM, Alcoa,
  Reynolds, paper mills, and the pollution of the Saint Lawrence
  Seaway and the Great Lakes

IT IS, TO UNDERSTATE IT dramatically, all very sobering. It stills the heart. It stirs the heart.

I look at my daughter, almost 3 years old. I wonder—what do I tell her about all this? How do I tell her? When? We talk about the rain a lot. (It rains a lot here.) We talk about how the Earth is thirsty, how the trees want a shower, how the grass is drinking the water. When do I tell her that acid rain is destroying the Adirondack forests to the northeast of us?

Born in 1948, I was raised in the "Glory Days," the go-get-em postwar years. The build-and-buy years. And now, 40 years later, the children I see playing on our street are part of what may be the last generation who will have the burdensome opportunity to say no.

It is unfortunate that our species seems to have waited for a body count of its own kind before realizing that we've seriously abused the place—the Earth, our community—we call home. Disease, disability, death, and despair—these might be eleventh-hour triggers that jolt us into awareness. A look at the U.S. institutions that deal in the business of health and environment—the Centers for Disease Control, the Environmental Protection Agency, the Occupational Safety and Health Administration, the American Medical Association, and so on—makes it clear that only now (and even now there is mostly denial) is there a trickle of recognition about the health/environment connection. And so, it is up to us to refuse to wait for more evidence before acting.

As women, we have distinctive ties to the ecological world. We are focusing more on these ties and reviving repressed thoughts about these ties—in our art, our science, our spirituality, our work, our everyday lives. I think it is critically important that we do not exclusively applaud or mythologize these ties (woman as eco-angel) or myopically bemoan them (woman as eco-victim). We need to get a grip on the many ways in which women/ecology relationships have emerged. We need to understand how we have been brutalized, been made vulnerable, become detached, become implicated in or complicit with ecological degradation, and how we can become challengers and restorers. Environmental health and the health of the environment is a prism through which we can see ourselves—with criticism, with appreciation—as passive or as active. Health as an ecological process is the visceral daily reality that forces us to face the crossroads at the end of the twentieth century.

I identify strongly with ecofeminism, feminist ecology, social ecology. Feminism and ecology are two beacons of hope for me. But for many women who are on the front lines of Earth-protection activities, who are most directly taking on those who are contaminating the rest of us, for many of those women, these labels and niches don't feel quite like home. And yet without these women we would have no resistance and little knowledge about what ails us. Many of the women I have in mind as I write have little to do with feminist studies or organizations and don't bother themselves with debates such as those between social ecology and deep ecology. They are the strong, impassioned women—often rebounding from grim health catastrophes—who are plainly and simply fighting for their lives.

What I want to do in this essay is look in the many mirrors that reflect who we are, what we are facing, how we are politically situated, and what we are doing and could be doing. I want to observe the ways in which women continue to fight the forces of environmental destruction and in so doing challenge frameworks for destruction. I want to argue that it is not only pollution and environmental disease that should be the focus of our efforts: we must also be vigilant and determined in the face of those "protectors"—in education, science, medicine and public health, and economic development—who would use gender and reproductive status (and race, class, susceptibility, and other identifiers) to accommodate us all to an industrial complex that would be only slightly improved, in a political atmosphere of increasing authoritarianism.

What is our life like as women living on this increasingly ravaged planet? What is there to learn, to watch out for? How do we experience the impact of pollution, deforestation, resource depletion, and so on? Unfortunately, if we look at what women are typically taught in most women's studies and in most women's health courses, we do not learn enough. No one can doubt the importance of learning about childbirth, birth control, eating disorders, sports, and so on. But all too often course curricula and texts present the decontextualized woman. We learn too little about women's work, about industrial policies impacting on women's health, or about the subtle and not-so-subtle environmental impositions that threaten us.

An ecological approach to learning about women and health would explore the array of roles, predicaments, and scenarios that is our collective biography. While this is only a beginning, the following provides a glimpse of what an ecological perspective could bring to our understanding. I want to focus here on some of the more disturbing scenarios—on scenarios that demand a response. I want to highlight not only the physical and ecological destruction wrought upon our lives, but the social and ecological conditions (legal, political, moral, emotional) that are making profound impacts on our lives. I will look at scenarios and circumstances that are in large part not of our making and at some of our actions in response.

THE DAMAGED WOMAN IN THE
DAMAGED ENVIRONMENT

In addition to the social abuse women suffer under patriarchy, industrialism, and modern science, there are very real biological hazards to be considered. Any orientation to women's health—theoretical or practical—that does not look at the ecological base of our health is incomplete and irresponsible. And yet, as I mentioned, most curricula and clinical practices offer a decontextualized, unecological view of women's biology and biography. There are many poorly researched, unanswered questions regarding the impact of environmental contamination on breast cancer, reproductive health, neurological functioning, and allergic diseases. We know very little about the cross-generational passage from mother to daughter of disease and disorders due to hazardous exposures. But, clearly, some proportion of women's ill-health has an environmental basis.[1]

A newly emerging and very controversial development in environmental health is the topic of "ecological illness" (or "chemical sensitivity," or "twentieth century allergy," to list just a few of the names used):

These illnesses . . . appear to stem from damage to the immune system, from either acute poisoning by toxic chemicals or from chronic, low-level exposures to many substances that ultimately overwhelm the system. The exact symptoms of ecological illness . . . may vary from person to person, but they generally involve an increasing intolerance to a wide range of chemicals, including ubiquitous substances like formaldehyde, pesticides, natural gas fumes, perfumes, scents and solvents. The EI victim may experience a wide range of disabling conditions, from a generalized weakness and joint or muscle pain to mental confusion, depression, and even hypertension, lung disease, heart disease and neurological disorders.[2]

Some researchers report that women are disproportionately likely to suffer from ecological illness (EI).[3] Certain questions must be addressed: Is the preponderance of women EI patients a demonstrable reality? If so, based on what? A biologically based toxics gender gap? Differential gender-based patterns of exposure? Socialized differences in symptom reporting and coping styles? Given that the EI syndrome is an amorphous array of difficult-to-diagnose symptoms, then women sufferers are also at risk of being discounted and demeaned. Researchers, clinicians, and feminists have long reported that women's medical complaints tend to be psychologized and trivialized by the medical establishment.[4]

On the one hand, we must reckon with the fact that our health is being damaged by the ecodestruction all around us. To what extent, in what ways, is not clear. On the other hand, the poorly grounded speculation and stereotyping about women's distinctive vulnerability is also damaging to us. I have used the words *damaged woman* somewhat facetiously. The damaged woman scenario is often a hair's-breadth away from the treatment of women as "damaged goods" – to be monitored, removed, labeled, treated, possibly rehabilitated, or made a lesson of. We need to look at the importance of the environment on women's health without making environmenal health a "women's problem."

WOMAN AS HAZARDOUS ENVIRONMENT
FOR THE NEXT GENERATION

One of the most sobering aspects of the ecological degradation we endure is the impact on our capacity to bear healthy children. In 1984, the Conservation Foundation reported that many scientists suspect or indict industrial pollutants as contributors to rising infertility, clusters of birth defects, "hot spots" of miscarriages, and the unusually early onset of menopause among some women. According to one researcher: "The womb is more sump than sanctuary."[5] Consider these selections from the growing reports on environmental reproductive health:

• Increasing numbers of birth defect clusters, especially in such industrial centers as Silicon Valley (California)

• Tragedies such as "Minamata disease" – extensive mercury poisoning, resulting in severe disabilities in the children of exposed pregnant women

• Elevated levels of PCBs, PBBs, and dioxin in mothers' milk; some researchers argue that present "background" or "average" levels may be hazardous.[6] Worst cases to date have been in Michigan (1983), Hawaii (1985), Arkansas–Oklahoma–Missouri (1986), and somewhat persistently in some parts of the Third World[7]

• Increasing reports of reproductive problems in the workplace – impotence, infertility, miscarriage, birth defects – due to such hazards as lead, ethylene oxide, DBCP, radiation[8]

Almost as troubling as the hazards themselves are the ways in which solutions are offered to or forced upon people. Protective/discriminatory/exclusionary policies are part and parcel of modern-day business-as-usual; that is, "the reproducers" or the "potentially pregnant" are classed as vulnerable and offered a kind of protection that usually only serves those trying to cover their liability. For example, in the workplace. "Fetal protection policies" are the means by which employers take the focus off their own hazard production by offering to "protect the unborn" by removing pregnant (or wanting-to-be-pregnant) women from hazardous zones.[9] In extreme cases, women have had themselves sterilized in order to keep their jobs and keep food on the table. More typically, practices include surveilling women's menstrual cycles or waiting for a woman to abort her pregnancy before placing her.

Most reasonable people would agree that a choice between a hazardous workplace and demotion or unemployment is no choice at all. But the management hoax continues. Women who are pregnant suffer either exposure or economic hardship. Women who are potentially pregnant, fertile but not wanting to get pregnant, are watched. Older infertile women are "allowed" to join men in the hazardous environment. Of course, the underlying falsehood is that reproductive toxics impact women, not men. The truth – now widely demonstrated – is that few contaminants affect women only and some affect men even more so.

Maureen Paul (an obstetrician and gynecologist focusing on occupational hazards) has just completed a "family, work, and health" survey of two hundred chemical and electronic plants in Massachusetts.[10] The vast majority offered no preventive, educational, or protective measures. One in five had "fetal protection policies" that removed women from hazardous zones. A small number offered voluntary transfer. This mix of ignorance, negligence, and selective protection accomplishes little. But, unfortunately, labor and women activists often unwittingly collude with industrial managers by applauding such "protections" — labor because it's fought hard for protections, reasonably wants some emergency measures for special cases, and is sometimes insensitive to working women's predicaments; women activists because they're relieved that someone is protecting the pregnancy and the baby.

This industrial protection racket becomes particularly pernicious when viewed in connection with all the other things — prenatal screening, alternative reprotechnologies — being hawked in the medical marketplace (see Irene Diamond's essay in this book). In many ways we have decreasing control over the environment for our reproductive health, the evolution of our pregnancies, the birth of our children; yet we are expected to be grateful for all that is provided, and we are treated as ingrates — even criminally liable — if we resist the package deal. It is all too easy to "assume pollution" and accept industrial relocation and obstetrical intervention, but they are responses to the symptoms, not the disease.

SUFFER THE CHILDREN:
MOTHER PROTECTOR/WOMAN WARRIOR

Not only do we witness or worry about children being born with environmentally caused problems, we also see "perfectly healthy children" disabled or destroyed by the contamination of their homes and communities. Love Canal, Woburn (Massachusetts), Times Beach (Missouri), rural Louisiana — the list grows of communities where children pay the price through the scourges of leukemia, neurotoxic disorders, and developmental problems.[11] Children "pick up" diseases by picking up their parents' workclothes and tools. Chemical sensitivity is fast becoming a haunting concern for parents, teachers, physicians, and psychologists who are seeing children with bizarre and baffling reactions to even low levels of contaminants. The "poisoned playground" and the "contaminated classroom" are now buzzwords for the reckless exposure of children to pesticides, paints, asbestos, and indoor air pollution. And there is deep trauma visited upon youngsters as they try to emotionally and morally deal with the reality of a dangerous environment. At Love Canal, social workers noted depression and a few suicides among teenage girls worried that they and their children would be "freaks" of some kind.[12] Mothers in toxically contaminated communities have become key environmental activists, and it is often the mothering of a wounded child that spurs them to act.

WOMAN AS BIOLOGICAL MARKER, AS RESEARCH SUBJECT, AS DATA

As those who conceive, bear, and breast-feed children, women are "interesting" to researchers. It is clear that the environmental impact upon human health, particularly reproductive health and the health of the nursing newborn, warrants more study. However, the politics of science being what it is, women are finding that the "quest for knowledge"—a quest that they may have initiated in their own community—is typically guided by the agendas of politicians, bureaucrats, industrialists, and career scientists.

"Woman as reproductive environment" has become a biological marker and significant point of data collection. This is certainly happening in the industrial environment where women's reproductive cycles are raw data for in-house research. In certain state departments of health and the federal Environmental Protection Agency (EPA) and the National Institute of Occupational Safety and Health (NIOSH), there is a growing momentum around reproductive risk assessment. Many of us would applaud the undertakings of selected researchers, provided that we are guaranteed our rights as research subjects, or, better yet, that we are involved in initiating and guiding the research. But all too often it doesn't happen that way.

Consider how some of the research on lactation and environmental exposure is conducted. Lactating women are a key biological marker of the bioaccumulation and transference of toxins. In the confusion at Love Canal, some women were told to "get ready for milk collection" several times; they nervously waited through many false starts; they were never given clear answers about the risk and were left to worry. In Oregon, women have been exposed to herbicide spraying. Kathy Williams, a nurse and environmental activist, reports on her research subject experience:

> The sample collectors told me I would be notified within six months of the result. Two years later, pregnant again, I was still trying to get the

results. After negotiations through my congressman, the EPA offered me my results—but only if I would sign an agreement not to make the results public. I declined. Although six months later the EPA announced that all samples tested negative, a "deep throat" within the agency told anti-spray activists that there had been positives.[13]

Organizations such as the National Women's Health Network have fought hard for the rights of women patients. We need to strengthen further both our rights as research subjects *and* our capacity to undertake participatory, meaningful, and accountable research. The Akwesasne Environment/Mother's Milk Project (Mohawk Nation, along the Saint Lawrence River) is especially sensitive to the threat of being colonized—as a people and as native women by nonnative researchers. Living with their water, air, and soil polluted by the surrounding industrial United States, the people are at high risk for environmental disease. The women there are pursuing their concerns: their breast milk may be both an interesting biomarker to ecological researchers and a grim symbol of their forced dislocation from the ecological world. While negotiating relations with state and federal officials, researchers, universities, laboratories, foundations, and other outside forces, the women are, in the words of project founder Katsi Cook, working to "develop a further understanding of our situation, to make well-formed choices, and to strengthen our community."[14]

WOMAN AS POLLUTER, BYSTANDER, BIT PLAYER IN OTHERS' AGENDAS

In looking at the reflections of ourselves and reckoning with who we are in relation to the ecocrisis, we must look at our own activities. Often we participate—unwittingly or with misgivings—in the mess around us. Sometimes this is because some of us, some of the time, really don't care and have been sold the whole game plan. Other times, we feel like helpless bystanders at a game we can't play and can't stop.

And often we are bit players in others' dramas ranging from progrowth "Bonanzas" to back-to-the-land "Daniel Boones." In the latter, women are expected to be ecological but on strictly patriarchal terms: "All too often, back-to-the-land means back-to-the-kitchen," observes Judy Smith (of the Women and Technology Project, based in Missoula, Montana). The build–buy–borrow–bonanza types give no second thoughts to squandering all resources and anybody's future. I want to focus on the bonanza boys with an example from the nuclear industry, which has waged a fairly sophisticated campaign to draw women to the "get yours" progrowth/environment-be-damned life-style.

The Atomic Industrial Forum (the major nuclear lobby) has been troubled by women's expressed concern with nuclear hazards. And so the forum launched Nuclear Energy Women (NEW), which has used a variety of means (conferences, lavish weekend retreats for women leaders, the targeting of women's organizations) to quell women's "irrational" fears. Women are told that they will gain a lot with nuclear energy—jobs, comforts, security—and are warned that they will suffer tremendously in a nonnuclear world crippled by darkness, crime, poverty, and global pandemonium.[15]

Many of us do get enmeshed in the madness. Not that we feel good about it. Many women don't have time to see where the madness begins and ends because we are busy surviving, even though we may be aware we are immersed in daily rituals of resource depletion and environmental pollution.

WOMAN AS SCAPEGOAT

Women as a class are often a convenient distraction or target for those who wish to avoid the reality of environmental degradation. Both the "fetal protection" approach and the "toxic gender gap" perspective are scapegoats of a sort. They allow environmental health to be a "women's problem," something women are particularly vulnerable around and/or worried about. Women's "delicate biology" and "fragile psychology" virtually become the cause of the problem.

A virulent form of sexist scapegoating appears among some of the "population people" who are ever watchful over women's "voracious" fertility and among some environmental organizations that blame both women and the developing world by condemning the overuse of the world's resources by the teeming masses. (It is less the masses and more the luxuried elites who exploit resources.) A particularly ugly rendition of this assault on "woman as baby-producer" is explored in Wolfgang Lederer's *Fear of Women* (New York: Harcourt Brace Jovanovich, 1968). In his chapter "Planetary Cancer," he profiles the pathological "uterine hunger" of "normal" women, the inundation of the world with their progeny. Basically, Lederer depicts an ecological disaster based upon the orgiastic, irrepressible procreativity of woman-as-carcinogen. This extreme example sheds light on how women's lives are often held in contempt by those who serve up formulas for final solutions to the global crisis.

There are other scapegoat activities that provide cover for those who endanger our health and the ecology. Not only have polluters continued to impair our genetic health, but under the guise of "selecting and protecting the weakest," some industrialists (with their scientists and physicians in tow) have perpetrated genetic screenings. These screenings supposedly winnow out the most chemically vulnerable; but, in fact, they single out people of African, Middle Eastern, and Mediterranean heritage, even though the evidence as to their vulnerability is specious. Such screenings—which are management vehicles for distraction and control—have been fought by coalitions of labor, environmental, civil rights, feminist, and progressive health activists. The denial of jobs to "reactors" and the "chemically sensitive" is another discriminatory smokescreen. The rational response to those who are chemically sensitive is not leperization—it is the acknowledgement that their very real predicament is a serious harbinger of worse things to come.

ACTIVIST UNDER ASSAULT:
"KITCHEN TABLE RESEARCHER," "HYSTERICAL HOUSEWIFE"

Some women who have taken on the industrial moguls, bureaucrats, and scientists have become remarkably empowered and effective. In many communities what has spurred action is "kitchen table research"—homegrown health surveys, independent sampling and lab testing, extensive literature reviews, mapping of suspected pollutants. This activity has been heralded by many. But more often than not it is met with a "kill the messenger" dismissal delivered with a strong sexist sting: "Women know nothing about, are afraid of, technology." "Women can handle the domestic front, not the industrial front." "Women tend toward hysteria, hypochondria, and malingering." Some of these women—held up to ridicule by public health authorities and political officials—are sometimes blamed for their children's illness ("It's something you've done—your genes or your parenting.").

Very often, industrial incidents of toxic exposure and/or disturbing symptoms are discounted if the majority of the grievants are women;

the term "industrial hysteria" is used in very gender-based ways. Men's complaints are taken as more serious signs of a "real" problem. Women activists often suffer isolation, abuse, and denial of appropriate official response and medical care. The stress of it all becomes an occupational hazard, a further threat to health and well-being.

Lois Gibbs, founder of the Citizen's Clearinghouse for Hazardous Waste (CCHW), is no stranger to the emotional costs of activism.[16] The contempt for the woman activist all too often becomes a part of the home scene. Family members (spouses in particular) and men in the community sometimes turn on her to distract themselves from their own fears, to rage with jealousy against the woman's newfound power and notoriety. At Love Canal, many women reported that as they worried about health, their husbands worried about declining property values brought on by the women stirring things up. One CCHW staff-person told me that "it seems every Monday morning we get calls from women who've endured abuse from husbands annoyed with their activities." To help women cope with this, CCHW called a special women's conference this past year that provided a safe place for women to explore how they've been transformed—for better or worse—and how to weather the close-range tensions on the family front.

WOMAN THE GATHERER:
SCAVENGING IN RAVAGED, CONTAMINATED LANDS

In the Third World, natural resource depletion and toxic contamination have reached epidemic proportions. Women are immersed in and responding to the crises of deforestation, desertification, resource decimation, pesticide contamination, and toxic dumping. Against this grim backdrop, women are still (especially as men flee to urban areas looking for work) the procurers and providers of essential resources: wood, water, food, fuel, health care. Women are having to search wider and longer for these resources—walking, hauling, lack of sleep, lack of food, lack of warmth are all part of the woman's day. Unregulated fast-paced industrialization, mounting Third World debt, and a cheapened labor force are the foundation for the international feminization of poverty. From pesticide-soaked fields in Africa to the electronic sweatshops of Korea to urban shanties in Brazil, women and their families are haunted by the spectre that they may not survive.

Women in the Third World form the base of ecological activism. They are more likely than men to be tied to their living environment through a deep knowledge of plants, animals, and local ecology.[17] And yet development agencies almost always bypass the women and give financial support to male leadership. The Women/Environment/Sustainable Development project (of the International Union for the Conservation of Nature and Natural Resources) is working to reverse this trend. Also, WorldWIDE—World Women in Defense of the Environment—supports projects such as the one initiated by Wangari Maathai, head of Kenya's National Council of Women, which involves rural women gathering seeds from indigenous trees and nurturing the emerging "green belts." Maathai notes: "Tropical forests are being destroyed by entrepreneurs, not by poor local women collecting twigs."[18]

CHALLENGING ENVIRONMENTAL POLITICS AND STANDING OUR GROUND

These depictions of the various places we inhabit in the broad social ecology challenge us to think about what we could be doing and what we've already started. I hope some things are clear from these reflections. First, the bleak, sometimes horrific, conditions that oppress us are created not only by the polluters, but also by the architects of policy, science, and health care who at best patch things up with distracting, ineffective, and sometimes dangerous "solutions." Second, we must not, and we must not let others, ghettoize environmental health as a "women's problem"; at best this practice can be patronizingly humane; more often it's misogynist victim-blaming. Third, our sense of ecology must include where people spend most of their waking hours—the workplace. The tacticians of industrial policy who recklessly pollute our rivers, our air, and our food also wage toxic warfare upon the people they employ. Ecologists and occupational health activists are long overdue in finding their common ground. Finally, we must persistently examine emerging health policy and politics for its impact on our health, our individual rights, our community life, and the possibility for a restored and healthy Earth.

I've already discussed the hazards of "fetal protection policies." Relatedly, we need to monitor the various reproductive health projects emerging around the country. The EPA's Reproductive Health Project warrants our attention. The EPA is finally taking reproductive health seriously and plans to include it in future risk assessments. But what is needed is an independent assessment of the risk assessment formula—an examination of how thorough and gender-balanced the research is and an insistence that the participants have access to data about their condition. Arkansas is one of the most advanced states in establishing a Reproductive Hazards Project that examines the link between clusters of birth defects and pollution zones. And the National Institute for Environmental Health Studies has been conducting a long-term evaluation of nine hundred nursing mothers and children to assess the impact of toxics in breast milk.

All such projects merit our attention. But we need to have access to the findings, and women involved as subjects need access to their records. We need to insist upon independent outside evaluations. We need to make sure that we are provided with—and provide each other with—the most practical and respectful implications of the research findings. For example, with breast milk studies, women are often given delayed and confusing advisories. The trauma resulting from such poorly conceived and poorly delivered research leaves some women scarred for an extended time.[19]

Another example of research activities to keep an eye on falls within the category of "toxics gender gap." In *Toxic Susceptibility: Male/Female Differences* (New York: Wiley-Interscience, 1985), Edward Calabrese concludes that women are the comparative toxic weaklings. But, Jeanne Stellman (director, Women's Occupational Health Resource Center) condemns the report for its selective vision:

> The data on sex differences are all over the map: sometimes males are more susceptible, sometimes females. But the author does nothing to synthesize this nor come to a conclusion about its implications. He doesn't address the basic issues of species variability but almost pretends that all males and all females respond alike. There is a distribution of responses within each sex, and usually, the variation within the sex is at least of the same order of magnitude as the variations between the sexes (with some exceptions, of course). This book is a disservice to serious debates about regulation and protection of both men and women from toxic substances.[20]

If women are deemed to be especially vulnerable, we may be offered special protections and restrictions and we may be held specially liable for our conduct and whereabouts in a toxic world. Instead of controlling pollution and polluters, we may be subject to more social control. Biologist Ruth Hubbard, among others, has expressed concern about the evolution of "prenatal torts" whereby pregnant women might be held liable for all fetal injuries. Hubbard quotes an attorney, Margery Shaw, who seems to be saying that a new mother could be punished for hazardous exposure:

> Once a pregnant woman has abandoned her right to abort and has decided to carry her fetus to term, she incurs a "conditional prospective liability" for negligent acts toward her fetus if it should be born alive. These acts could be considered negligent fetal abuse resulting in an injured child. . . . Withholding of necessary prenatal care, improper nutrition, exposure to mutagens and teratogens, or even exposure to the mother's defective intrauterine environment . . . could all result in an injured infant who might claim that his right to be born physically and mentally sound had been invaded.[21]

Obviously, there is much for us to watch, respond to, challenge, and change. Some of these quiet developments in law, science, and industry are not typically under the careful review of those interested in either women's health or ecology. Clearly, our mission is *not* to "restrict the delicate sex" from active life in a complex world, but to change that world. Our mission should be to criticize and challenge the gender politics of environmental research and policies. Our inspiration can be the emerging organizations that are exploring and living out the women-health-ecology connection (see "Resources" below). Our commitment must be to nurture in each other the strength and vision that are so desperately needed if we are to survive and thrive with a sense of being truly at home on this Earth.

RESOURCES

• Akwesasne Environment/Mothers' Milk Project, c/o Katsi Cook, 226 Blackman Hill Road, Berkshire, NY 13736
• Citizens' Clearinghouse for Hazardous Waste, Women and Family Stress Project, P.O. Box 926, Arlington, VA 22216 (703-276-7070)
• COSHs (Coalitions or Committees or Councils on Occupational Safety and Health). These are a network of twenty-five grass-roots educational and advocacy organizations around the United States. COSHs address general occupational health hazards, reproductive hazards, and conditions for women workers, and are increasingly work-

ing with the environmental movement. For a national listing, contact: Alice Hamilton Occupational Health Center, 400 8th Street SW, Washington, DC 20006 (202–457–0540)

• *Daybreak: American Indian World Views.* This is a quarterly publication with focus on ecology, community, survival, women's perspectives: P.O. Box 98, Highland, MD 20777 (301–854–0499)

• National Women's Health Network, 1325 G Street NW, Washington, DC 20005 (202–347–1140): The Committee on Occupational and Environmental Health provides information and advocacy; it is preparing a resource guide.

• Nurses Environmental Health Watch, 655 Avenue of the Americas, New York, NY 10010: They do research and provide education and advocacy; they are also available for consultation and workshops and publish a quarterly newsletter, *Health Watch.*

• Occupational and Environmental Reproductive Hazards Clinic and Education Center, University of Massachusetts Medical Center, 55 Lake Avenue N, Worchester, MA 01655

• *Women and Environments,* Centre for Urban and Community Studies, 455 Spadina Avenue, Toronto, Ontario M5S 2G8, Canada: journal and network directory

• Women-Environment-Sustainable Development. Contact: Irene Dankelman, Netherlands IUCN Committee, Damrak 28–30, 1012 LJ, Amsterdam, Netherlands (020–261732): information exchange and resource guide

• Women's Occupational Health Resource Center, 117 Saint Johns Place, Brooklyn, NY 11217 (718–230–8822): newsletter, fact sheets, clearinghouse

• WorldWIDE, World Women in the Environment, 1250 24th Street NW, Washington, DC 20037 (202–331–9863): newsletter, *Directory of Women in the Environment*

Vandana Shiva

DEVELOPMENT AS A NEW PROJECT OF WESTERN PATRIARCHY

"DEVELOPMENT" WAS TO HAVE BEEN a postcolonial project. It was to have been a choice for accepting a model of progress in which the entire world remade itself following the example of the colonizing modern West without being subjected to the subjugation and exploitation that colonialism entailed. The assumption was that Western-style progress was possible for all. Development thus implied improved well-being of all and was equated with the Westernization of economic categories—of needs, of productivity, of growth. Concepts and categories about economic development and natural resource utilization that had emerged in the specific context of industrialization and capitalist growth in a center of colonial power were raised to the level of universal assumptions and applicability in the entirely different context of the need to satisfy basic needs for the people of the newly independent Third World countries. Yet, as the German socialist Rosa Luxembourg has pointed out, the early industrial development in Western Europe necessitated the permanent occupation of the colonies by the colonial powers and the destruction of the local "natural economy." According to Luxembourg, colonialism is a constant necessary condition for capitalist growth. Without colonies, capital accumulation would grind to a halt.[1] "Development" as capital accumulation and the commercialization of the economy for the generation of "surplus" and profits thus involved the reproduction not merely of a particular form of creation of wealth but also the reproduction of the associated creation of poverty and dispossession. A replication of economic development based on commercialization of resource use for commodity production in the newly independent countries created internal colonies.[2] Development was thus reduced to a continuation of the process of colonialization. It was an extension of modern Western patriarchy's

189

economic vision based on the exploitation or exclusion of women (of the West and non-West), on the exploitation and destruction of nature, and on the exploitation and destruction of other cultures. That is why, throughout the Third World, women, peasants, and tribal peoples are struggling for liberation from development as they earlier struggled for liberation from colonialism.

The U.N. Decade for Women was based on the assumption that the improvement of women's economic position would automatically flow from an expansion and diffusion of the development process. Yet by the end of the decade it was becoming clear that development itself was a problem for Third World women. Insufficient and inadequate "participation" in development was not the cause for women's growing underdevelopment. Their underdevelopment arose from their enforced but asymmetric participation in the process of development in which they bore the costs but were excluded from the benefits. Developmental exclusiveness and dispossession aggravated and deepened the colonial processes of ecological degradation and loss of political control over an area's sustenance base. The only discontinuity was that now it was new national elites, not a colonial power, which masterminded the exploitation on the grounds of "national interest."

Danish development expert Esther Boserup has documented how women's impoverishment increased during colonial rule.[3] Colonial rulers, who had spent a few centuries in subjugating and crippling their own women into deskilled, deintellectualized appendages, limited colonial women's access to land, technology, and employment. The economic and political processes of colonial underdevelopment bore the clear mark of modern Western patriarchy. While large numbers of both women and men were impoverished by these processes, women tended to lose more. The privatization of land for revenue generation displaced women more severely, eroding their traditional land-use rights. The expansion of cash crops undermined food production, and women were often left with meager resources to feed and care for children, the aged, and the infirm when men migrated or were conscripted into forced labor by the colonialists. And the development process has deepened, instead of reversing, the processes of underdevelopment of women under colonialism. As a collective document of women activists, organizers, and researchers observed at the end of the U.N. Decade for Women: "The almost uniform conclusion of the Decade's research is that, with a few exceptions, women's relative access to economic resources, incomes, and employment has worsened, their burdens of work have increased, and their relative and even absolute health, nutritional and educational status has declined."[4]

Development projects have destroyed women's productivity both by removing land, water, and forests from their management and control, as well as by the ecological destruction of soil, water, and vegetation systems so that nature's productivity and renewability have been impaired. While gender subordination and patriarchy are the oldest of oppressions, through development they have taken on new and more violent forms. Patriarchal categories which define destruction as "production" and regeneration of life as "passivity" have generated a crisis of survival. Passivity as an assumed category of the "nature" of nature and women denies the activity of nature and life. Fragmentation and uniformity as assumed categories of progress and development destroy the living forces that arise from relationships within the web of life and the diversity in the elements and patterns of these relationships.

The economic biases against nature, women, and indigenous peoples are captured in this typical analysis of the "unproductiveness" of traditional natural societies: "Production is achieved through human and animal rather than mechanical power. Most agriculture is *unproductive*, human or animal manure may be used but chemical fertilizers and pesticides are unknown. . . . For the masses these conditions mean poverty."[5]

The assumptions are obvious. Nature is unproductive. Organic agriculture based on nature's cycles of renewability is unproductive. Women and tribal and peasant societies embedded in nature are also unproductive. Not because it has been demonstrated that in cooperation they produce fewer goods and services for needs, but because it is assumed that production only takes place when it is mediated by technologies for commodity production, even when such technologies destroy life. A stable and clean river is not a productive resource in this view. It needs to be "developed" with dams to become productive. Women, sharing the river as a commons to satisfy the water needs of their families and society, are thus not involved in productive labor. When they are replaced by man's engineering, water management and water use become productive activities. Natural forests are unproductive according to Western patriarchy. They need to be developed into monoculture plantations of commercial species. Such development becomes equivalent to maldevelopment—development deprived of the feminine, the conserving, the ecological principle. The neglect of nature's work in renewing herself and of women's work in producing sustenance in the form of basic vital needs is an essential part of the paradigm of what I call maldevelopment—which sees all work that does not produce profits and capital as nonwork or unproductive work. As German sociologist Maria Mies has pointed out, this concept of "surplus" has a patriarchal bias because from the point of view of nature and women it is not based on material surplus produced over and above the requirements of the community.[6] It is stolen and appropriated through violent modes from nature (which needs a share of her produce to reproduce herself) and from women (who need a share of nature's produce to produce sustenance and ensure survival).

There is no universal and neutral concept of productivity. Productivity means different things from different perspectives. From the point of view of capitalist patriarchy, productivity is a measure of the production of commodities and profit. From the point of view of Third World women, productivity is a measure of producing life and sustenance. That this latter productivity has been rendered invisible does not reduce its centrality to survival. It merely reflects the domination of modern patriarchal economic categories that see only profits, not life.

MALDEVELOPMENT AS THE DEATH OF THE FEMININE PRINCIPLE

Maldevelopment is a new source of male/female inequality. Anthropologist Alice Schelegel has shown that under conditions of subsistence the interdependence and complementarity of the separate male and female domains of work is the characteristic mode based on diversity, not inequality.[7] This traditional male/female equality in diversity is threatened by the integration of self-provisioning cultures into the maldevelopment model that makes Western technological man the measure of all work. The dominant mode of perception that creates maldevelopment is based on reductionism, duality, and linearity. It cannot understand equality in diversity. It cannot understand how forms and activities can be equally significant and valid even though different. The linear reductionist view superimposes the roles and forms of power of the Western male on women, all non-Western peoples, and even on nature. Based on these Western male-oriented concepts and values, nature, women, and indigenous Third World peoples become "deficient," in need of development. Diversity—and the unity and harmony in diversity—become epistemologically unattainable in this linear reductionist context. Maldevelopment is thus synonomous with women's underdevelopment (increasing sexist domination) and with nature's underdevelopment (deepening ecological crises). Commodities have grown, but nature has shrunk. The poverty crisis of the Third World arises from the increasing scarcity of water, food, fodder, and fuel associated with increasing maldevelopment and its ecological destruction. And this poverty crisis touches women most severely because with nature they are the primary sustainers of society. The Western development model based on the neglect of nature's work and women's work has become a source of this deprivation of basic needs.

Maldevelopment is the violation of the integrity of a living, interconnected world, and it is simultaneously at the root of injustice, exploitation, inequality, and violence. It involves the simultaneous subjugation of nature and women. It arises from limited patriarchal thought and action that regards its self-interest as universal and imposes it on others in total disregard of the needs of other beings in nature and society. Action guided by such myopic and reductionist self-interest violates nature's harmony, no longer allowing it to renew and maintain itself and thus creating the now familiar expressions of ecological instability and crises. Justice, equality, and peace are intimately tied with ecological stability. Recognition of nature's harmony and action to maintain it are preconditions for distributive justice. This is why Gandhi said that "Earth provides enough to satisfy every man's need but not for some people's greed."

Maldevelopment is rooted in identifying a narrow Western patriarchal bourgeois interest as universal, a partial as the whole. Violence arises from imposing this part on a diverse and integrated world. It arises by destroying wholeness in the mind, seeing separation where it should see unity. Woman is alienated from and dominated by man, nature is separated from and exploited by man, and society is torn apart by fragmented thought and action, by projecting duality, divisions, and dichotomies where they do not exist.

In practice, this fragmented, reductionist, dualist perspective gives rise to the violation of the integrity and harmony of people and nature and the violation of the harmony between men and women. It ruptures the cooperative unity of the masculine and feminine, and puts men, deprived of the feminine principle, above and thus separated from nature and women. The violence to nature, as symptomized by the ecological crisis, and the violence to women, as symptomized by women's subjugation and exploitation, arise from this subjugation of the feminine principle.

Maldevelopment is thus development deprived of the creative life force and power of the feminine principle. In maldevelopment, nature and women are viewed as the "other," as the passive nonself. Activity, productivity, and creativity are removed as qualities of nature and women and turned into exclusive qualities of men. Nature and women are transformed into passive objects to be used and exploited.

TWO KINDS OF GROWTH,
TWO KINDS OF PRODUCTIVITY

Maldevelopment is usually called "economic growth" measured by the gross national product (GNP). Jonathan Porritt, a leading ecologist, has this to say about GNP:

> Gross National Product—for once a word is being used correctly: Even conventional economists admit that the heyday of GNP is over, for the simple reason that as a measure of progress, it's more or less useless. GNP measures the lot, all the goods and services produced in the money economy. Many of these goods and services are not beneficial to people, but rather a measure of just how much is going wrong; increased spending on crime, on pollution, on the many human casualties of our society, increased spending because of waste or planned obsolescence, increased spending because of growing bureaucracies: It's all counted.[8]

The problem with GNP is that it measures some costs as benefits (for example, pollution control) and fails to measure other costs completely. Among these hidden costs are the new burdens created through ecological destruction. These costs are invariably heavier for women. (The increased costs involve longer walks for water, fodder, and fuel as the industrialized sector's boundless appetite for nature's resources rapes and destroys the Earth.) It is hardly surprising, therefore, that as GNP rises, it does not necessarily mean that either wealth or welfare is increasing proportionately.

I would argue instead that GNP is becoming increasingly a measure of how real wealth, the wealth of nature and the wealth produced by women for sustaining life through providing for basic needs, is rapidly decreasing. When commodity production as the prime economic activity is introduced as development, it destroys the potential of nature and women to produce life and goods and services for basic needs. More commodities and more cash mean less life—in nature through ecological destruction and in society through denial of basic needs. Women are devalued because of the devaluation of their work that cooperates with nature's processes and because of the devaluation of the output of their work that satisfies needs and ensures sustenance. But precisely because more maldevelopment has meant less sustenance of life, there is a new imperative for the recovery of the feminine principle as the basis for a development that is conserving and ecological.

This involves, first, a recognition that the categories of "productivity" and "growth" that have guided maldevelopment and have been taken to be positive, progressive, and universal are in reality restricted patriarchal categories. When viewed from the point of view of nature's productivity and growth, and the point of view of women's production of sustenance, these categories are seen to be ecologically destructive and a source of gender inequality. The resource and energy intensity of the production processes they give rise to demand ever increasing resource withdrawals from the natural ecosystems. These excessive withdrawals disrupt essential ecological processes and convert renewable resources into nonrenewable ones. For example, a forest provides inexhaustible supplies of diverse biomass over time if its "capital stock" is maintained and it is harvested on a sustained yield basis. The heavy and uncontrolled demand for industrial and commercial wood, however, exceeds the regenerative capacity of the forest ecosystems and over time destroys them. Women's work of collecting water, fodder, and fuel is thus rendered more energy- and time-consuming. Sometimes the damage to nature's intrinsic regenerative capacity is impaired not directly by overexploitation of a particular resource but indirectly by damage caused to other natural resources related through ecological processes. Thus, excessive logging in catchment areas of streams and rivers destroys not only forest resources but also a stable, renewable supply of water. And resource-intensive industries do not merely disrupt essential ecological processes by their excessive demands for raw materials, they also destroy and disrupt vital ecological processes through pollution of vital resources. In spite of a severe ecological crisis the paradigm continues to operate because resources continue to be available, though at the cost of denying them to the vast majority of people and destroying ecological systems. The lack of the due recognition of nature's processes for survival as factors in the process of economic development shrouds the political issues arising from resource transfer and resource destruction.

The ideological and limited Western concept of "productivity" has been universalized with the consequence that all other costs of the economic process have become invisible. These invisible forces come from the increased use of natural resources. Energy specialist Amory Lovins has described this as the amount of "slave" labor at present at work in the world.[9] According to him, each person on Earth, on average, possesses the equivalent of about 50 "slaves," each working a 40-hour week. Our global energy conversion from all sources (wood, fossil fuel, hydroelectric power, nuclear power, and so on) at the present time is approximately 8×10^{12} watts. This is more than twenty times the energy content of the food necessary to feed the present world population at the U. N. Food and Agriculture Organization's standard diet of 3,600 calories a day.

The "productivity" of the Western male compared to women or Third World peasants is not intrinsically superior. It is based on the inequality in the distribution of this "slave" labor. The average inhabitant of the United States, for example, has 250 times more "slaves" than the average Nigerian. If Americans "lost" 249 of these 250 "slaves," how efficient would they be? In the meantime, these resource- and energy-intensive processes of production divert resources away from survival and hence from women. What patriarchy sees as "productive" work is at the ecological level highly destructive. The second law of thermodynamics predicts that resource-intensive and resource-wasteful economic development must become a threat to the survival of the human species in the long run. Political struggles based on ecology in the industrially advanced countries are rooted in the conflict between long-term survival options and short-term overproduction and overconsumption. Political struggles of women, peasants, and tribal peoples based on ecology in countries such as India are far more acute and urgent since they are rooted in the immediate threat to the options for survival of the majority of the people.

In the market economy, the organizing principle for natural resource use is the maximization of profits and capital accumulation. Nature and human needs are managed through market mechanisms. Demands are restricted to those registering on the market. The ideology of development is in large part based on a vision of bringing all natural resources into the market economy for commodity production. When these resources are already being used by nature to maintain her production of renewable resources and by women for sustenance and livelihood, the diversion of resources to the market economy generates ecological instability and creates new forms of poverty for women.

TWO KINDS OF POVERTY

In a book entitled *Poverty: The Wealth of the People,* an African writer draws a distinction between poverty as subsistence and misery as deprivation.[10] It is useful to separate a cultural conception of subsistence living as poverty from the material experience of poverty as a result of dispossession and deprivation. Culturally perceived poverty is not real material poverty. Subsistence economies that satisfy all basic needs through self-provisioning are not poor in the sense of being deprived. Yet the ideology of development declares them poor. In this ideology people are defined as poor because they do not participate overwhelmingly in the market economy and do not consume Western-style commodities produced for and distributed through the market. They are perceived as poor if they eat millet grown by women for self-consumption and not the commercially produced and commercially distributed and processed food sold by global agribusiness. They are seen as poor if they live in self-built housing from natural materials like bamboo and mud instead of cement houses. They are seen as poor if they wear handmade and indigenously designed garments of natural fiber instead of Western clothes made of synthetic fibers. But subsistence does not mean a low physical quality of life. On the contrary, millet is nutritionally far superior to most processed foods. Housing built with local materials is better adapted than cement to the local ecology. Natural fibers and local dressing habits are in tune with local climates. The cultural perception of prudent subsistence as poverty has provided the legitimization for the development process as a poverty-removal project. But, instead, as a culturally biased project, it destroys wholesome and sustainable life-styles and creates real material poverty, or misery. Cash crop production and food processing take land and water resources away from sustenance needs and exclude increasing numbers of people, largely women, from their entitlement to food. "The inexorable processes of agriculture—industrialization and internationalization—are probably responsible for more hungry people than either cruel or unusual whims of nature. There are several reasons why the high-technology–export-crop model increases hunger. Scarce land, credit, water, and technology are pre-empted for the export market. Most hungry people are not affected by the market at all. . . . The profits flow to corporations that have no interest in feeding hungry people without money."[11]

The Ethiopian famine is in part an example of the creation of real poverty by development aimed at removing culturally perceived poverty. The displacement of nomadic Afars from their traditional pasture-land in Awash Valley by foreign commercial agriculture led to their struggle for survival in the fragile uplands, degrading the ecosystem and leading to the starvation of the cattle and the nomads.[12] At no point has the global marketing of agricultural commodities been assessed against the new conditions of scarcity and poverty that it has induced. This new poverty is no longer cultural and relative. It is absolute, threatening the very survival of millions on this planet. And at the root of this new material poverty lies an economic paradigm that cannot see beyond profits and the market. It cannot assess the extent of its appetite for natural resources, and it cannot assess the impact of that appetite on ecological stability and survival.

This economic system was created in the very specific historical and political context of colonialism. Under these specific conditions, the input for which efficiency of use had to be maximized in the production centers of Europe was industrial labor. For the colonial interests it was therefore rational to improve the efficiency of the use of labor even at the cost of the wasteful use of nature's wealth. This limited definition of productivity has, however, been illegitimately universalized to all contexts. Thus, on the plea of increasing productivity, labor-reducing technologies have been introduced even where labor is abundant and cheap, and resource-demanding technologies have been introduced where resources are scarce and already used fully for sustenance production. Traditional economies with stable ecology have shared with industrially advanced affluent economies the ability to use natural resources to satisfy basic vital needs. But the latter differ from the former in two essential ways. First, the same needs are satisfied in industrial societies through longer technological chains requiring higher energy and resource inputs and excluding large numbers of people without purchasing power. Second, these societies generate new and artificial requirements and wants to create a demand for increasing production of industrial goods and services. Traditional economies are not advanced in the context of satisfying nonvital needs. But in the context of satisfying basic and vital needs, they are often more than sufficient. Amazonian tribes have for many thousands of years had their needs more than satisfied by the rich rain forest. Their poverty begins with the destruction of the forest. And the story is the same for the Gonds in Bastar, India, or the Penans of Sarawak, Malaysia.

Economies based on indigenous technologies have been viewed as backward and unproductive because of the distorted concept of patriarchal productivity. The destruction of ecologically sound traditional technologies often created and used by women along with the destruction of their material base through the introduction of resource-demanding and ecologically destructive modern technologies is generally the reason behind the creation of female poverty in societies that have been subjected to bearing the costs of economic growth for other groups, regions, or countries.

The contemporary poverty of the Afar nomad is not rooted in the inadequacy of traditional nomadic life. It is rooted in the diversion of the productive pastureland of the Awash Valley. The erosion of the resource base for survival is increasing because of the demands for resources by the global market economy. This commercial exploitation has no built-in safeguard against the destruction of the processes of renewability of natural resources. The costs of resource destruction are externalized and unequally divided among various economic groups in the society. They are borne largely by women and those who satisfy their basic material needs directly from nature. Ecological degradation worsens the chances for the survival and well-being of such groups. Rural development specialist Gustavo Esteva has called "development" a permanent war waged by its promoters and suffered by its victims,[13] and specialist Claude Alvares calls it the Third World War: "A war waged in peace time, without comparison but involving the largest number of deaths and the largest number of soldiers without uniform."[14]

The paradox and crises of development arise from the mistaken identification of culturally perceived poverty as real material poverty and the mistaken identification of the growth of commodity production as solving basic needs. But the growing ecological crises and the ecological roots of poverty and the threat to survival indicate that this "development" is leading to a shrinking pie for the peoples of the Third World. It is not helping the pie to grow bigger. There is less water, less fertile soil, less genetic wealth as a result of the development process. Since these vital natural resources are the basis of nature's economy and women's survival economy, their scarcity is impoverishing women, marginalized people, and ecosystems in an unprecedented manner. Markets flourish as they perish.

The old assumption that with the development process the availability of goods and services would automatically increase and poverty would decrease is now under serious challenge from women's ecology movements in the Third World even while it continues to guide development-thinking in centers of patriarchal power. Survival is based on the assumption of the sanctity of life. Maldevelopment is based on the assumption of the sacredness of "development." The recovery of the feminine principle would allow a transcendence and transformation of the patriarchal foundations of maldevelopment. It would redefine growth and productivity as categories linked to the production—not the destruction—of life.

The recovery of the feminine principle is thus simultaneously an ecological and a feminist political project that legitimizes the ways of knowing and being that create wealth by enhancing life and diversity and that delegitimizes the knowledge and practice of resource destruction as a basis for capital accumulation.

Irene Diamond

BABIES,
HEROIC EXPERTS, AND
A POISONED EARTH

BABIES, ONCE PRIMARILY dealt with within the world of women, are now the subject of theological proclamations, medical surveillance, and international policy. The possibilities posed by the so-called new reproductive technologies, which divide bodies into readily manipulable parts, have added new elements of commodification and sci-fi fantasy to the historic mysteries of human fertility. Yet, despite all the public and scholarly attention that surrounds the topic of baby-making, what is perhaps most remarkable about this debate is the fragmentary and partial nature of the discussion. Can feminists, in particular those who are concerned about the survival of the planet, add clarity? Can ecofeminism provide a fuller picture of the issues than either feminism or ecology alone?

In the wake of the media drama over surrogate mothers and especially the fate of Baby M, which has framed the challenges in terms of the appropriateness or inappropriateness of contracts, it has become even more difficult to bring the contemporary restructuring of human pro-creation and birth into view. Whether women in patriarchal society can freely choose to enter into contracts to rent their wombs is a very real question. The liberal feminist view, that any questioning of the right to make and be held to contracts demeans women as a class, very conveniently ignores the differences in life opportunities among women. The possibilities for exploitation that are intrinsic to surrogate mother-hood in market societies cannot be denied.[1] Nonetheless, I want to argue that new technologies that assist with the seemingly benign tasks of helping infertile women have babies in their own bodies and of helping all mothers have "normal" babies pose profound threats to the dignity and well-being of human life itself.

The new opportunity of having experts provide information as to what kind of baby (what sex, what physical characteristics) a pregnant women is likely to bear reshapes the experience of pregnancy at the same time that it devalues the lives of the living who may be of the "wrong" sex or chromosomal structure. This focus on the threats that hide within bodies enables us to look away from the threats to life that our culture has created. The biologist Ruth Hubbard, who has been an especially astute analyst of the toll of medical progress, notes, "As the world around us becomes more hazardous and threatens us and our children with social disintegration, pollution, accidents, and above all nuclear war, it seems as though we seek shelter among the hazards that we are told lurk within us."[2] Moreover, the more we focus on the fertility problems of humans and ignore the ways in which humans are poisoning the Earth, the more we move toward a world where the complete and total control of baby-making by heroic experts is considered prudent and wise. Birth on a thoroughly poisoned Earth is likely to be so problematic that the choice of nonintervention will be totally lost. Machine-made babies will be the order of the day.

The scenario I have painted is not a particularly appealing one. One might very well argue that it is beside the point, indeed meaningless, to speculate about what birth would be like when the Earth is fully poisoned. Despite men's dreams of becoming gods, it is most unlikely that women or men would be alive if the Earth were no longer alive. (Considering that most evidence suggests that the Earth can live without us, while we cannot live without its fruits, my hunch is that a poisoned Earth would live on without the "benefit" of one of its species.) My reason for even engaging in such seemingly silly speculations is to bring the issue of new reproductive technologies out of the narrow medical and legal contexts in which it is typically discussed and into an arena where it is possible to see the links between the well-being of babies and the well-being of the Earth.

The push to regulate and monitor, which emerges in varying degrees from the expressed interests of medical researchers, lawyers, doctors, genetic counselors, and client-consumers, typically assumes that the birth of healthy babies is a function of equitably distributed diagnostic medicine. Access to the most advanced clinical techniques is the perceived critical issue. Some ethicists and legal scholars worry about how to settle complicated custody issues. Others concern themselves about appropriate rules to govern the use of laboratory-created human embryos. Within the confines of the debate there are differences of opinion. In discussions of the different procedures that accompany in vitro fertilization, for example, a few commentators, most especially spokespersons for the Catholic church, worry about the sanctity of human life.[3] But, for the most part, the dominant discussion places its faith in the power of professional expertise to alleviate the individual trauma of infertility or the fear of malformed babies. The notion that the health of individual bodies is related to the health of the social body and the ecosystem that sustains all bodies recedes far into the background as heroic experts focus in on the microcomponents of baby-making.

This discussion of reproductive technologies, which grips our imaginations through media portrayals of brave scientists at the frontiers of medicine struggling to help women with their needs, has not gone unchallenged by feminists. Writers such as Gena Corea, Renate Duelli Klein, and Robyn Rowland have characterized the newest stage of reproductive technology as yet another stage in the age-old male supremacist war against women's reproductive powers.[4] As Renate Klein aptly observes, "The new aspect of the new reproductive technologies is that now it is parts of women which are used—and abused—to control the reproduction of the human species. The technodocs have embarked on dissecting and marketing parts of women's bodies: eggs, wombs and embryos. Women are being dismembered."[5] These activists and critics have raised important questions about the invasiveness of in vitro fertilization and medical researchers' apparent lack of concern with the risks and dangers the procedures pose for women's long-term health. They point to the physical and psychological trauma women experience in clinics and the low actual birth rate. Their insistence that men are seeking to appropriate women's reproductive capacities serves to underscore both the masculinist character of scientific "objectivity" and the very real possibility of the complete medicalization and commodification of all phases of human procreation and birth.

The observation that the technodocs' "advances" of the last decade have occurred in the midst of grass-roots feminist efforts to demedicalize and depathologize human birth lends support to the idea that medical advances disguise a male counterattack.[6] The apparent tightening of medical control through the routine use of surveillance mechanisms through all phases of pregnancy, from prenatal genetic screening and ultrasound imagery to fetal monitoring during delivery, as well as the use of in vitro fertilization for a broad range of infertility problems, may indeed demonstrate an element of gender conflict.

Yet this notion of an unmitigated attack on women, which for a

number of feminist critics is signaled by sex-predetermination technologies that could eliminate women as a group before birth, does not
fully capture the microforces that propel the industrialization and
patenting of life. To understand the advance of technologies that appear to give individual women precise knowledge of their efforts to
achieve or maintain healthy pregnancies, we cannot ignore the long-term
historical forces that valorize predictability, control, and scientific evidence. Here we face a central paradox of contemporary feminism that
I can only note. Although recent feminist scholars have profoundly
criticized the presumed objectivity of scientific practice, feminism as
an intellectual and social movement has its roots in the Enlightenment.
That is, the ideals that feminism proclaims are themselves intimately
entwined, indeed indebted, to the modern worldview that the phenomena of society and the natural world are proper objects for the exercise
of human manipulation and control.

It is for this reason that, for many feminists, technologies that promise maximum individual choice and control with respect to the timing
of reproductive decisions and the "products" of pregnancy are seen
and applauded as enhancing women's freedom. For feminists who are
primarily interested in establishing the rights of procreation and child
rearing for individuals who do not fit within traditional definitions of
the family, the crucial issue is access to technological advances: "If
reproductive technology makes it possible for an unmarried person
to have her or his own child, it is discriminatory and socially unwise
to deny that person the right to procreate simply because she or he
may be unable to find a suitable spouse, be unwilling to marry, or object to heterosexual intercourse."[7] That is, in a world where everything
"should" be manipulated to better serve human happiness, rights
become the mechanism for eradicating all barriers to the technologically
feasible. We must also take into account that this vision of individual
freedom and technological modes of (re)production is fully implicated
in the commodity logic of our society. When we consider the economic
growth potential of this new colonization of procreation and birth it
is little wonder that medical experts who help people have the babies
they want are heralded as the harbingers of the new age.

We might imagine that ecologists who have defined the problem
of the contemporary world as one of "overpopulation" might be critical
of the new reproductive technologies. But here again the modern ethic
of control and management, which is intrinsic to managerial ecology
and the emergence of the idea of a "population" to be regulated, make

contemporary prenatal selection technologies especially appealing.[8] Many of today's population control advocates are particularly fond of the use of sex preselection in the Third World as a mechanism to reduce the birth rate. The reasoning is that with the ability to "plan" births through the abortion of female fetuses, couples would no longer "keep trying" to get a highly desired son. In some scenarios the birth of far more boys than girls would reduce the population because there would be fewer women to bear children.[9] However, the appeal of genetic screening as a mechanism of population control is considerably more complicated than the manipulation of sex ratios.

Concern about size of populations has been linked to concern about the quality of populations since the nineteenth century, and in the 1970s this linkage resurfaced with the new focus on the population explosion. The secretary of the American Eugenics Society argued that "American society, if it takes its responsibility to future generations seriously, will have to do more than control the size of its population . . . [it] will have to take steps to insure that individuals yet unborn will have the best genetic and environmental heritage possible."[10] The president of the American Association for the Advancement of Science focused on the rights of children, stating that:

> In a world where each pair must be limited on the average to two offspring and no more, the right that must become paramount is . . . the right of every child to be born with a sound physical and mental constitution, based on a sound genotype. No parents will in that future time have a right to burden society with a malformed or a mentally incompetent child. . . . Every child has the inalienable right to a sound heritage.[11]

In a society of isolated individuals where progress is measured in terms of scientific advance, experts' concern with the health of "populations" readily translates into complex forms of social control.[12] Whereas overt eugenics has usually taken the form of the sterilization of the "feebleminded" and those of "inferior" races, today the notion of the right of a child to be born healthy provides the impetus for monitoring the "correct" behavior of all pregnant women.[13] "Quality" control is maintained through the complexities of normalization. Obstetricians now routinely advise women to take advantage of the best available tests lest the obstetrician be sued in the name of a future child. Maximizing access to prenatal screening is justified to funding bodies as a cost-savings device that will reduce the state's long-term medical costs.[14]

The erosion of social commitment to babies and adults who require special support is particularly troublesome when we note that feminist advocates for persons with disabilities argue that, in many cases, the problem is not the disability but how people are treated because of it. These advocates question the whole medical view of disability as tragedy and ask further what the much heralded ability to conquer disabilities through encouraging women not to bear babies with disabilities means for the value of the lives of persons with disabilities.[15]

If one thing is clear from this discussion it is that there is no sure or easy response to the new "choices" that are posed by reproductive technologies that allow baby-making to be separated from traditional male/female mating and allow us to peer into the mystery of pregnancy. The emerging world of gene therapy, fetal surgery, and nurseries outside the womb holds the promise that medical "bad news" needn't mean the termination, death, or severe disablement of a wanted fetus. Since I first began hearing of them, I have been extremely suspicious of these technologies that seek to eliminate the risks and uncertainties of life. I take seriously the charge that unrestrained manipulation of the apparent components of reproduction moves easily from the lending of a helping hand to the production of human beings to specification. And I am very queasy about how we measure the success of our assorted interventions. The birth of an apparently healthy baby is surely very tangible, but what about the fate of that baby through the course of her life, and what about the fate of the generations as yet unborn? The medical profession's short-term "product" focus takes little account of the long-term consequences of actions that maximize control today. As biochemist Erwon Chargaff warns, "In manipulating processes worked out by nature in the wisdom of millions of years one must be aware of the danger that our shortcuts may carry a bleeding edge."[16]

These are issues that are constantly on my mind. Yet after a new marriage, a miscarriage, and a diagnosis of fibroids, I found that I, too, wanted doctors and machines to provide answers and comfort. When one doctor told me that it could be difficult, that they might have to decide to go in and get the baby out, but I should be encouraged because the local hospital was doing a good job of keeping 6-month-old babies alive, I rebelled. I felt pretty certain that I would never consent to participate in such a scenario, but in discussing the issues with my husband, who was deeply drawn to the possibility of a child, I began to wonder about the difference between saving a fetus and more routine operations for a sick child. After miscarrying again, and becoming pregnant once more, my deep reservations about sonograms faded. I felt I needed to know if this fetus was still alive. I agonized about what to do about amniocentesis, but decided to at least go through the standard counseling process to see what it was all about from the inside. When I explained some of my reservations, that I felt testing was akin to trying to play God, the genetics counselor quickly responded that counseling didn't deal with "morals." I asked why the recommended age for amnio in this city was now 34, and she confessed that she thought it was because of the greater availability of services. Yet she agreed that such availability might not be the best reason to recommend the procedure. I left feeling pretty confident and strong; I had seen how the system operated, and I felt I could resist. Even though I was the "advanced" age of 41 and would have to endure bewildered queries from family and friends, I was going to accept "risks." After all, my mother had given birth to me when she was my age. She didn't know what all this fuss about tests was all about today.

But after I miscarried and became pregnant again, I was 6 months older and found it somewhat more difficult to dismiss the numbers that seemed to be stacked against me. Whereas earlier I had concentrated on the risks of the procedure itself and thought how silly it would be to endanger a pregnancy I had been hoping for for 2 years, now I began to admit to myself that at my age, with two grown children, my desire for a child might not be strong enough to care for one with special needs. I was beginning to struggle with these new thoughts when the doctor asked about amnio. By this time we had our prepared response, but the doctor's fatherly advice about what *his* wife would do, in the midst of my own requestioning, left me emotionally vulnerable and confused. The tests now seemed reassuring if not necessary. Yet how could I live with myself given my condemnations of the system? I finally decided I would go ahead because my criticisms concerned the routinization of screening, not the technology per se.

When the day for my amnio finally arrived I was feeling pretty good physically. I assumed my bouts of morning sickness and just plain sickness had passed because I had gotten past the difficult first trimester. The initial sonogram showed, however, that I was no longer pregnant—the fetus had died. In our initial shock and despair, it was somehow comforting to hear the geneticist tell me and my husband that given the three losses, it would be appropriate to test our genes for a transposed chromosome. If this were the case, my chances of giving birth to a normal baby were low, but even then we shouldn't be discouraged because with proper checking they had gotten other people successfully through pregnancies. On the way home, as I took note of my feelings, I thought, "How could I ever criticize a woman who chose in vitro fertilization?"

When I got home I realized that what the doctor had meant by "checking" was chorionic villi sampling, a diagnostic chromosome procedure similar to amniocentesis that can be done as early as 8 weeks rather than the 15 weeks for amnio. I knew that the test was still considered experimental in some places, but now I realized that if I got pregnant again, I might actually "choose" the less tested procedure to provide what I thought of as protection against another second-trimester miscarriage. I would want to know earlier that the pregnancy was doomed. Yet, I also realized that in a very real sense I had been blessed. What if the fetus had not died and I had had the amnio and been told that the chromosomes were not "normal"? Just that afternoon I had seen two children: a teenager in a wheelchair unable to hold his head up being fed by his mother, and a young boy about 12, who had that angelic look that some Down's syndrome children have, walking along very zestfully with an older brother or friend. Those two images within a half-hour of each other were a vivid reminder that prenatal testing does not tell how severe a child's problems will be. I had been spared from having to make a decision about life with a diagnostic category that did not distinguish between these children.

As the days passed, I became obsessed with trying to determine if our problems were a result of my husband's working in a nuclear submarine plant as a teenager and spending many summers swimming in the bay that adjoined the plant. (The knowledge that a childhood friend of his had given birth to a baby with cancer was additional impetus for concern.) Upon mentioning this concern to the counselor, I received a prompt call from the geneticist who wanted to assure me that there was no relationship between our problems now and whatever radiation exposure my husband may have had as a youth.[17] But when the diagnostic test we were waiting for was completed, there was some initial confusion. My name had been accidentally placed on the vial with my husband's blood sample. Although the test had been negative, because of the mislabeling the lab technicians thought that the sample had been contaminated since they had found male chromosomes in "female" blood. When they discovered what had happened, they offered me a free test. (Since the initial hypothesis was that my husband had a transposed chromosome, only his blood had been sampled, and the test had showed that this was not the case.) It was assumed we would avail ourselves of this opportunity. But, by this time, the healing that comes with the passage of time gave me the strength and perspective to say "No thank you." The information that this seductive system could produce was not likely to produce a baby or the wisdom we needed to cope with the uncertainties we faced.

I began this essay by asking whether ecofeminism could provide some greater clarity on the contemporary restructuring of procreation and birth. My own recent negotiation through the world of baby-making (which did not include clinics and lawyers' offices where alternative conception technologies are pursued) has impressed on me that there are no right or wrong answers for individual women. And I have no illusion that an ecological lens will somehow eliminate the pain of infertility or the anxiety of pregnant mothers for the health of their children. Indeed, the ethics of interconnectedness that I think we need to pursue is very different from the dominant instrumental ethic that assumes that the vulnerabilities of the body can be mastered and conquered.

Whereas this dominant masculinist ethic leads to dissecting human reproduction into ever more micro and more "manageable" parts, with the explicit goal of improving the operation of the perceived components, alternative ethics of interconnectedness would take heed of the intricate webs that link the birth and well-being of all animals—human as well as nonhuman—with the well-being of the Earth's ecosystems.[18] In a fragmented culture that is ambivalent if not fearful of women's bodies, where the language of liberation is wedded to entities with rights, and where dominant images increasingly stress the importance of "one's own child," it is tremendously difficult to comprehend ecosystemic and social webs, even those that are intuitively reasonable. Yet try we must, for the alternatives range from some combination of the poisoning of all life on Earth to more thoroughgoing mechanized control over more and more aspects of life.

Today human infertility is the current scourge of heroic experts. And the technologies of noncoital reproduction that are designed to cure individual infertility have been the focal point of public controversy. The congressional Office of Technology Assessment contends in a major 1988 report on infertility that "the demand for infertility services has increased rapidly in recent years, despite the fact that the actual incidence of infertility has not."[19] The report's emphasis on the more rapid increase in demand reminds us of an important feature of the operation of power in contemporary society—how the construction of new categories of disease shapes the need for new medical technologies.[20] At the same time it is equally important to remember how the medical practice of diagnosing and treating discrete components of human reproduction fractures our awareness of the processes of species regeneration. For example, we're not interested in how today's infertility might be linked with yesterday's desire for the most efficient forms of birth control. Why bother to take responsibility for our bodies when today's technologies promise answers to today's desires. The threat that environmental contamination poses for the entire process of regeneration is simply not an issue in this system of microcontrol.

It has been argued that in an economy built upon a growing trade in toxic materials, drugs, and radiation, babies are the best "canaries" we have—that pregnancy can provide a warning much like the canary did for coal miners.[21] Clusters of infertility, miscarriages, contaminated breast milk, and birth defects can be important signals. But increasing the use of prenatal screening, expanding the use of genetic screening in toxic workplaces, encouraging people to check before marriage about the compatibility of their genes, and making alternative reproduction technologies available can help hide those signals. The advantage of the latter, of course, is that the power of heroic experts is extended, the toxicities of late capitalism persist, and the poisoning of the Earth can continue. Thus, the challenge of transforming our relationships with each other and with the Earth is postponed.

Irene Javors

GODDESS IN THE METROPOLIS: REFLECTIONS ON THE SACRED IN AN URBAN SETTING

I AM SITTING ON THE E TRAIN in New York City en route home. Across from me sits a disheveled man eating a donut and talking to himself. Gesticulating wildly, he breaks off pieces of donut and offers them to the air. He speaks to invisible guests asking them if they would like more tea and cake. Then he offers more pieces of donut to the air. The floor is covered with his offerings of generous hospitality. A woman sitting next to me comments, "What is that man doing, feeding ghosts?"

I laugh, yet behind my laughter is revulsion, irritation, and a desire to bolt. I feel like I am in a dream—a nightmare of bizarre happenings. But from my heart a voice says, "Stay with this, what you are seeing is holy." I respond, "What is so holy about a lunatic feeding donuts to the air waves?" The voice intones, "He is one of the parts of you that you most dread."

By the time I get home, I realize that I am in total confusion about the meaning of what is holy or sacred. I have witnessed something that would seem a profanation of the sacred; yet, a part of me is telling me that, in fact, the donut man is holy.

I ponder this paradox. I pull *Webster's Seventh New Collegiate Dictionary* from my bookshelf and find the following definitions for *holy* and *sacred*. Webster defines the former as coming from the Old English word *hal*—"whole, more at whole" and the latter as coming from the Middle English *sacren*—"to consecrate." Also, Webster offers the Old French *sacrer* as meaning "holy or accursed." Both *holy* and *sacred* are defined as something or someone "set apart for the service or worship of deity."

These definitions give me a great deal to think about. A string of associations fills my thoughts: holy—whole—to make more whole—sacred—consecrate—make holy—blessed, accursed, set apart—and polarities, the "donut man" as sacred *and* profane.

I question my attachment to holiness/sacredness as something, someone beautiful. Up to this point, I have not thought about the idea that holiness includes what we call "ugliness"—the darker side of life. I realize that my thinking is dualistic. I have been viewing life in either/or rather than either/and terms.

Western culture teaches us to think in dualities. We are raised to believe that there is a right and a wrong, a good and a bad, beauty and ugliness. We are taught that it is far better to be right, good, and beautiful. We fear and hate what our society considers to be wrong, bad, and ugly. All of these words reflect a socially constructed shared reality; yet, we use them as if they reflect absolute truth.

From my studies of the *I Ching*, Taoism, and the Goddess, I understand that life is continual process and that all polarities are reconciled within nature. Nature is symbolized by the construct of the triple Goddess. Each of her aspects mirrors the natural cycle of life, death, and rebirth.

In the West, she is Artemis (creatrix), Selene (preserver), Hecate (crone, destroyer). In the East (India), she is Shakti, Karuna, Kali. The Goddess creates, preserves, and destroys worlds. Her dance is change.

The Goddess lives in the city. She is present in all of her manifestations. However, we have great difficulty dealing with her as Hecate/Kali, the destroyer/crone. We fear the "gifts" that she brings us—age, change, deterioration, decay, death. She is an alchemist who finds the seeds for new life within the compost heap of decomposing forms. We fear her and run from her dark side; by so doing, we blind ourselves to her holiness.

Every morning as I leave the subway station at Fourteenth Street and Seventh Avenue in Manhattan, I say, "Good morning," to a beggar who has taken up residence about 15 feet from the entrance. He has all his possessions surrounding him: dirty blankets, shopping bags, used tin cans, newspapers, and a small transistor radio that is forever playing country/western music. He lives in filth and decay.

I watch as people pass by him. All avert their eyes and rush up the stairs to get away. The first time I noticed him, I also rushed by. Now I stop and have a few words with him. He is always very pleasant.

When I see him, I feel very sad. I think this is wrong, he should not live this way.

I cannot accept his life because he reminds me of the precarious nature of all life. He frightens me. He is the embodiment of my worst fears—isolation and ever impending disease and death.

I see this man as a manifestation of Hecate/Kali. He sits on his blanket and silently challenges me to question my life; in doing so, he serves as a catalyst for change. He forces me to face the specter of death on both a physical and ego level.

His material poverty might conceal great spiritual wealth. He teaches that there are two sides to the coin of life; he is both profane and holy, sacred and accursed. Like the "donut man," he forces me to look at myself, my attachments, my polarities, my illusions. He is the sword of Kali that cuts through all deception.

Whenever I chance to walk along Fourteenth Street and Fifth Avenue, I pass by a young, pretty woman who seems to live on this particular corner. She wears layers of clothing and several hats. She talks to herself. She communicates with others only to ask for spare change or a cigarette. She leans against a store wall and waits. From what I can see, her whole life is about waiting.

She engenders various reactions from people. Many times I have heard women comment, "She is so pretty, how did she get this way?" Men come up to her, call her Honey, and make rather lewd remarks. Oblivious to all of this, she just smiles and continues to wait.

She upsets people because she is a pretty beggar. In our culture, this is a contradiction in terms. If you are beautiful you are "supposed" to have all sorts of wonderful things happen to you, especially if you are a woman. Beauty is a key to success—a ticket that gets a woman into the world of male acknowledgement and recognition.

A pretty beggar bothers us. She does not dress for success or race purposefully to a 9-to-5 job in some huge male corporation or collude with society's teaching that she should use her physical beauty to attract men. She is not concerned with "making it" in any way, shape, or form.

She is an aspect of Hecate/Kali. She forces me to look at my assumptions about beauty and ugliness. She asks me to look at how I objectify my body in order to be attractive to men. With the sword of Kali, she cuts through my vanity and demands that I let go of my overattachment to my body. She helps me to transcend the duality of beauty/

ugliness by showing this dichotomy to be illusion. These qualities are two sides of the same coin and cannot be divided: they are a whole unto themselves.

Our society is terrified of death. We do everything imaginable to distract ourselves from our fear of dying. We expend a tremendous amount of energy running away from our own mortality. We are obsessed with control because on some deep level we know that no matter what we do we cannot avoid death.

Hecate/Kali will not let us forget that death is a necessary part of life. In all of her manifestations, the dark Goddess dares us to confront the death of old ways. She reminds us that nothing is permanent and change is inevitable.

The holy ones: the donut man, the subway beggar, and the "pretty woman who waits" confront us daily. They demand that we "wake up" and see life and death dance their exquisite *pas de deux*. The Goddess jolts our senses and prods us to give up our self-absorption. She destroys all the weapons we use to fight change and death. There is no security. There are no insurance policies against mortality.

In urban centers, Hecate/Kali teaches us that we heal ourselves and become whole when we reunite with the cycles of nature. She shows us that what we most fear in external reality—isolation, poverty, disease, loss of control, ugliness, death—are but the shadows and demons of those aspects of our inner worlds that are ruled by ego.

In spiritual terms, ego is defined as that which separates us from being, nature, the Goddess. Aspects of the ego are fear, the need to control and dominate, vanity, insecurity, dualistic thinking, excessive materialism, and a pathological need to be beyond the laws of nature.

Hecate/Kali destroys the ego. In so doing, she opens us up to our true being—our spiritual essence. She wants us to become one with her, with nature. She teaches us that we heal ourselves when we accept and reunite with the cycles of the natural world.

The city is nature. The people are holy. The land is sacred. In so loving the world, the Goddess in the metropolis dances amidst the concrete and garbage, embracing us all.

Cynthia Hamilton

WOMEN, HOME, AND COMMUNITY: THE STRUGGLE IN AN URBAN ENVIRONMENT

IN 1956, WOMEN IN SOUTH AFRICA began an organized protest against the pass laws. As they stood in front of the office of the prime minister, they began a new freedom song with the refrain "now you have touched the women, you have struck a rock." This refrain provides a description of the personal commitment and intensity women bring to social change. Women's actions have been characterized as "spontaneous and dramatic," women in action portrayed as "intractable and uncompromising."[1] Society has summarily dismissed these as negative attributes. When in 1986 the City Council of Los Angeles decided that a 13-acre incinerator called LANCER (for Los Angeles City Energy Recovery Project), burning 2,000 tons a day of municipal waste, should be built in a poor residential, Black, and Hispanic community, the women there said "No." Officials had indeed dislodged a boulder of opposition. According to Charlotte Bullock, one of the protestors, "I noticed when we first started fighting the issue how the men would laugh at the women . . . they would say, 'Don't pay no attention to them, that's only one or two women . . . they won't make a difference.' But now since we've been fighting for about a year the smiles have gone."[2]

Minority communities shoulder a disproportionately high share of the by-products of industrial development: waste, abandoned factories and warehouses, leftover chemicals and debris. These communities are also asked to house the waste and pollution no longer acceptable in White communities, such as hazardous landfills or dump sites. In 1987, the Commission for Racial Justice of the United Church of Christ published *Toxic Wastes and Race*. The commission concluded that race is a major factor related to the presence of hazardous wastes in residential communities throughout the United States. Three out of every five Black and Hispanic Americans live in communities with uncontrolled toxic sites; 75 percent of the residents in rural areas in the Southwest, mainly Hispanics, are drinking pesticide-contaminated water; more than 2 million tons of uranium tailings are dumped on Native-American reservations each year, resulting in Navajo teenagers having seventeen times the national average of organ cancers; more than 700,000 inner city children, 50 percent of them Black, are said to be suffering from lead poisoning, resulting in learning disorders. Working-class minority women are therefore motivated to organize around very pragmatic environmental issues, rather than those associated with more middle-class organizations. According to Charlotte Bullock, "I did not come to the fight against environmental problems as an intellectual but rather as a concerned mother. . . . People say, 'But you're not a scientist, how do you know it's not safe?' I have common sense. I know if dioxin and mercury are going to come out of an incinerator stack, somebody's going to be affected."

When Concerned Citizens of South Central Los Angeles came together in 1986 to oppose the solid waste incinerator planned for the community, no one thought much about environmentalism or feminism. These were just words in a community with a 78 percent unemployment rate, an average income ($8,158) less than half that of the general Los Angeles population, and a residential density more than twice that of the whole city. In the first stages of organization, what motivated and directed individual actions was the need to protect home and children; for the group this individual orientation emerged as a community-centered battle. What was left in this deteriorating district on the periphery of the central business and commercial district had to be defended—a "garbage dump" was the final insult after years of neglect, watching downtown flourish while residents were prevented from borrowing enough to even build a new roof.

The organization was never gender restricted but it became apparent after a while that women were the majority. The particular kind of organization the group assumed, the actions engaged in, even the content of what was said, were all a product not only of the issue itself, the waste incinerator, but also a function of the particular nature of women's oppression and what happens as the process of consciousness begins.

Women often play a primary part in community action because it is about things they know best. Minority women in several urban areas have found themselves part of a new radical core as the new wave of environmental action, precipitated by the irrationalities of capital-intensive growth, has catapulted them forward. These individuals are responding not to "nature" in the abstract but to the threat to their homes and to the health of their children. Robin Cannon, another activist in the fight against the Los Angeles incinerator, says, "I have asthma, my children have asthma, my brothers and sisters have asthma, there are a lot of health problems that people living around an incinerator might be subjected to and I said, 'They can't do this to me and my family.'"

Women are more likely than men to take on these issues precisely because the home has been defined and prescribed as a woman's domain. According to British sociologist Cynthia Cockburn, "In a housing situation that is a health hazard, the woman is more likely to act than the man because she lives there all day and because she is impelled by fear for her children. Community action of this kind is a significant phase of class struggle, but it is also an element of women's liberation."[3]

This phenomenon was most apparent in the battle over the Los Angeles incinerator. Women who had had no history of organizing responded as protectors of their children. Many were single parents, others were older women who had raised families. While the experts were convinced that their smug dismissal of the validity of the health concerns these women raised would send them away, their smugness only reenforced the women's determination. According to Charlotte Bullock:

> People's jobs were threatened, ministers were threatened . . . but I said, "I'm not going to be intimidated." My child's health comes first, . . . that's more important than my job.
>
> In the 1950s the city banned small incinerators in the yard and yet they want to build a big incinerator . . . the Council is going to build something in my community which might kill my child. . . . I don't need a scientist to tell me that's wrong.

None of the officials were prepared for the intensity of concern or the consistency of agitation. In fact, the consultants they hired had concluded that these women did not fit the prototype of opposition. The consultants had concluded:

Certain types of people are likely to participate in politics, either by virtue of their issue awareness or their financial resources, or both. Members of middle or higher socioeconomic strata (a composite index of level of education, occupational prestige, and income) are more likely to organize into effective groups to express their political interests and views. All socioeconomic groupings tend to resent the nearby siting of major facilities, but the middle and upper socioeconomic strata possess better resources to effectuate their opposition. Middle and higher socioeconomic strata neighborhoods should not fall at least within the one mile and five mile radii of the proposed site.

. . . although environmental concerns cut across all subgroups, people with a college education, young or middle aged, and liberal in philosophy are most likely to organize opposition to the siting of a major facility. Older people, with a high school education or less, and those who adhere to a free market orientation are least likely to oppose a facility.[4]

The organizers against the incinerator in South Central Los Angeles are the antithesis of the prototype: they are high school educated or less, above middle age and young, nonprofessionals and unemployed and low-income, without previous political experience. The consultants and politicians thus found it easy to believe that opposition from this group could not be serious.

The intransigence of the City Council intensified the agitation, and the women became less willing to compromise as time passed. Each passing month gave them greater strength, knowledge, and perseverance The council and its consultants had a more formidable enemy than they had expected, and in the end they have had to compromise. The politicians have backed away from their previous embrace of incineration as a solution to the trash crisis, and they have backed away from this particular site in a poor, Black and Hispanic, residential area. While the issues are far from resolved, it is important that the willingness to compromise has become the official position of the city as a result of the determination of "a few women."

The women in South Central Los Angeles were not alone in their battle. They were joined by women from across the city, White, middle-class, and professional women. As Robin Cannon puts it, "I didn't know we all had so many things in common . . . millions of people in the city had something in common with us—the environment." These two groups of women, together, have created something previously unknown in Los Angeles—unity of purpose across neighborhood and racial lines. According to Charlotte Bullock, "We are making a difference . . . when we come together as a whole and stick with it, we can win because we are right."

This unity has been accomplished by informality, respect, tolerance of spontaneity, and decentralization. All of the activities that we have been told destroy organizations have instead worked to sustain this movement. For example, for a year and a half the group functioned without a formal leadership structure. The unconscious acceptance of equality and democratic process resulted practically in rotating the chair's position at meetings. Newspeople were disoriented when they asked for the spokesperson and the group responded that everyone could speak for the neighborhood.

It may be the case that women, unlike men, are less conditioned to see the value of small advances.[5] These women were all guided by their vision of the possible: that it *was* possible to completely stop the construction of the incinerator, that it is possible in a city like Los Angeles to have reasonable growth, that it is possible to humanize community structures and services. As Robin Cannon says, "My neighbors said, 'You can't fight City Hall . . . and besides, you work there.' I told them I would fight anyway."

None of these women was convinced by the consultants and their traditional justifications for capital-intensive growth: that it increases property values by intensifying land use, that it draws new businesses and investment to the area, that it removes blight and deterioration—and the key argument used to persuade the working class—that growth creates jobs. Again, to quote Robin Cannon, "They're not bringing real development to our community. . . . They're going to bring this incinerator to us, and then say 'We're going to *give* you fifty jobs when you get this plant.' Meanwhile they're going to shut down another factory [in Riverside] and eliminate two hundred jobs to buy more pollution rights . . . . They may close more shops."

Ironically, the consultants' advice backfired. They had suggested that emphasizing employment and a gift to the community (of $2 million for a community development fund for park improvement) would persuade the opponents. But promises of heated swimming pools, air-conditioned basketball courts and fifty jobs at the facility were more insulting than encouraging. Similarly, at a public hearing, an expert witness' assurance that health risks associated with dioxin exposure were less than those associated with "eating peanut butter" unleashed a flurry of derision.

The experts' insistence on referring to congenital deformities and cancers as "acceptable risks" cut to the hearts of women who rose to speak of a child's asthma, or a parent's influenza, or the high rate of cancer, heart disease, and pneumonia in this poverty-stricken community. The callous disregard of human concerns brought the women closer together. They came to rely on each other as they were subjected to the sarcastic rebuffs of men who referred to their concerns as "irrational, uninformed, and disruptive." The contempt of the male experts was directed at professionals and the unemployed, at Whites and Blacks—all the women were castigated as irrational and uncompromising. As a result, new levels of consciousness were sparked in these women.

The reactions of the men backing the incinerator provided a very serious learning experience for the women, both professionals and non-professionals, who came to the movement without a critique of patriarchy. They developed their critique in practice. In confronting the need for equality, these women forced the men to a new level of recognition—that working-class women's concerns cannot be simply dismissed.

Individual transformations accompanied the group process. As the struggle against the incinerator proceeded to take on some elements of class struggle, individual consciousness matured and developed. Women began to recognize something of their own oppression as women. This led to new forms of action not only against institutions but to the transformation of social relations in the home as well. As Robin Cannon explains:

> My husband didn't take me seriously at first either. . . . He just saw a whole lot of women meeting and assumed we wouldn't get anything done. . . . I had to split my time . . . I'm the one who usually comes home from work, cooks, helps the kids with their homework, then I watch a little TV and go to bed to get ready for the next morning. Now I would rush home, cook, read my materials on LANCER . . . now the kids were on their own . . . I had my own homework. . . . My husband still wasn't taking me seriously. . . . After about 6 months everyone finally took me seriously. My husband had to learn to allocate more time for baby sitting. Now on Saturdays, if they went to the show or to the park, I couldn't attend . . . in the evening there were hearings . . . I was using my vacation time to go to hearings during the workday.

As parents, particularly single parents, time in the home was strained for these women. Children and husbands complained that meetings and public hearings had taken priority over the family and relations in the home. According to Charlotte Bullock, "My children understand, but then they don't want to understand. . . . They say, 'You're not spending time with me.'" Ironically, it was the concern for family, their love of their families, that had catapulted these women into action to begin with. But, in a pragmatic sense, the home did have to come second in order for health and safety to be preserved. These were hard learning experiences. But meetings in individual homes ultimately involved children and spouses alike—everyone worked and everyone listened. The transformation of relations continued as women spoke up at hearings and demonstrations and husbands transported children, made signs, and looked on with pride and support at public forums.

The critical perspective of women in the battle against LANCER went far beyond what the women themselves had intended. For these women, the political issues were personal and in that sense they became feminist issues. These women, in the end, were fighting for what they felt was "right" rather than what men argued might be reasonable. The coincidence of the principles of feminism and ecology that Carolyn Merchant explains in *The Death of Nature* (San Francisco: Harper & Row, 1981) found expression and developed in the consciousness of these women: the concern for Earth as a home, the recognition that all parts of a system have equal value, the acknowledgment of process, and, finally, that capitalist growth has social costs. As Robin Cannon says, "This fight has really turned me around, things are intertwined in ways I hadn't realized. . . . All these social issues as well as political and economic issues are really intertwined. Before, I was concerned only about health and then I began to get into the politics, decision making, and so many things."

In 2 years, what started as the outrage of a small group of mothers has transformed the political climate of a major metropolitan area. What these women have aimed for is a greater level of democracy, a greater level of involvement, not only in their organization but in the development process of the city generally. They have demanded accountability regarding land use and ownership, very subversive concerns in a capitalist society. In their organizing, the group process, collectivism, was of primary importance. It allowed the women to see their own power and potential and therefore allowed them to consolidate effective opposition. The movement underscored the role of principles. In fact, we citizens have lived so long with an unquestioning acceptance of profit and expediency that sometimes we forget that our objective is to do "what's right." Women are beginning to raise moral concerns in a very forthright manner, emphasizing that experts have left us no other choice but to follow our own moral convictions rather than accept neutrality and capitulate in the face of crisis.

The environmental crisis will escalate in this decade and women are sure to play pivotal roles in the struggle to save our planet. If women are able to sustain for longer periods some of the qualities and behavioral forms they have displayed in crisis situations (such as direct participatory democracy and the critique of patriarchal bureaucracy), they may be able to reintroduce equality and democracy into progressive action. They may also reintroduce the value of being moved by principle and morality. Pragmatism has come to dominate all forms of political behavior and the results have often been disastrous. If women resist the "normal" organizational thrust to barter, bargain, and fragment ideas and issues, they may help set new standards for action in the new environmental movement.

Julia Scofield Russell

THE EVOLUTION
OF AN
ECOFEMINIST

Breathe. Feel the air enter your lungs. Breathe. Feel millions of oxygen atoms permeating your lung membranes, entering your bloodstream, being delivered to every cell in your body, fueling the fire of life within you. Mother is feeding you. She feeds you and sustains your life with every breath.

Let your consciousness move now down to your feet. Keep going down through the floor, to the ground. Penetrate the ground with your consciousness as though you were growing roots into the Earth. Deeper and deeper. Sense her massiveness. Her ever-abidingness.

Feel her hold you to her. Gravity is her embrace. Feel her love. Allow her love to flow into you, up through the soles of your feet, through your legs and torso to your heart, your shoulders, your head. Bathe in her love. Breathe.

Let her love permeate every cell. Let your heart fill with her love. Let it swell with love, from her, for her.

She nurtures you in every way.

The air you breathe is her.

The food you eat is her.

Let your love and gratitude grow. Let it flow out to her, to Father Sun, and to all your brothers and sisters of the plant and animal kingdom.

We are all mother's children, beloved by her, nurtured and protected from the harsh reality of outer space.

I THINK, PERHAPS, THE SINGLE most important fact to be known by every person on the planet is that the Earth is a living being. This is ancient wisdom. Lost and now refound. James Lovelock learned it by comparing the Earth's atmosphere to that of other planets in his book, *Gaia: A New View of Life on Earth* (New York: Oxford University Press, 1979). But it can be learned in many ways.

I learned it from a compost pile, in an initiation whose beginnings were humble indeed. I constructed three bottomless boxes, 18 inches square and about 6 inches high, according to instructions I came across in *Woman's Day*. I placed the boxes on top of one another, covered them with a piece of plywood and began disposing of my table scraps in there. Occasionally, I would add a handful of dirt.

After about 6 weeks the pile almost filled the boxes. It was time to turn it. I took the box off the top and placed it on the ground next to the others. Then I dug in with my hand spade to transfer the top layers into the box I had just removed. I was assailed by a revolting stench of vomit! I was horrified. As I proceeded down further the odor began to change, but not for the better! It smelled intensely like human feces!

What was going on? *Woman's Day* had said nothing about this! I switched the second box to the new site. Ugh! Now it began to smell like dog or cat feces. Not much better than human, but I kept on and soon began to perceive a barnyard scent. Having spent some years as a girl in dairy country, this smell of horse and cow manure I recognized at least as something more earthy, less a putrefying waste. The farmers had used manure to fertilize their fields.

Now I was down to the bottom box. I lifted it and placed it on top of the other two. My next spadeful revealed something amazing! I didn't quite know what at first. It was dark, dark brown and somewhat chunky. I gingerly leaned forward for a whiff. It smelled—clean! I took a piece of it in my hand. It was crumbly. I smelled it again. It smelled like the ground after a spring rain! No doubt about it. It was soil! Fresh, rich, clean soil.

As I crouched there with this fragrant new soil in my hand, my mind boggled and the knowledge came through loud and clear: The Earth turns everything given to it into itself, just as my body does and all living bodies do. The Earth is a living being!

I know now that the ghastly odors I encountered as I turned the pile were due to the lack of air circulation. Lack of oxygen causes anaerobic digestion, which is characterized by foul odor. An aerated pile does not smell bad.

However, it was that progression of smells from vomit through feces to soil that enabled me to recognize that it was a process of digestion that was taking place, and it was this recognition that was the great learning for me. Needless to say, this learning has changed and continues to change my life, as I think it must anyone's life, who learns it. Sometimes it is very painful, as when I see the abuses being heaped upon the Earth's body: toxic wastes, ozone depletion, species extinction, desertification, smog, acid rain, famine, forest death, poverty, cancer, genocide, dead rivers and lakes, nuclear contamination.

Many of our cities are, by now, actually uninhabitable, though we continue to live in them, wondering why we are miserable, sick, furious, frightened. But moving out of the cities is no escape. Toxic waste will find you wherever you are. It will bubble up in your backyard, seep into your drinking water, or waft on a summer breeze into your bedroom and nursery.

"Progress" is mindlessly polluting our air, sea, soil, minds, souls, and bodies. The mad absurdity of the entire socioeconomic/cultural structure is evident. Ecofeminists have realized that we must question the entire civilization that mankind has contrived—all of its values, its goals, its achievements. It is not merely antifeminine, it is antihuman, antilife.

We have discovered that we cannot ignore the larger sickness to rail against isolated symptoms for we then betray ourselves and the world. To succeed merely in the limited objectives of social equality is to succeed in locking ourselves more tightly into a system that is fatal to us all.

It is true that our civilization has been robbed of the healthy balance of masculine and feminine influence necessary for survival. We women must manifest our half of the whole. But not a tacked-on half. Our course is to permeate the whole, changing it all.

As victim consciousness fades, we are discovering that which we uniquely have to give as women, female human beings, aware children of our Mother Earth, loving kin to all our relatives in this biosphere. It's becoming clear to us that women's liberation cannot be separate from the liberation of all—men, women, children, old, middle aged, Black, White, Yellow, Red, and mixed, rich and poor, animals, plants, and Mother Earth herself—from the tyranny of the conqueror society that now dominates the world. Whether it calls itself capitalistic, communistic, socialist, democratic, republican, multinational, or whatever is incidental to the primary characteristic they all share—the drive to conquest, the exploitation of women, nature, and each other.

How do we move from a conqueror society to a nurturer society? First, we should recognize that the process is already well under way. We're facilitating meetings instead of running them, we're mediating disagreements instead of litigating them. We can and have introduced a new style of management into business that acknowledges the whole individual. We're spearheading social responsibility in investment and economics as though people and the Earth mattered. The Green movement is growing, worldwide. Citizen diplomacy is creating person-to-person peace. The patriarchal psychology of Freud is being superseded by a more nurturing and wholistic view of the human personality. The illusion of pure objectivity is disappearing with the emerging reality of quantum physics. Health care is becoming care of the whole person rather than symptom suppression.

We can and do write books, hold conferences, join groups, go to meetings, vote, sponsor legislation, lobby our representatives, participate in campaigns, and run for office ourselves. Perhaps we demonstrate and commit civil disobedience. All this is important and effective and needs to be done.

Yet there is still another level of empowerment, commitment, and opportunity that is often overlooked when we discuss social change and that is the essential role our individual life-styles, our everyday choices and behavior, play in maintaining the status quo or effecting change. I call it the politics of life-style and I think it is a distinctly feminine politics in that it is both inner and universal, personal and all-inclusive. It is based on the understanding that lasting societal transformation begins with and rests on transformation of the individual.

It may be hard at first to see how our life-styles are political. So I should begin by explaining what I mean by politics. I define the word in a broader sense than is usual. Economist Hazel Henderson defines the politics to which I'm referring in *The Politics of the Solar Age.* She says:

> I am talking about all the newer "politics by other means," the more fundamental politics of: redefining issues and reshaping questions; restating old "problems"; re-visioning alternative futures, alternative lifestyles; reweaving the split between work and leisure, the "public" and "private" sectors, money and wealth, "success" and well-being, psychic riches and deeper human satisfaction. I am talking about the new "issue politics," which is supplanting geographical politics, not in its narrow, vengeful form but in the broader issues: the politics of planetary awareness and ecological understanding, and the new demands growing out of it: global laws concerning equitable resource use, new conflict-resolution mechanisms, universal human rights, freedom of information and media access, a new international economic order, and a global framework of accountability for multinational corporate enterprises and the impacts of science and technologies.[1]

What is the justification for such a wholistic definition of politics?

It is generally thought that we may choose to become politically involved and take part in the political process at special times, in special places, but that it is something that normally takes place elsewhere and involves other people, the famous "they" and "them." It is politicians, we think, who choose to live and work in the so-called political arena full time. There are the parties and the platforms, the elections and the coups, all of them seen as sometimes affecting us but separate from us, from our daily lives.

But are they? Is the body separate from the head? Are the fingers separate from the hand? In a certain way, yes. But in a more important way, no. They are all parts of one body. All the parts are affected by the actions and general health of all the other parts, and all those parts and their interrelationships make up the whole body. A finger with nerves that don't send or receive messages is severely handicapped, as is a hand with missing or paralyzed fingers. And the body as a whole is handicapped by any damaged or unhealthy limb or organ.

We're all part of a body politic, presently in the form of a nation, and that body politic derives its character, its health, its effectiveness, its very existence from us. We are its lifeblood, its nerves, its brain. *It will not function without our continual cooperation.* For instance, its present economic structure depends on our agreement to use Federal Reserve banknotes as the measure of exchange between us and to consume certain things at a certain rate and hundreds and thousands of other actions and nonactions that support the status quo.

At the same time, a body, a nation, exists in a larger context in which it functions as a part. The nation exists in the context of all nations that make up the whole political body of humanity. And all of humanity exists in a biosphere that is the body of the whole Earth. We exist as part of a seamless whole in which everything is connected to everything else. Seen in this context, I think, it is evident that the movies we choose to see, the food we eat, what we throw away and where, our relationships, our means of livelihood—everything—has effects that emanate out from our personal lives into our society and ultimately the whole living planet.

If we go to meetings and stage demonstrations protesting industrial pollution or unfair employment practices and then get in our car and stop off on our way home to buy the products manufactured by those same companies, we may be doing more to perpetuate the problems than alleviate them. When we consume goods and services without regard for their environmental and social costs, we are supporting technologies and policies that are laying waste to our world. If we resort, or accede, to domination and exploitation in our personal and business lives, we are practicing modes of behavior that are bringing us to the brink of disaster on an international scale. Do we protest government spending on nuclear weaponry, yet continue to fund it through our taxes?

Not that we should stop protesting, but we also need to start changing *ourselves*. Healing the planet begins with us, in our daily lives.

There has been something in me that has always striven for integration and suffered from the fragmentation and compartmentalizing that is the normal life-style of today. But it wasn't until my thirties that I began to encounter writings by others who found today's demands and deprivations onerous and stressful. Rachel Carson[2] documented the havoc our way of life was wreaking on our natural environment, and before I knew it almost everything I picked up was confirming my long, albeit secretly held, objections to the typical middle-class U.S. life-style—its goals, its values, its products and by-products, its technologies, and on and on down the list.

As my ecological consciousness grew, I perceived that our species was behaving as a cancer on the Earth. Through unlimited and un-differentiated growth, we are infecting and spreading our toxic wastes throughout the world. But I also saw that I had the choice to live as a healthy cell, joining with other healthy cells, to function as part of the Earth's immune system. This was the genesis of Eco-Home, a demonstration home in Los Angeles for ecological living in the city. Our focus is on reducing the toxicity our habit of clumping together has on our environment by bringing an ecologically sensitive consciousness to our everyday lives.

At Eco-Home we reduce and recycle our wastes, we conserve energy and water, and we support decentralized, nonpolluting, renewable resource energy production. We have climate-appropriate and organic food gardens, and we're developing a demonstration home to model all these systems and more. We support local organic food growers through an organic farmers' market. We support the development of a local exchange trading system and help each other find or create right livelihood. We make socially responsible investments and, in cooperation with the Co-op Resources and Services Project (CRSP), we have our own revolving loan fund that will provide capital for ecologically sound businesses. Also in cooperation with CRSP, we're sponsoring the creation of an ecologically integrated community here in Los Angeles. In general, then, we work to promulgate a view of reality that recognizes the interrelatedness of all phenomena.

We take our role as consumers seriously and fulfill it thoughtfully. We understand that when we purchase a product we are supporting the entire system that produced it. We are also responsible for its effect on us and our world while we own it and even after we no longer want or need it. What is its effect then? Does it trash up our landscape? Does it pollute the water or the air or the soil? Or is it recyclable, reusable. Does it conform to the law of the circle—the fact that the Earth's natural life-support systems are circular. There is no "out." Everything is in the system, and everything we put into the system comes back to us, for good or for ill. If the product can be reused or recycled, it is life supporting. If it can't be, it follows the law of entropy, increases chaos, and is antilife. We try to support life in everything we do and to withhold our support from products and processes that degrade life in any way.

We withdraw support from companies and/or practices that are socially and ecologically damaging. We support those that are ecologically sound and ethical. If there aren't any, we start our own with our friends. When confronted with blockage or even sabotage in personal or business life, we recognize it as an opportunity to practice win/win conflict resolution instead of resorting to legal, physical, or even psychological revenge. We bring our lives into harmony with the natural cycles and systems that sustain life.

As we transform ourselves, we transform our world. Not later. Now. Simultaneously. How can this be so? The practice of the politics of lifestyle springs from an understanding of how things actually happen rather than the linear, cause-and-effect model. As we align ourselves with the regenerative powers of the Earth and the evolutionary thrust of our species, we tap abilities beyond the ordinary. We move into the Tao.

How do you initiate this process in your life? You can start just about anywhere. You can start with recycling, with your means of transportation, with your diet and food-buying practices, with composting, with your relationships, with meditation, tax resistance, right livelihood, housing, gardening, conservation—it's up to you. What seems easiest, most obvious, or most urgent to you? Start there.

Most important: start becoming aware of yourself as an integral part of the body of humanity, and the body of humanity as a child of Mother Earth, still cradled in her womb with all our brothers and sisters of the plant and animal kingdoms. Doing the meditation that opens this essay every day will help to build your conscious bonding with her. A new sense of security will subtly alter your consciousness. As your awareness grows, so will your actions be informed by greater sensitivity to the impact you're having on all around you. Mothering Earth in your everyday life will become a personal imperative.

And so we move, from a conqueror society to a nurturer society.

Rachel L. Bagby

DAUGHTERS OF GROWING THINGS

I am a farmer's daughter
daughter
of daughter
of daughter

of women
who
knew
what to plant
during which growing moon

I am a grandchild
of harpist

music
of growing things

RACHEL L. BAGBY,
"Bringings Up and Comings Round"

THIS ESSAY TELLS OF AN ONGOING EFFORT to maintain mutually nuturing relationships with nature, human and elemental, in the midst of a low- and no-income urban village community of about 5,000 people. *Webster's New World Dictionary* reserves the use of the word *village* for certain types of living units located in the country. Yet, despite its location within the city of Philadelphia, the area on which this essay focuses meets every other qualification listed under "village community" in that it is comprised of a group of houses, is larger than a hamlet, functions as a self-governing political unit, and has several half-acre plots that are worked by the community.

Philadelphia Community Rehabilitation Corporation (PCRC) is the

231

institution through which this work is accomplished. Momma—Rachel Edna Samiella Rebecca Jones Bagby—is the woman who founded it PCRC's operating budget is financed from the $4,000 in rents collected each month, a yearly bazaar (complete with prizes for the best sweet potato pie), and a seemingly infinite number of chicken dinners, plant sales, and bus trips to Atlantic City. It employs a regular staff of three to five and numerous independent contractors. Every summer a handful of teenagers get their first work experience there. It's "repeopling" program has renovated and rented more than fifty formerly vacant homes and created a twelve-unit shared-house.

And then there are the gardens, the focus of this essay.

The material was culled from more than forty cassette recordings of phone conversations between me and Momma—between Northern California and North Philadelphia, Pa.—over the past 3 years. It is essential to have Momma tell her stories in her own, inimitable voice. While the interview format comes close, we are still working on a hybrid form of prose and musical notation that will do the rhythms and melodies of her speech justice. What may seem to be misspellings and grammatical errors are intentional, ways of honoring Momma's voice. Much of her power in the community comes from her *way* with people. Much of that way is communicated in her manner of speaking.

DAUGHTER: How much land do you have?
MOTHER: I think it's about 5 acres. I imagine if you measured it, it would be about 5 acres. All the different lots we have.
DAUGHTER: And how do you choose your lots for the gardens?
MOTHER: We didn't choose the lots. We just got the lot that we could get. These were empty lots, in other words. Rather than to grow weeds, we just begged the city to let us have them. And we paid for some of them, too. [At a cost of about $500 per half acre.] Some of them are really ours; we own.
DAUGHTER: So these were empty lots?
MOTHER: They were all empty lots, yes, and we just got them, we asked for them in order to make the place look better than growing a whole lot of weeds. We just grow something that's more useful—food and flowers. Make it beautiful. And the food is outta sight. Rather than to grow weeds. Why sit and grow weeds when you can do something with it? So this is what we did, and it's working, and it's spreading. We have a meeting now every month.

DAUGHTER: We'll come back to the meetings. First tell me how much food you get from the garden.

MOTHER: Out of that garden? We made more tomatoes than we could use and still have tomatoes coming out of our ears. Green peppers, too. And we still have them.

DAUGHTER: So what did you do? Can them?

MOTHER: Yeah, we canned them. And the tomatoes are canned. Remember I told you? Tomatoes are canned, the peppers are canned, and I have a lot of the greens canned. Vegetables we don't buy. Peas we dried. We still got dried peas. California black eyes. And it yields a lot because, see, what you do is as fast as one crop get through, you plant another one until the frost falls. In the winter, we can't plant; before then we plant winter greens. We plant okra, then we plant potatoes; we plant cucumber; and then we plant carrots. You know, so we just put different things in as food. We just keep things going until the frost falls.

DAUGHTER: So you rotate the crops?

MOTHER: We rotate the crops. That's how you yield more. Right now, we're planting some seeds, as soon as, next week we'll be planting seeds so we can set them outdoors when the weather breaks.

DAUGHTER: How did you have to prepare the land? And what was the original shape? Wasn't there glass and bottles and all that?

MOTHER: We just took hoes and rakes and stuff and raked it. Dug it as deep as the plants will grow, and raked all that stuff and put it out.

DAUGHTER: What?

MOTHER: We dug with something called a grub hoe and just paid some boys for just going in and digging it up. Tole them, "Just dig it as deep as the food will grow."

DAUGHTER: How deep is that?

MOTHER: About as deep as my leg.

DAUGHTER: So that if you stood up, your waist would be at the cement?

MOTHER: My knee would be in the ground.

DAUGHTER: So we're talking maybe 2 feet?

MOTHER: Yeah, 2 or 3 feet. What we did, we did that and then we asked for top soil and had folks go out in the park and get the horse manure from the park.

DAUGHTER: What park?

MOTHER: Woodside Park, right here. You remember Woodside Park! The stables—the drippings from the horses. Stable compost, they call it. Stable manure. It's one of the largest parks in the United States! That's right! See, when you come, you're in such a hurry you forgot all the good parts. All you see is these raggedy places. But there are some good parts.

DAUGHTER: I know Momma. The best part in Philadelphia is *you*!

MOTHER: Well . . . There are some good parts. Anyway, that's where we get the compost. We go out there and get it and it don't cost anything. Just go out there and haul it.

DAUGHTER: It's free.

MOTHER: Yeah. You don't pay for that! It's there for the getting. It makes such good dirt. You heap it up, all that stuff. That's how your crop grows.

DAUGHTER: Now, you said you paid some boys to do it.

MOTHER: We had two or three boys and we paid the men to dig it up for us. We didn't have a plow. I know how we used to do it in the South, turn it with the turnplow and two horses. But we didn't have the turnplow here, so we just paid the men to dig it up and dig it deep and they had to dig it right.

DAUGHTER: How long did they work on this?

MOTHER: It didn't take them long. Took 'em like 2 days.

DAUGHTER: And you paid some young boys to work on it, too?

MOTHER: Yes, about $3 an hour even.

DAUGHTER: So they were employed for that little bit. How old were they?

MOTHER: One was—I think the best worker was 14. His name was Joey, I think. I can't remember his name. I called him Joey.

DAUGHTER: So after they turned it, they plowed it up and then hauled out all that they dug up?

MOTHER: No, we took the rake and raked up what wasn't too good. Raked up as much as we could. They, you set it out and they picked it up, then you paid them to get rid of it is what we did.

DAUGHTER: There's still glass and stuff down there, but the food just grows around it?

MOTHER: That's what I'm saying. That's what we did.

DAUGHTER: Then you got the horse drippings?

MOTHER: We got that from the horse stables before we raked up the place and had it all chopped up in there together.

DAUGHTER: Oh, I see. So first you turned it by digging it up, then you put the drippings down and turned it all up together?

MOTHER: Right. Then chop it up again.

DAUGHTER: Who did the planting?

MOTHER: Well, I supervised the planting.

DAUGHTER: Who helped you?

MOTHER: Most everybody helped.

DAUGHTER: Women, men, about how many people?

MOTHER: Six of us.

DAUGHTER: Do you plant from seeds?

MOTHER: You plant from seeds, some of them were planted from seeds and some of them were plants we bought. The ones that we couldn't get enough plants up from seeds we bought.

DAUGHTER: What did you buy?

MOTHER: Red cabbage and carrots, more or less we bought those seeds. And all the herbs, I bought those seeds. But see, once you plant them, you don't plant them the next year.

DAUGHTER: They just come back?

MOTHER: Yes. Now I did say *all*. I'm wrong, because thyme you don't plant anymore, the peppermint you don't plant, so many of the stuff you don't plant anymore. You just plant it one time and it comes back every year.

DAUGHTER: And you timed it all based on the moon?

MOTHER: Yes. I always plant according to the moon. According to that, I plant. According to the light I know when to plant.

DAUGHTER: So how much did it cost for . . . ?

MOTHER: Oh! I forgot!

DAUGHTER: I know Momma, just try to estimate for seeds and . . .

MOTHER: I think the tools were quite expensive.

DAUGHTER: Let me ask you the full question, all right? The whole question is, how much did it cost for the seeds, the plants, the hoes, the other equipment that you got, paying the boys? How much do you think all that cost?

MOTHER: Well, the land was about $1,000 for the land. And we put the fence up. I think that wire fence was $1,300—cyclone fence. Then we used the boys 2 days and I paid them, that was $3 an hour. There was two boys, $3 an hour for 16 hours. The seeds run you less than a dollar a pack, you know, and I didn't get but one pack each because I had about five or six different herbs, so that's what the seeds are.

DAUGHTER: But you got other plants.

MOTHER: The plants will run you about $1.50 to $2.00. Say, about $10 worth of plants. That's not the seeds, though. The seeds were about $5 for all the seeds, say, $10 for the seeds. That's just an estimate, now.

DAUGHTER: And the equipment?

MOTHER: Well, we bought . . . We don't have to buy equipment every year. We bought about $200 worth of equipment, but we don't buy that every year.

DAUGHTER: Well, you don't buy the land or the fence every year either It looks like your yearly cost is $20 for the seeds and plants.

MOTHER: Yes, you can put about $20 or $25 for the year. For the seeds themselves, and the plants. They just use the equipment over and over again.

DAUGHTER: That $25 feeds how many people for how long?

MOTHER: About twelve households for one season. When spring comes, you start all over again.

DAUGHTER: So it feeds you for the fall and the winter, doesn't it?

MOTHER: Yeah, that's one season. During the summer we eat a lot out of there. We don't have to can it.

DAUGHTER: So it feeds you year round? Vegetables.

MOTHER: Yeah. Vegetables year round. I told you. Vegetables we don't buy.

DAUGHTER: That's a big savings, Momma.

MOTHER: I'm trying to get these folks to realize that.

DAUGHTER: What happens at your meetings? You said the meetings have been growing.

MOTHER: We trying to get them to realize how much they save by doing this. And spread it. Because the city has so many vacant lots so they can plant these things. This is what we're trying to get them to do and show them the value of having, of doing this. We see so many of them lazy, they say they can't do, but you *can* do it.

DAUGHTER: You say the meetings have been getting bigger?

MOTHER: Yes. I think the meetings have been getting larger and more valuable.

DAUGHTER: How many people come to the meetings?

MOTHER: We had forty-nine last week.

DAUGHTER: And you're meeting once a week?

MOTHER: Once a month.

DAUGHTER: Who comes to these meetings?

MOTHER: Just people that're interested in planting gardens. Neighborhood people. And now we're letting them see how the food looks canned.

DAUGHTER: That's what you do in your meetings? What else do you do? It sounds like a real educational program.

MOTHER: That's what it is! See how it look canned, and also how it tastes.

DAUGHTER: You give them samples?

MOTHER: Yes. I just thought of that out of my head, you know, but it's a lot of work.

DAUGHTER: How many meetings have you had?

MOTHER: We had one last month. And this month we'll have another one. We plan to have one every month.

DAUGHTER: You're building up to planting season? How did you get people interested before, since you've just started the meetings? This is the first time you've had them, right?

MOTHER: This is the first time I started the meetings.

DAUGHTER: You just go around and talk to people?

MOTHER: Like door-to-door campaigning. Door-to-door education.

DAUGHTER: You are such a jewel on this planet, Momma. You are wonderful!

MOTHER: (*Quietly*) What do you mean?

DAUGHTER: What do you mean what do I mean? You really are. I don't know. It's real unusual what you're doing and you're helping people and you're keeping that connection between the Earth and people and . . .

MOTHER: You know what? (*Laughs*) We help ourselves when we help others. You can't help yourself unless you, you have to help somebody, too.

DAUGHTER: Tell me a little about your background. *I* know it. *You* know it, but tell me again so I can get it on this tape.

MOTHER: See, what give me the idea to do this, is I just got sick and tired of walking by weeds. Absolutely a disgrace to me. Instead of growing weeds, if weeds can grow where there's nothing but cement and bricks and stuff, if weeds can grow in there, something else can grow also. And you have the weeds taller than I am. People be afraid to go by Twenty-first Street. That's where we had to go to go to the store, and people would snatch pocketbooks and run over you, and you couldn't find them in the weeds. So that's how we got started with that. Now, when I was home, I came up on the farm . . .

DAUGHTER: Home where?

MOTHER: South Carolina. I came up on a farm. My father was a farmer.

And I loved it. We grew our stuff there. I really loved it. To sit there and get in a field of watermelon and walk on watermelons from one end to the other. I thought it was fun.

DAUGHTER: To walk on them? And they wouldn't bust?

MOTHER: When they were smaller, you know. When they get ripe, they get tender.

DAUGHTER: You mean when they're smaller, they're harder?

MOTHER: Yes. And I was little, too. Anyway, what I'm trying to say is he would grow so many watermelons that you could hardly see the ground. That's just how [many] there were. Sweet taters, peanuts, all kinds of beans, white potatoes. So, I learned that he would plant his stuff at a certain time. Some I have forgotten, but he would get the *Farmer's Almanac*. . . .

I plant things in the ground when the sign of the moon . . . you plant the fish. In that *Farmer's Almanac*. Like the carrots. I won't plant carrots from the corner of the moon. I plant like beans and those kind of things that go on top of the ground. Anything underneath, you plant the fish. And peas, you plant them on the twins and your leaves will be hanging with beans and stuff. I'll never forget that, because I used to have to drop that stuff. I used to love to do that, too; drop the seeds in the ground.

I knew how to drop them. I knew how to take my hand and put it in so it won't spread out. I put it in right down and I could bend then, you know, when you're young you can bend, you can buckle. And I would take my hand and put it right down in the ground. I would do an acre or so a day and wouldn't think nothing of it. And I loved it. It's just in me. That's all.

I like to see things grow instead of wasting. And all these vacant lots you can't, you don't have the money to put houses on all them, but you can buy a little dollar worth of seeds and put on them. Can't put houses on them, but you sit and eat stuff that comes from them. Look at the flowers that are so pretty. That sort of thing. So this is what started. And everybody, it's spreading, you know.

DAUGHTER: It's really wonderful Momma. I'm wondering about how Philadelphia Green [a horticultural society devoted to assisting neighborhood revitalization efforts] and how the city [of Philadelphia] got involved. You approached the city, right? The city wasn't doing it at first, right?

MOTHER: No, but then we approached the city to help us, because I found out they could help us do a lot. That's how I got in with them. Anything that I think can give us a hand, because we need a lot of help out here. Anybody that can give us a hand we approach them. The Philadelphia Green can have a lot of things; they can help with the tools, they can send out people to help, now like we don't have those tapes and stuff. They have that and they bring it out and show these different gardens on these tapes and tell you what it's all about.

DAUGHTER: You mean video tapes?

MOTHER: Video tape. They have that, so then they bring it out for us. But if you don't ever ask for it, you won't get it.

DAUGHTER: Philadelphia Green has existed for a while, hasn't it?

MOTHER: See, that started when you were here, because when I was over at ACDC [Advocate Community Development Corporation], I planted the first garden over there. You were in high school and I was there working ACDC.

DAUGHTER: It was 1970?

MOTHER: Yes, something like that. I planted the first garden over there.

DAUGHTER: And Philadelphia Green existed then?

MOTHER: They existed then and I got involved when we first got the plants, the little pots to put flowers on the steps. That was Philadelphia Green. Ever since then. That's how I got started. That's why I worked there as long as I did because I was glad to be involved with people, you know. And these gardens and stuff. Now we have it ourselves. So it's a joy. It's work, but it's a joy, and we're opening a park.

DAUGHTER: What else are you planning?

MOTHER: Well, we're planning to do more gardening. We're trying hard not to slide backward. We're trying to go forwards. Add a little bit more each year.

DAUGHTER: What else are you doing?

MOTHER: Gardening, shared housing, and regular housing. We're also getting tutoring for literacy, starting to teach some people how to read and get jobs. We just started that. That's the tutoring I been wanted. I want to get that going in a big way.

DAUGHTER: Do you still have training programs for kids to get employment?

MOTHER: Yes, we still have that job bank, that's what we call that. So people can get a job. So that's it. And it keeps you going, too, just like those different directions on the *Farmer's Almanac.*

DAUGHTER: Keeps you out of trouble, too.

MOTHER: Well, I never get in too much trouble no way. I have a whole lot I can do. See, I've always been able to keep myself busy. I've never been able to not have anything to do. See, I can sit and crochet. I want to sew. I piece quilts. There's so much you can do. My goodness! If I wasn't doing that [work with PCRC] I'd stay in this house here a month and don't even go to the door and work the whole time.

DAUGHTER: How do you think what you do relates to ecology, relates to the Earth? How do you talk about that?

MOTHER: Well, I talk about it like I always do, 'cause this is where you see the real nature of the universe. The real one, without . . . before it's transformed into different things. Because even children don't have the least idea of the food they eat. What grows in the ground, what grows on top, what good for blood, what good for different things. A lot of adults don't have any idea. So that's how I relate it to everyday living.

You get firsthand . . . everybody get a firsthand look at real nature. That's how I see it. That's how I love it. You can see it come up, you can see it grow and you see how it grows, and see it dies if you don't take care of it. That tells you something.

DAUGHTER: What does it tell you?

MOTHER: It tells you that if you're not taken care of, tells you, you got to take care of whatever you have. If you don't it will die then, or grow wild like the things in the fields, out in the woods. God has created things to stay alive without being taken care of but you can't try to, like to say, try to tame them. If you try to tame them you have to give them some of that that they get ordinarily. But the Earth is created so that everything should be taken care of.

DAUGHTER: By somebody or something?

MOTHER: By nature, and then if you interfere with it . . .

DAUGHTER: Say that again, the Earth was created . . .

MOTHER: To take care of everything on Earth. It's supposed to be taken care of. That's why, man, they say, has been made the highest of all things, because we're supposed to take care of the things that we cultivate. We're supposed to take care of them. And if we're not going to take care of it let it grow wild, the Earth will take care of it.

DAUGHTER: But if you interfere . . .

MOTHER: Right. If you interfere with it, and we must if we can survive. See, we must interfere because we need these things *to* survive. And it goes around and around. See, we need these things to survive therefore when you plant something you hafta take care of it. If you don't, it'll die. Either you take care of it or leave it alone.

DAUGHTER: What kind of resistance have you met?

MOTHER: People not wantin' to work. They don't want to get their hands dirty. They don't want to, not want to work, what I mean is, you take a lot of mothers don't want to wash the greens, they don't wanna dig down and get the carrots from the ground, they don't want to get the turnips from the ground. That's dirt. When they get it it's in the store and they clean, so to speak. So a lot of them rather go to the store and get it. I say, "How long it's been in that store? You can get it right from here and clean it, put it right in your pot or eat it like it is. Put it in your salad and you get the real, all the vitamins."

So you have resistance, people say, I can't bend down, can't bend over, or my fingernails too long. They don't tell you that but you look at the fingernails and know they're too long to do any work. So that's the resistance you get. You get a lot of that, 'cause we are uneducated to the facts. And not just that, but in a lot of things. We just don't seem to understand.

But I feel as though our children would better understand how to take care of things and would have a better feeling of the things around them, you know. It begins when you're, you know, small really.

DAUGHTER: Do you work with children a lot in the garden?

MOTHER: I love to, yes. I generally have them in there and showing them the grass from the weeds and from the plants and how it looks and how they grow, too. The grass grows, too. The weeds grow, too. That's part of nature. They say, "What good are they?" This can be a fertilizer for next year. "What!? Weeds!?" You let them sit there and rot and that replenish the Earth. See, everything has a cycle. See, those the kinda things.

DAUGHTER: How do you get the children in there?

MOTHER: All you have to do is open the gate and say "Come on children." If I had more strength I'd have all the kids in there, but I don't have the strength anymore and I can't get anyone interested in the children. The mothers say, yeh, take the children so they can sit down and look at television. But all the kids that I have met want to get out there in the garden and they beg you to let them come in and help. It takes a lot of time with children. And I don't have that much time trying to do all these other things. But I would just have someone to just go with them. I don't have that. The mothers not interested anymore. "I gotta look at my soap opera."And they are their children. "Here, you can take 'em, I gotta look at my soap opera. I'll give you money. Take 'em to such and such a thing. You take 'em while I sit and watch my soap opera, or do anything else." So those opposition you get now.

DAUGHTER: And what kind of hope do you have? Even with that opposition, how do you keep on going?

MOTHER: Faith. I know out of all of that, it may be one or two that you'll get through to. Even with one, I'll be thankful. You know. Faith. Just keep on going. You do that with children, all of them will not end up in jail. Some of 'em come out all right. But you don't look for a whole lot. You don't expect a whole lot.

DAUGHTER: Why do you think that if you show them the living things that will help them straighten up?

MOTHER: It help, it helps them to . . . I think it will help them to appreciate the beauty of the Earth, and of nature; we call it mother nature.

DAUGHTER: Do you think it helps them appreciate the beauty of each other and their abilities?

MOTHER: This is the thing. If you can appreciate the Earth, you can appreciate the beauty of yourself. Even if this has beauty, I, too, have beauty. The same creator created both. And if I learned to take care of that I'll also take care of myself and help take care of others. See, taking care of yourself and appreciating yourself is the first step. But you can't go with a child and say that. You know, you show 'em this and they'll say, "ummmm," you know, some of these other things'll come to them themselves, or "if this is it, then I, look at me." Then they won't feel so let down all the time. Sometime we fail in trying to do that.

DAUGHTER: What do you mean you may fail?

MOTHER: Sometime you may fail, the children may not get it. They may not. Like I say, you may get one or two. That's what I mean. I am who I am whether I'm black, blue, or brown. I'm a human being. Therefore, I stand for just as much right as you stand for although my color is different, you see. I'm no less than you are regardless of my color.

DAUGHTER: You see the children move past some of that as a result of working?

MOTHER: Yes. Yes. They compare sometimes so you let them see pictures of other children working, say, "Well, I can do it as well as he can do it."

DAUGHTER: You show them pictures of other children working?

MOTHER: Right. And then see that's giving them confidence in themselves that they can do things, too, other than throw a ball and bat a ball. Other than break out people's windows and curse in the street. "If they can stop and make things, make a beautiful plant, so can I." Some of them will stop and say that. And they'll tell you, "Let's do our garden."

DAUGHTER: Do you have special meetings for children?

MOTHER: Special meetings, special workshops. They don't have the same workshops as the adults. Yes.

DAUGHTER: The organization has special meetings?

MOTHER: For children. We have to.

DAUGHTER: What age groups?

MOTHER: We have all ages.

DAUGHTER: From what? Starting where?

MOTHER: Acch! We have some small 'cause the, uh, the 8-year-old wanna bring the 2-year-old. Some of 'em so little, but we don't turn them away. Long as they can walk and talk, they come. From 3 up. But we don't limit the age group.

DAUGHTER: What's the oldest?

MOTHER: Well, the teenagers get so . . . but we have some teenagers help us with the others though. We have some as long as they in school and don't have a job.

DAUGHTER: And how many children are you working with?

MOTHER: Oh! I don't know.

DAUGHTER: Give me an estimate.

MOTHER: (*Sigh*) Look like to me it's 'bout fifty or more. Because of the fact—uh, it's more than that. But I can't work with the children like I want to. That's the only thing. I want to work with them on a regular basis. Like I would like to work with those children every week. Have just 2 hours or 3 hours every week working with the kids. You'd be surprised to see the difference. With all this stuff going on you have to create agencies that's going to work with the children to help, because in every state of the universe—I don't know 'bout, I haven't read much about the foreign states—there're abandoned children. Because of crack, because of alcohol, or because of this or because of that, you name it.

We gon' have to learn to set up something to work with these kids because outta that, one of those abandoned children you get one or two children, one or two kids that will carry on, that will not use and will not do the stuff that they were abused by. See, because a lot of people think that if you don't beat a child it's not abuse, but there're other ways to abuse children. And more damaging, or just as damaging. It's a whole lotta ways to abuse children. I know.

DAUGHTER: How often do you meet with the children?

MOTHER: Well, see, it depends. Like right now I'm not meeting with them because I'm with this housing. Usually it's during the summer. But see that isn't the way it's supposed to . . . not like I would like to have it. I would like to have a year-round program for the children. You gotta have a place, you gotta have money, you gotta have those things to do this with. We have a meeting like at Christmas. Last week was a Christmas workshop. Then we have a fall workshop.

DAUGHTER: Special workshops.

MOTHER: Yes. That isn't enough for them.

DAUGHTER: What did you do during the fall workshop?

MOTHER: Fall workshop we had making pumpkins and Thanksgiving. That was the fall workshop. Making pumpkins and playing in the hay. Things like the old folks do, like they did before. Some children had never seen a bundle of hay and had something like a hay ride, you know, put it up and let you slide down on the hay.

DAUGHTER: Where did you have that?

MOTHER: In the yard, in the garden.

DAUGHTER: As part of the composting?

MOTHER: Right. So see, that was fall, that's just one time. Then we had a workshop for Christmas, how you make decorations, that's another time. . . . During the winter, you work from the proceeds of the fall. But it isn't enough to get through. I feel as though if we could work constantly with the children we could reach more of them. Now it takes a smart child to remember from this

workshop to that workshop how it connects. But see, the majority of them can't get it.

DAUGHTER: What do you mean, "how it connects"?

MOTHER: Okay, we get the pinecones, we only can get the pinecones
certain time of year. And we tell them that this pinecone has
matured, it's grown, and now we can do this with it. But now
how many children gonna remember that when we make them
for Christmas. So then see, it's too big a gap to reach most children
now. It's too big a gap between them.

DAUGHTER: So, you want them to see the process, to see the stages?

MOTHER: That's it. It's very sad to me, 'cause they missing so much.
It's really sad. Go around, you see all these children in the street,
you see all these babies having babies, it's sad. Sad times.

DAUGHTER: So, how do you maintain what you *are* doing with the
adults, through all that resistance? I know you said you have those
door-to-door campaigns sometimes. But how do you pass their
resistance?

MOTHER: Just keep on talking to them and showing them different
things.

DAUGHTER: Do you work one-on-one with them?

MOTHER: You have . . . it's better. A lot of times it's better. You get
better results to work one-on-one because everyone is different.

DAUGHTER: And what kind of articles do you read?

MOTHER: Well, like I was reading the article we had in the paper couple
Sundays ago 'bout abandoned children and how many children
in this state, I was talking about this state, that has been abandoned. And how they were talking about they didn't have enough
workers to work closely with these children and how these crack
mothers and drunken fathers and crack fathers just put the children out in the street. And just last week, last week?, this week,
the mother stole a car and was renting them out to people and
sending her son out to make sure the car came back and one
16-year-old find it out and killed the boy. Those kind of things. . . .

DAUGHTER: So, when you're working with the folks you read them
articles like that and . . .

MOTHER: And I say, "Now, this is the type of mother you don't wanna
be. You had these children and you have a responsibility whether
you take or accept it or not." I say not just mothers have responsibility, fathers, too, but, where the fathers? If you know where

the fathers are, you love them so much you won't turn them in. Then if you won't turn them in, you work for your child, that's all. You work and do it.

DAUGHTER: What age group are you talking about?

MOTHER: All these mothers now are having children. Most of 'em are teenagers. Most of 'em are young children. Most of them are babies themselves.

DAUGHTER: And these are the same mothers whose children you get and take to the garden?

MOTHER: Yes, a lot of them. And a lot of these mothers we take to the garden are young. Most of 'em young. I don't think I have an old person with a child that we take to the garden. Most of 'em these young mothers. I can't think of a one.

DAUGHTER: What do you do? How do you get to them? You just go up to their house or what do you do?

MOTHER: And ask them would you like for your child to join, and then the children come and ask you. A lot of them come and ask you.

DAUGHTER: The children do?

MOTHER: Right. Then we go to the house. So I got Helen working with me now and another lady to head up that project. I hope it'll work well. Get the children involved. Went in the block and took every name of a child that wanted to work. And asked to work. You didn't have to ask them. And then went to the mothers and had the mothers to agree and asked them to come and help us. Only two came out. The others had something else to do. They didn't have time to come. "I give you some money but I don't have time." You know. Those kinda things.

DAUGHTER: And how many children were there?

MOTHER: Oh Jesus, we had about twenty-some-odd. 'Round thirty-three or thirty-four children and two parents.

DAUGHTER: And how about the old folks that you do have working on the garden. You go door to door with them, too?

MOTHER: Yeh, some of them like to work in the garden. The older folks.

DAUGHTER: And what do you call older? What age group?

MOTHER: Well, the ones without children mostly. 'Cause I have one lady . . .

DAUGHTER: That's over forty or how old?

MOTHER: Over 40, yeh. Over 40. They come to the garden because they love it. And they never done it before and they say they learning. So they enjoy it. Over 40, I got over 40 up to how old? I think

we had a 90-year-old man working in the garden, but he not able
to come anymore. But he worked 'til he was 90-something years
old. We give him a plaque for being the oldest gardener that we
had. And he had the prettiest garden we had.

DAUGHTER: He did now? Was he from the South?

MOTHER: Yep.

DAUGHTER: Do you have a bunch of folks from the South working?

MOTHER: Yes. He couldn't read, but he'd have you to read it to him
and he would catch it as you read it and go do just what you say

DAUGHTER: Read what now?

MOTHER: Like the directions on the paper how you plant? You read
it out to him, he won't miss a thing. He go right on and do it

DAUGHTER: So everybody has a place?

MOTHER: Right. That's it. So that's how it's done, but it takes a lot of
time and a lot of . . . When everybody says it's hard because it
takes a lot of time. It takes a lot of time with these people to
counsel them. It's a lot of time. And you can't do it in a hurry
and you can't do it one time and you can't limit the times that
you hafta do it. You have to do it until it gets done. That's all.

DAUGHTER: But you do see some results?

MOTHER: Well, yes, you see a good bit of results. I saw a good bit of
results this summer when we plant those, were putting those
plants out. They said the plants were not gonna stay. The children
themselves didn't destroy any of the plants. They watched out
for the plants. And they enjoyed the street. They played ball but
none of the ball broke those plants. They watched out for it. Close
as it is. They watched out for it and that was marvelous.

When you have your vision, that's one step, as you go through
one it'll go to the next step. And you follow it, nothing gonna
be unturned, everything will work in place.

DAUGHTER: But if you follow it?

MOTHER: Yeh, and keep on praying. Can't stop. Can't stop 'cause too
much out here. And a lot of times you may have to change sometimes. Who knows? You know what I mean?

DAUGHTER: You may have to change directions a little bit.

MOTHER: Right. May have to change your directions. So you have to
keep in touch always. You have to, have to constantly think it
over and . . . you know . . . pray for guidance 'cause you don't
know when you have to change. So when time come to change
you know to change. 'Cause I pray for my strength and my health

and guidance so that I can go 'head. 'Cause I have to pray for the words to be right to go talk to some of these parents 'cause some of them may get insulted. You have to pray for that patience. I pray for that patience and understanding.

DAUGHTER: It takes a lot of patience?

MOTHER: Oh, yeh. Ha! Don't start without patience, honey.

Catherine Keller

WOMEN AGAINST WASTING THE WORLD: NOTES ON ESCHATOLOGY AND ECOLOGY

> to waste: v.t. 1. to lay waste; devastate 2. to use up;
> consume; to wear out 3. to emaciate; to cause to be consumed
> or weakened, as by overuse, disease, or the like; to enfeeble
> 4. to expend needlessly, carelessly, or without valuable result;
> to squander . . . see RAVAGE
>
> MERRIAM-WEBSTER

> Time is short, since the deterioration of some life-support
> systems appears to be accelerating.
>
> STATE OF THE WORLD 1988

> Then I saw a new heaven and a new earth, for the first
> heaven and the first earth had vanished, and there was no
> longer any sea. I saw the holy city, new Jerusalem, coming
> down out of heaven from God, made ready like a bride adorned
> for her husband.
>
> REV. 21:1

THE EARTH IS BEING WASTED—devastated, with a violence echoed by the crude contemporary idiom of "waste the sucker"; it's being used up, its profound resources squandered, its lush abundance consumed, its complex surfaces worn out. Yet this apocalyptic sort of message would not be worth repeating if it weren't also the case that there is still great life and responsiveness in the Earth as well. This is no time for despair—and there is no time for despair. Yet something in us readily succumbs to a sense of futility, something perhaps more than, yet related to, the objective configuration of economic and political forces laying waste our planet. So I want to begin to ask: What is the connection between the flagrant, accelerating waste of our world and the contemporary recrudescence of the myth of the Apocalypse? Do women have, as women, a specific response to make? I will not try here to offer any definitive answers; at present I am more interested in getting these questions formulated, in feeling a way into their tensions and possibilities.

Here is how the melodramatic voice of the connection sounds to me: "Waste her! Go ahead, use 'er up! Devastate, consume, expend, squander, ravage, Daddy will give us a new one. The final rapture is almost here!"

This is not the voice of any single belief: it is a voice uttered from the whirlwind symbiosis of born-again Christian apocalypticism and military/industrial consumerism, from an unprecedented alliance of reactionary premodernism with hypermodern greed that reared its gleaming head during the decade of the 1980s. Listen to what it says: "Waste not want not? Haste makes waste? Old wives' tales—make way for the new bride! Who needs the warnings of ecofreaks, antinuclear fanatics, and witch women who don't understand that the Lord has made all good things for our use: to use up before the millennium. Not to waste is to waste—make haste, Jesus is coming! Fill the Earth and subdue 'er!—that was God's command at the beginning. Now, at the end, let's dispose of that which was created to be at man's disposal."

Let me be clear: such a caricature does not reproduce the sincere faith of many born-again Christians, or any evangelical doctrines. I mean to evoke something more pervasive, more systemic, than the influence of the U.S. right-wing Christian movement, than even of its televangelists, those dispensationalist apocalypticists preaching the imminent demise of the world, preceded by their own rapture before the tribulations.[1] The power of the televangelists has been interrupted by the revelation that, at least in the realm of personal morality, they do not live by the absolutes they preach; and the rightest momentum of the 1980s may not sustain itself through another presidency. But regardless of the next moves of the religiopolitical right, the apocalyptic myth has been influencing and will continue to influence the course of planetary history. That is, the expectation of an end-time and of an end of time has, I believe, defined the limits of Western patriarchal consciousness, Christian, Jewish, and secular. Perhaps all the more effectively because largely unconsciously, the imagery that concludes the Bible has conveyed a formative framework for the end of history.

To the extent that this is true, it should come as no surprise that the paths of Western technological and political development have led us to the threshold of annihilation. Nor is it an accident that the masses of middle-class White humanity—including at this moment White middle-class women—who unlike people of color and the poor usually have no urgent matters of social survival facing them, do not rise up and make this end-of-the-world scenario *stop*. Of course, the most concrete reason that we as a class let it continue is because of our dependence upon ecological and military exploitation to sustain anything even vaguely resembling our middle-class life-styles. Our helplessness before the modern state generates both a widespread lack of belief in truly sustainable options and a sense of the futility of resistance.

I am claiming, however, that this economic dependency itself reflects artificial limits upon the imagination. Participants in Christian civilization, which extends far beyond the bounds of belief, have been preprogrammed by ancient visions to expect that when the going gets rough, the world will go. Apocalypticism leads some to a fervent hope for the end, which promises a new beginning, and others to a gloomy resignation to global destruction. These have always been the two sides of the apocalyptic consciousness: hope and despair.[2] Because of the literally apocalyptic situation of this late modern period, both of these attitudes side with omnicide.

Nuclear annihilation continues to be an option, one preferred by many for its impressive capacity to fulfill "God's" prophecy in such passages as Rev. 16:17f:

"Then the seventh angel poured his bowl on the air; and out of the sanctuary came a loud voice from the throne, which said "It is over!" And there followed flashes of lightning and peals of thunder, and a violent earthquake, like none before it in human history, so violent it was."[3]

But the nuclear and ecological threats are twin manifestations of the same source: the unchecked power of the military/industrial establishment, subliminally inspired and justified by apocalyptic assumptions of an end of history.

Within this textual context I will focus more on that form of doomsday annihilation that is already well underway: in the moment-by-moment "end of the world" proceeding through the tangible, cumulative, daily destruction of the physical environment. This we feel now all the time, this doom, this dread, this rage, quite apart from the pervasive nuclear anxiety. For instance, let's talk about the weather. It is again today, as I write, too hot for this time of year. I have winced each time native New Jerseyans (I haven't lived here long) shook their heads and said, "It just doesn't seem right. Maybe my memory mistakes me, but June was always more pleasant than this." "Springs have been getting shorter and shorter." I have felt a wretched gratitude if someone indicated that this is just a variation within a normal pattern. Maybe we still have time . . . But, of course, the information is now suddenly everywhere and unavoidable: that the warming pattern of the greenhouse effect, based especially on the burning of fossil fuels and the accumulation of now a century of industrial waste gases, has almost certainly begun, much sooner than scientists expected. I notice that sometimes I choose not to mention these things, as though it is impolite in the course of a simple discussion of the heat; at other times, a kind of apocalyptic rudeness overtakes me, and I say, "Well, unless we do something it is only going to get worse." This morning even that bastion of establishment "balance," the *New York Times*, took on the issue as its leading editorial: "The Greenhouse Effect? Real Enough." The editorial pointed out that, in the face of a disastrous drought unlike any this country had known, and the fact that "four of the last eight years—1980, 1981, 1983 and 1987—have been the warmest since measurements of global surface temperatures began a century ago, and 1988 may be another record hot year," measures should be taken and suggested a set of crucial means for slowing the greenhouse warming (including encouragement of nuclear energy development).[4]

Quite apart from moments of political consciousness, these end-time winces, semiconscious mixes of acknowledgment and denial, fill our days with nagging little apocalyptic tensions. We wonder whether to use bottled water even for making coffee and then wonder how to find out whether the bottled water comes from a nontoxic water source. Habits and plans shift, to outings that do not center around prolonged exposure to the sun. In this summer of 1988, people who previously didn't think about skin cancer, now, with a certain ruefulness, mention the ozone layer and wear a hat to play tennis, wear #35 sun block even for an hour in the sun.

It is good news that the news is finally getting around. We may get to widespread action. This end-time is not irreversible, yet, though some of the damage may be. But the prospect of a permanently scarred planet, like that of a person who comes out of a mugging with some scars, is no reason to shut down hope—yet isn't there something within all of us that seems to give up the future with each new wave of ecological bad news? To sustain action may require naming the apocalyptic element that has embedded world destruction within a vision of Divine providence moving history from creation to conclusion. The mythic miasma of a few apocalyptic texts, operating out of context and unconsciously, seems to preform our sense of time and history.

As you read the following two passages, remember recent heat waves, droughts, and media attention to the greenhouse effect, and consider the effects of the passages' juxtaposition on you:

> By 1987, what had become known as the ozone "hole" was twice the size of the continental United States. Though the hole involves a series of as yet poorly understood chemical reactions, it could portend an unexpectedly rapid ozone depletion globally and translate into lowered crop output and rising skin cancer and eye damage as more ultraviolet radiation reaches the earth.[5]

> The fourth angel poured his bowl on the sun; and it was allowed to burn men with its flames. They were fearfully burned; but they only cursed the God of heaven for their sores and pains, and would not repent of what they had done. (Rev. 16:8ff)

Obviously there is a certain fit—and fundamentalists are far more expert than I at matching biblical "prophecies" to current events. They read (and always have) these parallels as evidence of the imminence of the last days. Others, taking a staunchly secularist view, may write off such parallels as coincidence. Let me say that if these are the only two options, I suspect the fundamentalists are closer to the truth. Close enough to succumb to a frightening distortion, a distortion already infecting the apocalyptic writers themselves. It is hard to miss the patriarchal, militarist dualism in the Book of Revelation. There may be a profound intuition at work in the vision of the oppressed community for which "John" wrote[6]—that *if* civilization continues along the route of the gross and violent imperial materialism symbolized by the "whore of Babylon" (and Rome), *then* globally scaled destruction, involving not only society but the cosmos, becomes inevitable. But even the critique of imperialism is couched in the terms of both religious and male chauvinism; a literalist mindset seems to turn the outcome into a vindictively foregone conclusion. There is a voice that even in me—who has a background quite the opposite of any Christian fundamentalism—whispers, "Maybe it is inevitable. Maybe there is no other way than the way of regeneration through destruction." This voice, in myself, does not feel authentic; it has a derivative, superstitious, despairing ring. But, for millions of persons in this country, this voice has become dominant, militantly evangelical, and committed to the belief that ecological and/or nuclear disaster, along with increasing political injustice and violence, are more or less inevitable signs of the times: that is, of the end of time.

For this reason it is best not to simply and angrily discount them, but to try to hear. It is not only that as the prophecies of Revelation seem to approach realization, we have reason to think they were on target; rather, this is a formative text deeply enough inscribed in Western consciousness to have found the means of its self-fulfillment. That is, as the early Christian movement became increasingly institutionalized, patriarchal, and, finally, with Constantine, the bearer of imperial power, such mythic imagery became part of the understanding of time, nature, and history that has shaped the course of Western development. So it is not that the text of the bowl and the burning sun literally predicted the hole in the ozone layer, but that the text may be the *sine qua non* for the hole. But the text could have been—and has been—realized in many other ways as well.

If this hypothesis—that the end-time myth serves as *sine qua non* of the present end-time threat—has any validity, then it behooves us to examine the connection between ecology and eschatology. *Ecology:* the study of the relationships among things. *Eschatology:* the study of end things. Is it as simple as this—that because the relationships among things, among everything—animal, vegetable, and mineral—have been neglected and violated and because patriarchal humanity has exploited rather than nutured its relationships to its environments that the literal "end" seems so imminent? That the degradation of relationships to means to ends in fact leads to end things? What relation does such degradation bear to Christian eschatology? Is eschatology a cause of the literal end? Is it also a resource against it?

Eschatology has traditionally referred to the final judgment and resurrection of the dead, to the inbreaking at any moment of the Divine realm, or to life after death. Early Christians as well as the Jews of the same period lived in high expectations, born of the classic prophecies, of a new heaven and earth, a new Jerusalem, envisioned originally as a just and harmonious world order in which humanity has ceased its wars and its exploitations and lives in harmony with a renewed eco-sphere. Apocalyptic eschatology is a radical development of that hope, taking the form of mythopoeic visions of end-times involving a cata-strophic end of history, a rapture of the saved, the sons of light, who are installed in triumphant glory along with the Messiah at the Second Coming, and a Final Judgment in which the sons of darkness receive, after gruesome tribulations during which they do not repent, the justice of eternal corporal punishment.

Of course, mainline Christianity quickly veered away from the early charismatic hope for an end to the world within the generation: it in-stitutionalized and individualized its eschatology and usually ignored the hallucinogenic excesses of the apocalyptic vision. Yet the funda-mentalist forms by which it has returned in our time do not suggest a marginal exception, but something more like the return of the re-pressed. The extravagant moral dualism of the apocalyptic perspective, which can resolve the tensions of worldly life only by destroying the world, has returned with the full secular force of U.S. industrial-imperial power in this decade. Reinforcing the moral dualism is a theological dualism, in which an absolutely transcendent Deity reigns from outside his "creation," utterly independent of that world. This in turn yields a temporal dualism of beginning and end: creation is at the start, and eschatology refers to a literal conclusion.

And so there is some causal link between the ancient vision of a world at the "disposal" of a controlling Lord and that world of dispos-able products, itself subject to human control and human disposal of its resources, brought into being by modern technology. The sacred story ends in the apocalyptic tribulations of the end-time, preordained by the Divine dominance; the secular derivative ends—despite its belief in endless progress and its repudiation of supernaturalism—in some combination of whimpers and bangs brought on by the ecocidal and omnicidal measures of a politics of domination. Although both present supposedly hopeful visions of the future, both involve the destruction of the Earth. The latter, with its vision of endless progress by way of endless exploitation, seems to have developed the science with which to effectively and unconsciously fulfill on a worldly plane the other-worldly vision of the apocalyptic. One can surmise that the develop-ment therefore of scientific modernity, despite its apparent secularizing focus, is still inspired by biblical apocalyptic. Both in fact drive toward the end of time and the world: neither respects the spatiotemporal rhythms of earthly ecology. And, for both, woman, in her association with bodiliness, becomes the metaphor and recipient of the subjugation and externalization of nature. Woman, as whore, old wife, witch, is the embodiment of time, which is to be used up, which is running away.[6]

The link between the kind of science and the kind of theology that worked together to create the present situation is suggested by biologist/physicist and Nobel recipient Ilya Prigogine: "The 'mechanized' nature of modern science, created and ruled according to a plan that totally dominates it, but of which it is unaware, glorifies its creator, and was thus admirably suited to the needs of both theologians and physicists. . . . The debasement of nature is parallel to the glorification of all that eludes it, God and man [sic]."[7] Prigogine and coauthor Isabelle Stengers never mention the additional parallelism so obvious to feminists, that of the debasement of woman to the glory of a *he-man* God and the men who bear his image. But let us return to the original text:

> Then I saw a great white throne, and the One who sat upon it; from his presence earth and heaven vanished away, and no place was left for them. (Rev. 20:1)

No place was left for them—the natural universe, whose extension is identical with the extension of space, loses place. This at the moment when its time is up. From the vantage point of White transcendence, the apotheosis of masculine rule, the One precludes the many. The universe seems to condense itself in the vision to a single unifying centerpoint, which realizes itself by annihilating the spatiotemporal world. A pristine simplicity is achieved, in which the New Jerusalem, the bride, of "gold bright as clear glass," of twelve gates each "being made from a single pearl," can be erected for the eternal bliss of the sons of light. "All this is the victor's heritage" (Rev. 20:21). The debasement of nature is parallel to the glorification of all that eludes it, God and man.

The architect of this "victor's heritage" glories in a cosmic minimalism: "The city had no need of sun or moon to shine upon it; for the glory of God gave it light (Rev. 21:22). "And there was no longer any sea." To elude nature is to elude its evolutionary complexity, to transcend diversity. That the sea is eliminated from the new creation is no accident: the first creation of Genesis inherits the old Babylonian identification of the sea with the primordial; with the female, chaos, the Tehom. The oceanic womb of life, construed in various Hebrew scriptures as a monster to be contained, is now eternally vanquished, replaced by the purely paternal creation. But even the relatively austere

diversity of planetary bodies is eliminated, and a glory-light of immaterial transcendence shines on the desired future. This drive to transcendent unity is, of course, a profound impetus in all patriarchal
spirituality, and it always achieves its ends at the expense of nature
and multiplicity. I am also suggesting that it pertains to the present
ecological situation.

Consider what is happening to planetary multiplicity today: "As
forests disappear, as the soils erode, and as lakes and soils acidify and
become polluted, the number of plant and animal species diminishes.
This reduction in the diversity of life on earth may well have unfore-
seen long-term consequences."[8]

Indeed. And the long term is precisely what the apocalyptic deadline
shortchanges for the sake of a specific sort of present intensity. (This
is an ironic reversal of original intent: what operates as self-denial for
the sake of future reward in fact functions to justify the systemic hedon-
ism that wastes the future for the sake of present consumption.) What
is the relation between the elimination of complexity and the elimination of the future? And what, precisely, is the ecofeminist relation?

Certainly modern complexity, ambiguity, and pluralism have created
a horror of any more "progress"—not without good reason! The syndrome of future shock accounts in part for the massive recursion to
simplistic, premodern, apocalyptic solutions to the moral and spiritual
perplexities of the late modern age. But why has it come to this?

Let me suggest, further, that the relation between complexity and
future concerns essentially the very nature of relatedness. To relate
is to complicate. Whether we imagine a relation to our body, a tree,
an intimate friend, an enemy, global society, or the ecosphere, to bring
consciousness to the relation is to sustain complexity. And quite apart
from any human consciousness, the evolutionary processes in nature
all demonstrate complexity within ecological relatedness.

We are, as is everything that is, an instance of becoming-in-relation.
Nothing is independent of anything else. This is the fundamental ecological vision, applicable to human culture as well as to nonhuman
communities. The others always influence us, however much we screen
out, deny, simplify. To embrace the influx of otherness into self, to
acknowledge that even what we despise becomes a part of our experience and therefore of ourselves—this is to live in the consciousness
of our interconnectedness. Yet the dominant cultures of the West have
systematically stifled this sort of consciousness. In the words of Agnes
Whistling Elk, a Canadian native shaman: "White people have this

thing that says, 'I'm not a snake. I'm not a squirrel. I'm something important.' They separate, and that's their tragedy.'"[9] This is a tragedy of momentous proportions, which threatens to annihilate the squirrels and the snakes, any native peoples who survived White genocides, and, of course, life itself, to which these White separatists seem to see themselves as an exception—precisely by separation.

Many of us have felt and argued that women have been the caretakers of relation, that the dominant separate self of the culture is the male ego. Yet we must at the same time acknowledge that inasmuch as this female relatedness has survived, it has been the very means of women's entrapment, our dependency. And the dependency is no more ecologically viable than the illusion of an independent ego; indeed, ironically, it has led to our own modes of separation, of social isolation as well as the disconnection from our bodily knowledge. So Agnes Whistling Elk may perceive rightly, as a woman of color, that all White people, including White feminists, suffer from a destructive and self-deceptive separation. Perhaps we—White women—can only begin to regain the wisdom and power of relation as we move into contact with non-White, nonpatriarchal, and nonmodern modes of connection with the physical world.

This relatedness does not present itself as something single, simple, or conclusive. Note, for instance, the extraordinary complexity of the spiritual paths of Native Americans and other shamanistic and Earth-centered peoples. Every bird or stone or ancestor might embody the sacred and needs to be heard, heeded, internalized as "medicine." Relatedness is not, as classical monotheism might have it, a matter of the One Other, or the One who is Other. At any moment we meet an infinite plurality, most of which we do indeed screen out, bundle and reduce into manageable perceptual and cognitive categories. To attune ourselves to this plurality means to live with the untold, indeed unspeakable, complexity it poses for us. For as we take in the many, we ourselves are many. The cohesion we achieve is not simple oneness, but, in philosopher and mathematician Alfred North Whitehead's language, a "composite unification." No unitary subject underlies—and therefore "controls"—the spatial and temporal multiplicity that informs every moment of our experience. Our nature is not that of a separate essence; rather, the nature of things—of all things natural, which nothing eludes but by self-deception—is this fluid complication out of which the "essence" of something must compose itself. The self arises, as does the self of every cosmic creature, moment by moment in new conjunctions of influence and creativity. Its continuity composes itself out of its creativity, as it spins long-term futures on the basis of its long-term memory. The deep past and the worldly future matter *naturally* to the connective self. For it knows its own emergence from and extension into an endless network of relations.[10]

If this is so, then relation is cumulative in its complexity. And time itself is the complex pattern of relationships. Complexity can no more be evaded than nature itself. At least if one is growing with and not against the grain of reality. To honor reality is to attend care-fully to the diversity of each moment—the many cannot be purged, wasted, flung like the devil: "the cowardly, the faithless, and the vile, murderers, fornicators, sorcerers, idolaters, and liars of every kind" into "the lake that burns with sulphurous flames" (Rev. 21:8).

The dualistic solution to the problem of evil is characteristic of the great monotheisms: simplification by Oneness never quite unifies reality, never quite works—it always has the cumulative impact of its discarded waste products to dispose of. (Hence sulphurous fumes?) No wonder time must end in some final conflagration—the cosmos cannot contain all the garbage. In this worldview that at the most intimate, emotional levels as well as the ecological and economic levels refuses to recycle the past, the force of denied diversity appears as chaos and evil. Thus, already in the first creation epic, the *Enuma Elish* (the Babylonian creation myth from the late second millennium B.C.), the male warrior God Marduk establishes his universe by conquering the first mother, the Great Goddess Tiamat—who as the primordial ocean is interpreted as a monster of chaos. The biblical version is the story of Genesis, in which the word of God creates His world out of the Tehom—the Hebrew equivalent of Tiamat.[11] So the Bible opens with the creation of a world out of the primal sea, in which chaos is not yet fully defeated; and the Bible ends with the destruction of that world, in which diversity and fluidity still had their ways, and its replacement by one with no sea. While we can argue that Genesis represents a critique and transformation of the warrior myth, in Revelation he returns full force: "From his mouth there went a sharp sword with which to smite the nations; for he it is who shall rule them with an iron rod" (Rev. 19:20).

This messianic figure, also called the "Lamb," mocks the relational complexity required by Jesus's own teaching of the justice of love, even of others and enemies. This second coming—less of Jesus than of the Babylonian Marduk—poses a simpler solution, the final solution. For

Jesus of Nazareth, eschatology referred, as with the earlier prophets, to a just version of *this* world, and its timing was unpredictable, even to himself. The point was to "pay heed, watch—for you know not the time" (Matt. 24:42). *Watch*—attend consciously, alert to the possibilities for relation and transformation flooding in upon us *now*. We are not to waste those opportunities, but to relish the eschatological banquet now, by opening community to include those who are radically other, poor, needy, disdained. In its better moments, the eschatological future is not a literal end but a creative edge—the moment of the fullness of time in which a new plenitude of relations is realized. Anxiety is healed not by elimination of complexity but by the cosmic trust of the lilies.

If time is the complex of relations in which diversity unfolds, then end-time is a logical consequence of the debasement of diversity and of relation. Temporality is the mark of physicality, of body and woman and all that complexity that resists control, that undermines the unitary ego, and that mocks the male hero. Relationship and sensuality have been assigned to women, and the Earth itself has been feminized and ravaged accordingly. Feminist theory has well mapped the long history of religious, philosophical, and scientific projection of "nature" onto woman's body and of woman's body onto the Earth. Ruling-class men, especially but not exclusively those raised within the domains of Western monotheism, have seen themselves as godlike exceptions to nature, diversity, and death. And so, along with women, the diversity of peoples, of races, of religions, and of species have suffered irreversible degradation during the course of patriarchal history. Yet it is not these suffering ones, but those who have inflicted the suffering who seem most to want out, who threaten to bring on the final death, the escape from time and relation and, by a perverse logic, from death itself. For apocalypticism portrays the death of everything as the way to the eternal life of the privileged few.

Science has been the needed and perhaps unwitting tool of the apocalyptic literalization. As Prigogine and Stengers analyze modern science, its classical insistence on a single, immutable, timeless, and universally dominant truth and its describing nature as a simple and homogeneous machine continued the theistic assumptions of simplicity and control—and of the transcendent mind of either scientist or God. But they offer an interesting hope by claiming that, at least in theory, contemporary science has moved to a new time-bound pluralism: "Both at the macroscopic and microscopic levels, the natural sciences have thus rid themselves of a conception of objective reality that implied that novelty and diversity had to be denied in the name of immutable universal control." They show how this shift has emerged along with a new valorization of time (which even Einstein could not accept), that is, of natural processes that are irreversible. Irreversibility is the basis of the thesis that order always emerges out of chaos (of randomness or irreversibility); that "today interest is shifting from substance to relation, to communication, to time. . . . Our universe has a pluralistic, complex character."[12]

Perhaps this new valorization of time, especially in conjunction with pluralism and relation, signals a certain conversion within the White male power elite. But in itself, such a theoretical shift is only interesting. We are now working under imperative deadlines. However, in conjunction with political movements linking ecology, social justice, and feminism, it signals an alternative to the deadly and self-contradictory mix of technological mechanism (based on time-reversible process) with apocalyptic eschatology (an archaic form of irreversibility: history moves from a beginning to an end).

What we need is a reduced and sensitive technology cooperating with the exhaustible, irreversible, spontaneous, and pluralistic character of the universe and the Earth. To achieve this we also need a new understanding of human socioecology—one that cherishes our own diversity rather than exploiting it through hierarchies of state, race, class, and gender. We therefore need to propagate a spirituality that imagines an open and sustainable future, one that looks lovingly on time as the garden of all the relations that have been and will be, that works practically to effect change where it is possible.

Such a spirituality cannot disconnect itself from the biblical heritage altogether. Some of us at least can afford to (and perhaps cannot afford not to) tap the eschatological energies of the classical prophets and of the Mary and Jesus of the synoptic gospels, for whom "prophecy" referred to the denunciation of injustices against the vulnerable and the vision of a lush future in *this* world for all who partake in justice and wisdom. None of these ancient texts come free of their own sexism and nationalism. We cannot find there a point of pure and undiluted liberation, yet there is much radical wisdom there to recycle.

When we revere the complexity of our own and each other's relations and situations, rather than seeking a feminist purity, we have the chance of extending our work effectively and multilaterally into the culture at large.

But here enters eschatology. For while apocalyptic eschatology may bear responsibility for the creation of a sense of time as coming to an end, in a larger and older sense, eschatology in the context of the prophetic cry for justice may be responsible for a sense of the irreversibility of history itself. That is, the sense of history as dramatic unfolding rather than cyclic repetition has its strongest sources in biblical consciousness.

A deliteralized, deapocalypticized eschatology can better serve the feminist project of a socially and historically responsible ecocentrism. Mary's *Magnificat*, for instance, proclaiming the eschatological "year of the Lord's favor," the "good news to the poor," suggests—like all liberation theology, biblical and contemporary—the opening of the sacred community to be realized now, though its fuller realization is still in the future. Such reformed eschatology might give us some leverage for addressing the end-time mode of eschatological consciousness with a modicum of empathy—therefore giving us the chance of affecting it. Without an ecocentric consciousness, liberation eschatology will neglect the natural environment for the sake of small gains now for the poor, undermining the soil, the water, and the air from which everyone's future must flow.

We also need an eschatological consciousness in the sense that we are *watching* now with acute consciousness of the risk to all life; that we are aware that though some processes of damage are still reversible, others are not; that we are in an edgy time, without endless time ahead—indeed, that we are in an end-time. The end of what time? Either of Earth's capacity to support human and most other societies; or of patriarchal history and its time sense (or lack thereof). That is, ending end-time means beginning again with a new, full concept of time—a time that has space for us all and a space that has time for us all—a helical time.

For such a concept of time we draw from whatever Earth-centered, native sources may still speak to us. From them we begin to learn the way of the creatures, of our creatureliness, so that our bodies, our ancestors, and our communities can again speak wisdom to and through us. Women in the past two decades have reopened access to Goddess religions in which woman was neither reducible to, nor separable from, Earth—any more than was any other earthly thing. In a culture that has led to an apocalyptic displacement of the universe in which we dwell, projecting a White warrior experience of alienation into the infinite, to be simply at home again, in our bodies, our worlds, is to become ecocentric: "eco," from *oikos*, the Greek word for "home," which is also the root of "economy." This will mean being at home on the edge of time, not fighting against time but with it. It will mean finding economic/ecological niches for all the wildness of diverse creatures who still, however nervously, populate our planet. Many, too many, are gone, irreversibly, forever. Many will be lost before there is time to save them. But we can take their memory into the creation of a future out of the sacred abundance remaining to us. There is no centralized rule in the universe, no simplicity that will save us. But there is the rhythm by which, again and again, we center ourselves, embody ourselves—make a home for ourselves—amidst the multiplicity. We need no new heaven and Earth. We have this Earth, this sky, this water to renew.

Yaakov Jerome Garb

PERSPECTIVE OR ESCAPE? ECOFEMINIST MUSINGS ON CONTEMPORARY EARTH IMAGERY

IN THE LATE 1980S WE STAND POISED on the cusp between modernity and postmodernity. Even as some of the Enlightenment's fondest visions and longings seem to have attained fulfillment in the last century's fantastic efflorescence of technological mastery, wide-ranging human and environmental devastation lead us increasingly to suspect that these visions may be bankrupt at their fundaments. The basic tenets of modernity's relationship to nature and the Earth are fast reaching their logical conclusions, and we stare in horror as we rush toward them.

This is the background for the emergence of a new image of the Earth that has taken deep root in the Western (and particularly U.S.) psyche during the last few troubled decades. Stewart Brand prised a photograph out of NASA's files to rapidly become *the* representation of the Earth in our times: the whole Earth image.[1] This photograph of the earth from space is now a hugely ubiquitous image: one cannot open a computer magazine or an environmental journal without finding it. Broadly resonant, it is just as likely to appear above the desk of a physicist working on the design of nuclear weapons as above that of the director of a nonprofit environmental organization; as likely to lend its appeal to a Sierra Club brochure as to an advertisement for tractors. It is also a strikingly powerful—almost numinous—image for some; some regard it as a modern mandala whose contemplation is credited with transformative powers and whose spread will single-handedly usher in a new era.[2]

DECONSTRUCTING NASA'S PHOTOGRAPH

In this essay I will explore this new icon (defined by my dictionary as "an object of uncritical devotion") that has come to represent our age. As ecofeminists we are doubly primed to be skeptical of modernity, of it's relationship to the Earth and nature, and of this latest image through which it represents our relationship with the planet. "All great simple images," says French philosopher of science Gaston Bachelard, "reveal a psychic state."[3] What, I ask, is the psychic state out of which this image springs? What can the whole Earth image tell us about the fundamental ways in which contemporary culture construes its relationship to nature? In a previous essay, I explored some of the ways in which the whole Earth image has been *harnessed* to convey a variety of environmentally destructive messages.[4] I discussed, for example, the ubiquitous media portrayals of the Earth as surrounded and contained, conquered and controlled, rendered into a dead artifact, mapped into a barren rectilinear monolith, and trivialized into a mere plaything. In this essay I will focus on some of the attributes of the whole Earth image which are *inherent* to it and thus cannot be explained away as the aberrant misuses of a particular graphic artist or advertising campaign.

My method in this iconoclastic task will be to systematically suspend our commonsense assumptions about this familiar photograph. "We must first rid ourselves of the notion that photographs simply present reality," says writer Susan Sontag, "they interpret it."[5]

For example, one of the most important features of the whole Earth image is the vantage point from which it is obtained: from the outside. We have left the Earth in order to get a better view, in order to see it all at once. Today we take this perceptual maneuver for granted; we regard the viewpoint of a spectator surveying a distant "landscape" as natural. But the urge to step back in order to gain perspective, in order to gain an encompassing vista, is new, as are the technical capabilities for depicting such a viewpoint. It is only in Renaissance Europe of the fourteenth and fifteenth centuries that we begin to see much evidence of this type of relationship toward portions of the Earth, in the physical sciences, literature, landscape painting, architecture, and the principles of garden design.[6] And if we look at the images surrounding this early experimentation with this new perspective we see that this horizontal extension of the landscape view is fraught with far-reaching implications: when we step back to get a better view we create not only a physical distance but a corresponding psychic aloof-ness. The landscape perspective gives rise to (or is symptomatic of) a sense of detachment and spectatorship, for we become disengaged *observers of* rather than *participants in* the reality depicted.

Another way of clarifying for ourselves the tremendous transfor-mation in worldview that accompanied the landscape perspective is through the metaphor of an architectural style that existed prior to this perceptual transformation: the Gothic cathedral. Yi Fu Tuan describes the perceptual assumptions embodied in these structures:

> The vertical cosmos of mediaeval man is dramatically symbolised by pointed arches, towers and spires that soar. The Gothic cathedral baffles modern man; a tourist with his camera may be impressed by the beauty of the nave with its aisles, transepts, radiating chapels, and the span of the vaults. [However] should he seek a position to set up his camera he will find that there is no privileged position from which all these features may be seen. To see a Gothic interior properly one has to move about and turn one's head. Outside the cathedral, the modern tourist may be able to get a good picture of the total structure from a distance. But in mediaeval times this was seldom possible. Other buildings clustered around the edifice and blocked the distant view. Moreover, to see the cathedral from a distance would diminish its impact of bulk and ver-ticality. The details of its facade would no longer be visible. The mediaeval cathedral was meant to be experienced; it was a dense text to be read with devout attention and not an architectural form to be merely seen. In fact, some figures and decorations could not be seen at all. They were made for the eyes of God.[7]

I think the implications for the whole Earth image are obvious. We were once surrounded by our world, experiencing it with all of our senses, participating in it with devout attention to its details—but we have left the cathedral. We *have* obtained a privileged viewpoint for our cameras, a place from which all features can be seen at once. *We* now possess, as the NASA control crew were fond of reminding us, the "God's eye view" of Earth, where nothing is hidden.[8]

The whole Earth image is a starkly literal representation of the Earth; our children now do not get their first impressions of Earth through the multidimensional language of myth and fable, through songs and stories told around the evening fire, but through a photographic im-age. A photograph aims for clarity and unambiguous representation; it is a representation that claims: "Look, things are what they seem."

For the first time in human history, our image of the Earth is not told to us by friends, elders, or family, nor is it gleaned through the direct experience of our own senses. The NASA image of the Earth is brought to us from the depths of cold space by immensely sophisticated machines to which only a few have access.

And since it is a literal rather than a mythic representation, the whole Earth image has no *telling:* it is verb-less, a snapshot, a single frozen instant. Photography, says Susan Sontag, tells us about how something looks, not about how it functions. Functioning takes place in time and must be explained in time. And since understanding is based on how something functions, only that which narrates can make us understand.[9]

Thus, there is a certain psychological flattening and impoverishment of understanding that occurs when a narrative and mythic Earth imagery is replaced by this static and literal photographic image. That is, the whole Earth image relies on sight alone to inform us about our planet. The smell of redwoods, the warmth of summer breezes, the sound of crickets at night (and even the unthinkable cold and silence of space – the location from which this image derives) are, quite literally, not part of the picture. The purely visual nature of the whole Earth image is not a trivial feature. Vision has been judged the preeminent sense in Western thought and as a defining idiom for the achievement of reliable knowledge.[10] Vision is a sense that allows us to perceive all elements of a manifold distinctly at once. It is a sense that operates without necessitating our engagement: We can see without being seen but not touch without at the same time being touched by the object of our perception. And it is a sense in which the advantage lies in distance, rather than proximity. All of these attributes can impart to vision – both as a sense and as a metaphor for knowing in general – a distancing flavor.

The historical shift toward an increasing reliance on the visual has been accomplished by a variety of allied changes in worldview, an entire "epistemology of the visual." Classicist Eric Havelock, for instance, in his analysis of the transition from an oral tradition to a literate culture in ancient Greece describes the associated changes "from identification and engagement to individualization and disengagement, from mimesis to analysis, from concrete to abstract, from *mythos* to *logos*.[11] This distancing, disengaged, abstract, and literalizing epistemology is quintessentially embodied in the whole Earth image where the visual mode of understanding is applied to the entire planet – to nature herself. From a distance of tens of thousands of miles away, transcendent, serene, and unaffected, we survey the whole Earth at once. "This is how the world is best perceived," declares the image. "This is the stance from which the Earth is to be known."

Feminist theorists have done some particularly important work on the role of the visual in modern culture, pointing out the stereotyped gender differentiation of preferred sensory modalities. They have examined the way in which sight has been construed as a particularly "phallic" sense and touch a particularly "feminine" one, and are critical of the corresponding hierarchy of worth, where vision — and the epistemological stance it embodies and implies — is elevated above the "baser," more participatory senses, such as touch. This critical analysis is particularly revealing as to the motivations and ramifications of the increasing emphasis on the visual mode of knowing within patriarchal culture, and it offers the hope of reclaiming a sense of the erotic which is based not "on the gaze which objectifies but on the touch which unites."[12]

The photographic amplifies our already large prejudice in favor of the visual. It places the final seal on the disengagement from participation that vision allows, on the standing back so that subject views object across a void. The photographic act can be a form of violence when it allows us to deny the subjectivity of what we view, when it transforms the external world into a spectacle, a commodity, a manipulable package. "There is an aggression implicit in every use of the camera," says Sontag. [Photography] is a "sexual aggressive act."[13] Others have talked about the "predatory" nature of the camera, contentions that are backed up by the frequent metaphoric equation of a camera with a phallus or gun.

These are strong words, but they contain a truth. Premodern people often shun being photographed; they regard it as soul-depriving, humiliating, a form of rape.[14] At the bottom of this persistent unease about being photographed is, perhaps, a sense that through the photographic act we may be denied our subjectivity, that rendered merely into objects in the world of another we will be denied the respect and mutuality that obtains between two subjects. The making (or taking) of an image at its origins was a magical activity, a means of appropriating or taking power over something;[15] understood in this light, our photographic icon of the Earth seems not quite so benign.

Women are particularly and painfully aware of these dynamics of visual objectification and photographic violence: both underlie voyeurism and pornography. Ecofeminism's basic insight—the deep structural resonances between men's violence toward nature and toward women—is nowhere more evident than in many of the uses we see of the whole Earth image; replace the earth with a woman in these images and they become the all-too-familiar fantasies of pornography.

A SINGLE EARTH, A WHOLE EARTH

Feminists (and postmodernists in general) have become wary of complete pictures, of single unifying viewpoints from which everything can be seen at once. Such integrative frameworks strive to hold all the parts together with no contradictions or incompleteness, no paradox or ambiguity. It has become our critical habit to wonder whose experience has been left out of these grand schemes, how the hegemony of the one-true-story is policed.

The whole Earth image is such a univocal model. Compare it with the fantastic variety of premodern images, the variety even within one kind of representation, such as the images of the earth Goddess. These early images present an unbridled and fecund multiplicity of Earth imaginings: my Earth is not your Earth is not her Earth, and could never be before the whole Earth image. With its single encompassing and privileged viewpoint, this contemporary image visually epitomizes the modern quest for a unified totalizing framework. Its mechanical reproducibility helps sweep away our piebald imaginings, and in our technological culture its photographic literalness renders competing images invalid—*seeing* is believing. The local knowledge that was informed by many senses evaporates in the face of this uniform global picture.[16] The same monotheistic impulse that replaced the pantheon with a single God and the plurality of psychic personages with a single heroic ego, has now given us a single Earth image.

Not only is the Earth of the whole Earth image singular, but it is also whole: healthy, unhurt, unmodified. From this elevated perspective, the Earth does look misleadingly unbroken, free of defect, unmodified and unhurt by human action. This is one of the features that has endeared the image to visionaries of the New Age and other philosophers of jubilant humanism. It is an Earth vision to match the humanistic psychologist's vision of the human: all transcendence and joy, resonating with a positive vibrance, full of health, unity, integration, openness, and a "green growing energy."[17] The *whole* Earth image presents us an

Earth without a shadow side, both literally and in the Jungian sense. (Contrast it to premodern mythic imagery of the Earth and its creation: these are full of monsters, dramatic deaths, blood, sweat, and urine, trickery, uncouth fornication, and decay of all sorts.)

Visions of unity inevitably contain their flip sides: the shadows of *un*holy unity and of fragmentation. The idealized image of the "whole" Earth does not include these shadow sides of modernity's unity and thus wards off anxieties about new and frightening historical realities.[18]

The first shadow of wholism is that a connecting, unified Earth can also be tyrannical, imprisoning, an entrapping web. While our hopes are now global, so is power and domination. Crisis, too, has become global, as global war, global pollution, global warming threaten us *as a species*, and the Earth *as a whole*.

The second shadow of wholism is fragmentation. The appearance of the whole Earth image coincides with a crisis of breaking down, of falling apart. The imagery and fears of fragmentation are everywhere, from the terror of global shattering through nuclear holocaust to the slower *dis*integration of the systems that maintain our air, our water, our food. Chromosomes are torn by radiation and toxins, there are holes in the ozone layer, spills into our oceans, cracks in our reactors, evolutionary lines are being truncated, top soil eroded. The fabric of life, it seems, is going to pieces, as if to warn us of the one-sidedness of these visions of glorious unity and integrity.

The whole Earth perspective provides us with a small, comprehensible, manageable icon—an easily manipulable token Earth that we can use to replace the unfathomably immense and overwhelmingly complex reality of the world which surrounds us. "A blue-and-white Christmas ornament," astronaut Russell Schweickart called it, while astronaut "Buzz" Aldrin talked of how "the earth was eventually so small I could blot it out of the universe simply by holding up my thumb."[19] For a brief while (or more extendedly through the vicarious experience of our photographic trophy), the tables are turned: we are larger than it; what was powerful and all-surrounding becomes background, diminutive, marginal—a little disk far away outside our window. What was pulsing with its own vitality and detail is rendered by distance into a static iconic abstraction. So, quite strikingly, some of the first responses to this image are belittlement, a patronizing bemusement. And we see so many images of the Earth as bauble, ornament, plaything: as beach ball, tennis ball, lollypop, yo-yo. . . .

What are the subliminal motivations for and consequences of this tokenization and trivialization? Are there dangers that attend the replacement of the myriad aspects of the Earth with this abstract token whose ubiquitous and mechanical repetition tend to make us forgetful of the reality it is supposed to designate?

Consider, for example, the computer game *Astrochase*. Our mission: to save the Earth from total destruction. The destruction of our planet is evidenced on the screen by (I quote here from the instruction manual): "first a pulsating of the galaxy followed by a spectacular explosion in which the fragments of the earth shatter in all directions. This is not only the end of our planet but the end of our game as well."[20] But have no fear, all can be restored by pressing the reset button. What nuclear end are our children rehearsing here? How does the easy reset assuage our anxieties about the very real possibility of ultimate nuclear destruction? How does the subliminal persistence of these illusions of a token Earth affect our decision making and that of our leaders regarding very real questions of the Earth's fate?

EXTRATERRESTRIALISM: THE ESCAPE FROM IMMANENCE

Western patriarchal thought is maintained through a ramified series of interrelated dualisms. Woman/man, matter/spirit, body/mind, emotion/reason, darkness/light, evil/good, nature/culture, subjective/objective—the list is long and familiar. In each case women have been associated with one extreme of these dualisms and become the repository for men's projections of their own disowned attributes. (Indeed, masculinity is often *defined* in terms of opposition to these repressed poles.)[21] Much of the task of feminism and feminist philosophy has been to examine the consequences of these dualisms, and to see through and beyond them. In particular, ecofeminism is beginning to examine and challenge the ways in which our relationship toward the Earth and nature is shaped by this web of gender-valenced oppositional categories.

It is against this background that we come to examine one of the most frightening themes apparent in the whole Earth image and its use: extraterrestrialism.[22] The extraterrestrial motif is rampant in popular U.S. culture, where science fiction, movies, video games, advertising media, all conjure up a plethora of images which spurn earthly habitation in the pursuit of fantastic, otherworldly futures. And the whole Earth image fits in well with these fantasies, for its origin and viewpoint are necessarily extraterrestrial; it is a rearward view of the earth, a view seen as we leave.

In particular, extraterrestrial imagery—and the extraterrestrial enterprise as a whole—draws its cultural potency from the same set of dualities we noted above.[23] And, first and foremost, the extraterrestrial project is a masculine one[24]—in practice certainly, and perhaps, as the poet W. H. Auden points out, in impulse, too:

> It's natural the Boys should whoop it up for
> so huge a phallic triumph, an adventure
>   it would not have occurred to women
>   to think worthwhile, . . . [25]

As we examine the imagery and myths that surround an extraterrestrial enterprise such as the space program, we find it to be in many ways an oversized literalization of the masculine transcendent ideal, an attempt to achieve a self-hood freed not only from gravity but from all it represents: the pull of the Earth, of matter, dependence on the mother, the body. *Out of the Cradle*[26] is the title of one book on space exploration, *Breaking the Bonds of Earth*,[27] the subtitle of another. "I viewed my mother quite differently when I was in the womb than I did after birth," says astronaut Schweickart in explaining the ways in which the view from space changed his perspective.[28] Man, the futurists tell us, can be free of dependence on Earth and come to live in artificial surroundings of his own creation.[29] The goal is not merely to gain access to "extraterrestrial resources;" much more is at stake: space exploration is seen as the cutting edge of "the evolution of human society and human consciousness."[30] "Should man fall back from his destiny," a NASA official warns us, "the confines of this planet will destroy him."[31] Notice the three actors here: *man,* his *destiny,* and the *Earth.* The whole drama is enacted along an axis of verticality (up = growth = destiny = future = space [= man]; down = regression = failure = Earth [= woman]), and the Earth's role is seen as destructive, confining, pulling man back from his destiny. Indeed, the whole patriarchal cultural project has been seen as an enormous extraterrestrial enterprise through which "man acquires a soul distinct from his body, and a superorganic culture which perpetuates the revolt against organic dependence on the mother."[32]

Such talk has a familiar ring to the psychoanalytically minded. Object relations theory, for instance, has a lot to tell us about the parallels or even causal relationships between the modern need for transcendence of matter and the Earth and the psychodynamics of men brought up by mothers within patriarchal arrangements of child rearing. Individuation for boys in a patriarchal culture involves movement away from the primary (maternal) other, so that maturity is equated with independence and lack of connectedness to the providing figure. The flip side of this independence is an unconscious fear of dependency, of being swallowed up by the immanence of the female body and by the world of matter in general. The earthy realities of the biological world, the body, and the female body especially, are resented as obstacles dragging the free, unencumbered subject back down to a merely "natural" existence. The powerful and pervasive resonances between violence toward nature and violence toward women in Western culture stem, perhaps, from this unconscious horror of physical immanence and dependency. Women come to represent the pulls of flesh and matter—threats to the disembodied purity of the spirit and the mind. Against this psychological background we can understand some of the deeper underpinnings of extraterrestrialism and its goals of radical independence and autonomy from embeddedness in the natural world. Such an understanding is important in an era when patriarchal culture has attained the technical capability to pursue these archetypal fantasies in ways that are increasingly literal, costly, and life threatening.

A multitude of whole Earth images plays upon these extraterrestrial themes. In many we see the Earth outgrown, transcended, and discarded, a worn and spent relic from humanity's childhood that can be trashed as we move on. ("Beam me up Scotty," says a bumper sticker, "this planet sucks!") Many focus on escape from the Earth through the mediation of high technology and imbue space and an extraterrestrial view of Earth with feelings of newness, adventure, and the promise of a glamorous, high-tech future "out there." Others portray evolution as a process of Earth transcendence, with the gaze of the human figures cast longingly on an Ultimate out there in space, rather than on the Immediate here on Earth.[33] Several portray disembodied cerebrums that hover far above the planet, their existence reduced to technologically effected control through pure thought alone.

The ways of thinking and feeling that produce this kind of imagery have very deep roots in Western religious thought. For premodern people, divinity was immanent in the natural world: there were gods of the rain and the wind, sacred energies in the hills and valleys, and plants and animals all had their own numinous presence. But the desert fathers who founded monotheism gradually replaced these by a single god, a God who was "out there," distant from the world. Spirit became separable from the world of matter and natural phenomena.

Monotheism's novel notion of a unitary and transcendent spirituality became increasingly entrenched over the centuries at the expense of an attunement with the world and its material process. From late antiquity through the early Renaissance it found complex expression in an outlook that classicist Hilary Armstrong refers to as "cosmic piety."[34] In this tremendously influential world picture the cosmos is very sharply divided into two parts with very different values: the Earth, that central region below the moon, and the upper cosmos, that spiritual and immaterial realm that lies *outside* and *above* this. Cosmic piety encouraged a radical disesteem for the Earth, that insignificant and lowly region we inhabit. "This central region below the moon in which [the earth] lies is low in every way and on every scale, and the earth is lowest in it. It is the darkest, dampest and dirtiest part of the universe, a kind of cosmic cesspit, full of corruption and decay." The only beauty and divinity available to humans was that which trickled down from the upper cosmos, with inevitable consequences for the desirable orientation of human endeavors; spiritual life, it was felt, prepares us for ascent to the true life of the soul in the heavens above through ridding us of all the dark impurities and passions associated with material existence in this lowest region. And as with all the other great splits in Western intellectual history, this one, too, was polarized in terms of gender. It was the hot, bright, dry, active, male, good, Divine principle that belongs to and aspires to this upper realm, and the cold, dark, moist, passive, female, evil principle that belongs below, and tends to pull us back down to the Earth's gross material corruption.

Though the stronger forms of this worldview no longer enjoy the explicit and unanimous credence they once did, their currents still run strongly in Western culture, often surfacing quite explicitly in the extraterrestrial enterprise. President Reagan, for instance, succinctly captured the essential mood of cosmic piety when he eulogized the astronauts killed in the 1986 space shuttle explosion. He spoke of them as heros killed in fulfillment of the glorious adventure of trying to "escape the surly bonds of earth to fly up and touch the face of God." Sound familiar? Divinity, the transcendent ethereal God whom we strive to emulate and approach, is *out there—above*; the surly bonds of Earth pull us back and hamper us in this transcendent quest. Was it not thus natural for NASA scientists to dub their newly attained whole Earth images as a "God's-eye view"?

As opposed to these contemporary recapitulations of cosmic piety, one of the central impulses of women's spirituality and other gynophilic spiritualities is to break down the division between a transcendent holy realm and the rest of existence. By once again valorizing and finding divinity in the natural world around us, in the "profane" cycles of human life, and in the female body, women and men have begun to break the series of dualities and thus the stranglehold of patriarchal value systems.

"BUT WHAT ABOUT ALL THE POSITIVE ASPECTS OF THE IMAGE?"

The whole Earth image, as we have seen, epitomizes in many ways— in the very fundaments of its construction—trends and notions in Western culture that are deeply problematic. It is not farfetched to call this image the *magnum opus* of patriarchal consciousness. Yet the whole Earth image was brought to light and is still being used by those who *rebel against* what is destructive in the Western relationship to the Earth: by peace activists, environmentalists, and proponents of a new Earth-based spirituality. Many people in these groups seem to be deeply touched by the image, sometimes to the point of evangelically sponsoring its distribution. The image, they claim, shows us the incredible beauty of the Earth. From this transcendent perspective the Earth seems one unit and the political borders over which so much blood is spilt illusory. They say the image reminds us of the Earth's fragility and of its preciousness as a sole oasis of green in the blackness of space.

How are we to understand this seeming contradiction. Can we explain or even justify the adoption of such a problematic image by those working to preserve the Earth? Does the whole Earth image have sufficient virtues to make it worthwhile despite the alienating impulse it embodies so deeply? Or should other images replace it, and if so which? I am not sure of the answers to these questions, though I can offer some speculative thoughts with which to approach them.

Perhaps these environmental and peace groups are sympathetic to the whole Earth image to the extent that they have unwittingly internalized the epistemological and ideological assumptions that underlie it. For example, though our critical faculties might utterly reject the deep assumptions that inform the pathos of a soap opera, its sentiments are still part of our emotional repertoire and might still have the power to move us. In the case of the whole Earth image, however, such unconscious assimilation of cultural moods is worrying, for the assumptions this image embodies and perpetuates are the very ones from which environmentally destructive behavior flows.

Another way to explain the strong emotions that the whole Earth image arouses among people who care for the planet is to tease these feelings apart more carefully. These are not, it seems to me, simply the warm enjoyment of a beautiful sight, the sunny appreciation of a glorious piece of natural history, a simple outflowing of communion with the natural world. Rather, our emotional responses to the image are bittersweet, tinged with an ache for that which the image makes us realize we have lost. We hover as gods above this perfect sphere so beautiful in its crystal clarity, but isn't there a deep ache of longing for a beauty we somehow cannot touch, a realization that we remain disengaged, that our communion is unconsummated—it is only from afar, only through the eye. Is our feeling when looking down at our Earth across so much empty blackness perhaps a little shiver of cold, a pang of loneliness as we realize how far we've gone, how far out we are? My suggestion is that the emotions this image arouses are due not so much to our sympathy for the worldview it presents, but to the way in which we recoil from it; the image's viewpoint is valuable because it reminds us that we have not yet attained it. We are stirred, in other words, by the parts of ourselves that *refuse* this cold distanced vision, and by our imagination's response that counters the stark abstraction of this space photo with concrete real and full-bodied images of communion with our planet—specific places, people, and creatures. The image graphically presents us with the cold consequences of what modernity is attempting, and we take fright, realizing this might not be what we want. Perhaps, as Daniel Noel has suggested, our culture needed to come this far out in order to return.[35]

One last explanation of the image's power to move us and a possible justification for an environmentalist use of the image may be that we can override the distancing and objectification that photography encourages, and salvage elements of an I-Thou relationship with the Earth. Is such a relationship possible despite the medium? If the objectification of the gaze occurs because of a *denial* of reciprocal communication, can our act of looking be a dialogue rather than an inspection? Can we "see without staring," and allow the Earth to speak to us through this image, to declare its subjecthood?[36] Can the whole Earth image be as richly imbued with our own personal meanings and concretely contextualized experience as a family photograph or a portrait of an old friend, rather than being an impersonal public image of a foreign vista rudely decontextualized by the camera? Can we, in other words, remake the image's meanings through the imaginative act we bring to our encounter with it, and if so what are the conditions that would make this possible? (The challenge of doing this seems homologous to that of creating a nonpredatory and nonvoyeuristic photograph of a human body, one that invites and conveys impulses of love and respect, mystery and communion, rather than objectification.) Only if these epistemological challenges are met, it seems to me, can the whole Earth image be salvaged and recreated by the spectator as a good way of relating to our home.[37]

DO WE NEED A NEW IMAGE?

But perhaps the contradictions of the whole Earth image are too weighty, and it should be abandoned altogether. What then should replace it?

Should we heed the call of many ecofeminists, to reclaim the image of Earth as a sacred Goddess? True, it renders the Earth into an organic dynamic entity, does not rely purely on the visual, and restores the multidimensionality of myth to our stories about the Earth and our relationship to it. But we should check carefully whether we really want to view our relationship with the Earth through genderized lenses. What baggage will carry over from one domain to another (especially in a culture whose relation to both women and mothers is as misogynous as ours is)? What are the consequences—for both Earth and women—of reinforcing this age-old alignment between them.[38] Where does Goddess imagery leave men? The choice between identification with a fierce roaming Sky God on the one hand and an all-encompassing, nurturing Earth Goddess on the other—what a caricatured and degenerate subset of the full range of archetypal possibility! Bring on the Sky Goddesses, the Earth Gods, and all the wild and fecund creatures of psychic life—restore to both men and women those richly creative images of self-hood and earth-hood so long banished from our culture.

Maybe we should be suspicious of the very way in which our mind tries immediately to find an alternative image. Isn't this impulse toward a single true image a manifestation of modernity's obsolete quest for a single privileged viewpoint that gives us the whole picture, the one true representation? Isn't this urge a product of the same monotheistic and centralizing tendencies that have gotten us into so much trouble in the first place? Isn't the fantasy that we can somehow contain the Earth within our imagination, bind it with a single metaphor, the most mistaken presumption of all? What would it be to live with multiple images of the Earth—fragmented, partial, and local representations that must always be less than the Earth we try to capture through them?

I opened with Gaston Bachelard's dictum that all great simple images reveal a psychic state. In reviewing the contemporary great simple image of the Earth, it does indeed seem as troubled as our times. Like our culture at the close of one era and the dawn of another, the image vacillates between objectification and communion, domination and love, escape and return. Poised on the cusp of modernity and postmodernity, we are, as philosopher of science Stephen Toulmin points out, in the throes of a transition to a world which "has not yet discovered how to define itself in terms of what it *is*, but only in terms of what it has *just-now-ceased to be.*"[39] Doesn't our dilemma with respect to future Earth images define our condition: all icons shattered but nothing to replace them? (Indeed, isn't our ability to ever again be comforted by a single unifying image forever broken?)

We have seen the ways in which various strands of modernity are inextricably woven into this image through which we represent the Earth, creating a fearful vision of domination and escape from participation in a living Earth. Yet we have also seen the ways in which the image has been used to gain a new sense of perspective on the planet and to warn us of our peril. But no matter which images we use to sustain us in our task, as environmentalists and feminists, we are aware that the time has come to reweave the future with different threads.[37]

Gloria Feman Orenstein

ARTISTS AS HEALERS: ENVISIONING LIFE-GIVING CULTURE

WE HAVE SUGGESTED IN OUR INTRODUCTION that ecofeminism as a political movement creates change in ways that break down the boundaries between concepts and roles previously seen as antithetical. In the creation of new cultures that neither pit humans against nature nor set them above it, but rather situate us within the cycles of the cosmos and celebrate the interconnectedness of all things, the arts have begun to play a major transformational part. This, in itself, makes ecofeminism a different kind of political movement, for instead of viewing the arts as adjuncts to political activity or as distractions from political activism, ecofeminism considers the arts to be essential catalysts of change.

The ceremonial aspect of art is now understood to be potent enough to raise energy, to evoke visions, to alter states of consciousness, and to transmit vibrations, thoughts, and images that, when merged with the energy of political acts (such as the protests at the Diablo Canyon nuclear power plant, the Livermore Weapons Lab, the Nevada Test Site, the women's peace camp at the Greenham military base in England, and the Women's Pentagon Action) can create a critical mass powerful enough to alter the energy field of the participants. The rituals enhance and augment the political actions, binding the participants together in a shared spiritual community and creating the opportunity for healing.

I am suggesting that what might be called the "ecofeminist arts" function ceremonially to connect us with the two powerful worlds from which the Enlightenment severed us—nature and the spirit world. If the severing of our intimate connectedness to the Earth, the sky, the dead, the unseen, and our ancestors was the accomplishment of the

Enlightenment, then ecofeminism calls for an *endarkenment*[1] — a bonding with the Earth and the invisible that will reestablish our sense of interconnectedness with all things, phenomenal and spiritual, that make up the totality of life in our cosmos. The ecofeminist arts do not maintain that analytical, rational knowledge is superior to other forms of knowing. They honor Gaia's Earth intelligence and the stored memories of her plants, rocks, soil, and creatures. Through nonverbal communion with the energies of sacred sites in nature, ecofeminist artists obtain important knowledge about the spirit of the land, which they can then honor through creative rituals and environmental pieces.

Ellen Marit Gaup-Dunfjeld is both a shaman and a poet. Her poetry is written in both Sami and Norwegian. When she translated some of her poems into English for me, I became aware of a fundamental difference between the ecofeminist arts and the arts of the postmodern movement in which language is self-referential and does not point to a prior existing, exterior reality. In one of her poems she chanted: "The word is not only the word / Something is behind it / If you are thinking / If you are seeking / You will find it / The word is not only the word." Her poem tells us that beyond the world of human creation lies the realm of the Great Spirit's creation. It is the function of the poem to allow words to lead us to worlds of nature and of spirit, not to make art rival nature or constitute a world sufficient unto itself. The realm of the Great Spirit's creation, which contains all that is seen and unseen, living and dead, is the realm to which art points. As a poet and shaman, Ellen Marit reconnects us to the powers of those worlds. Her poetry translates the language of the Earth Mother into human words. But it is the song of the Earth Mother than we must hear by listening sensitively to the sounds made by the human poet:

> And the wind up in the mountain is whistling
> Don't you hear the wind *yoiking?*
> Our Mother Earth is speaking: "Don't give me to strange people
> But protect me from them
> Because this is your mountain
> And your river and your lake
> Don't sell your inheritance
> Because it is the biggest inheritance you can leave to your next of kin."

The shaman/poet becomes the intermediary between humans and the Earth Mother, translating the messages of nature into words that are communicable to human ears that have become deafened to the meaning of the sounds of the natural world. Ecofeminist poetry such as Ellen Marit's topples our human arrogance. It situates humans within the cosmos, linking us once more to nature and to the Great Spirit. It brings us the songs of the wind, of the birds, the suffering of the creatures, and the messages of the Earth Mother.

During the 1970s and 1980s in the West, women writers and artists, inspired by Susan Griffin's *Woman and Nature: The Roaring Inside Her*,[2] began to conceive of a culture that would revolutionize our relationship to nature and postulate a world in which spirit resides in matter. Griffin linked a feminist cultural vision to an ecological vision of interconnectedness: "Because we know ourselves to be made from this earth, and shaped like the earth, by what has gone before . . . we know this earth is made from our bodies. For we see ourselves, and we are nature. We are nature seeing nature. We are nature with a concept of nature. Nature weeping. Nature speaking of nature to nature."[3]

The ecofeminist arts often invoke the symbol of the Great Mother (the Goddess) in order to emphasize the interconnectedness of three levels of creation, all imaged as female outside of patriarchy: cosmic creation, procreation, and artistic creation. Thus, the Goddess has begun to function as an emblem of healing in the ecofeminist arts, for it is the image of the Great Mother that heals the splits between the material and the spiritual, the human and the nonhuman, the mind and the body, and the sacred and the profane that have dominated patriarchal civilizations in the West for the last several thousand years. The Goddess signifies that all forms of life, both human and nonhuman, and culture and the arts are all interconnected through their creation by an agency originally imaged as female.

Through public and private rituals, ceremonies, and art performances, contemporary "feminist matristic" artists – artists who reclaim ancient Goddess iconography and symbols – resanctify the Earth to create an ecstatic rebirth of a new culture from the womb of the Great Earth Mother. This new cosmogony reclaims as well the 35,000 years of history in which cosmic creation was imaged as female by decentering patriarchal history, reducing it to a small period of 5,000 years within the larger framework of matristic history.[4]

These art rituals are rites of evocation and transformation, mythic reenactments of a journey back to the matrix of being, to our sacred origins in the womb of the Great Earth Mother. During the enactment and performance of these art rituals, we come into closer contact with the subtle energy forces that shape, mold, and create reality. The ritual permits us to live a new myth, to *experience* its cosmogony and its symbols, its traditions, its modes of expression. As we enter the ritual, we begin to embody these new knowledges and new feelings. Ritual hastens the processes of community creation and alliance building, of psychic transformation, and personal and group empowerment.

When I speak of new images in connection with the reclamation of the Goddess, I do not mean that contemporary women artists recreate an ancient past as if they knew exactly how it occurred historically. Nor would they wish to return to that past, even if they could know more about it than current excavations have made possible. On the contrary, in reclaiming the Goddess, ecofeminist artists are actually reconnecting with a source of empowerment by reconstructing images relating our current moment of ecofeminist rebirth to images and symbols derived from a tradition that empowered women for more than 35,000 years. These new images, then, fuse modern meanings with ancient symbols to create highly charged signs that transmit this energy to contemporary women. The image of a woman with her arms uplifted, derived from the Cretan Goddess, is one example of how the reclaimed Goddess image is used by Ana Mendieta, many of whose works depict women rising from the Earth with their arms raised in a pose reminiscent of the ancient Goddess of Crete whose uplifted arms wielded powerful serpents.

Let us look briefly at the work of several of these artists to get a sense of the way in which the art rite or work functions to reconnect us with nature and the spirit world.

California artist Vijali has been sculpting the Great Earth Mother in sacred rocks and boulders that she finds in sites all over the world. Indeed, in order to view her works, one needs to visit them with a map in hand, for they are located in mountains and forests, far from the main road, and a hike and a picnic are usually part of the process of reaching and seeing them. Thus, her art brings us directly into nature.

As a child, Vijali was introduced to meditation. She entered a Hindu convent at the age of 14 and lived there until she was 25. She experienced the luminous energy by which humans are interconnected with nature during the many hours she spent meditating. When she left the convent and embarked on her artistic path, she underwent still more intense experiences channeling healing energies. She found that in order to ground those energies, she had to live and sculpt in the mountains. She would see energy moving in the stones, and at those peak moments she experienced a oneness with everything. It is this vibrant life energy that she expresses in her art. Her work enables us to experience our own interconnectedness with nature, particularly since the journey to see her sculptures consists of a ritual in which one spends at least half of the day out of doors. As I prepared, for example, to visit her sculpture of the *Great Winged Ones,* I thought about bringing food along, about the weather, and about the ways in which I relate to the natural world rather than to an art gallery. Once I arrived at the piece, I experienced a slowing down of time as I became attuned to the site. Her stone sculptures flow with their natural setting, which is their home. Her work also aligns us with site-specific energy flows, the telluric currents and natural processes in the environment. We take a day out to see one artwork, and make the experience of it the focus of our journey. The sculpture ultimately draws us closer to nature, making us conscious of the subtleties of each sensation in the landscape.

Vijali describes her new work, the *World Wheel,* as being inspired by the Native-American medicine wheel. She plans to create a series of environmental sculpture and performance events around the world, in sites in Spain, Italy, Greece, Israel, Egypt, the Soviet Union, India, Tibet, China, and Japan. She sees the *World Wheel* as a rite to bring about global peace and understanding to help us survive and heal the planet and ourselves. The first performance took place in Malibu, California, on the occasion of the Harmonic Convergence during the summer of 1987.[5] Vijali worked closely with a community of local performance artists and people interested in spirituality and ecology to create a site-specific event evocative of a changing mythos, one creating an Earth-revering culture. She created a medicine wheel from rocks and objects found at the site while participants danced, chanted, and created healing ceremonies throughout the night.

Another ecofeminist artist is New Yorker Helene Aylon. In 1982 she rescued some soil from a Strategic Air Command weapon base. The soil was placed in pillowcases and then transported in an "Earth Ambulance" of her creation to the United Nations, where it was carried down the steps to the U.N. Plaza on stretchers as if it were a wounded body. At the U.N., a 14-day sleep-out was held to show concern for the Earth.

In *Sister Rivers,* a ritual that took place at the Kama River in Japan, Aylon conceived of the Earth as the Mother, and of her rivers as vital arteries and veins of the living mother planet. In the piece, two young Japanese women came to the Kama River and placed rice and seeds into two pillowcases. They then sent the cases down the river to Hiroshima and Nagasaki, where other women awaited their arrival. The women there added soil from Hiroshima and Nagasaki to the seeds and rice already in the pillowcases and sent them sailing down the river. Aylon plans to continue to sail pillowcases down the rivers of the world, gathering soil from various parts of the planet within them, making everyone conscious of the need to rescue Mother Earth.

Chicago artist Fern Shaffer collaborates with photographer Othello Anderson to explore the place of humans on Earth and the meaning of all kinds of natural phenomena. Shaffer dresses in different shamanic costumes in order to communicate with the sacred powers of the land through shapes, colors, vibrations, and gestures reminiscent of ancient ritualists who were once in touch with these sacred energies. Through rituals held at different sites in different climates and at different times of the planetary cycles, Shaffer and Anderson are learning to use the language of art to commune with the invisible energies that inhabit these sites. The rituals, though done with only one or two people present, are posited on the understanding that since everything is interconnected, the artist's visit to the site and her energy exchange with it may touch off a chain of reactions associated with the webs and networks of the Great Mother and may produce a healing. Shaffer often performs her rituals at sites where she feels nature needs healing, and these sites often turn out to be places where nuclear reactors have been located. Her colorful, flamboyant costumes introduce feminist matristic resonances and, she hopes, create transformations in the atmosphere that may begin the healing process of the site and send the healing vibrations out into the surrounding community, hopefully leading to healing there as well.

New York performance artist Mierle Laderman Ukeles works with the New York Sanitation Department as its official artist in residence. She does what she calls "maintenance art"—art that maintains the Earth and keeps it clean and healthy. In 1976 she began working with and holding discussions with three hundred sanitation workers. She realized that the gestures the sanitation workers use when cleaning are similar to those of painters and asked the sanitation workers to consider an hour of their regular day's work as art. In 1983 she choreographed *Ballet Mechanique* with six sanitation trucks and their sweepers. She also has made a mirrored garbage truck that becomes a social mirror in which people on the streets can see themselves reflected as troops of Earth-maintenance people and planetary healers. From 1978 to 1980 she walked around New York City shaking hands with sanitation workers and thanking them for keeping the city alive.

At present she is producing *Flow City*, a public artwork done in conjunction with the sanitation department at the Fifty-ninth Street pier on the Hudson River. This complex work involves building a viewing platform with explanations of the movements of the barges that carry the city's refuse to Staten Island. In this piece, some of the barges will return with fresh dirt, thus demonstrating a complete recovery cycle. The public will be able to see the waste they produce and that the Earth can transform some of it back again into a healthy form, thus leading to the understanding that they are connected both to the waste and to the Earth.

In *Gaia, Mon Amour*, French-California performance artist Rachel Rosenthal demonstrates her discovery of the Earth as a living being. Rosenthal's creation of Gaia depicts the immensity and the wrath of a powerful Earth Mother. Rosenthal's Gaia shatters and challenges all our preconceptions. Gaia roars and bellows, expresses her anger at how she is being killed. Rosenthal realizes that man has taken the Earth Mother hostage, but that Gaia is actually powerful, supremely intelligent, and anything but passive. Yet humans are living as parasites on the Earth and by killing their host are killing themselves as well. Gaia teaches Rosenthal important lessons about nature and the place of humans in the cosmos. In this performance piece, Rosenthal rocks and keens against a Native-American backdrop depicting the sacred land. She drums and chants for an end to rape and ecocide, for a time when all humans will revere the Earth as Native Americans do.

One might well think of ecofeminist visual arts as medicine journeys and of ecofeminist literature as medicine stories created in order to bring about a healing of the Earth.

For example, in Ursula K. Le Guin's novel *Always Coming Home*, which creates an ethnography of the Kesh, a people living in the distant future, the oral tradition is very much alive. In fact, it is as sacred and as important as any written tradition. The ecological basis of the Kesh's literary tradition includes the firm belief that, like everything else that is alive, books are mortal—they also die. Thus, the Kesh clear out and recycle their books every few years in a kind of ritual to make room for new books. After all, why should forests be destroyed if paper can be recycled to print new books? The mantic function of the storyteller has been restored in the Kesh world. Like shamans, their artists (dancers, painters, shapers, and makers) journey to the gap between the worlds and come back with words and tunes. Like shamans, they go into confusion and come back with patterns. What they bring back can be understood as ecological memory. It is expressed in this way: "It was the universe of power. It was the network, field, and lines of the energies of all the beings, stars and galaxies of stars, worlds, animals, minds, nerves, dust, the lace and foam of vibration that is being, itself, all interconnected, every part of another part and the whole part of each part, and so comprehensible to itself only as a whole, boundless and unclosed."[7]

The Kesh also have a keen sense of community and "continuity with the dirt, water, air, and living creatures of the Valley."[8] They return home to die because they feel themselves to be intimately connected to their bioregion and its soil. Before they slaughter an animal, they address its spirit, thus showing respect for all souls. The Kesh have chosen not to live a "high tech" life because they value the health of the planet above personal comfort.

If we look upon ecofeminist literature as medicine stories, we can understand that its function is to teach us lessons about healing. These stories illustrate ways in which we can reconnect with the sources of our powers of transformation. They also show us how the patriarchal heroic ethic has led to the death of nature and how a radical new ethic must evolve in order for the planet to survive. From this perspective it is interesting to note that in an ecofeminist novel such as *Always Coming Home*, the protagonist is not a single hero, but an entire culture.

These stories ask us to look beyond words and beyond appearances. They ask us to reconnect with the very source of all creation, to affirm life, and to honor Gaia's intelligence and feelings as we would those of our own mother, which she is. Ecofeminist writers tell tales about how, in recovering our lost senses and powers through reconnecting with nature and the spirit world, we can bring forth life out of the wasteland and restore the Grail, the great cauldron of regeneration that is the Earth herself.

Because ecofeminism does not postpone the creation of a culture that restores the vital links between the natural world, the human world, and the spirit world, artists as visionaries are valued as important creators in the process of change. These artists are not writing political theory. Their narratives involve the imagining of various solutions, some of which lead us beyond the impasse of the dualism of culture versus nature, and some of which recapitulate that dualism by reversing it, maintaining that it is imperative now to value nature over culture. What is most important for us to understand is that ecofeminist artists are, indeed, taking journeys, visualizing many possibilities, presenting us with alternative visions, and gleaning knowledge that can only be obtained via the imagination. It is imperative that we go about the task of creating an alternative society and a culture that is interconnected with nature *now,* and that we look to our artists for a multiplicity of images that will enable us to transform the world before it is too late.[9]

Notes

ECOFEMINISM: OUR ROOTS AND FLOWERING

1. See, for example, the introduction and essays in Charlene Spretnak (ed.), *The Politics of Women's Spirituality* (Garden City, NY: Doubleday/Anchor, 1982).
2. My favorite is G. Tyler Miller, *Living in the Environment*, 4th ed. (Belmont, CA: Wadsworth, 1985).

HOW TO HEAL A LOBOTOMY

1. Dorothy Dinnerstein, *The Mermaid and the Minotaur* (New York: Harper & Row, 1986).
2. See her essay, "Invoking the Grove," in Judith Plant (ed.), *Healing the Wounds* (Philadelphia: New Society Publishers, 1989). See also Deena Metzger, *Looking for the Faces of God* (Berkeley, CA: Parallax Press, 1989).
3. In Starhawk, *Truth or Dare* (New York: Harper & Row, 1987), p. 1.
4. See Stephen Hawking, *A Brief History of Time* (New York: Bantam, 1988).
5. Personal communication. See also Gloria Feman Orenstein, *The Reflowering of the Goddess* (Elmsford, NY: Pergamon Press, Athene Series, 1990).
6. See Paula Gunn Allen, "Tribal Cultures." *Revision* 9 (no. 1: 1986).

THE GAIA TRADITION AND THE PARTNERSHIP FUTURE:
AN ECOFEMINIST MANIFESTO

1. Riane Eisler, *The Chalice and the Blade* (San Francisco: Harper & Row, 1987), p. 31.
2. James Mellaart, *Catal Huyuk; A Neollthic Town in Anatolia* (New York: McGraw-Hill, 1987).
3. Marija Gimbutas, *The Goddesses and Gods of Old Europe*, rev. ed. (London: Thomas & Hudson, 1982).
4. Quoted in Eisler, *Chalice and the Blade*, p. 36.

THE ORIGINS OF GOD
IN THE BLOOD OF THE LAMB

1. E.O. James, *Origins of Sacrifice: A Study in Comparative Religion* (Port Washington, NY: Kennikat Press, 1948), p. 37.

2. Ibid., p. 41.
3. Joseph Campbell, *Myths to Live By* (Toronto: Bantam Books, 1972), p. 40.
4. Ibid., p. 33.
5. James, p. 37.
6. Ibid., p. 38.
7. Quoted by Peter Furst, "The Shamanic Universe," in *Stones, Bones and Skin* (Toronto: Arts Canada, 1977), p. 14.
8. Ibid.
9. Julian Jaynes, *The Origins of Consciousness in the Breakdown of the Bicameral Mind* (Boston: Houghton, Mifflin, 1976), pp. 405, 407.
10. Andreas Lommel, *Shamanism: The Beginnings of Art* (New York: McGraw-Hill, 1966).
11. Mercea Eliade, *Shamanism: Archaic Techniques of Ecstacy* (New York: Pantheon, 1964), p. 12.
12. James, *Origins of Sacrifice*, p. 40.
13. Frances Moore Lappé and Joseph Collins, *Food First: Beyond the Myth of Scarcity* (Boston: Houghton Mifflin, 1977).
14. This paper was first published in *Anima* 12 (no. 2: Spring 1986): 139–43.

THE ELEUSINIAN MYSTERIES:
ANCIENT NATURE RELIGION OF DEMETER AND PERSEPHONE

1. Quoted by C. Kerenyi, *Eleusis: Archetypal Image of Mother and Daughter* (NY: Pantheon, 1967). p. 15.
2. Quoted by Jane Ellen Harrison, *Prolegomena to the Study of Greek Religion* (London: London Press, 1962), p. 267.
3. George Mylonas, *Eleusis and the Eleusinian Mysteries* (Princeton, NJ: Princeton University Press, 1961), pp. 14, 33–49.
4. See Kerenyi, *Eleusis*, p. 8.
5. Thelma Sargent, trans., *The Homeric Hymns* (New York: Norton, 1973), p. 79.
6. See Harrison, *Prolegomena*, pp. 123, 285; Lewis R. Farnell, *The Cults of the Greek States*, Vol. III (New Rochelle, NY: Caratzas Brothers, 1977), pp. 75–85.
7. Quoted by Richard Trapp, "The Eleusinian and Dionysian Mysteries," paper presented at the Classics and Philosophy Colloquium, October 1982, San Francisco State University.
8. Harrison, *Prolegomena*, pp. 120–1, 128, 157, cites Plutarch as identifying Isis and Demeter.
9. See Harrison, *Prolegomena*, p. 122.
10. Charlene Spretnak, *Lost Goddesses of Early Greece: A Collection of Pre-Hellenic Mythology* (Berkeley, CA: Moon Books, 1978), pp. 103–10.
11. Sargent, *Homeric Hymns, p. 13.*
12. See C. Kerenyi, *The Gods of the Greeks,* trans. Norman Cameron (New York: Thames and Hudson, 1951), pp. 45–46, 67.

13. Harrison, *Prolegomena*, p. 564.
14. Quoted by Paul Friedrich, *The Meaning of Aphrodite* (Chicago: Chicago University Press, 1978), p. 161.
15. H. G. Evelyn-White, *Hesiod, the Homeric Hymns and Homerica* (Cambridge, MA: Harvard University Press, 1914), pp. 288–91.
16. Harrison, *Prolegomena*, pp. 273, 548–53, 562–6.
17. Quoted by Kerenyi, *Eleusis*, p. 41.
18. Homeric "Hymn to Demeter," in Edouard Schure, *The Mysteries of Ancient Greece: Orpheus, Plato* (Blauvelt, NY: Rudolf Steiner, 1971), p. 75.
19. For somewhat differing accounts of the 9 days of rituals, see Mylonas, *Eleusis*, chap. 9; Farnell, *Cults of the Greek States*, pp. 164–91; Harrison, *Prolegomena*, pp. 151–61.
20. See Kerenyi, *Gods of the Greeks*, p. 12.
21. Schure, *Mysteries of Ancient Greece*, p. 111.
22. Quoted by Trapp, "Eleusinian and Dionysian Mysteries" (Cicero, *The Laws*, 2.36).
23. This essay is a shortened and revised version of my article, "The Eleusinian Mysteries of Demeter and Persephone: Fertility, Sexuality and Rebirth," *Journal of Feminist Studies in Religion*, 4 (no. 1: Spring 1988).

THE WOMAN I LOVE IS A PLANET;
THE PLANET I LOVE IS A TREE

1. Quoted by Susan Cady, Marian Ronan, and Hal Taussig, *SOPHIA: The Future of Feminist Spirituality* (San Francisco: Harper & Row, 1986), p. 29.

RETHINKING THEOLOGY AND NATURE

1. See Carol Christ, "Finitude, Death, and Reverence for Life," in *Laughter of Aphrodite: Reflections on a Journey to the Goddess* (San Francisco: Harper & Row, 1987), chap. 12.
2. Gordon Kaufman, *The Theological Imagination: Constructing the Concept of God* (Philadelphia: Westminster, 1981), p. 226. Kaufman's modern post-Kantian perspective caused him to overstate the separation between divinity, humanity, and nature in Jewish religion, but he is correct in stating that the Jewish conception of Yahweh as ruling nature through a covenantal relation with humanity represented a fundamental departure from earlier views of the relation of God, humanity, and nature.
3. Ibid., pp. 215–6, 225.
4. Susan Griffin, *Woman and Nature: The Roaring Inside Her* (New York: Harper & Row, 1978), p. 227.
5. Ibid., p. 226.

6. Ibid., p. xvii.

7. Ibid., p. 227.

8. Ibid., p. 1.

9. Ibid.

10. Ibid., pp. 226, 227.

11. Ibid., p. 226.

12. Gordon Kaufman, *Theology for a Nuclear Age* (Philadelphia: Westminster, 1985), p. 35.

13. Ibid., pp. 35–36.

14. Ibid., pp. 44–45.

15. Ibid., pp. 20, 28. Also see my "Embodied Thinking: Reflections on Feminist Theological Method," *Journal of Feminist Studies in Religion* 5 (no. 1: Spring 1989): 7–16.

16. Kaufman, *Theology*, pp. 37, 46.

17. Alice Walker, *The Color Purple* (New York: Pocket Books, 1982), p. 178.

18. Public Lectures. See also *The Holy Book of Women's Mysteries*, Vol. 1 (Los Angeles: Susan B. Anthony Coven 1, 1979), pp. 9, 11.

19. Kaufman, *Theology*, p. 59.

20. Ibid., p. 50.

21. Ibid., p. 52.

22. Walker, *Color Purple*, pp. 178–9.

23. Paula Gunn Allen, *The Sacred Hoop: Recovering the Feminine in American Indian Traditions* (Boston: Beacon Press, 1986), pp. 119, 60.

24. Simone de Beauvoir, *The Ethics of Ambiguity*, trans. Bernard Frechtman (New York: Philosophical Library, 1948), pp. 135–6.

25. For the particular dangers of an ethic of self-sacrifice for women, see Valerie Saiving, "The Human Situation: A Feminine View," in Carol Christ and Judith Plaskow (eds.), *Womanspirit Rising: A Feminist Reader on Religion* (San Francisco: Harper & Row, 1979), pp. 25–42.

26. Kaufman, *Theology*, p. 44.

27. Allen, *Sacred Hoop*, p. 60.

28. Lynn V. Andrews, *Flight of the Seventh Moon: The Teaching of the Shields* (New York: Harper & Row, 1984), p. 52.

29. Martin Buber, *I and Thou*, 2nd ed., trans. Ronald Gregor Smith (New York: Scribner's, 1958), p. 8.

30. Griffin, *Woman and Nature*, p. 190.

31. Ntozake Shange, *for colored girls who have considered suicide when the rainbow is enuf* (New York: Macmillan, 1976).

32. This essay grew out of discussions in my class God and the Prehistoric Goddesses at Harvard Divinity School and was presented as a public lecture in the divinity school's Women's Studies and Religion Program on March 4, 1987. Constance Buchanan, Gordon Kaufman, Naomi R. Goldenburg, Judith Plaskow, and Mara Keller provided helpful comments on earlier drafts.

POWER, AUTHORITY, AND MYSTERY: ECOFEMINISM AND EARTH-BASED SPIRITUALITY

1. Starhawk, *Truth or Dare: Encounters with Power, Authority, and Mystery* (San Francisco: Harper & Row, 1989), pp. 341–2.

CURVES ALONG THE ROAD

1. Susan Griffin, *Woman and Nature: The Roaring Inside Her* (New York: Harper & Row, 1978), p. 187.
2. The above remarks were made as part of a speech delivered in March of 1987. On October 18, 1989 NASA launched Project Galileo, a shuttle that carried 50 pounds of plutonium, enough to kill every person on Earth. If an accident had occurred within the Earth's 22,000-mile gravitational pull, radioactive material would have been spread all over the planet.
3. Griffin, *Unremembered Country* (Port Townsend, WA: Copper Canyon Press, 1987), pp. 131–3.

ECOFEMINISM AND FEMINIST THEORY

1. Françoise d'Eaubonne, "Feminism or Death," in Elaine Marks and Isabelle de Courtivron (eds.), *New French Feminisms: An Anthology* (Amherst: University of Massachusetts Press, 1980).
2. See Karen Warren, "Feminism and Ecology: Making Connections," *Environmental Ethics* 9 (no. 1: 1981): 3–20.
3. See Alison M. Jaggar, *Feminist Politics and Human Nature* (Totowa, NJ: Rowman and Allanheld, 1983).
4. Merlin Stone, *When God Was a Woman* (New York: Harcourt Brace Jovanovich, 1976).
5. See Dorothy Nelkin, "Nuclear Power as a Feminist Issue," *Environment* 23 (no. 1: 1981): 14–20, 38–39.
6. Carolyn Merchant, "Earthcare: Women and the Environmental Movement," *Environment* 22 (June 1970): 7–13, 38–40.
7. Donna Haraway, "A Manifesto for Cyborgs," *Socialist Review* 15 (no. 80: 1985): 65–107.
8. Sherry Ortner, "Is Female to Male as Nature Is to Culture?" in Michelle Rosaldo and Louise Lamphere (eds.), *Woman, Culture, and Society* (Stanford, CA: Stanford University Press, 1974), pp. 67–87.
9. Carolyn Merchant, "The Theoretical Structure of Ecological Revolutions," *Environmental Review* 11 (no. 4: Winter 1987): 265–74.
10. See Jeanne Henn, "Female Farmers—The Doubly Ignored," *Development Forum* 14 (nos. 7 and 8: 1986); and Gillian Goslinga, "Kenya's Women of the Trees," *Development Forum* 14 (no. 8: 1986): 15.

HEALING THE WOUNDS: FEMINISM,
ECOLOGY, AND THE NATURE/CULTURE DUALISM

1. One of the major issues at the United Nations Decade on Women forum held in Nairobi, Kenya, in 1985 was the effect of the international monetary system on women and the particular burdens women bear because of the money owed the "first world," particularly U.S. economic interests, by developing countries.
2. It is one of the absurd examples of newspeak that the designation "pro-life" has been appropriated by the militarist right to support forced childbearing.
3. See especially Murray Bookchin, *The Ecology of Freedom* (Palo Alto, CA: Cheshire Books, 1982). Of the various ecological theories that are not explicitly feminist, I draw here on Bookchin's work because he articulates a historical theory of hierarchy that begins with the domination of women by men, making way for domination by race and class, and the domination of nature. Hence the term "social" ecology. *The Ecology of Freedom* presents a radical view of the emergence, and potential dissolution, of hierarchy. Social ecology is just as concerned with relations of domination between persons as it is with the domination of nature. Hence it should be of great interest to feminists.
4. Sophocles, *Antigone*, trans. Elizabeth Wychokoff, in David Green and Richard Lattimore (eds.), *The Complete Greek Tragedies*, Vol. II: *Sophocles* (Chicago: University of Chicago Press, 1959), pp. 170–1 (lines 335–70).
5. Hans Jonas, *The Imperative of Responsibility: In Search of an Ethics for the Technological Age* (Chicago: University of Chicago Press, 1984), p. 136.
6. See Alison M. Jaggar, *Feminist Politics and Human Nature* (Totowa, NJ: Roman and Allanheld, 1983).
7. Alice Schwarzer, *After the Second Sex: Conversations with Simone de Beauvoir*, (New York: Pantheon, 1984), p. 103.
8. Virginia Woolf, *Three Guineas* (New York: Harcourt, Brace & World, 1938).
9. Peter Kropotkin, *Mutual Aid: A Factor in Evolution* (Boston: Porter Sargent, 1914).
10. See the works of scientists Lynn Margolis and James Lovelock, especially *Gaia: A New Look at Life on Earth* (New York: Oxford University Press, 1982).
11. See Cherrie Moraga and Gloria Anzuldua, *This Bridge Called My Back* (New York: Kitchen Table Press, 1983); Gloria Joseph and Jill Lewis, *Common Differences: Conflicts in Black and White Feminist Perspectives* (Garden City, NY: Doubleday/Anchor 1981); and Bell Hooks, *Feminist Theory: From Margin to Center* (Boston: South End Press, 1984). Audre Lorde has written eloquently of the problems of attempting to "use the master's tools to disassemble the master's house" and the implicit racism of heretofore definitions of "theory": see Audre Lorde, *Sister Outsider* (Trumansburg, NY: Crossing Press, 1986).
12. Luisah Teish, *Jambalaya* (San Francisco: Harper & Row, 1986).

13. These traditions are complex, and there are critical differences among them. Each has an ancient, and total, cosmology and set of practices, and while it is possible to find commonalities, creating a willy-nilly, random patchwork is not a brilliant new synthesis. That is the problem with the incoherent mush called "new age spirituality" or its slightly more secular version, the "human potential movement." Each religious tradition requires instruction (which may be in an oral or written tradition, or both), study, and the discipline of practice. I also don't know that traditions and cultures that apparently have an antidualistic perspective when it comes to the relationship between human and nonhuman nature are *necessarily* not sexist, xenophobic, or hierarchical in other contexts.

14. See Jean Baudrillard, *The Mirror of Production* (St. Louis: Telos Press, 1975).

15. In raising these issues I am in no way advocating the criminalization of women who market their eggs or wombs. If there is to be criminalization, the purveyors, or pimps, should be penalized, not the women. And obviously, there are critical economic and class issues here.

16. See especially Zillah Eisenstein, *The Radical Future of Liberal Feminism* (New York: Longman, 1981).

17. One exception is Carolyn Merchant, who has written a socialist feminist analysis of the scientific revolution, *The Death of Nature: Women, Ecology and the Scientific Revolution* (New York: Harper & Row, 1979). See also, Carolyn Merchant, "Earthcare: Women and the Environmental Movement," *Environment* 22 (no. 4: June 1981): 38–40.

18. Nancy Hartsock, *Money, Sex and Power* (Boston: Northeastern University Press, 1983); and Alison M. Jaggar, *Feminist Politics and Human Nature* (Totowa, NJ: Roman and Allanheld, 1983).

19. Cultural feminism is a term invented by feminists who believe in the primacy of economic (as opposed to cultural) forces in making history, but cultural feminists are proud of their emphasis.

20. On the social, mindful nature of mothering see the work of Sara Ruddick, especially "Maternal Thinking," *Feminist Studies* 6 (no. 2: Summer 1980): 342–67; and "Preservative Love and Military Destruction: Some Reflections on Mothering and Peace," in Joyce Trebilcot, (ed.), *Mothering: Essays in Feminist Theory* (Totowa, NJ: Rowman and Allanheld, 1983), pp. 231–62.

21. Catherine Caufield, *In the Rainforest* (Chicago: University of Chicago Press, 1984), pp. 156–8.

22. See Edward Hyams, *Soil and Civilization* (New York: Harper & Row, 1976).

23. See Petra Kelly, *Fighting for Hope* (Boston: South End Press, 1984) for a practical, feminist Green political analysis and program, with examples of ongoing movements and activities.

24. I am indebted to ecofeminist sociologist and environmental health activist Lin Nelson for pointing out to me why the feminist health movement is yet to become ecological.

25. See Elizabeth Fee, "Is Feminism a Threat to Scientific Objectivity?" *Inter-*

national Journal of Women's Studies 4 (no. 4: 1981): 378–92. See also Sandra Harding, *The Science Question in Feminism* (Ithaca, NY: Cornell University Press, 1986) and Evelyn Fox Keller, *Reflections on Gender and Science* (New Haven, CT: Yale University Press, 1985).

26. See, for example, Evelyn Fox Keller, *A Feeling for the Organism: The Life and Work of Barbara McClintock* (San Francisco, Freeman, 1983).

27. The cross-cultural interpretations of personal freedom of anthropologist Dorothy Lee are evocative of the possibility of such an ideal of freedom. See Dorothy Lee, *Freedom and Culture* (Englewood Cliffs, NJ: Prentice-Hall, 1959).

ECOFEMINISM AND THE POLITICS OF RESISTANCE

1. Howard Hawkins, "The Potential of the Green Movement," *New Politics* 5 (Summer 1988): 86–87.

2. Michel Foucault, "Michel Foucault: An Interview," *Edinburgh Review* (1986): 59.

3. Michael Hoexter, "It's Not Easy Being Green," *New Politics* 5 (Summer 1988): 106–18.

4. Ibid., p. 118.

5. For discussion of the Amherst, MA, conference, see Jay Walljasper, "The Prospects for Green Politics in the U.S.," *Utne Reader* (September/October 1987): 37–39. For the social ecology position on deep ecology, see Murray Bookchin, "Social Ecology versus Deep Ecology," *Socialist Review* 18 (July-September 1988): 9–29. For a critique of social ecology from a deep ecology stance, see Kirkpatrick Sale, "Deep Ecology and Its Critics," *The Nation* (14 May 1988): 670–5.

6. Catherine MacKinnon, "Feminism, Marxism, Method, and the State: An Agenda for Theory," *Signs* 7 (Spring 1982): 515–44. Donna Haraway gives an astute critique of MacKinnon's "radical reductionism" in "A Manifesto for Cyborgs: Science, Technology, and Socialist Feminism in the 1980s," *Socialist Review* 80 (1985): 65–107. MacKinnon's more recent full-length work, *Feminism Unmodified* (Cambridge, MA: Harvard University Press, 1987), exacerbates rather than lessens the reductionism of her earlier work.

7. Jana Sawicki, "Identity Politics and Sexual Freedom: Foucault and Feminism," in Irene Diamond and Lee Quinby (eds.), *Feminism and Foucault: Reflections on Resistance,* (Boston: Northeastern University Press, 1988), pp. 177–91.

8. Michel Foucault, *The History of Sexuality,* trans. Robert Hurley (New York: Vintage, 1980), pp. 92–96.

9. Leonie Caldecott and Stephanie Leland, eds., *Reclaim the Earth: Women Speak Out for Life on Earth,* (London: Women's Press, 1983); Anne Witte Garland, *Women Activists: Challenging the Abuse of Power* (New York: Feminist Press, 1988).

10. As Foucault has suggested about his work on madness joining ranks with that of R. D. Laing, alliances are formed whenever a we emerges through shared questions rather than through a we "previous to the question." See Foucault, "Polemics, Politics, and Problemizations: An Interview," in Paul Rabinow (ed.), *Foucault Reader*, (New York: Pantheon, 1984), p. 385.

11. Wilmette Brown, "Roots: Black Ghetto Ecology," in Caldecott and Leland (eds.), *Reclaim the Earth*, p. 73.

12. Ibid., p. 84.

13. Charlene Spretnak, "Introduction," in Charlene Spretnak (ed.), *The Politics of Women's Spirituality* (New York: Anchor Books, 1982), p. xvii.

14. Gayatri Chakravorty Spivak, "Feminism and Critical Theory," in Gayatri C. Spivak, *In Other Worlds: Essays in Cultural Politics* (New York: Routledge & Kegan Paul, 1987), p. 89.

15. Ibid., pp. 91–92.

ECOFEMINISM AND DEEP ECOLOGY:
REFLECTIONS ON IDENTITY AND DIFFERENCE

1. Bill Devall and George Sessions, *Deep Ecology: Living as if Nature Mattered* (Salt Lake City: Peregrine Smith, 1985), p. 67.

2. For a sustained critique of deep ecology for its emphasis on anthropocentrism as opposed to androcentrism, see Ariel Kay Salleh, "Deeper than Deep Ecology: The Ecofeminist Connection," *Environmental Ethics* 6 (1984): 339–45.

3. See Nancy Chodorow, *The Reproduction of Mothering* (Berkeley: University of California Press, 1978).

4. Dorothy Dinnerstein, *The Mermaid and the Minotaur: Sexual Arrangements and Human Malaise* (New York: Harper & Row, 1967).

5. Randall L. Eaton, "The Hunter as Alert Man: An Overview of the Origin of the Human/Animal Connection," in Randall L. Eaton (ed.), *The Human/ Animal Connection* (Incline Village, NV: Carnivore Journal and Sierra Nevada College Press, 1985), pp. 9, 121.

6. Ibid., p. 47.

7. José Ortega y Gasset, *Meditations on Hunting*, trans. Howard B. Wescott (New York: Scribner's 1985), p. 121.

8. Ibid., pp. 121, 124.

9. Aldo Leopold, *Sand County Almanac* (Oxford: Oxford University Press, 1949), p. 229.

10. Ortega, *Meditations on Hunting*, p. 123.

11. Ibid., pp. 92, 121.

12. Ibid., p. 29.

13. Leopold, *Sand County Almanac*, p. 227.

14. Ibid., p. 232.

15. Ibid., p. 227.
16. Ortega, *Meditations on Hunting*, p. 88.
17. Leopold, *Sand County Almanac*, p. 230.
18. The parallel attitude toward women is not difficult to discern: Men are "lured" by women's "beauty." Women are possessed by acts of violence such as pornography and rape.
19. Ortega, pp. 96–97.
20. Leopold, *Sand County Almanac*, p. 227.
21. Ibid., p. 227.
22. Ibid., pp. 239, 228.
23. Ortega, *Meditations on Hunting*, p. 98.
24. Quoted in Devall and Sessions, *Deep Ecology*, p. 75.
25. Ibid., p. 188.
26. Warwick Fox, "Approaching Deep Ecology: A Response to Richard Sylvan's Critique of Deep Ecology," *Environmental Studies Occasional Paper 20*, University of Tasmania, 1986.
27. Quoted in Devall and Sessions, *Deep Ecology*, p. 101.
28. An example of this danger may be found in the philosophy of Spinoza which provides an important inspiration for deep ecologists. Spinoza argued that the attainment of a higher self was to be achieved through a correct understanding of God/Nature—that is, through a unification of Mind with Nature. This understanding, however, did not include a respect for animals, for whom Spinoza felt deep contempt: "It is plain that the law against the slaughtering of animals is founded rather on vain superstition and womanish pity than sound reason" [Note I to prop. xxxvii, pt. IV of the *Ethics*. In R. H. M. Elwes (trans.), *The Chief Works of Benedict de Spinoze*, vol. II (New York: Dover, 1955), p. 213.] Although deep ecologists dismiss Spinoza's speciesism as an "anomaly" (see Devall and Sessions, *Deep Ecology*, p. 240), this disparity should underline some of the perils of grounding one's morality in an abstract conception of unity rather than a felt sense of connection to individual beings.
29. A study by Stephen Kellert and Joyce Berry confirms that there are, in fact, dramatic differences in men's and women's attitudes toward animals. See "Attitudes, Knowledge, and Behaviors toward Wildlife as Affected by Gender," *Wildlife Society Bulletin* 15 (no. 3: Fall 1987): 363–71.
30. Charlene Spretnak, ed., *The Politics of Women's Spirituality*, (New York: Anchor Books, 1982), p. xvii.

DEEP ECOLOGY AND ECOFEMINISM:
THE EMERGING DIALOGUE

1. See also my essay, "Feminism, Deep Ecology, and Environmental Ethics," *Environmental Ethics* 9 (Spring 1987): 21–44.

2. John Rodman, "Four Forms of Ecological Consciousness Reconsidered," in Donald Scherer and Thomas Attig (eds.), *Ethics and the Environment* (Englewood Cliffs, NJ: Prentice-Hall, 1983).

3. For a penetrating critique of moral extensionism, see John Rodman, "The Liberation of Nature?" *Inquiry* 20 (1977): 83–131.

4. Arne Naess, "Identification as a Source of Deep Ecological Attitudes," in Michael Tobias (ed.), *Deep Ecology* (San Diego, CA: Avant Books, 1984), pp. 256–70.

5. Warwick Fox, "Deep Ecology: Toward a New Philosophy for Our Time?" *The Ecologist* 14 (1984): 194–204.

6. Support for this "nodal" conception of the self is often drawn from the many recently published books on the "new physics." Alfred North Whitehead's "philosophy of organism" constitutes perhaps the most complete metaphysical appropriation of quantum theory. His writings have much to say to deep ecologists and ecofeminists.

7. Rosemary Radford Reuther makes this point particularly well in *New Woman, New Earth: Sexist Ideologies and Human Liberation* (New York: Seabury Press, 1975).

8. For an outstanding feminist reinterpretation of the emergence of patriarchy in human history, see Marilyn French, *Beyond Power: Women, Men, and Morality* (New York: Summit Books, 1985).

9. See Carl G. Jung, *Symbols of Transformation*, trans. R. F. C. Hull (Princeton, NJ: Bollingen Series XX/ Princeton University Press, 1976) and Erich Neumann, *The Origins and History of Consciousness*, trans. R. F. C. Hull (Princeton, NJ: Bollingen Series XLII/ Princeton University Press, 1970).

10. Ken Wilber, *Up from Eden: A Transpersonal View of Human Evolution* (Boulder, CO: Shambhala, 1983).

11. Ken Wilber, *The Atman Project* (Wheaton, IL: Quest Books, 1980); see also, *Up from Eden*.

12. Ariel Kay Salleh, "Deeper than Deep Ecology: The Eco-Feminist Connection," *Environmental Ethics* 6 (1984): 339–45.

13. Jim Cheney, "Eco-Feminism and Deep Ecology," *Environmental Ethics* 9 (1987): 115–45.

14. Ibid., p. 133.

15. Marti Kheel, "The Liberation of Nature: A Circular Affair," *Environmental Ethics* 7 (1985): 135–49.

16. The environmental philosopher Kheel has in mind in her critique is J. Baird Callicott, particularly his essay "Animal Liberation: A Triangular Affair," *Environmental Ethics* 2 (1980): 311–38.

17. Catherine Keller, *From a Broken Web: Separation, Sexism, and Self* (Boston: Beacon Press, 1986).

18. Ibid., p. 114.

19. Ibid.

20. Ibid., p. 161.

21. See, especially, Gary Snyder, *Turtle Island* (New York: New Directions, 1974); *The Old Ways* (San Francisco: City Lights, 1977); *The Real Work* (New York: New Directions, 1980).

22. Cheney, "Eco-Feminism," p. 139.

23. Ibid., p. 140.

24. Ibid.

25. Ibid., p. 144.

SEARCHING FOR COMMON GROUND:
ECOFEMINISM AND BIOREGIONALISM

1. Peter Berg and Raymond Dasmann, "Reinhabiting California," in Peter Berg (ed.), *Reinhabiting a Separate Country: A Bioregional Anthology of Northern California* (San Francisco: Planet Drum Foundation, 1978), pp. 217–8.

TOWARD A WOMANIST ANALYSIS OF BIRTH

1. Alice Walker, *In Search of Our Mother's Gardens* (San Diego: Harcourt Brace Jovanovich, 1983), pp. xi, xii.

2. Stanislav Grof, *Beyond the Brain—Birth, Death, and Transcendence in Psychotherapy* (Albany: State University of New York Press, 1985), p. 252.

3. Barbara Ehrenreich and Dierdre English, *Witches, Midwives and Nurses: A History of Women Healers* (Old Westbury, NY: Feminist Press, 1973).

THE PLACE OF WOMEN IN POLLUTED PLACES

1. Two key resources are: Wendy Chavkin, *Double Exposure: Women's Health Hazards on the Job and at Home* (New York: Monthly Review Press, 1984) and the *Women's Occupational Health Resource Center Newsletter*.

2. Earon Davis, "Ecological Illness," *Trial* (October 1986): 34.

3. See Iris Bell, *Clinical Ecology: A New Medical Approach to Environmental Illness* (Bolinas, CA: Common Knowledge Press, 1982).

4. K. J. Lennane and R. J. Lennane, "Alleged Psychogenic Disorders in Women: A Possible Manifestation of Sexual Prejudice," *New England Journal of Medicine* (February 8, 1973): 288–92.

5. "How Serious are the Hazards to Reproduction?" *Conservation Foundation Letter* (May-June 1984).

6. Arnold Schecter, "Comparisons of Human Tissue Levels of Dioxin and Furan Isomers in Potentially Exposed and Controlled Patients Fifteen Years after Cessation of 2,3,7,8–TCDD Environmental Contamination" (Paper presented to the American Chemical Society National Meeting, Washington, DC, April 13-18, 1986).

7. World Health Organization, "Organohalogen Compounds in Human Milk and Related Hazards" (Report on WHO Consultation, Bilthoven, Netherlands, January 9–11, 1985).

8. U.S. Office of Technology Assessment, *Reproductive Health Hazards in the Workplace* (Washington, DC: Government Printing Office, 1985).

9. Joan Bertin, "Reproductive Health in the Workplace," in Nadine Taub and Sherrill Cohen (eds.), *Reproductive Laws for the 1990's: A Briefing Handbook* (Clifton, NJ: Humana Press, 1988).

10. Maureen Paul, "A Survey of Corporate Practices Regarding Reproductive Hazards in the Massachusetts Chemical and Electronic Industries" (Paper presented at the American Public Health Association Annual Meeting, Boston 1988).

11. See, for example, Paula DiPerna, *Cluster Mystery: Epidemic and the Children of Woburn, Massachusetts* (St. Louis: C. V. Mosby, 1985).

12. Tracy Freedman, "Love Canal Children: Leftover Lives to Live," *The Nation* (May 23, 1981): 624–7.

13. Kathy Williams, "Slashburning and Herbicides: The Politics of Caring," *Health Watch* 7 (no. 4: 1987): 1.

14. Katsi Cook, "A Community Health Project: Breastfeeding and Toxic Contaminants," *Indian Studies* (Spring 1985): 15.

15. Lin Nelson, "Promise Her Everything: The Nuclear Power Industry's Agenda for Women," *Feminist Studies* 10 (Summer 1984): 291–314.

16. Lois Marie Gibbs, *Love Canal: My Story* (Albany: State University of New York Press, 1982).

17. See Irene Dankelman, *Women and Environment: Alliance for a Sustainable Future* (London: Cambridge University Press, 1987).

18. Quoted by Diana Page, "Women Head the Way in Ecuador and Kenya," *WorldWIDE News* (November 1986): 1.

19. For example, see Sherry Hatcher, "The Psychological Experience of Nursing Mothers upon Learning of a Toxic Substance in the Milk," *Psychiatry* 45 (1982): 172–81.

20. Jeanne Stellman, "Book Review: Edward Calabrese's *Toxic Susceptibility: Male/Female Differences*," *Women's Occupational Health Resource Center News* 8 (no. 2: 1987): 11.

21. Ruth Hubbard, "Personal Courage Is Not Enough: Some Hazards of Childbearing in the 1980's," in Rita Arditti, Renate Klein, and Shelly Minden (eds.), *Test-Tube Women: What Future for Motherhood?* (London: Pandora Press, 1984), p. 345.

DEVELOPMENT AS A NEW PROJECT OF WESTERN PATRIARCHY

1. See Rosa Luxembourg, *The Accumulation of Capital* (London: Routledge & Kegan Paul, 1951).

2. An elaboration of how "development" transfers resources from the poor to the well endowed is contained in J. Bandyopadhyay and V. Shiva, "Political Economy of Technological Polarisations," *Economic and Political Weekly* 17 (November 6, 1982): 1827–32, and J. Bandyopadhyay and V. Shiva, "Political Economy of Ecology Movements," *Economic and Political Weekly* 23 (June 11, 1988): 1223–32.

3. Esther Boserup, *Women's Role in Economic Development* (London: Allen and Unwin, 1970).

4. DAWN, *Development Crisis and Alternative Visions. Third World Women's Perspectives* (Bergen, Norway: Christian Michelson Institute, 1985), p. 21.

5. M. George Foster, *Traditional Societies and Technological Change* (Delhi: Allied, 1973).

6. Maria Mies, *Patriarchy and Accumulation on a World Scale* (London: Zed Books, 1986).

7. Alice Schelegel (ed.), *Sexual Stratification: A Cross Cultural Study* (New York: Columbia University Press, 1977).

8. Jonathan Porritt, *Seeing Green* (Oxford: Blackwell, 1985), p. 121.

9. Amory Lovins, cited in S. R. Eyre, *The Real Wealth of Nations* (London: Edward Arnold, 1978).

10. Cited by R. Bahro, *From Red to Green* (London: Verso, 1984), p. 211.

11. S. R. Barnet, *The Lean Years* (London: Abacus, 1980), p. 171.

12. P. Koehn, "African Approaches to Environmental Stress: A focus on Ethiopia and Nigeria," in R. N. Barrett (ed.), *International Dimensions of the Environmental Crisis* (Boulder, CO: Westview Press, 1982), pp. 253–89.

13. Gustavo Esteva, "Regenerating People's Space," in S. N. Mendlowitz and R. B. J. Walker (eds.), *Towards a Just World Peace: Perspectives from Social Movements* (London: Butterworths and Committee for a Just World Peace, 1987).

14. C. Alvares, "Deadly Development," *Development Forum* 11 (no. 7: 1983): 3–4.

BABIES, HEROIC EXPERTS, AND A POISONED EARTH

1. I am suggesting here that exploitation is not inherent in the phenomenon of one woman bearing a child for another. Whether such a situation is exploitative derives from the larger social context. Imagining an egalitarian society in which the motivations to give to another are not shaped by power and economic hierarchies is difficult to do in the contemporary world, but I am most reluctant to subscribe to a view of surrogacy that condemns it on the grounds of its inherent biological or psychological wrongness.

2. Ruth Hubbard, "Personal Courage Is Not Enough: Some Hazards of Childbearing in the 1980's," in Rita Arditti, Renate Duelli Klein, and Shelly Minden (eds.), *Test-Tube Women: What Future for Motherhood?* (London: Pandora Press, 1984), p. 343.

3. In the Vatican's report, "Instruction on Respect for Human Life and Its

Origin and on the Dignity of Procreation," in vitro fertilization is condemned because "such fertilization entrusts the life and identity of the embryo into the power of doctors and biologists and establishes the domination of technology over the origin and destiny of the human person." Interestingly, treatments that involve fertilization inside the body and do not obtain sperm by masturbation are acceptable. Thus, a technique known as gamete intra-fallopian transfer (where doctors extract a woman's egg from the ovary, combine it with sperm, and inject it directly into the fallopian tube) is acceptable if the sperm is collected in a condom worn during intercourse and the condom is perforated to allow the possibility of natural fertilization. See Gail Vines, "Perforated Condom Offers Loophole in Papal Rules in IVF," *New Scientist* (March 19, 1987): 19.

4. See, for example, Gena Corea, *The Mother Machine* (New York: Harper & Row, 1985) and G. Corea et al. (eds.), *Man-Made Women* (Bloomington: Indiana University Press, 1987).

5. Renate Duelli Klein, "What's 'New' about the 'New' Reproductive Technologies?" in Corea, *Man-Made Women*, p. 66.

6. See Pamela S. Summey and Marsha Hurst, "Ob/Gyn on the Rise: The Evolution of Professional Ideology in the Twentieth Century," *Women and Health* 11 (Summer 1986): 103–22.

7. Note, "Reproductive Technology and the Procreative Rights of the Unmarried," *Harvard Law Review* 98 (January 1985): 685.

8. For a discussion of the origins of managerial ecology, see Carolyn Merchant, *The Death of Nature* (New York: Harper & Row, 1980), chap. 10; and for a discussion of the emergence of a "population," see Michel Foucault, *The History of Sexuality* Vol. 1 (New York: Pantheon, 1978), pp. 25–26.

9. John Postgate, "Bat's Chance in Hell," *New Scientist* 58 (April 5, 1973): 16, as cited by Christine Overall, *Ethics and Human Reproduction* (Boston: Allen & Unwin, 1987), p. 29.

10. Carl J. Bajema, "The Genetic Implications of American Lifestyles in Reproduction and Population Control," in Noel Hinrichs (ed.), *Population, Environment and People,* (New York: McGraw-Hill, 1971), p. 70.

11. Bentley Glass, "Science: Endless Horizons or Golden Age?" *Science* 171 (1971): 23–29, as cited in Hubbard, "Personal Courage."

12. This new ability to monitor "health" before birth points to an expansion of the arenas for surveillance and regulation. For example, in a manual for physicians and genetic counselors, *Genetic Disorders and the Fetus* (New York: Plenum Press, 1986), p. 11, Aubrey Milunsky argues that "genetic counseling is best offered routinely and systematically prior to marriage."

13. See the discussion in Hubbard, "Personal Courage," pp. 345–8.

14. In 1986, the state of California chose to launch a statewide alpha-feto-protein screening program even though the President's Commission for the Study of Ethical Problems recommended against routine screening. In arguing

for the adoption of the program, the California Commissioner of Genetic Services emphasized that $3.7 million would be saved for Medi-Cal if 90 percent of the women found to be carrying severely deformed babies chose abortions. See Robert Steinbrook, "In California, Voluntary Mass Prenatal Screening," *Hastings Center Report* (October 1986): 4–7.

15. See, for example, Anne Finger, "Claiming All of Our Bodies: Reproductive Rights and Disabilities," and Marsha Saxton, "Born and Unborn: The Implications of Reproductive Technologies for People with Disabilities," in Arditti et al., *Test-Tube Women*, pp. 281–312.

16. Irwin Chargaff, "Engineering a Molecular Nightmare," *Nature* 329 (May 1987): 199.

17. See Rosalie Bertell, *No Immediate Danger* (London: Women's Press, 1985), for a discussion of the health effects of radiation exposure.

18. Tom Muir and Anne Sudar, "Toxic Chemicals in the Great Lakes Basin Ecosystem—Some Observations," (Burlington, Ontario, Canada: Water Planning and Mangement Branch, Inland Waters/Land Directorate, Ontario Region, November 1987), provides a valuable overview of ecosystem contamination as it affects human and nonhuman reproduction.

19. U.S. Office of Technology Assessment, *Infertility: Medical and Social Choices* (Washington, DC: U.S. Government Printing Office, May 1988), p. 56.

20. The report notes, for example, that one of the factors contributing to the rise in identified infertility is the tendency of couples to classify themselves as infertile more quickly because of a desire to condense childbearing into a shorter interval. Measuring the actual incidence of infertility is thus nearly impossible. Bearing in mind the ways in which social factors shape our perception and hence our ability to measure, it is worth noting that the report includes secondary infertility (in which couples have at least one biological child) in its category of infertility. Primary infertility (childlessness) doubled from 500,000 in 1965 to 1 million in 1982. See pp. 50–55.

21. Erik Jansson, "The Causes of Birth Defects, Learning Disabilities, and Mental Retardation in Relation to Laboratory Animal Testing Requirements and Needs" *National Network to Prevent Birth Defects News* (June 14, 1988), argues that the child and fetus share a far greater susceptibility to toxic exposure "because rapidly dividing cells and migrating cells have been shown to be much more susceptible to radiation and toxins. Also, the child and fetus lack the enzymes in many cases to metabolize and excrete toxins."

WOMEN, HOME, AND COMMUNITY:
THE STRUGGLE IN AN URBAN ENVIRONMENT

1. See Cynthia Cockburn, "When Women Get Involved in Community Action," in Marjorie Mayo (ed.), *Women in the Community* (London: Routledge & Kegan Paul, 1977).

2. All of the quotes from Charlotte Bullock and Robin Cannon are personal communications, 1986.

3. Cockburn, "When Women," p. 62.

4. Cerrell Associates, *Political Difficulties Facing Waste to Energy Conversion Plant Siting* (Los Angeles: California Waste Management Board, 1984), pp. 42–43.

5. See Cockburn, "When Women," p. 63.

THE EVOLUTION OF AN ECOFEMINIST

1. Hazel Henderson, *The Politics of the Solar Age: Alternatives to Economics* (Garden City, NY: Anchor/Doubleday, 1981), p. xiii.

2. Rachel Carson, *Silent Spring* (Boston: Houghton Mifflin, 1962).

WOMEN AGAINST WASTING THE WORLD:
NOTES ON ESCHATOLOGY AND ECOLOGY

1. Grace Halsell, *Prophecy and Politics: Militant Evangelicals on the Path to Nuclear War* (Westport, CT: Lawrence Hill, 1986), provides a useful introduction to the subject.

2. For an excellent collection of essays on the varieties of contemporary apocalypticism, see Saul Friedlander (ed.), *Visions of Apocalypse: End or Rebirth* (New York: Holmes and Meier, 1985).

3. This is the famous Armageddon passage, responsible for the fundamentalist conviction. [See also Hal Lindsay, *The Late Great Planet Earth* (Grand Rapids, ID: Zondervan, 1970) (a book that seems to have sold more copies than any book since the Bible), who argues that God has foreordained a nuclear Armageddon. This necessitates unconditional support of the policies of Israel, as the Jews must be "ingathered" before it can occur.] This and subsequent biblical citations are from *The New English Bible* (New York: Oxford and Cambridge University Presses, 1970).

4. *The New York Times* (June 23, 1988), p. A22.

5. Lester R. Brown (ed.), *State of the World 1988: A Worldwatch Institute Report on Progress Toward a Sustainable Society* (New York: Norton, 1988).

6. See Carolyn Merchant, *The Death of Nature: Women, Ecology and the Scientific Revolution* (San Francisco: Harper & Row, 1980), for an excellent account of the link between the rise of modernity, the witch persecutions, and the industrial assault on nature.

7. Ilya Prigogine and Isabelle Stengers, *Order Out of Chaos: Man's New Dialogue with Nature* (New York: Bantam, 1984), p. 51.

8. Brown, *State of the World 1988*, p. 8.

9. As cited, whether altogether literally or not I cannot tell, by Lynn Andrews in *Medicine Woman* (San Francisco: Harper & Row, 1981), p. 107.

10. I have argued all this extensively in *From a Broken Web: Separation, Sexism and Self* (Boston: Beacon, 1986).

11. Ibid. For source references and a discussion of the hero myth, notably of Marduk, in its connection to the separative impulses of patriarchal selfhood, see Chap. 3.

12. Prigogine and Stengers, *Order Out of Chaos*, pp. 8f.

PERSPECTIVE OR ESCAPE? ECOFEMINIST MUSINGS
ON CONTEMPORARY EARTH IMAGERY

1. Stewart Brand, "The First Whole Earth Image," in Michael Katz, et al. (eds.), *Earth's Answer: Explorations of Planetary Culture at the Lindisfarne Conferences* (New York: Lindisfarne Books, 1977), pp. 184-9.

2. A young man awakes with a vision of putting the whole Earth image in the hands of every citizen around the planet as a way of promoting global consciousness (his four-color 2-inch-diameter stick-on stamps are now available for the asking). See "Sticking with the Only Planet We've Got," *Earth Island Journal* (Fall 1988): 5.

3. Quoted in Susan Griffin, *Pornography and Silence: Culture's Revenge Against Nature* (New York: Harper & Row, 1981), p. 82.

4. Yaakov Garb, "The Use and Misuse of the Whole Earth Image," *Whole Earth Review* 45 (March 1985): 18-25.

5. Susan Sontag, *On Photography* (New York: Farrar, Straus & Giroux, 1973).

6. See the chapter "From Cosmos to Landscape," in Yi Fu Tuan, *Topophilia* (Englewood Cliffs, NJ: Prentice-Hall, 1974), pp. 129-49.

7. Ibid., p. 137.

8. E. M. Courtright (ed.), *Exploring Space with a Camera* (Washington, DC: U.S. Government Printing Office, 1968).

9. Sontag, *On Photography*, p. 23.

10. See Yaakov Garb, "Attitudes toward Nature: An Analysis of Visual Imagery," in D. DeLuca (ed.), *Essays on Perceiving Nature* (Honolulu: University of Hawaii, 1988), pp. 148-62.

11. Eric Havelock, *Preface to Plato* (Cambridge, MA: Harvard University Press, 1963).

12. The quote is from Susan Rubin Suleiman (ed.), *The Female Body in Western Culture: Contemporary Perspectives*, (Cambridge, MA: Harvard University Press, 1986). See also Evelyn Fox Keller and Christine R. Grontkowski, "The Mind's Eye," in Sandra Harding and Merrill B. Hintikka (eds.), *Discovering Reality* (Dordrecht, Holland: D. Reidel, 1983), pp. 207-24. For a powerful application of such analysis to a contemporary issue, see Rosalind Pollack Petchesky, "Fetal Images: The Power of Visual Culture in the Politics of Reproduction," *Feminist Studies*, 13 (no. 2: Summer 1987): 263-92.

13. Sontag, *On Photography*, pp. 7, 14–15.

14. See Rob Kostka and Ben Kerns, "On the Photographic Image," *Spring: An Annual of Archetypal Psychology and Jungian Thought* (1984): 181–93. See also Neil Everndon, *The Natural Alien: Humankind and Environment* (Toronto: University of Toronto Press, 1985), "on staring," pp. 88–94.

15. Sontag, *On Photography*, pp. 154–5.

16. The whole Earth image reflects our present geographic experience. Whereas, for example, California Mono Native Americans typically spent their entire lives within a radius of a dozen miles and came to know that place with a level of intimacy we can scarcely imagine, the transportation and life-style of most contemporary culture make places increasingly accessible, interchangeable, and less individual; the "global citizen's" knowledge of and attachment to the natural features of any given place, however, is usually superficial: being everywhere we are nowhere.

17. See James Hillman, *Re-Visioning Psychology* (New York: Harper & Row, 1975), pp. 64–70 and 240–1 for a withering examination of humanistic psychology's naive avoidance of pathology.

18. See Peter Bishop's important comments on the emergence of idealistic holism and its lurking shadows in his "The Shadows of the Holistic Earth," *Spring: An Annual of Archetypal Psychology and Jungian Thought* (1986): 59–71. Interestingly, Bishop points out that it is the science of ecology that has most recently provided the language for this holism with its descriptions of organic systems in terms of harmony, balance, interdependence, unity, and totality (p. 62).

19. Russell Schweickart, "No Frames, No Boundaries," in Michael Katz, William Marsh, and Gail G. Thompson (eds.), *Earth's Answer* (New York: Lindisfarne Books, 1977), pp. 3–13, quote on p. 12. Aldrin's remark is quoted in Kevin W. Kelley, *The Home Planet* (New York: Addison-Wesley, 1988).

20. *Astrochase: Program Instructions* (Place: First Star Software, 1982).

21. Thus, for instance, "rationality" is defined in terms of transcendence of the feminine: see, for example, Genevieve Lloyd, *The Man of Reason: "Male" and "Female" in Western Philosophy* (Minneapolis: University of Minnesota Press, 1984). See also Eva Feder Kittay, "Woman as Metaphor," *Hypatia* 3 (no. 2: 1988): 63–86.

22. I first encountered a discussion of the extraterrestrial motif in Zoe Sofia's remarkable essay "Exterminating Fetuses: Abortion, Disarmament, and the Sexo-Semiotics of Extraterrestrialism," *Diacritics* 14 (Summer 1984): 47–59.

23. Listen to the words of nuclear physicist and proponent of space exploration Freeman Dyson: "Man would defeat the World, its limited resources and living space, by leaving the planet for free-floating colonies in space. Man would defeat the Flesh, its various diseases and infirmities, with the aid of bionic organs, biological engineering, and self-reproducing machinery. Man would defeat the Devil—the irrational in his nature—by reorganiz-

ing society along scientific lines and by learning intellectual control over his emotions" [from a talk entitled "The World, the Flesh, and the Devil," given in London, 1972, and quoted in Kenneth Brower, *The Starship and the Canoe* (New York: Harper & Row, 1978), p. 33].

24. On the masculinity of the space project and it's scientists, see Ian Mitroff, "Science's Appolonic Moon: A Study in the Psychodynamics of Modern Science," *Spring: An Annual of Archetypal Psychology and Jungian Thought* (1974): 102–12.

25. W. H. Auden, "Moon Landing," in Charles Muscatine, et al. (eds.), *The Borzoi College Reader* (New York: Knopf, 1971), p. 469.

26. William K. Hartmann, et al. (eds.), *Out of the Cradle: Exploring the Frontiers Beyond Earth* (New York: Workman, 1984).

27. John S. and Ruth A. Lewis, *Space Resources* (New York: Columbia University Press, 1987).

28. Quoted in Franck White, *The Overview Effect: Space Exploration and Human Evolution.* (Boston: Houghton Mifflin, 1987), p. 201.

29. On the mythic themes of radical self-sufficiency and a masculine techno- logical birth, and on the relation of these to the extraterrestrial project, see Sofia, "Exterminating Fetuses." James Hillman's brilliant exposition on the upward transcendent drive of *puer aeternus* (the archetypal figure of the eternal youth) is highly relevant for any discussion of the extraterrestrial impulse, though space precludes incorporating this perspective here. See Hillman, *Puer Papers* (Dallas: Spring, 1979).

30. See White, *Overview Effect*, p. xviii. For one shockingly explicit portrayal of the transcendence of earthbound existence as evolution's cutting edge, see the front cover of the February 1981 issue of *Futurist*.

31. Quoted by Loren Eiseley, "The Last Magician," in *The Invisible Pyramid* (New York: Scribner's, 1970), p. 153.

32. Norman O. Brown, *Life Against Death: The Psychoanalytic Meaning of History* (New York: Columbia University Press, 1959).

33. The terminology here is Eric Erickson's: "Man's ultimate has too often been visualized as an infinity which begins where the male conquest of outer space ends, . . . The Ultimate, however, may well be found to reside in the Immediate, which has so largely been the domain of woman and of the inward mind." From *Identity: Youth and Crisis* (New York: Norton, 1968), p. 294.

34. Hilary Armstrong, "The Divine Enhancement of Earthly Beauties: The Hellenic and Platonic Tradition," in H. Read and H. Armstrong (eds.), *On Beauty* (Dallas: Spring, 1987), pp. 41–73.

35. Daniel Noel, *Approaching Earth: A Search for the Mythic Significance of the Space Age* (Warwick, NY: Amity House, 1986).

36. Everndon, *The Natural Alien*, p. 95. The ideas in this paragraph rely strongly on his analysis in "Seeing and Being Seen: A Response to Susan Sontag's Essays on Photography," *Soundings* 68 (Spring 1985): 72–87.

37. For the beginnings of an attempt to reclaim for feminist discourse the sense of vision (and thus the notion of objectivity) as embodied, situated, and partial rather than transcendent, conquering, and omniscient, see Donna Haraway, "Situated Knowledges: The Science Question in Feminism and the Privilege of Partial Perspective," *Feminist Studies* 14 (no. 3: 1988): 575–99.

38. As Ynestra King points out, there are three possible directions for feminism with respect to the woman/nature connection. The first calls for women to abandon their alignment with nature, which they see as a source of perpetual devaluation. [See, for example, Sherry B. Ortner, "Is Female to Male as Nature Is to Culture?" in M. Rosaldo and L. Lamphere (eds.), *Woman, Culture, and Society* (Stanford, CA: Stanford University Press, 1974), pp. 67–87.] The second reaffirms this alignment but turns patriarchal assumptions on their head through a valorization of the "feminine." [See, for example, Mary Daly, *Gyn/ecology: The Metaethics of Radical Feminism* (Boston, Beacon Press, 1978.)] King herself represents the third direction that attempts to transcend the very duality between nature and culture out of which such (false) choices arise. See Ynestra King, "Toward an Ecological Feminism and a Feminist Ecology," in J. Rothschild (ed.), *Machina Ex Dea* (New York: Pergamon, 1983), especially pp. 122–3. See also Elizabeth Dodson Grey, *Green Paradise Lost* (Wellesley, MA: Round Table Press, 1979). A further discussion of the benefits and pitfalls associated with the adoption of feminine imagery for the Earth appears in Charlene Spretnak's talk, "The Concept of Earth as Bountiful Goddess in Pre-Indo-European Cultures of Old Europe," in the *Proceedings of the National Audubon Society Expedition Institute Conference Is the Earth a Living Organism,* 1985, University of Massachusetts, Amherst. (Available on microfiche from the U.S. Department of Education, ERIC, or through the National Audubon Society Expedition Institute, Sharon, CT 06069.)

39. Stephen Toulmin, "Death of the Spectator," in *The Return to Cosmology: Postmodern Science and the Theology of Nature* (Berkeley: University of California Press, 1982), p. 254.

40. This is a written version of a talk that was illustrated with a slide presentation of almost a hundred images, including many premodern ones. For technical reasons, these could not be printed in this collection, and the essay has been modified to stand alone. Several of the images appear in my earlier essay, "The Use and Misuse of the Whole Earth Image," *Whole Earth Review* 45 (March 1985): 18–25.

ARTISTS AS HEALERS:
ENVISIONING LIFE-GIVING CULTURE

1. The term *endarkenment* was coined by Merlin Stone in "Endings and Origins," *Woman of Power* 8 (Winter 1988): 29.

2. Susan Griffin, *Woman and Nature: The Roaring Inside Her* (Boston: Beacon Press, 1978).

3. Ibid., pp. 223, 226.

4. Based upon the Goddess figurines known as the Venus of Willendorf dated from 35,000 B.C.

5. See Jose Arguelles, *The Mayan Factor: Path Beyond Technology* (Santa Fe: Bear & Co., 1987).

6. Ursula K. Le Guin, *Always Coming Home* (New York: Harper & Row, 1985).

7. Ibid., p. 290.

8. Ibid., p. 90.

9. For further discussion of the ecofeminist arts, see Gloria Feman Orenstein, *The Reflowering of the Goddess* (Elmsford, NY: Pergamon Press, Athene Series, 1990).

Selected Bibliography

Abram, David. "The Perceptual Implications of Gaia." *The Ecologist* 15 (1985): 96–103.

Allen, Paula Gunn. *The Sacred Hoop: Recovering the Feminine in the American Indian Tradition.* Boston: Beacon Press, 1986.

Alvares, C. "Deadly Development." *Development Forum* 11 (no. 7: 1983): 3–4.

Bahro, Rudolf. *From Red to Green.* London: Verso, 1984.

Baudrillard, Jean. *The Mirror of Production.* St. Louis: Telos Press, 1975.

Berman, Morris. *The Reenchantment of the World.* New York: Bantam, 1984.

Bertell, Rosalie. *No Immediate Danger: Prognosis for a Radioactive Earth.* London: Women's Press, 1985.

Bird, Elizabeth. "The Social Construction of Nature: Theoretical Approaches to the History of Environmental Problems." *Environmental Review* 11 (1987): 255–64.

Bishop, Peter. "The Shadows of the Holistic Earth." *Spring: Annual of Archetypal Psychology and Jungian Thought* (1986): 59–71.

Bookchin, Murray. *The Ecology of Freedom.* Palo Alto, CA: Cheshire Books, 1982.

Bordo, Susan. *The Flight to Objectivity: Essays on Cartesianism and Culture.* Albany: State University of New York Press, 1987.

Brown, Norman O. *Life Against Death: The Psychoanalytic Meaning of History.* New York: Viking Press, 1959.

Caldecott, Leonie, and Stephanie Leland. *Reclaim the Earth: Women Speak Out for Life on Earth.* London: Women's Press, 1983.

Cameron, Anne. *Daughters of Copperwoman.* Vancouver: Press Gang Publishers, 1981.

Caufield, Catherine. *In the Rainforest.* Chicago: University of Chicago Press, 1984.

Chavkin, Wendy. *Double Exposure.* New York: Monthly Review Press, 1984.

Cheney, Jim. "Ecofeminism and Deep Ecology." *Environmental Ethics* 9 (no. 2: Summer 1987): 115–45.

Christ, Carol. "Embodied Thinking: Reflections on Feminist Theological Method." *Journal of Feminist Studies in Religion* 5 (no. 1: Spring 1989): 7–16.

––––– *Laughter of Aphrodite: Reflections on a Journey to the Goddess.* San Francisco: Harper & Row, 1987.

Connexions Collective. "Environment: From the Ground Up." *Connexions: An International Women's Quarterly* (special issue) (no. 6: Fall 1982).

Cook, Alice, and Gwyn Kirk. *Greenham Women Everywhere: Dreams, Ideas and Actions from the Women's Peace Movement.* Boston: South End Press, 1983.

Cook, Katsi. "A Community Health Project: Breastfeeding and Toxic Contaminants." *Indian Studies* (Spring 1985): 14-16.

_____, and Lin Nelson. "The Seven Generations: Community Epidemiology and Environmental Protection in Indian Country—Lessons from a Mohawk Women's Health Project." Paper presented to the Annual Meeting of the American Public Health Association, Washington, DC, 1985.

Corea, Gena. *The Mother Machine.* New York: Harper & Row, 1985.

Daly, Mary. *Gyn/Ecology: The Metaethics of Radical Feminism.* Boston: Beacon Press, 1978.

Dankelman, Irene, and Joan Davidson. *Women and Environment in the Third World.* London: Earthscan, 1988.

D'Eaubonne, Françoise. "Feminism or Death,'" in Elaine Marks and Isabelle de Courtivron (eds.), *New French Feminisms: An Anthology.* Amherst: University of Massachusetts Press, 1980, pp. 64-67.

Devall, Bill, and George Sessions. *Deep Ecology: Living as if Nature Mattered.* Salt Lake City: Peregrine Smith Books, 1984.

Dinnerstein, Dorothy. *The Mermaid and the Minotaur: Sexual Arrangements and Human Malaise.* New York: Harper & Row, 1977.

DiPerna, Paula. *Cluster Mystery: Epidemic and the Children of Woburn, Massachusetts.* St. Louis: C. V. Mosby, 1985.

Eaton, Randall. "The Hunter as Alert Man: An Overview of the Origin of the Human/Animal Connection," in Randall L. Eaton (ed.), *The Human/Animal Connection.* Incline Village, NV: Carnivore Journal and Sierra Nevada College Press, 1985, pp. 8-21.

Eisler, Riane Tennenhaus. *The Chalice and the Blade: Our History, Our Future.* San Francisco: Harper & Row, 1987.

Elkington, John. *The Poisoned Womb.* New York: Viking/Penguin, 1985.

Esteva, Gustavo. "Regenerating People's Space," in Saul H. Mendlovitz and R. B. J. Walker (eds.), *Toward a Just World Peace: Perspectives from Social Movements.* London: Butterworths, 1987, pp. 271-98.

Everndon, Neil. *The Natural Alien: Humankind and Environment.* Toronto: University of Toronto Press, 1985.

_____. "Seeing and Being Seen: A Response to Susan Sontag's Essays on Photography." *Soundings* 68 (Spring 1985): 72-87.

Foucault, Michel. *The History of Sexuality*, Vol. 1. New York: Pantheon, 1978.

_____. *Power/Knowledge: Selected Interviews and Other Writings, 1972-1977.* New York: Pantheon, 1980.

Fox, Warwick. "On Guiding Stars to Deep Ecology: A Reply to Naess." *The Ecologist* 14 (1984): 203-4.

Garb, Yaakov. "The Use and Misuse of t.1e Whole Earth Image." *Whole Earth Review* (March 1985): 18-25.

_____. "Virtual Reality." *Whole Earth Review* (Winter 1987): 118-20.

Gibbs, Lois. *Love Canal: My Story.* Albany: State University of New York, 1982.

Gilligan, Carol. *In a Different Voice: Psychological Theory and Women's Development.* Cambridge, MA: Harvard University Press, 1982.

Gimbutas, Marija. *The Goddesses and Gods of Old Europe, 6500–3500 BC: Myths and Cult Images.* Berkeley: University of California Press, 1982.

Goslinga, Gillian. "Kenya's Women of the Trees." *Development Forum* 14 (no. 8: 1986): 15.

Grey, Elizabeth Dodson. *Green Paradise Lost.* Wellesley, MA: Round Table Press, 1979.

_____. *Sacred Dimensions of Women's Experience.* Wellesley, MA: Round Table Press, 1988.

Griffin, Susan. *Made from This Earth.* New York: Harper & Row, 1982.

_____. *Pornography and Silence: Culture's Revenge Against Nature.* New York: Harper & Row, 1981.

_____. *Woman and Nature: The Roaring Inside Her.* New York: Harper & Row, 1978.

Haraway, Donna. "Manifesto for Cyborgs." *Socialist Review* (no. 80: March–April, 1985): 65–107.

_____. "Teddy Bear Patriarchy: Taxidermy in the Garden of Eden, New York City, 1908–1936." *Social Text* 11 (1984/1985): 20–64.

Harper, Barbara, Marvin Legator, and Michael Smith. *The Health Detective Handbook: A Guide to the Investigation of Environmental Health Hazards by Nonprofessionals.* Baltimore: Johns Hopkins University Press, 1985.

Heizer, Robert Fleming. "World View of California Indians," in Robert Fleming Heizer and Albert B. Elsasser, *The Natural World of the California Indians.* Berkeley: University of California Press, 1980, pp. 202–20.

Henn, Jeanne. "Female Farmers—The Doubly Ignored," *Development Forum* 14 (7 and 8; parts 1 and 2).

Hillman, James. *The Myth of Analysis: Three Essays in Archetypal Psychology.* New York: Harper & Row, 1975.

_____. "Peaks and Vales: The Soul/Spirit Distinction as Basis for the Differences between Psychotherapy and Spiritual Discipline," in James Hillman (ed.), *Puer Papers.* Dallas: Spring Publications, 1979, pp. 54–74.

_____. *Re-Visioning Psychology.* New York: Harper & Row, 1975.

Horkheimer, Max, and Theodore W. Adorno. *Dialectic of Enlightenment,* trans. Jon Cumming. New York: Herder and Herder, 1972.

Hyams, Edward. *Soil and Civilization.* New York: Harper & Row, 1976.

Jaggar, Alison M. *Feminist Politics and Human Nature.* Totowa, NJ: Rowman and Allanheld, 1983.

Jain, Shobhita. "Women and People's Ecological Movement," *Economic and Political Weekly* 19 (no. 41: October 13, 1984): 1788–94.

Jaynes, Julian. *The Origin of Consciousness in the Breakdown of the Bicameral Mind.* Boston: Houghton Mifflin, 1976.

Jonas, Hans. *The Imperative of Responsibility: In Search of an Ethics for the Technological Age.* Chicago: University of Chicago Press, 1984.

_____. "The Nobility of Sight," in Hans Jonas, *The Phenomenon of Life: Toward a Philosophical Biology.* Chicago: University of Chicago Press, 1966, pp. 135–52.

Keller, Catherine. *From a Broken Web: Separation, Sexism, and Self.* Boston: Beacon Press, 1986.

Keller, Evelyn Fox, and Christine R. Grontkowski. "The Mind's Eye," in Sandra Harding and Merrill B. Hintikka (eds.), *Discovering Reality.* Dordrecht, Holland: D. Reidel, 1983, pp. 207–24.

Kellert, Stephen, and Joyce Berry. "Attitudes, Knowledge, and Behaviors Toward Wildlife as Affected by Gender." *Wildlife Society Bulletin* 15 (no. 3: Fall 1987): 360–78.

Kelley, Kevin W. *The Home Planet.* New York: Addison-Wesley, 1988.

Kelly, Petra. *Fighting for Hope.* Boston: South End Press, 1984.

Kheel, Marti. "The Liberation of Nature: A Circular Affair." *Environmental Ethics* 7 (Summer 1985): 135–49.

King, Ynestra. "Toward an Ecological Feminism and a Feminist Ecology," in J. Rothschild (ed.), *Machina Ex Dea.* New York: Pergamon Press, 1983, pp. 118–29.

Kolodny, Annette. *The Land before Her: Fantasy and Experience of the American Frontier, 1630–1860.* Chapel Hill: University of North Carolina Press, 1984.

Kubrin, David. "'Burning Times': Isaac Newton and the War Against the Earth," in *Proceedings of the Conference Is the Earth a Living Organism.* Boston: University of Massachusetts, 1985. (Available from National Audubon Society Expedition Institute, Washington, DC, and on microfiche from the U.S. Department of Education–ERIC.)

LaBastille, Ann. *Women and Wilderness.* San Francisco: Sierra Club Books, 1980.

LaChapelle, Dolores. *Earth Wisdom.* Boulder, CO: Guild of Tutors Press, 1978.

Latin American and Caribbean Health Network. "Campaign Against Toxic and Dangerous Agricultural, Industrial and Consumer Products." *Women's Health Journal* (Santiago, Chile: ISIS International) 1 (1987): 11–15.

Leopold, Aldo. *Sand County Almanac.* Oxford, England: Oxford University Press, 1949.

Lloyd, Genevieve. *The Man of Reason: "Male" and "Female" in Western Philosophy.* Minneapolis: University of Minnesota Press, 1984.

Lowe, Donald. *History of Bourgeois Perception.* Chicago: University of Chicago Press, 1982.

MacCormack, Carol, and Marilyn Strathern (eds.), *Nature, Culture and Gender.* New York: Cambridge University Press, 1980.

Macy, Joanna, with Arne Naess, Pat Fleming, and John Seed. *Thinking Like a Mountain: Towards a Council of All Beings.* Philadelphia: New Society, 1988.

McLuhan, Marshall. *The Gutenberg Galaxy: The Making of Typographic Man.*

Toronto: University of Toronto Press, 1962.

Merchant, Carolyn. *The Death of Nature: Women, Ecology, and the Scientific Revolution*. San Francisco: Harper & Row, 1981.

———. "Earthcare: Women and the Environmental Movement." *Environment* 22 (June 1987): 7–13, 38–40.

———. "Ecofeminism." *The New Internationalist* (no. 171: May 1987): 18–19.

———. *Ecological Revolutions*. Chapel Hill: University of North Carolina Press, 1989.

———. "The Theoretical Structure of Ecological Revolutions." *Environmental Review* 11 (no. 4: Winter 1987): 269–74.

Mies, Maria. *Patriarchy and Accumulation on a World Scale*. London: Zed Books, 1986.

Murphy, Yolanda and Robert F. *Women of the Forest*. New York: Columbia University Press, 1974.

Naess, Arne. "The Deep Ecological Movement, Some Philosophical Aspects." *Philosophical Inquiry* 8 (1986): 10–13.

———. "Identification as a Source of Deep Ecological Attitudes," in Michael Tobias (ed.), *Deep Ecology*. San Diego, CA: Avant Books, 1984, pp. 256–70.

Nelkin, Dorothy. "Nuclear Power as a Feminist Issue." *Environment* 23 (no. 1: 1981): 14–20, 38–39.

Noddings, Nel. *Caring, a Feminine Approach to Ethics and Moral Education*. Berkeley: University of California Press, 1984.

Noel, Daniel. *Approaching Earth: A Search for the Mythic Significance of the Space Age*. Warwick, NY: Amity House, 1986.

Norwood, Christopher. *At Highest Risk: Environmental Hazards to Young and Unborn Children*. New York: McGraw-Hill, 1980.

Ortner, Sherry B. "Is Female to Male as Nature Is to Culture?" in M. Rosaldo and L. Lamphere (eds.), *Woman, Culture, and Society*. Stanford, CA: Stanford University Press, 1974, pp. 67–87.

Peterson, Abby, and Carolyn Merchant. "Peace with the Earth: Women and the Environmental Movement in Sweden." *Women's Studies International Forum* 9 (no. 5: December 1986): 12–18.

PhilaPOSH (Philadelphia Area Project on Occupational Safety and Health), *Getting Job Hazards Out of the Bedroom: The Handbook on Workplace Hazards to Reproduction*. Philadelphia: Author, 1988. (511 North Broad Street, Suite 900, Philadelphia, PA 19130.)

Plant, Judith. *Healing the Wounds: The Promise of Ecofeminism*. Philadelphia: New Society, 1989.

Plaskow, Judith and Carol P. Christ, eds. *Womanspirit Rising: A Feminist Reader in Religion*. New York: Harper & Row, 1979.

Pratt, Annis. "Women and Nature in Modern Fiction." *Contemporary Literature* 13 (no. 4: Autumn 1972): 476–90.

Rodman, John. "Four Forms of Ecological Consciousness Reconsidered," in

Donald Scherer and Thomas Attig (eds.), *Ethics and the Environment*. Englewood Cliffs, NJ: Prentice-Hall, 1983.

Ruether, Rosemary. *New Woman: New Earth*. New York: Seabury Press, 1975.

Salleh, Ariel K. "Deeper than Deep Ecology: The Ecofeminist Connection." *Environmental Ethics* 6 (1984): 339–45.

Shiva, Vandana. *Staying Alive: Women, Ecology and Development*. London: Zed Press, 1988.

Shkilmyk, Anastaia. *A Poison Stronger than Love: The Destruction of an Ojibway Community*. New Haven, CT: Yale University Press, 1986.

Sjöö, Monica, and Barbara Moore. *The Great Cosmic Mother: Rediscovering the Religion of the Earth*. San Francisco: Harper & Row, 1987.

Sofia, Zoe. "Exterminating Fetuses: Abortion, Disarmament, and the Sexo-Semiotics of Extraterrestrialism." *Diacritics* 14 (Summer 1984): 47–59.

Sontag, Susan. *On Photography*. New York: Farrar, Straus & Giroux, 1973.

Spretnak, Charlene. *Lost Goddesses of Early Greece*. Boston: Beacon Press, 1981.

_____, ed. *The Politics of Women's Spirituality*. New York: Anchor Press, 1982.

_____. *The Spiritual Dimension of Green Politics*. New Mexico: Bear & Co., 1986.

_____, and Fritjof Capra. *Green Politics: The Global Promise*. New Mexico: Bear & Co., 1986.

Starhawk. *Dreaming the Dark*. Boston: Beacon Press, 1982.

_____. *The Spiral Dance: A Rebirth of the Ancient Religion of the Great Goddess*. San Francisco: Harper & Row, 1986.

_____. *Truth or Dare*. San Francisco: Harper & Row, 1988.

Stone, Merlin. *When God Was a Woman*. New York: Harcourt Brace Jovanovich, 1976.

Teish, Luisah. *Jambalaya: The Natural Woman's Book of Personal Charms and Practical Ritual*. San Francisco: Harper & Row, 1985.

Third World Organizing, the Center for. *Toxics and Minority Communities*, Oakland, CA, 1986. (595 Martin Luther King Junior Way, Oakland, CA 94609.)

Toulmin, Stephen. "Death of the Spectator," in Stephen Toulmin, *The Return to Cosmology: Postmodern Science and the Theology of Nature*. Berkeley: University of California Press, 1982, pp. 237–54.

Tuan, Yi-Fu. *Space and Place: The Perspective of Experience*. Minneapolis: University of Minnesota Press, 1977.

_____. *Topophilia*. Englewood Cliffs, NJ: Prentice-Hall, 1974.

U.S. Office of Technology Assessment. *Reproductive Health Hazards in the Workplace*. Washington, DC: U.S. Government Printing Office, December 1985.

Von Strum, Carol. *A Bitter Fog: Herbicides and Human Rights*. San Francisco: Sierra Club Books, 1983.

Walker, Alice. *Living by the Word: Collected Writings, 1973–87*. San Diego, CA: Harcourt Brace Jovanovich, 1988.

Warren, Karen. "Feminism and Ecology: Making Connections." *Environmental Ethics* 9 (no. 1: 1987): 3-20.

Wilber, Ken. *Up from Eden: A Transpersonal View of Human Evolution.* Boulder, CO: Shambhala, 1983.

Worster, Donald. *Nature's Economy: The Roots of Ecology.* San Francisco: Sierra Club Books, 1977.

Zimmerman, Michael. "Feminism, Deep Ecology and Environmental Ethics." *Environmental Ethics* 9 (Spring 1987): 21-44.

About the Contributors

SALLY ABBOTT, M.A., teaches classes on prehistoric Goddess worship at Cal State Hayward, John F. Kennedy University and U.C. Extension in the San Francisco Bay Area. She is a poet and fiction writer, and her work has been published in *Anima, The James Joyce Quarterly, Moving Out, Psychological Perspectives,* and other journals.

PAULA GUNN ALLEN teaches Native-American studies at the University of California, Berkeley. She is the author of *Shadow Country* and four other books of poetry, of the novel *The Woman Who Owned the Shadows,* and the collection of essays *The Sacred Hoop: Recovering the Feminine in American Indian Traditions.*

RACHEL E. BAGBY is an elder who nurtures life on Earth. She founded and directs the Philadelphia Community Rehabilitation Corporation (PCRC), which operates gardening, housing, employment, and literacy programs.

RACHEL L. BAGBY is a composer, performer, writer, lawyer, and associate director of the Martin Luther King Papers Project at Stanford University. She works with the Woman/Earth Institute to gather and publish wisdom from elders who nurture life on Earth. She recently released her first recording, *X the Lines.*

CAROL P. CHRIST is the author of *Diving Deep and Surfacing: Women Writers on Spiritual Quest, Laughter of Aphrodite: Reflections on a Journey to the Goddess;* and coeditor of *Womanspirit Rising: A Feminist Reader on Religion* and *Weaving the Visions: New Patterns in Feminist Spirituality.* She was Stauffacher Visiting Professor of Religion at Pomona College in 1988, and currently lives in Greece where she wrote the essay in this volume.

IRENE DIAMOND lives with three generations of her family in Eugene, Oregon, where she teaches at the University of Oregon and participates in local Green politics and related ecofeminist educational activities. Her most recent book, *Feminism and Foucault: Reflections on Resistance,* was coedited with Lee Quinby. She is currently working on *Resisting the Logic of Control: Feminism, Fertility and the Living Earth.*

RIANE EISLER is the author of *The Chalice and the Blade: Our History, Our Future.* She is the codirector of the Center for Partnership Studies in Carmel, California. She is a member of the General Evolution Research Group, an associate editor of *World Futures,* and an international peace activist. Her earlier books include *Dissolution* and *The Equal Rights Handbook.* She has contributed to many other publications, including the first *World Encyclopedia of Peace,* and such journals as *Futures, The Human Rights Quarterly, The International Journal of Women's Studies,* and *Political Psychology.*

YAAKOV JEROME GARB is a doctoral student in the Graduate Group in Science and Mathematics Education at the University of California, Berkeley, where he also teaches a course on environmental ethics.

SUSAN GRIFFIN is a writer who lives in Berkeley, California. Her writings include *Woman and Nature: The Roaring Inside Her, Pornography and Silence: Culture's Revenge Against Nature,* and a recent collection of poetry, *Unremembered Country.* She is currently working on a book entitled *The First and the Last: A Woman Thinks about War.*

CYNTHIA HAMILTON has been active in grass-roots organizing for over a decade and was a participant in the effort to halt construction of the solid waste incinerator in Los Angeles, the subject of her essay in this volume. She received her B.A. in political science from Stanford University and her Ph.D. in political science from Boston University. She is currently an associate professor in the Pan African Studies Department at California State University, Los Angeles.

IRENE JAVORS is a psychotherapist in New York City and a poet. Her book of poems, *Mists of Memory,* was published in 1988 by Empress Press. She gives lectures and workshops on topics related to creativity and the sacred.

CATHERINE KELLER teaches constructive theology at Drew University and is the author of *From a Broken Web: Separation, Sexism, and Self.*

MARA LYNN KELLER received her Ph.D. in philosophy from Yale University. She is a lecturer in philosophy, global peace studies, and women's studies at San Francisco State University. She has been active in the civil rights, peace, and women's movements since the 1960s and is a Rosen method bodywork practitioner. She is currently working on a book, *The Mysteries of Demeter and Persephone: Mother-Daughter Goddesses of Fertility, Sexuality, and Rebirth.*

MARTI KHEEL is a vegetarian, ecofeminist, animal liberation activist, and writer. She is cofounder of Feminists for Animal Rights and has been active in the animal liberation movement for the last 10 years. Her articles have appeared in *Between the Species, Creation, Environmental Ethics, New Catalyst, Woman of Power,* and *Womanspirit.* She is currently a doctoral student at the Graduate Theological Union, Berkeley, California.

YNESTRA KING teaches at Lang College at the New School for Social Research in New York. She was an organizer of the Women's Pentagon Action and is a cofounder of WomanEarth Institute. Her forthcoming book, *Women and the Reenchantment of the World,* will be published by Beacon Press.

CAROLYN MERCHANT is chair of the Department of Conservation and Natural Resources at the University of California, Berkeley. She is author of *The Death of Nature: Women, Ecology and the Scientific Revolution* and *Ecological Revolutions*. Her articles have appeared in *Environment, The New Internationalist, Environmental Review,* and *Women's Studies International Forum.*

LIN NELSON is on the staff of the Central New York Council on Occupational Safety and Health, is cochair of the National Women's Health Network Committee on Occupational and Environmental Health, and is a consultant to the Akwesosne Mohawk Mother's Milk Project. She hopes to see—and be part of—stronger ties (more effective, more appreciative) between the feminist, ecology, Third World/Fourth World, and workers' health movements.

GLORIA FEMAN ORENSTEIN is an associate professor of comparative literature and teaches in the Program for the Study of Women and Men in Society at the University of Southern California in Los Angeles. She is the author of *The Reflowering of the Goddess* and *The Theatre of the Marvelous: Surrealism and the Contemporary Stage.* She has published widely on women in the arts and cocreated the Women's Salon for Literature in New York City.

JUDITH PLANT is a writer and journalist whose work focuses on creating sustainable human communities. She is actively involved in the bioregional movement, both globally and locally. She is editor of *Healing the Wounds: The Promise of Ecofeminism* and coeditor of *The New Catalyst,* a journal of social and political change from British Columbia.

LEE QUINBY teaches English and American Studies at Hobart and William Smith Colleges in Geneva, New York. Her work has appeared in *The American Historical Review, Criticism,* and *Signs.* She is coeditor of *Feminism and Foucault: Reflections on Resistance* and is currently completing a book entitled *The American Resistance: Studies in Aesthetic Ethics.*

ARISIKA RAZAK is a midwife, healer, and spiritual dancer. She is director of Nurse-Midwifery Services at Highland General Hospital in Oakland, California. Her emphasis is on Third World women's health, alternative birthing, and spiritual and cultural aspects of birthing. She views dance as a vehicle for the personal and individual expression of spirit. She is currently working with Hallie Ingelhart and Karen Vogel in creative expansion of the concept of Womanspirit: a joyous creation of postpatriarchal, twenty-first century forms of play, work, relationship, and worship.

JULIA SCOFIELD RUSSELL, after attending Bennington College, studied under two Zen masters for 18 years learning the disciplines of patience, selfless devotion, and nonattachment. She availed herself of the educational resources of Los Angeles and the world in fields as diverse as black holes, early childhood education, permaculture, metaphysics, and alternative economics. In 1980 she founded Eco-Home, a demonstration home for urban ecological living. She is active in the Green movement, serves on the board of directors of the Los Angeles County Agriculture Development Corporation, and publishes the newsletter *Ecolution*.

VANDANA SHIVA is the director of the Research Foundation for Science and Ecology in Dehra Dun, India, and the author of *Staying Alive: Women, Ecology and Development in India*. After receiving a doctorate in theoretical physics, she worked for the Indian Institute for Management in Bangalore. In keeping with her family's tradition of activist women, she devotes time to the *Chipko* movement, speaking, writing, and helping out as circumstances demand.

CHARLENE SPRETNAK is the author of *Green Politics: The Global Promise* (with Fritjof Capra), *Lost Goddesses of Early Greece,* and *The Spiritual Dimension of Green Politics,* and is the editor of *The Politics of Women's Spirituality.* She is a cofounder of the Green Committees of Correspondence, the major Green politics organization in the United States.

STARHAWK is the author of *Dreaming the Dark: Magic, Sex, and Politics, The Spiral Dance: A Rebirth of the Ancient Religion of the Great Goddess,* and *Truth or Dare: Encounters of Power, Authority, and Mystery.* A feminist and peace activist, she holds an M.A. in psychology from Antioch West University and teaches at several San Francisco Bay Area colleges. She travels widely, lecturing and giving workshops. In San Francisco, she works with the Reclaiming collective, which offers classes, workshops, and public rituals in the Old Religion of the Goddess, called Witchcraft.

BRIAN SWIMME, PH.D. (gravitational systems), is the author of *The Universe Is a Green Dragon* and teaches courses in cosmology at College of the Holy Names, Oakland, California.

MICHAEL E. ZIMMERMAN is a professor of philosophy at Tulane University. Author of *Eclipse of the Self: The Development of Heidegger's Concept of Authenticity,* he has also written essays on deep ecology and ecofeminism. His new book, on Heidegger's concept of modern technology, will be published by Indiana University Press in 1990. His interest in "applying" philosophy to contemporary social concerns is reflected in his appointments as clinical professor of psychiatry at Louisiana State University Medical School and clinical professor of psychology at Tulane Medical School.